Vera, Thank you
for your support!

Lauri

PUNISHED *for* PURPOSE

From Out of the Darkness
Came a Powerful Healing Light

LAURI BURNS

WingSpan Press

First Edition 2010

Printed in the United States of America

Published by WingSpan Press
Livermore, CA
www.wingspanpress.com
The WingSpan name, logo and colophon are the trademarks of
WingSpan Publishing.

Publisher's Cataloging-in-Publication Data

Burns, Lauri L.
Punished for purpose / Lauri Burns.
p. cm.
ISBN: 978-1-59594-346-0 (hardcover)
ISBN: 978-1-59594-373-6 (pbk.)
1. Adult child abuse victims—Biography. 2. Prostitution.
3. Heroin abuse. 4. Foster parents.   I. Title.
RC569.5.C55 B87 2010
362.76—dc22
2009944202

10 9 8 7 6 5 4 3 2 1

Acknowledgments

Cover photographs copyright Image Source/Getty Images
and Sarah May Bates

Front cover concept and images: Sarah May Bates of DDB LA

Cover design: Jacqui Hatzikokolakis

Photos of the author: Leonard Ortiz, *The Orange County Register*

Photo of Central Islip Psychiatric Center, Islip, New York:
Jason Krieger (www.hoursofdarkness.com)

Editing: Christine Patrick and David Collins

PUNISHED *for* PURPOSE

1

SITTING AT THE VANITY IN MY SUITE ONBOARD THE ROYAL Caribbean cruise ship I took a deep breath, collected my thoughts and closed my laptop. I had written a good deal in the privacy of my cabin, but had barely scratched the surface. Recounting my life thus far had been painful, and realizing how much of the nightmare still remained untold overwhelmed me. There were many days when I could only write a line or two, most days I couldn't write at all. On this particular day, I felt like I had made some real progress. Living through this life once was plenty for anyone to endure, but now I was voluntarily reliving it through my writing. Was I crazy? I couldn't say, but any thought of stopping was countered with the hope that I might help someone. Even if I only helped one person to take a different path, my nightmare would serve a higher purpose, and somehow out of all of this badness would come something good. The moment I began my story, I knew I couldn't turn back; regardless of how long it took me, I was compelled to get it all out. Although I was on a roll that particular morning, I needed to stop. The ship had docked at shore and it was time to pack up and prepare to disembark. The fog horn would sound any moment and I hadn't even started packing. With my laptop now closed, my mind kept on writing.

As I rushed around the room, grabbing my belongings and shoving them into my suitcase, I got that ominous feeling one gets when a great vacation nears its end. My cell phone remained on the side of my bed where I had set it several days ago in the off position. I figured preserving battery power would be good, as there was no signal out at sea. As a sign of defeat and a confirmation that my vacation was nearly over, I retrieved it, turned it on, and set it back down. Better to jump right back into action than to delay it any further.

As expected, less than a minute later it jingled alerting me that messages were waiting. Conflicted by my desire to know who had called and my unwillingness to punctuate the end of my cruise, I could only stare at the pestering phone. The longer I procrastinated reconnecting to my life on land, the more my curiosity grew. Conceding to the inevitable, I gave in, picked it up and dialed my voicemail…To listen to your voice messages, press 1.

"Hi Lauri, it's Mom. Oh, I forgot you're on the cruise. Good luck with your speech honey, call me when you get home." Beep.

"Lauri, this is Michael Gold. I'm a social worker at St. Martin's Hospital. We have your father here with us and he's made some statements. I need you to call me back as soon as possible. My office number is…"

I grabbed a pen and paper off the nightstand and wrote down the number. A range of emotions bombarded me. *What could he have possibly done this time?* I thought I had closed out the past when I shutdown my laptop, but I was wrong. I couldn't have possibly prepared myself for this call. Feeling trapped, I set the phone down and stood by the cabin's small window and stared out at the vast blue sea. I began to talk to myself in my head. I often do this when I need some inner coaching and this was certainly one of those times. *You can do this…you are a grown woman Lauri…it's all different now. Breathe in and breathe out… just dial…and breathe.* Thoughts adrift, I was snapped back to reality by the ship's booming fog horn. I regained my composure, reached for my phone and slowly dialed. I was relieved to hear the machine at the other end, as it extended my vacation a few more minutes.

"This is Michael Gold. I'm not in the office right now, but please leave me a message and I'll call you back as soon as I can." Beep.

"Hello Michael, this is Lauri Burns; I'm returning your call. I apologize for the delay but I was on a cruise and had no signal. Please return my call as soon as possible; I will keep my phone close by."

From the loudspeaker above a man's voice declared, "Blue tags on deck for departure." I shoved my cell in my back pocket, threw my remaining things into my suitcase and headed for the lobby. Exiting the elevator, I joined the long line of passengers who had arrived before me. My children, who shared their own cabin, showed up shortly thereafter and filed in behind me. "Did you comb your room to make sure you got everything?" I asked. Mary mumbled yes in that child annoyed by a bothersome parent tone, Chantel smiled and nodded and Danielle responded with a chipper, "Yepper! Went through it twice!"

Seconds later, the phone rang. Reluctantly, I retrieved it from my pocket, "Hello, this is Lauri."

Then I heard the deep familiar voice on the other end. "Lauri Burns, this is Michael Gold."

"Yes?" I responded.

"There was an incident involving your father and he's been here with us for a few days. Up until yesterday he told us he had no family. Today he's saying he has one daughter. He gave us your number." *Although I have two sisters, I was too intrigued to interrupt.*

"It seems that your father was planning on taking his life and that of a lady named Lydia. Do you know Lydia?" *I made that sound one makes when answering yes to a question without saying any words,* "Mmm hmm."

As he continued to talk, I dropped my bags and slowly walked away from the line. I found refuge in a shaded area behind the lounge, crouched down and closed my eyes. Was this really happening? *Now?...*

"Your father had called his Rabbi and his brother-in-law and told them he and Lydia made a suicide pact and wanted to be left alone so that they could die in peace. Someone called the police. When they arrived, your father wouldn't come out of the house. From the doorway, they could see two guns on the table behind him."

"They ordered him out of the house and told him to kneel down on the lawn. Although he came outside, he told them he couldn't kneel down because of a recent knee surgery. Apparently, they didn't believe him so they took him down physically. It appears he was injured and he's very upset."

My vacation was clearly over. I continued listening. "Now he's saying he did some bad things and he's going to be put away.

Do you know what he's talking about?" Again, I somehow replied, "Yes."

2

I FLASHED BACK 20 YEARS AGO TO A VISIT WITH MY THERAPIST AT THE time. I was 24 years old sporting long black hair down to the middle of my back, dark liquid eyeliner emphasizing the intensity of my large brown eyes and torn jeans that exposed my knees and butt. These were my favorite jeans—as reckless as my state of mind. Underneath the jeans, I wore black fishnet stockings to conceal my skin. While that might have lured some in, my large black steel toed boots and anger kept most at bay.

The therapist calmly asked, "When did you first become suicidal?" It was precisely at that moment that I realized that I had no recollection of ever wanting to live. As far back as I could remember I wanted to die. I responded with a simple, "I don't remember."

Unable to extract an emotional response out of me after several weeks of treatment, she suggested we try an exercise. "I want you to ask little Lauri how she feels about what we've been discussing and I want little Lauri to respond. I've done this before and it seems to work quite well. I am going to give you a pen. Since you normally write with your right hand, I want little Lauri to respond with her left hand. We use this method to access our inner child. I'll leave the room so you don't feel any pressure from me. Any questions before I go?"

What did she think, I was Sybil or something? Although I thought she was out of her mind, I did as she instructed. Shortly thereafter, she came back into the room excited to hear what "Little Lauri" had written. I looked her in the eyes and said, "Sorry, I'm not Sybil. No little Lauris came out while you were gone. It's just me in here." And I slid the paper toward her.

It had been a long time since I had felt any emotion about my past. I was cold. Like watching a movie about another person, I was completely disconnected from anything that had happened in my life. She looked at my sloppy response and somewhat dejected, read it aloud...*I don't feel anything. It was a long time ago.*

3

I SAT WITH MY MOTHER RECENTLY TO DISCUSS MY CHILDHOOD. AT first she was reluctant, but began to open up when I assured her that I was emotionally stable and needed to know. Although I could recall the broad strokes, I couldn't remember the details. I assured her that anything she could tell me would help. Although somewhat undecided, she began to talk.

My mother married my father at the young age of twenty-one. My father was five years older than she was and seemed to be a great catch. Having joined the Navy right out of high school, he studied to be an airplane mechanic. By the time he proposed to her, he had a full time job at the local airline and a beautiful new Mustang Coupe. Wanting to escape her father's control, it couldn't have progressed fast enough. Within six months of my dad's proposal, they were married.

With my dad's meager wages they were able to rent a small one bedroom apartment in Rosedale, a suburban neighborhood in the borough of Queens, N.Y. By the time my mom was twenty three, my sister Nadine was eleven months old and my dad had advanced in his career. Having a good understanding of airplane mechanics, he had completed a training program and landed a job as a Flight Engineer with a major airline. Things appeared to be going very well until a few months later.

In September of 1962, the airline went on strike. Having just begun his career, with a family to support, my father had nothing to fall back on. When the paychecks stopped, he spiraled downward. That was just about the time my mom realized she was pregnant with me.

When my mom revealed the situation to my dad, he was furious.

Although it wasn't my fault, my mom said, he resented me before I was even born. As my mother's stomach grew, my father's anger intensified. Never having agreed to a second child, he was convinced that by getting pregnant, she had intentionally disobeyed him. Although as an infant I was incapable of doing anything to upset my father, the moment I was born, I became his number one target.

My mother, father and sister, Nadine all shared that tiny one bedroom apartment. When he was home, my father demanded that my bassinette be placed in the hallway just outside the front door of our apartment. Aware that it was not only wrong, but also dangerous, my mother did so reluctantly. By this time she had already established a fear of defying my father. She did as she was told. Having just left the hospital as a newborn, I was not welcome in our home. During the night, if my mother heard cries from the hallway, she would sneak out to feed me, while trying desperately not to wake my father.

To make matters worse, whenever she fed me I would throw up, and cry again. My mom was a nervous wreck. Stuck in the hallway, crouched down over my small bassinette, she was terrified of waking my father. It wasn't until I was ten weeks old that my mother took me to a doctor. He quickly determined that I wasn't keeping the food down because I was allergic to the formula I was being fed. Bottom line—I was alienated and alone, agitated and hungry from the start. Not being a psychologist, I can't say for sure how this situation affected me, but I suspect being cast aside as an infant is at the core of my lifelong sense of aloneness.

I was twelve weeks old when my parents purchased their first home. It was a charming little three bedroom house in a pleasant suburban community on Long Island, called Smithtown. The house was bright white with conservative little black shutters and neat as a pin. With two small strips of green lawn lining the driveway and a lamppost by the walkway, it couldn't have been nicer. We lived in a quaint little neighborhood populated by young families. The grocery store was just around the block and there was an elementary school within walking distance.

Being so young at the time, I don't remember much about Smithtown other than the birth of my little sister, Alyssa. She was born when I was nearly four years old. I still recall anxiously waiting for her arrival from the hospital. Before leaving for the hospital, my mother announced that she would be bringing home a baby and presented Nadine and I with small porcelain dolls to prepare us.

Like a little porcelain doll herself, the excitement when I saw Alyssa for the first time was life changing. For the next few weeks when the adults left her room, I would sneak in and stand alongside her crib, wrap my fingers around the bars and whisper to her. With large dizzy eyes, she strained to focus on the musical chimes that hung above her. Although I knew she was too young to understand me, I imagined she knew exactly what I was saying.

We only lived in Smithtown until I was six, but, according to my mother, my father's abuse started there. She remembered like it was yesterday. I was three years old at the time it began.

Nadine and I were fighting over a toy in the basement. My dad ran down the flight of stairs, grabbed my arm and yanked it so hard that my mother thought it had been disjointed. She watched as my dad dragged me to the side of the room and continued to hit me. She pleaded with him to leave me alone yelling, "Stop! You don't even know what happened!" Soon thereafter, she discovered that Nadine was at fault, not me. When she told my dad, he seemed disinterested. With a painful sigh, my mom told me that from that day forward my dad instinctively came after me whenever anything or anyone had upset him. For the next several years, beating me was his only remedy for expelling his rage.

From Smithtown, we moved to an upscale neighborhood on the outskirts of Long Island called Centerport. We lived in a neighborhood called Golden Bridge Estates. When we first moved there it was just a dirt road and a lot of trees. I can still remember the smell of the wood as our house was being built and the sound of my sneakers on the thin plywood that covered the foundation. Within a few years of moving there, the development had grown. The neighborhood was complete with large homes, lush landscaping and a great expanse of woodsy areas in the backdrop. Our house was a on a large hill with a brick stairway lining the way up.

The foyer was both elegant and inviting with a large glass chandelier hanging above and a wide view of the surrounding rooms. The formal living room was off to the left, complete with off-white carpeting and a baby grand piano. This room was rarely used, with the exception of family pictures and my older sister's short-lived piano lessons. It was common knowledge that this room was off limits and for "looks" only. The formal dining room was off to the right and used mainly for Passover dinners. The family room was straight ahead complete with French doors and a view of the redwood deck out to the woods. Immediately above the chandelier was the grand balcony, which offered a preview to the second level sewing room.

Our neighbors were all well to do, the majority Catholics. Most of the moms stayed at home and the fathers were doctors, lawyers and a few organized crimers that the neighborhood kids assumed were car salesmen due to the constant change of vehicles. The impromptu arrival of a small fleet of flashy new Cadillacs and the finely dressed men that drove them seemed ordinary to us kids.

It was breathtakingly beautiful in Centerport. I loved the first snow. Nothing was better than walking outside in my pj's with my snow coat and boots on. I'd fall into the soft bed of crystals and flop my arms and legs to create snow angels or crack off the longest icicle hanging from the rooftop and sit on the front steps licking it. The brisk cement pierced my flimsy pajamas and awoke my senses as the sun sparkled off the white blanket surrounding me.

In autumn, the swirling winds reminded me that Halloween was just around the corner. As the wind blew on my face, I'd strut around in my sneakers crunching the crisp orange and golden leaves covering the ground. The change of seasons was always majestic to me. It gave me the sense that there was something bigger out there, but I couldn't begin to imagine what it was.

About a mile from our home was a place called the Old Barn. It was a big red barn that had been converted into a general store. While known for selling horse and pet supplies, the other kids and I were drawn there by "the table." Situated to the left just beyond the entrance, was the most magnificent table you could imagine. Some of the best candy you could buy sat on that small wooden table. There was Bazooka, fun sticks with flavored sugar, baseball cards and candy necklaces. All of which sold for less than a quarter. But the candy wasn't the whole draw; it was also the journey to the barn.

The walk from our house to the barn was about a mile through the woods and over a red bridge that rested on top of giant wooden legs and appeared to be held together by little more than rusted chains and old nails. It swayed and creaked as I walked over its 2" x 4"s. Train tracks weaved through the forest and eventually made their way under the bridge. I never knew where the train was coming from or going to, but whenever I heard that whistle blow, I knew it was time. With my candy in tow, I would race to the bridge, sit on the edge and hang my legs through the chains. As the powerful steel monster approached, the bridge would vibrate and rattle. With my hands tightly gripping the chains and my feet stretched straight out, I was ready for the ride. When it finally passed beneath me, its mighty force caused the entire expanse to shake so intensely that it bounced me around like a huge roller coaster. Although it never fell and was probably much more stable than I ever could have imagined, the thought of it giving way was enough excitement to keep me coming back for more.

From as far back as I could remember, I loved anything that promised to give me a jolt. As a small child I was crazy about scary movies. I was a dedicated fan of *Creature Feature*, *Frankenstein* and *King Kong*. *The House that Dripped Blood* was also one of my all time favorites. As the beatings from my dad escalated, I often imagined that like Carrie at the prom, I could use my powers to get revenge on him or anyone else that hurt me. Although it didn't work, I never gave up day-dreaming about it.

To the outside observer, everything in my life seemed perfect. My sisters and I attended public school, went to Temple twice a week and were Bat Mitvah'ed, as was expected in a nice Jewish family. We had cleaning people since the time I can remember and never seemed to lack anything monetarily. I had brief singing lessons, played the viola and, although I revolted immensely, I joined the Brownies as soon as I was old enough. Everything was beautiful on the outside, but when the doors were closed and the outsiders were gone, it was very different. A dream on the outside and a nightmare within. As a child I would have welcomed a quiet death rather than to endure another day.

4

THE BEATINGS CONTINUED. WHENEVER THEY STARTED, MY MOM would rush to the door and scream at my father to stop. Although he persisted as if she wasn't even there, I felt somewhat comforted knowing that she at least cared. I will always remember the day she stopped coming to the door. At first, I thought she couldn't hear us but, a few beatings later, I realized she just wasn't coming anymore. As clearly as I recall a small sense of safety with her at the door, I remember the feeling of being an accepted casualty. It was acceptable that I be beaten from that point forward. The loneliness and desperation fueled a silent ongoing discussion between me and God..."*It is clear you hate me...just let me die!*" I had a diary filled with large dark curse words directed towards my dad and God. With an inability to confront my dad due his size and anger, God received the brunt of it. After all, he chose this place for me.

Being raised Jewish I always knew there was a God and I was keenly aware that he knew me. Although you'd think that was a good thing, it was not in my case. The only logical explanation that I could come up with for my circumstances was that I had done something bad in a past life. Maybe I had been a witch or something. That was why I was being punished in this life. My perception of God was that he knew who I was and we both knew that I was sentenced to this house because of my sins. There were many times in my childhood when I would scream at God, "*I hate you!*" I believed that if I angered him enough, he would just let me die. He never did, and that only made matters worse.

My father's beatings always ended the same way. He would expel all of his anger until exhausted and say, "Now get up, give me a hug and tell me that you love me." If I refused, the beating would resume until I gave in. I still recall the violent revulsion that erupted within me as I forced myself to hug him and tell him that I loved him. In order to survive, I did as I was told. Getting physically abused was painful enough, but being forced to show love to a man that repulsed me was nothing less than torture. As time went on, I became numb to my innate emotional reactions and I merely existed with little or no response from within. I became cold and detached from my body.

As my father's beatings escalated, so did my self-hatred. By the age of five, I was completely alienated from everyone and was prone to throwing myself down flights of stairs, banging my head on the walls and punching myself in the face. The harder I punched myself and the larger the bruises, the better. I wanted everyone to know, especially my parents, that I got it! I am worthless! I knew I was worth nothing and maybe if I hurt myself enough, they would stop hurting me. I never got the desired affect; the beatings only got worse. And now my entire family's attention shifted to ongoing talk about something being wrong with me, or more directly, my brain. This only fueled more self-hatred.

In addition to my self-injurious behavior, I also started to become violent with others. My first act of violence was in nursery school. There was a girl in my class that was much larger than the other children and her tongue hung out. In a world of her own, she would often be staring off into nowhere, with her mouth wide open, tongue out the side and drool running down her chin. In clothing too small to cover her protruding belly, she looked like a giant baby. Everything about her made me angry. It was all I could do not to yell, "*What the hell is wrong with you! You look stupid!*" She needed to be hurt. Since she was twice my size, I had to be creative.

I was eventually able to get her alone. In a soft whisper, I said, "Come here." Without much of a response, she drifted towards me. I guided her to the large wooden stairway and said I wanted to play house. When she agreed, I told her I would be the parent and she would be the child and it was time for bed. Pointing to the stairs, I asked her to lie down. I told her to close her eyes. As soon as she was relaxed, I put my foot on her ribs and shoved her down the stairs as hard as I could. With each thud, her body tumbled downward until it finally rested at the bottom of the stairs. Hurt and disoriented, she slowly got up and began weeping. By the time she found the teacher she was hyperventilating so badly that she could barely speak. She struggled to tell her what had happened and dragged her by the arm to point me out. Thinking ahead, I was already gone. By the time she saw me again, the teacher had stopped listening. I don't recall feeling any guilt that day, only relief that I didn't get caught.

I stored more rage than you could ever think possible in the tiny body of a five-year-old, and I had to contain it. Clearly, I never felt five. From as far back as I can remember, I had much more serious problems to deal with than most kids my age. At snack time in nursery school, they served cookies and juice. In an attempt to stay invisible, I sucked my cookies. I always thought that if they heard me crunching they might notice I was there. I did everything I could to avoid communication. I was sure if someone talked to me, they too, like my family might think I was crazy. Having the kids make fun of me would be more than I could handle. I would lose control, and then they would all know. As you can imagine, it takes a long time for a Chips Ahoy to melt down, but the fear of being noticed overrode the impulse to chew. While the other kids my age were learning how to share and play with others, I was becoming adept at survival skills.

By the time I was six, I was acutely aware of both my dad's mood and his location within the house. Regardless of what I was doing, if he was home, I instinctively knew where he was. I knew the sound of his walk just by the weight of his body, even without shoes. When I heard his voice, I quickly registered the tone. As I got older, I became skilled at anticipating a beating by the sound of his voice and the pace of his steps as they hit the floor. Like a skilled war veteran, I knew where to find cover, regardless of my location. Sometimes it was in the attic, alongside the fireplace or on many occasions in my closet, behind my clothes. This was always the scariest because the open area beneath my clothes left my legs fully exposed. But with no other option, and under the bed being obvious, it was all I had. I had studied him long enough to know that in the midst of a rage, he would instinctively come after me, but he never had the patience to search me out. Frustrated, he would storm out of my room, verbally abuse my mom and leave the house. But the fear that this would change was always with me as I shook behind the clothes, trying my best not to breathe. Another favorite hiding place was in the attic near the sewing room, which would eventually become Nadine's room. At the time she was moved there, I was told this was a privilege provided to the eldest sibling. Over the years I became suspicious about the real intent of her seclusion.

In the long run, the bathroom became my safest haven, with the lock on the door providing an extra level of safety. Although my dad knew where I was, he never kicked in the door. He must have realized at some level that he would be the one to fix it. I guess you could say he was a rational rageaholic. Knowing I was in there, he would simply submit to waiting me out. My fear would always outlast his anger. I spent many nights curled up in a ball on the small, soft rug in front of the sink with my feet tucked close beneath me to avoid the chill of the cold porcelain floor.

I was always thankful for my father's job. Being a flight engineer, he and his crew were gone on trips at least three days a week. Although I was thankful for the reprieve, the time he was home between trips seemed far too long.

When I was about seven years old, my parents brought home a dog. Her name was Pepper. She was a beautiful fawn pug. Pepper was the first living creature I would ever bond to as a child, and also the last. Up until that point, the thought of dying was always a welcome one. But now that she was there it was different. From that point forward, I wasn't alone. Greeting me the moment I came home, she was always by my side. On the nights in the bathroom, on the small rug, she would curl up beside me and I would drape my arm over her. As she drifted to sleep, her purr-like snore would comfort me and remind me that she loved me. As small as she was, I don't know if I felt protected by Pepper or if I felt I had to protect her. I think it was a little of both. The pain that I felt the day my dad kicked her off of the stoop and into the snow, yelling, "Get out there and go you stupid mutt!" was unbearable. It was much easier for me to withstand his abuse than to watch Pepper get hurt. When Pepper became a target as well, I was conflicted with committing suicide, as it meant leaving Pepper alone with my dad.

One day Pepper didn't greet me when I came home. She was always so excited to see me and, sensing my approach, would be waiting anxiously for me when I entered the house. On this particular day, she was nowhere to be found. I searched everywhere for her, but came up empty handed. When I eventually asked my mom where she was, she sadly proclaimed that, "We gave her away." Although we had had Pepper for at least seven years, my mom said she had suddenly become allergic to her. Attempting to ease my pain, she told me that she had dropped her off with a lady who owned a farm. In spite of my constant pleas, they never took me to see her. To this day, I will never know if Pepper actually went to that farm or if my dad had done something to her. No one in my family ever discussed Pepper again. It would be many years later before I would ever bond again.

Although I didn't care anymore, my dad continued playing games with my head, trying to hurt me. One summer day he brought home a kitten for me. She was an orange and white tabby that I named Lacey after my best friend at school. My friend Lacey was a redhead with an upbeat personality. Although Lacey was my best friend, she knew nothing of the insanity of my family. Lacey's family was over-the-top normal, so I pretended mine was as well, out of fear of being judged. Lacey the kitty was a little ball of innocence. She was a wonderful contrast to my solemn life and access to love that I so desperately needed, but had lost the capacity to accept. I can still remember a certain excitement as I would near the house from school just knowing that I would find Lacey in my room.

One day I came home and Lacey was gone. When I asked where she went, my dad would only say, "Gone." He continued to bring home kittens and take them away. After a short time, I lost interest in the new kittens. Although he continued to beat me, his psychological torture no longer affected me.

The only person who ever hugged me other than my father was my grandmother. My Grandma Rose and Papa Joe lived in a tiny one bedroom, upstairs apartment in Bushwick New York. My grandma was a short, overweight woman, who projected nothing but love for us, and Papa was a frail, quiet man with a cane, who rarely spoke. Upon arriving at their apartment, Grandma Rose would mutter something in Yiddish and grab each kid for a huge hug.

She would wrap her arms around us and hug us as tightly as she could. As she closed in on me, I would be smothered up within her huge breasts and pillows of human cushion. I would seize with panic the moment she grabbed me. It was as if my body had a memory all of its own and it would react as if I had just been beaten. I would never pull away because I wouldn't want to hurt her feelings, but the inner eruption was almost unbearable. It was a fierce storm of anger, coupled with an uncontrollable urge to scream out in tears. The feeling of being enclosed in the grasp of another person's arms spelled fear and loss of control for me at a young age. I was able to think my way through it by repeating in my head...*it is almost over...she's not going to hurt you...it is almost over...it is almost over...*I was only able to breathe again when she finally released me.

She was a sweet old lady who threw on her apron the minute we arrived and spent our entire visit in the kitchen pushing food on us. She'd always say, "Nosh, nosh" in her broken Yiddish accent and watch us eat to our heart's content. As soon as everyone finished, she'd immediately start cleaning. That woman was always doing something around the apartment, somehow never finding the time to join us at the table. While our conversations with Grandma Rose were limited due to her inability to speak English, she spoke volumes with her enormous heart. It would be years before I would learn how such a gentle and loving woman raised such an angry and overbearing man. My Papa, on the other hand, was a mystery. He died while I was young and I never learned much about him because my father never spoke of him.

Although we visited my dad's parents regularly, we were much closer with my maternal grandparents, Nanny and Poppy.

Nanny and Poppy lived in a charming little house in Newtown, New York. Nanny was a small woman, a bit overweight, good-natured and well-educated. She was an English teacher in her day and it was evident in both her communication and crossword puzzle skills. She never seemed to sleep; she was always made up with her hair curled and dress pressed. She was subservient to my grandfather's needs. Poppy on the other hand, with grey hair almost to his shoulders, was an old beatnik. He spent the majority of his time in his big leather chair by the large bay window in front of their house. With a cigarette smoldering in the ashtray next to him, he always seemed to have a full martini and a fresh olive. With legs outstretched on his stool, reminiscing about life in the day, he was perfectly content.

Nanny was very close to my mom, while Poppy seemed to be closer to my dad. We would visit them often for dinner and family get-togethers. They were nice people, but I never felt a connection. I mean you can only take so much of meaningless conversation like, "how is school?" and "what did you do this summer?" when you are living in a situation so hostile that you hate yourself and everyone around you. I could never understand why no one said anything about what was really going on. Surely they knew about the problems with my dad? My mom must have mentioned it. After all, she saw and heard the beatings regularly. No one cared. The failure to mention it kept me alienated from everyone.

I will always remember the day Poppy finally said something. I was eight years old. My father and grandfather were having a heated conversation in our kitchen. I don't think they knew I was home because I had learned to be very quiet when my dad was around. I had become accustomed to doing everything possible to avoid his detection. I overheard my grandfather say, "If you don't stop hitting that kid, she'll never grow up normal." This was the first time I ever heard anyone discuss the beatings. Those words were so foreign and so sought after that I felt not only a sense of shock, but also a sense of panic. My grandfather's validation confirmed the intensity of the situation. It was no longer just in my head. It was real—very real.

Although it was never mentioned again, I instantly felt something for my grandfather that I had never felt for another human being. As a child, I never would have used the word "love" unless it was in reference to my feelings for Pepper. My parents never said I love you and they certainly never hugged us, unless, of course, it was after a beating. The lack of understanding for when and why a beating would occur, coupled with my family's decision to cover everything up, made it impossible for me to trust. I revolted at the thought of ever bonding with anyone— ever. But that one simple statement did something. From that day forward, I always felt a sense of safety around Poppy. Someone knew.

My grandfather's words confirmed the intensity of the situation, but also my desperate need to somehow get out. Unfortunately, not having experienced any sense of safety in my world or having a physical plan of escape, I thought my only way out was suicide. As time went on, my self-injurious behaviors took control and I began to develop strange personality defects.

By the time I was ten, I had developed another personality but, unlike a schizophrenic, I was aware of my duality. I knew the other me as Licorice. I'm not exactly sure why, but I got the name from a wiry brindle Boxer we had. I only became Licorice when I was around Alyssa. I spoke in a strange voice and acted like a child. Alyssa played the role of my mother and I referred to her as "Alyssa Ma."

When I was Licorice, Alyssa would tend to my needs as if I was a child. Lying in my bed, I would say, "Aly Ma, I am cold and I am also hungry." Alyssa would say, "Oh don't worry, Aly Ma will take care of you." She would grab a blanket and softly tuck it around my body and say, "Now, now baby, I will get you something to eat…would you like some cereal?" I would nod my head yes. She would promptly leave the room and return with a snack from the kitchen. Still pretending I was a baby, she would say, "Do you want Aly Ma to feed you?" I would nod my head yes and she would sit on the side of the bed and feed me my food.

I only recall feeling vulnerable enough to be dependent and childlike when I was Licorice. Alyssa was six at the time and I knew she would never hurt me. To this day, Alyssa and I have never discussed Licorice again. She knew I was being hurt by our dad and we both knew this was her only way of helping me.

5

A S I GOT OLDER, I BEGAN PUSHING ALYSSA AWAY, JUST AS I HAD
everyone else. I shunned her and verbally abused her. I had a
strong desire to be isolated and could no longer accept comfort in any
form from anyone. By my own design, I was completely alone.

As best I can remember, Alyssa was not around a lot when the
abuse was happening. A few years ago she confided in me that she spent
a good deal of time hiding on the roof during those incidents. She told
me she couldn't stand to hear the sounds associated with the beatings.
Although it was horrific for me, it must have been scary as hell for
her. She was so small. When I think about it today, it breaks my heart
knowing how alone Alyssa was. She was so tiny and afraid. Out of
desperation, she climbed by herself up the side of the house onto a very
high roof. She often stayed up there for hours without anyone missing
her. As a matter of fact, I don't think anyone ever asked her where she
was until our conversation thirty-five years later. For all intents and
purposes, she was invisible. I can only imagine how alone she felt.

My relationship with my older sister Nadine was completely
different. I never felt close to her. It was as if she, like my dad, didn't
want me around. It had been that way for as long as I could remember.
I thought little of it, until the whispering started. I was about eleven
when I first heard my mom and sister talking to others about "something
being wrong with Lauri."

When approaching the kitchen it was not out of the ordinary to
hear my mom on the phone quietly talking to her friends about me.
Never about what my father was doing, but only about me and my crazy
outbursts. The mere idea that she never mentioned my father would

bring on an immediate explosion. I would run into the room and grab anything I could, and throw it to the floor. As it shattered into tiny pieces, I would scream, "I hate you! I fucking hate you!" The crazier and louder, the better...I had to stop her from talking. As I learned from my father, your point is most clearly heard when it is felt. I used fear to control her when my father wasn't around.

That was also about the time that Nadine starting whispering and alienating me from the other kids. Whether we were with cousins or friends, she would make sure they were off somewhere else, in a place where I wasn't invited. They would go in her room and as I approached, she would say, "Everyone can come in, except Lauri." After the door slammed, I would hear muffled whispers and then giggles. This only solidified my hatred and distrust for my family. Distance from Nadine I was certainly used to, but when she turned others against me, I turned from her and never looked back. Nadine was my dad's favorite. Being gone two or three days at a time, my dad often returned home from work bearing a single gift. It was always for Nadine. They seemed to have a special bond. Her efforts to isolate me, and her relationship with my dad fueled the violence within me. Over time, I developed an immense hatred towards her.

I have come to define my dad as a "rageaholic." At a young age, I knew he was different from other fathers, but I thought he was just weird. He was violent, irrational and prone to enormous mood swings, but I had no idea what that meant or why he behaved that way. While I don't really remember him drinking until I was a bit older, whenever he did drink, he became more volatile, more unpredictable and much more dangerous.

In order to cope, I did everything possible to rationalize or justify my dad's behavior. I desperately needed to convince my friends that he was normal. I feared that if they thought otherwise, they might think something was also wrong with me. With my whole family already against me, the last thing I needed was to give anybody else a reason to alienate me. It was one thing to be alone by choice; it was something entirely different to have everyone shun you.

The beatings continued throughout my childhood, sometimes regularly and sometimes intermittently. They rarely came as a result of my behavior. More accurately, my father beat me whenever he needed to vent about anything or anyone. To him, I was like one of those punching bags that many men keep in the garage. In addition to the irregularity of the occurrences, the methods also varied. Beatings with a belt occurred most frequently, but in the midst of a rage, a shoe was a close second. The one thing he avoided without question was my face. Even though he seemed to lack any form of control, he always made sure the impact occurred on my back, my legs or my butt.

As my home life intensified, the thought that it would ever get better dissipated. Knowing there was no rescue team coming, daydreaming and fantasizing was all I had left. My favorite daydream was the "spacemen." We would all be asleep in the wee hours of the night when the doorbell rang. Alarmed by the hour, my parents would rush to the door. There they would be greeted by two men in white jumpsuits (I don't know where I thought they were coming from; NASA?) Dismissing all formalities, they would get straight to the point. *"We need to see Lauri. We found her real family; there was a mix-up at the maternity ward."* Needless to say, they never showed.

Knowing my rescue team wasn't coming, I worked with what I had. The following is a good example of superb rationalization and coping mechanisms developed for optimal success in an abusive home: My dad's driving. My dad drove as if there was no speed limit and the lines were there simply to provide unemployed painters a pay-check. Curbs? They were used like the walls of a pool table. He used them to bank off, keeping him somewhat within the automotive playing field.

Although I only hung around with a few girls from school, none of them ever rode with my father a second time. One time was plenty. One girl even told me that her mother forbade her from ever riding with my father again. I was appalled. Although deep inside I knew they were right, I needed to convince them otherwise. I would rationalize his behavior by saying, "Don't you know my dad's an airline pilot? He's used to going 550 miles per hour in the plane. You try doing that all day and night and then slowing down to 50 afterward. He's safer going a hundred than most people are going the speed limit!" Although I deplored him, I did everything I could to defend him. It was all so confusing. After all, he was the only dad I had.

On one occasion, when I was around seven years old, we drove to Nanny and Poppy's for dinner. While we visited them on a regular basis, this trip was specifically planned so we could pick up a spare bed they had offered us. In those days, it seemed customary for every family to own at least one station wagon. Ours was white and brown with wood paneling on the sides, tan leather seats and matching carpet in the "way back," the open space behind the back seat.

For long trips like this one, my sisters and I would make sure to bring coloring books. Not to color on, of course, that would be too normal. We were simply maximizing our investment in my dad's crazy driving. We would sit in the way-back on the coloring books as my dad turned corners at high speeds and weaved through the traffic. As he sped down the road, we would slide around the way-back with our behinds on the coloring books and our hands tightly clenched on the sides of the book. This was the Burns' E-Ticket ride.

The drive up and dinner went as usual that night, but I clearly remember my dad and grandfather struggling to get the bed out of the house and on top of the car. Once content that it was properly situated, they worked hard to secure it tightly with a long piece of rope. On the way home my sisters and I fell asleep, as was customary on long drives at night.

When we arrived home, we were woken up to the sound of my dad screaming. "Get out of the car!" Although I was still half asleep, I clearly recall him looking around and yelling, "Where the hell is the bed?!" I had no idea I was supposed to be watching it. Luckily he was so distracted by where the bed had gone; I made it out unscathed that night.

I didn't think about that incident until many years later. Now, as an adult driver, I can't imagine how he didn't notice a queen size bed flying off the roof of the car. Certainly, the average person would have felt such a substantial change in weight, or if not that at least spot the bed in the rear view mirror bouncing around the freeway in busy traffic. Evidently he saw and felt nothing.

Believe it or not, in addition to my dad's rage he was also the family clown. He was not quite as entertaining as he thought, and his jokes were usually "off" in a big way. Not surprisingly, the humor generally capitalized on the weaknesses of others. After delivering a punch line, he'd wait for his audience to laugh while they looked at him skeptically. Although the laughs never came, he never tired of trying to be the funny man. I could never reconcile how he thought I would accept him as the "funny man" when he was the scariest man I knew.

From a young age, I used sarcasm and humor to deflect the pain I was feeling. Although I feared my dad tremendously and wanted to be nothing like him, I eventually emulated not only his warped sense of humor, but also his appetite for violence.

I had a strange recurring dream when I was a child. In my dream, there was a war outside of my house. There were explosions, shooting and people were dying. I was alone in the house and all of the doors were locked. I was safe. Both versions of my dad, the funny one, and the violent one, stood outside the locked front door begging me to let them in. Although they were pleading for their lives, I never allowed either of them in. Not knowing which one was which, I remember thinking that I would rather let them both die, than to allow the wrong one in.

When I first watched Jack Nicolson in "The Shining," his character seemed all too familiar. Whenever my dad entered the house, I immediately assessed his state of mind. I never knew what to expect. My ability to quickly assess his mood saved me from many beatings. Ironically, that same skill would help save my life in later years.

Even though my mom kept our house organized, she herself was a mess. Our home was always picture perfect. It actually looked like no one lived there. To give you an understanding of how accurate that is, let me tell you about "the bench." Right inside our front door was a bench. I guess it would most resemble the bench at a piano, except this bench was stained to match the golden browns in the felt on the wallpaper.

Yes, I said felt. This was the 60's—you could pet your wallpaper. As a kid coming in from school it was customary after walking two miles to get home and put my books on the bench right inside the door and head for the kitchen. That is, unless mom was home. If she was home, the first thing she would say is, "Who left books on the bench?" I could never understand why it was there. My mom had the house spotless at all times; she could tell whether we were in a room by the fingerprints on the table. I realize now that was probably the only part of her life she still had control over, so in this area she overcompensated.

On the top of our fireplace lay a large pile of family photo albums. The pictures were filed chronologically and dated all the way back to my parent's childhood. My dad's pictures started when he was around nineteen, but my mom's pictures went back to the time she was a toddler. I distinctly remember the ones from when she was a teenager. Smiling from ear to ear, surrounded by friends, she was absolutely radiant. She had silky long caramel brown hair, a figure to die for, and a beautiful smile. I can only tell you that the woman I called mom had features that resembled the girl in the pictures, but the twinkle in her eyes was long gone. Depression hung over her like a dark veil. By the time I was five she was fragile, nervous and withdrawn, and emotionally unavailable. Yet, I knew in my heart that she did the very best she could.

My best memories of my mom center around the nights I had bad dreams and the times I was sick. When I was little, I often had nightmares. In an effort to help me to feel safe, she would sit in the rocking chair alongside my bed until I fell back to sleep. She was also very nurturing when I was sick. I suffered from pneumonia several years in a row and, while I was bedridden, she made sure to bring me tea with cream and toast with jelly. On several occasions, she also brought home my favorite comic book, "Archie and the Gang." To this day, although I can't rationally explain it, I actually enjoy being sick. It's the only time I truly allow people to nurture me.

Other than the pneumonia, I rarely got sick. That is, other than the problems with my head. I was about eleven when the blackouts started. It felt like when you stand up too quickly, and the room rocks and fades to black. For me, this could happen at any time. Without notice, and with my eyes open, whether sitting or standing, the light faded. The first time it happened, I was in my fourth-grade classroom. One minute I was looking at the teacher and the next it was dark. It was like the lens on a camera, slowly closing. I could still hear him talking, but it was more of an amplified echo. Within less than a minute, I was back. Not wanting to be wimpy, I didn't tell anyone at first. I actually thought it was kind of cool. It allowed me to drift away. After about a month, I told my mom. The only reason I told her was to gain attention, similar to when I was sick. My mom took me to the doctor. He gave me something called an EEG. My head was measured and my scalp was marked with a pen. The technician then glued electrodes on my head and connected me to a machine. Could things get any stranger? My God, my mom and I both knew the problem was a result of being hit by my dad, but since she never brought it up, neither did I. After finding nothing on the EEG, the doctor prescribed Dilantin.

In an attempt to understand both the blackouts and violent outbursts, while still denying the effect my dad had on me, my mom continued taking me to doctors and psychiatrists. In addition to the Dilantin, I was prescribed a variety of medications, but for some reason, I took Melarill, a medication used to treat schizophrenia, the longest. After several EEGs revealed nothing, my mom pursued "other" alternatives. One day she brought home a pile of books on psychic experiences. I later learned that she obtained these books from a support group on space travel that she had attended.

A small group of strangers met regularly in a basement to discuss out-of-body experiences and their ability to travel beyond. Somehow, my mom had connected this stuff to the blackouts I was having. She would have done anything rather than admit the reality of our situation. I think at some level, if she were to admit what had really happened to me, she would be unable to face herself for not intervening sooner. I was completely unaffected by her mention of the visits with space travelers. I had learned long ago that neither of my parents was truly connected to reality.

My mom gave me the medicine every day. I liked being taken care of, so I had no problem taking it. My father on the other hand didn't like it. He hated the attention I was getting from my mom and he was also threatened by my relationship with the doctors. Afraid I would say something, he needed it to end. When my mom and I were at the store one day, he threw all of the medicine away. Upon our arrival home, I heard him screaming at her in the kitchen. "The doctor is an idiot! You know your own kid, she isn't suffering from anything. It's all an act! She doesn't need this shit because there's nothing wrong!"

As my father's anger accelerated, so did my out of control behaviors. When he was away on trips, things at home deteriorated. Much like him, when I didn't get my way, I would force my way with violence. Afraid of me, my mom and sisters would simply give in. Much like a volcanic eruption, anger would explode from every part of my being with no warning. I would break things, punch holes in the walls, and leave whenever I wanted. They had absolutely no control over me. My behavior also changed with my dad. After his beatings I would open my window and scream; I would cry louder than you could possibly imagine. I wished the neighbors would hear my screams and call the police. Eventually, the police did intervene, but not in the manner I had hoped for.

6

B Y THE SUMMER FOLLOWING SIXTH GRADE, I WAS ALIENATED FROM everyone and everything. I perfected consciously cutting myself off from the effect of my father's beatings. I no longer cried when he hit me. I had become a stone that couldn't be broken. I worked hard to reprogram my brain to think that pain didn't actually hurt. I thought if I could do this, I could endure anything. I had become the dark and disruptive person my father had always seen me as being. I was always in trouble anyway, so when it came to trouble, I thought, "*Bring it on.*"

Convinced that my dad would have preferred a boy, I started to see myself as one and frequently got into fist-fights with other boys. When it came to a fight, my mental state was, *Go ahead F with me, I can take whatever you can dish out.* And lord knows I could. Even by the age of thirteen, I wasn't a big girl, ninety-six pounds when soaking wet, but I could endure pain like no one I knew.

I possessed no practical fighting skills. I was just a skinny, hyper, child overflowing with rage at both my father and God. I was an irrational, reckless and explosive mess. I couldn't control my actions and never thought of their repercussions. As I saw it, there was no future to worry about anyway. Someday I would successfully take my own life and I knew it. I walked through life with a hair-pin triggered, automatic response system. The anger in my dad's eyes was a mirror to my soul. I had become the person he wanted me to be...worthless.

In addition to fighting regularly, I started smoking cigarettes, shoplifting, and hitchhiking. I thrived on the feeling of being bad. It provided me with a sense of power and control that was missing in every other part of my life. I made a habit of hitchhiking uptown, or sometimes I would skitch. Skitching is sliding on the icy roads using your boots like skates. I would wait by the stop sign, hiding behind a tree. When a car pulled up and stopped, I would quickly creep up behind the car and grab onto the bumper. It was dangerous, but exciting. I would slide on my boots on the slick road and let off as the car began to slow down again. When I got uptown I would go into the five and dime and steal. I would steal stupid things…fake jewelry, gum, candy. It didn't really matter what, it was the excitement of getting away with it. And frankly I thought they have so much stuff anyway, they will never notice.

One of the many innocent people who endured my wrath was my sixth grade teacher, Mr. Simmons. We struggled constantly. Mr. Simmons made a practice of yelling at me, which was probably well deserved because at this point I thrived on negative attention. But, it was clear from the very start that his yelling would only provoke more negativity and problematic behavior from me. My unspoken message was always, "Mister, you have no idea the abuse I can endure; you couldn't scare me if you tried little man."

I used to put tacks on his chair every morning to remind him that I was there. Each time he sat on them, I was amused. I could never understand how he would forget and sit right down day after day. It was customary for me to leave the classroom when Mr. Simmons turned his back to the class to write on the chalkboard. I often ventured outside of the classroom to explore the halls. Other times, I left through the sliding doors that led to the woods. Out there, at least I could smoke. Although I got caught on many occasions, it was not a deterrent. The trips to the principal's office had little impact on me. If anything, it gave me a stamp of approval with the rest of the reckless kids, and that was worth every moment of lecture.

Although I took my share of the class's attention, the biggest troublemaker in our class was Jerry. Not only was he the class clown, but he was even more disruptive than I was. I always admired the way he could have the entire class roaring with laughter while he was being lectured by the teacher. Jerry easily took command of the whole room;

31

that kid had real talent and I, of course, aspired to be more like him. Although we both harassed Mr. Simmons most of the year, by the end of the year we felt the need to take it up a notch. We devised a plan to paint the classroom and recruited a handful of moderate troublemakers to assist us. There was a rainbow of plastic paint jars under the sink in the back of the classroom. Although they were intended to be used during the art portion of class, we were going to use them to redecorate the room.

The plan was as follows: As Mr. Simmons was writing on the chalkboard, I would quietly creep toward the back of the room, but this time instead of my usual exit routine, I would crawl under the sink and into the paint cabinet and shut the door. We assumed Mr. Simmons would think I had left the classroom as usual. I would sit in the cabinet until school ended. When I heard Mr. Simmons turn off the lights and shut the door, I would climb out and open the sliding door to let my conspirators in. We would then let our artistic juices flow and paint the entire room and everything in it.

Everything went as planned, up to the point where I opened the door to let the conspirators in. Jerry was standing by himself. Everyone else had chickened out. Having to appear to be tough, neither Jerry nor I had the courage to be the first one to wimp out. We decided to proceed as planned.

I chose green and Jerry chose yellow. We painted the chalkboard, the books, and the inside of Mr. Simmons' briefcase, as well as his glasses. I spent the remainder of that year smiling inwardly while looking at him wearing those green-rimmed glasses. It was all a big laugh and we were the center of attention for a good week. Although we were proud of our prank, one of the original crew let the principal in on our plan. I was on cloud nine until they told my dad. Surprising, he didn't beat me. I was so confused. When it seemed like I actually deserved to be punished, he did nothing. From thereon in, Mr. Simmons made a routine of having the class sit quietly while he spun Simon and Garfunkel's "The Sound of Silence." I never knew what we were supposed to derive from that song, and having listened to it again recently, I am still not sure.

It was also during that summer, that my parents converted the large upstairs sewing room into a bedroom for Nadine. Nadine was adamant that Alyssa or I were never allowed to enter her room without an invitation. Needless to say, those invitations only came when she thought she could gain something from our presence. If she wasn't looking for information, she generally wanted cigarettes. It was also around this time that Nadine's alliance with my dad became more evident and his behavior became more erratic. It seemed we were all changing roles. My mom was taking more and more prescription pills, Nadine was becoming more secretive and I was becoming more "boy like." And Alyssa by this time was completely invisible.

One afternoon my father bolted into the house and yelled, "Come here kids, I have a surprise for you!" When we entered the kitchen, he was proudly holding a small metal cage containing two white rabbits. He told us they were both girls and he would be making a home for them in the yard. Within a few hours, he had built a pen out of wood and chicken wire for them to live in.

It wasn't until the first snowfall that we realized his plan had gone wrong. One morning, while sitting at the breakfast table eating Captain Crunch and staring out of the large bay windows, I saw what looked like small snowballs moving around the pen. Unsure of what I was seeing, I retrieved the BB gun and went outside to find out that we were now the proud owners of eight rabbits. True to form, my dad had mistakenly brought home one female and one male rabbit. We said nothing. If you visit Centerport these days, you'll find a large population of white rabbits inhabiting the forest.

It became customary for me to assume my father's role whenever he was away. I protected my sisters and was always there to handle anyone that bothered them. I welcomed any excuse for a good fight. My father had two guns. He had a handgun, which he carried in a holster under his airline uniform, and slept with under his pillow. He also kept a BB gun over the fireplace to protect our rabbits. When he was away and we heard sounds, I was now the one who grabbed the BB gun.

It was routine in our family for the kids to attend day camp during the summer time, but now that Nadine was older, she opted out. Alyssa and I would load the bus reluctantly at about 8 a.m. with our God-awful camp packs on our backs preparing for a day of sweat and sports. I never excelled at any sport, unless go-cart driving counts, and even then I must admit, I was more prone to attempt to exit the track for a "free style" ride than go around the pre-planned, rock lined path. The way I saw it, if you got the cart, make it count! I was banned from the activity for a month after crashing into the go-cart shack in a reckless attempt to spin out on a patch of dirt.

When it came to sports, I was a disaster. I clearly remember standing on the hot baseball field as they picked teams. The captains would begin calling out the names of the most valued players, while I stood off to the side kicking rocks, hoping they would forget I was there so that I could go explore in the woods...but a few minutes later, the moment of truth. It's just me and the fat kid that can't run. Now this is humiliation at its best—you could hear in the most disgusted, defeated tone of voice..."OK, we'll take Claire, if you take Burns."

The assignment of positions was even better. They created a whole new position for me. It was the 'get your ass as far out into the field as you can go and still hear us and stand there' position. I can tell you that on more than one occasion, I had been out there so long and was so uninterested that by the time the ball did come my way, it just rolled right past me, which only served to increase their love for me.

For the majority of our childhood, Nadine was an outcast. She had braces, frizzy hair and was a recluse of sorts. Although we went to the same school, no one at our school knew I had a sister. We were that estranged from each other.

In the summer of '75 Nadine was reborn. Braces off, a functional round brush and several hours of baking in the sun with baby oil and *poof*...the new Nadine! She hooked up with some boys that drove fast cars, partied hard and liked loud rock and roll. Her whole life changed overnight.

By this time, she was smoking pot regularly. Shortly thereafter, I began smoking pot as well. People often ask me, when did you take your first drink...or drug? I always find this question amusing because as Jews, we are started on Grape Concord Manischewitz the moment we come out of womb. We have it for Passover, Chanukah and sometimes at Temple on Friday nights. I clearly do not remember my first drink, but I can tell you this, I love Grape Concord Manischewitz wine. I recently attended a Bar Mitzvah where a small girl about nine years of age was walking around with a tray with small plastic cups of wine on it. From beneath the tray, little hands were coming up from small people who could not even see what they were reaching for. These are my people. Clearly I do not remember my first drink.

Smoking pot was something entirely new. I can't say for sure whether I was more into the spaced out feeling or the feeling of knowing I was being bad. I loved being a troublemaker and acting tough and this only enhanced those feelings. From the time I started smoking pot, no matter what the weather was like, if I felt like getting high I would hitchhike to a friend's house.

One day we had a snow storm, the schools were closed and we were stranded at home with no electricity. A living hell gone worse. I decided to take my chances and hitchhike to my friend Lacey's. As I walked out of the front door, my mom chased out after me. The winds were so strong that I was struggling to stay upright and the snow was coming down so fast that it stung my face with its tiny cold pellets. My mom yelled, "You can't go out in this weather Lauri Burns! Are you crazy?!" I just kept on walking. I was thinking how courageous an act this will be and how impressed Lacey would be when she sees that I was tough enough to hitchhike in this weather.

By that summer I was hitchhiking on a regular basis. One day, on my way to town, I was picked up by a man who unexpectedly veered off the road and headed into the woods. I was scared to death. Both my heart and mind went racing out of control. I had no idea what was happening, but I knew it was bad. Eventually, he stopped and reached into his side door to retrieve something.

Before he could reveal what he was looking for, I instinctively, screamed out, "I have a knife and will cut you open like a fucking pig and watch your blood spill out all over you!"

It was such a random thing to yell, but it was just what came out when I opened my mouth. Taken aback, the man promised not to hurt me. He said he just wanted to get high, and at that point I could see he had a small pipe and some weed in his hand. Given my outburst, and the nature of my threats, he immediately took me out of the woods. I was a bit embarrassed, but also impressed that I scared the man enough to make him exit the woods. I felt powerful. I don't know exactly where my courage came from that day. I never told anyone about this event because I was sure I would have been blamed for putting myself in that position.

For reasons I will never understand, this was about the time my parents began allowing us to smoke cigarettes in our bedrooms. What a confusing life. I was getting beat up for doing nothing and when I was actually doing something worthy of reprimand, it was deemed acceptable. Needless to say, I enjoyed the liberty and so did many of our friends. Lord knows none of the other parents allowed this.

7

THE YEAR I TURNED THIRTEEN WAS AN ESPECIALLY TOUGH ONE. ON New Year's Eve, Poppy died while blowing up balloons. I had lost the only person who had ever tried to protect me. With both Pepper and Poppy gone, I was alone and more depressed than ever.

Over the next few months, I spent a good deal of time with the Cantor at our temple preparing for my Bat Mitzvah. The Cantor is the person at temple in charge of the singing. Just like churches have choirs, temples have Cantors. At temple it is customary for the Cantor to initiate the songs (mostly sung in Hebrew) and the congregation to follow.

Because the entire Bat Mitzvah consists of singing in Hebrew, I had a lot of prep work to get ready. It is customary to sing out of tune at the Bat Mitzvah. The melody in the songs fluctuates very quickly from alto to tenor and back again for no apparent reason. The songs, like my life, made no sense, but I did it.

I distinctly remember standing on stage during the ceremony chanting in a language I didn't understand. Although my family sat in the audience directly in front of me, I didn't know them and they didn't know me. We had never exchanged meaningful words at any level. It was like an out of body experience. There I was amongst my immediate family and fifty of their closest friends and no one really knew me or what I was going through. For all intents and purposes, I was alone.

It was around this time that my dad's anger towards my mom intensified. Their hatred toward one another was palpable. You could feel it the minute they walked into a room. His verbal abuse toward her was relentless. As his anger accelerated, so did her prescription drug intake.

Over the next few months, my mom made a habit of packing her bags, setting them by the door and screaming, "I'm leaving you f... ing kids...you're on your own!" But after a few hours of ranting and raving she would return the bags to her room. After the first few times, we became immune to her antics. I often wondered if she had actually packed her bags or if they were sitting there completely empty. Shortly after my Bat Mitzvah, she left for real. By that time we were so accustomed to the suitcase packing thing that no one noticed. It wasn't until the next day when she didn't return that we realized she might have actually done it this time. Bottom line, it was a relief. I was glad someone had finally gotten out.

Initially, she only left for a few weeks, promising to return if my father were to leave. A few weeks later, my dad left and she moved back in. My parents continued to swap living in the house for short periods of time. Depending on who was there, we were given explicit instructions about what to say and do to protect that parent.

In addition to the discussions about the breakup, my dad and Nadine seemed to be having more than their share of secret chats. It wasn't long after that, my dad moved out of the house again and Nadine stopped eating. Our parents were so busy fighting that they failed to notice. She was in the ninth grade and weighed less than eighty pounds the day she fainted. She was pale as a ghost and she had dark circles under her eyes. I knew the moment it happened that it was directly related to my father's leaving. I couldn't put the pieces together as to why. She was immediately hospitalized for anorexia. She was fed intravenously and returned home a week later and a few pounds heavier. It was never discussed again.

After a few months, my mom finally left for good. She moved to California with little more than what she had in her pocket. She promised to send for us as soon as she was able to secure a place to live. Although I believe she wanted to take us with her, her lack of resources made that impossible. My dad controlled all of the money. By the time she left, we all knew she needed to go. Her pill intake was at an all time high and she too had become verbally abusive. She was falling apart. Although I would have given anything to go with her, I was just glad someone finally got out. Like many of those scary movies I used to watch, I was keenly aware that the person leaving, if not killed by the bad guy first, usually returned with help. Since we were with the bad guy, her chances of returning were very good.

8

So, suddenly we were alone with our father. If i had any idea what I was in store for, I might have felt differently about my mom's leaving, but it was too late. The first sign that I was in trouble was when the walk-in closet in my parent's room was converted into a liquor storage area. Large brown boxes lined the floor. Each box contained several bottles of Smirnoff's vodka. In addition to the bottles in the closet, it was customary to see a cold bottle in the freezer. He never spoke a word about the alcohol to us, but he warned us about the closet. "If I find out that anyone went near my closet, they will regret it."

Simply stated, we knew to comply. My dad never raised a hand to either of my sisters, but having witnessed his abuse on me was enough. We all stayed away from the closet. I never actually saw him drink, but the change was evident in his behavior. He became more unpredictable than ever and significantly more volatile. I retreated so far inward that I felt as though I didn't even exist.

It was customary by the time I was thirteen to spend my free days hanging out at McDonalds with friends. Hitchhiking was always the preferred method. It provided me with the excitement and freedom that I needed to feel alive. Somehow it made me feel in control, and I desperately needed that. I will never forget the day my dad offered to give me a ride. Although every impulse inside of me screamed no, I knew to deny his request would only trigger his anger. Right after he started the car, I realized I had forgotten my house key. Knowing he would be mad if I left without it, I said, "One sec' dad, I forgot my key."

I bolted out of the car and ran up to my room as fast as I could. Although I didn't see it immediately, after ruffling through some things, I spotted it. Whirling around to get back down to the car before he got upset, I turned for the door. That was when I noticed he had followed me up. Before I could register any response, he punched me in the face. That was the first time he actually knocked me out. When I came to a few seconds later, I stood up on wobbly legs, gave him the customary hug and told him I loved him. Silently, we returned to the car and proceeded to McDonalds.

With my mom gone, my dad's relationship with my sister Nadine became weirder than ever. He put more energy into making her do and say things to protect him and she readily complied. Their private conversations became more and more frequent. It didn't make any sense. The more they conspired with one another, the more nervous I became. I knew whatever they were up to, it wasn't good. My only hope was to avoid them at all cost.

I was startled when my dad entered my room one night and demanded, "You need to get out of the house!" It was after dark on a school night. Both Nadine and Alyssa were home, but he was only talking to me. I had no idea what he was up to, but I didn't ask questions. I immediately got up and started walking. He followed me down the hall into the foyer and as I exited the front door he said, "You stay outside until I am ready to let you back in." He promptly shut the door and locked it. Not wanting to disobey him, I left our property. Well almost. I walked down the big hill in front of our house and sat on the curb. There was nowhere to go. I sat...and sat...and sat...The longer I was there, the colder it grew and the more my mind raced. *What were they doing in there?* With my dad's drinking and erratic behavior, I wasn't sure they were *doing* anything. Maybe he would fall asleep and forget about me. Almost an hour later, my butt began to ache from the hard cement curb. In an attempt to relieve the soreness, I fell back onto the soft grass. *Well, if he doesn't let me in, I will sleep out here...*

Big mistake. Wet with moisture from the night air, I was now wet and cold. *What the hell were they doing in there?* I thought of knocking on the door of one of the kids I knew from the bus stop, but what would I say? Can I come in? Any kid my age would be doing homework or preparing for bed. Due to the unexpected nature of the request, I had not thought to bring a jacket; I had no idea I was going to be locked outside. Looking back at my house, I saw no sign of activity. The whole house looked dim with the exception of my bedroom light, which remained on. When I turned back around, I noticed Debbie's house across the street.

Debbie was a few years older than me. They had moved in less than a year ago and we became friends. It was actually her five-year-old sister Tabatha that drew me over there the first time. She was a perfect little angel, silky straight black hair and the biggest brown eyes you ever saw. Anytime I saw her outside, I would offer to watch her for their mom. Now looking over at their house, I noticed that all of the front windows were brightly lit. *Hell, it was worth a try.* I walked over.

When I saw the expression on her mom's face, I knew I had made a mistake. "Lauri, what are you doing here? It is after nine, Debbie is asleep." Completely embarrassed I said, "Oh...sorry" and quickly walked away. What an idiot. She must think I am crazy. As far as I was concerned, everyone knew I was crazy...the neighbors, my parents, my relatives...what did it matter anymore. I had sat on the curb for a good thirty minutes more by the time I heard the latch on our front door release. Before I could turn to look, he was gone, but the door was left unlocked. These lockouts continued and as things got stranger, I started to piece the puzzle together.

I was sitting in the den watching TV when Nadine sat down on the other end of the couch. Not really acknowledging her I just continued to watch my show. When the commercial came on, she said, "Hey, dad took me somewhere last night...to a big dinner party." She appeared to be bragging. With not much of a response, I just looked at her. "He introduced the people...he said they were his family...and he told them I was his girlfriend...and he kissed me." What? Ha? I had no idea what she was talking about. Was everyone losing their minds? Although mortified, I didn't know if she was making up a story or telling me the truth. Even as crazy as my dad was, this was hard for even me to buy. I was sure she was lying. She walked away abruptly and it was several years later before I ever thought about it again. When I did remember it, I thought it was a dream. Today I know it wasn't.

Believe it or not, with all of this going on, we still had normal activities. Alyssa and I had day camp all summer long. Nadine, on the other hand, stayed home because she was "older." Most of the time, it was just her and my dad at the house, but when he was at work, she had the house to herself. And she used it. It became customary to hear tunes from Led Zeppelin, ELO or Peter Frampton erupting from our house before I even exited the camp bus. This was music to my ears in more ways than one. It meant my dad was gone, there was a party in the house and, by default of being a resident, I was invited. Inside, there was always a bunch of older boys whipping up screwdrivers in my dad's blender. I liked the screwdrivers and hanging out with the boys. Nadine was usually out of sight, in her upstairs room with her "new" boyfriend.

Although my romantic interests were minimal I did have a few experiences. My first secret love affair was in nursery school. There was a small Italian kid with jet black hair and long bangs that hung over his eyes. His name was Michael. Michael used to always say, *"There's something fishy going on around here..."* I loved that kid! I never made contact with him and hid whenever he approached me, but I was crazy about him. Most of all, I went to extraordinary lengths to ensure Michael never heard me crunching my cookies.

I also had a "boyfriend" agreement with one of the boys that used to visit the house with Nadine's friends. We would get drunk and kiss on the couch. I will never forget the feeling when he phoned our house to tell me it was over. I can best describe it as a state of shock. Although I don't remember really caring that much for him, I remember the feeling of being dumped. It was horrible. From that point forward, if I was ever dating anyone, I was always the first one out and I never got attached.

When my dad was gone on trips, we occasionally had someone stay with us. Usually it was a lady in her fifties who really didn't talk to us, but more often than not, we were alone. I started to invite friends to spend the night. This was something I rarely did when my parents were married, but now that we had the house to ourselves, it was great.

Janice was the one that spent the night the most often. Janice was a very big stoner and hung out with a lot of older kids. Although she was my age, she seemed a lot older.

It was a Saturday the last time Janice spent the night. My dad had left on a trip earlier that morning. Janice had planned to spend the night and we were going to hang out the next day. She was over by 7 p.m. The plan was to wake up, hitchhike to McDonalds and smoke. It seemed like all we ever did was go to McDonalds, eat fries, hang around with a dozen or so of our friends and smoke cigarettes. Every so often, the day was spiced up by a good fight.

The next morning Janice and I woke up as planned and hit the bathroom to get ready for our day. With my dad gone, this was just the break I needed. After we showered and put on our makeup, we realized the blow dryer was gone. This was strange, but I knew there must have been a logical reason. I don't know why I thought that, nothing was ever logical around this place. Needless to say, we looked everywhere a reasonable person would have left a blow dryer. I looked in my sister's rooms, the other bathrooms and coming up empty handed, I gave up. Janice, on the other hand, not knowing our house, just searched aimlessly. After almost twenty minutes with no success, we gave up. It was clearly gone. I assumed Nadine had taken it out with her and forgot to bring it home. It was a serious chick crisis, my hair was a frizz ball and I certainly wasn't going to McDonalds like that. Our plans were off.

I can still recall the sinking feeling I had when I heard the basement door open. At that point I forgot all about McDonalds and the missing blow dryer. The only person who ever came up through the basement was my dad. The basement was the entryway from the garage to the house. Although we weren't doing anything wrong, his mere presence created paranoia and fear. I was sure he was out for the night; this was not in the plan. I heard his footsteps coming down the hall and I yelled from the bathroom, "Dad, have you seen the blow dryer?" No response. I heard him enter his room and set his suitcase and pilot's cap down. It was an Airline cap made out of blue cloth with a hard plastic rim for a secure fit. It had a firm bill with gold wings affixed and the name of the Airline he worked for. It was customary for my dad to empty all of his change from his pockets into his cap prior to setting it down. When it hit the chair at the end of his bed, I could hear the rumbling of the change. I now had an acute sense of where my dad was at all times.

A few seconds later, he exited his room. Then I heard his retreat down the basement stairs into the far end of the shop. The shop was my dad's "man cave." It was where he withdrew when he wanted to get away from everybody without leaving the house. As you entered, there were several large natural wood shelves neatly stocked with tools, paint and hardware. He had converted an area toward the back into a gym. The shop was my father's sanctuary. When he was in there, we never entered. A few moments later, I heard him coming up the stairs and re-entering the main part of the house.

From the bathroom, I could see as he turned the corner that he was holding the blow dryer in his hand. Although I was confused as to why the blow dryer would have been in the shop, I dared not ask any questions. He often did crazy things like this to start a fight and I wasn't interested in bringing one on. As he entered the bathroom, he lifted the blow dryer over his head and yelled, "I told you to stay out of my fucking closet!" It was immediately apparent to me that Janice had opened the door to his liquor closet during our search. I had forgotten to tell her about the closet!

He began beating me, using the blow dryer as a weapon. The moments that followed went very quickly. With every step he took towards me, I took a step back. My back hit the wall and I was trapped. There was a small space between the toilet and the wall. He continued to hit me and I cowered into the space attempting to use the toilet as a barrier. When he missed, I heard the crunch of the plaster in the wall. The next few minutes were just a blur. When Janice appeared at the door, I was thrust back into the room, like a drunken person awaking from a black-out. Janice's presence plunged into our world like a cold sharp knife into the small of our backs. When she let out a gasp, my father immediately spun around, redirecting his attention toward the door. We all quickly assessed the enormity of what we were about to take in…My father's shock of having his behavior witnessed, Janice's alarm and my humiliation while my worlds collided from the tough cool exterior I had grown so accustomed to presenting, to the frail scared child stuck between the toilet and the wall.

As both Janice and my father made eye contact, the look of shock resounded in their eyes. Both of them were instantly transported out of their safety zones. Although for different reasons, the shock was equally resident. No one uttered a world. Janice, confused and embarrassed, retreated quickly down the hall to the kitchen phone and my dad went to his room, closed the door and engaged the lock. This was the first time anyone besides my family had ever witnessed my dad's abuse.

Before I knew it, we were at Janice's house. Although I know her mother picked us up, I have no recollection of the drive to her house. I was in a state of shock and disbelief. I do remember sitting with Janice's parents in their living room as they told me that everything would be okay. They said they would help me, but I couldn't imagine how. I thought if they talked to the authorities or worse yet, to my father, I would be beaten like never before.

While I genuinely appreciated their interest, the entire conversation was surreal to me. I had never discussed the situation regarding my father with anyone before. To be more accurate, I didn't actually talk with Janice's parents. It took all I had just to listen and nod while they did all the talking. I was completely uncomfortable. I remember nothing else of the next few hours until the phone in the kitchen rang.

I could only hear Janice's mom's side of a conversation. I could tell by the content being discussed, as well as the fact that she continually glanced my way to see if I was listening, that she was now talking to my father. "Oh, so she is undergoing treatment for that? Yes, these kids can get themselves into a lot of trouble. Yes, it isn't good." Then something about my medication and she politely finished off with, "Oh, I understand," and hung up.

Without saying a word, she retreated into the living room and was talking quietly with Janice's dad. I assumed my father must have lied in order to protect himself and I was sure that she was passing that information on to her husband as fact. A few minutes later, she returned to the kitchen and told me that my dad would be coming to get me shortly. Although I already knew, she told me that she had talked to him and assured me that things would be okay now. Rather than feeling relieved, I was thinking how naïve this woman was. I appreciated her effort, but she had no idea what she was dealing with.

I vividly recall my dad in the foyer of their home. I was on the stairs and Janice stood behind me. As he thanked Janice's parents for taking care me, I was feeling sick to my stomach with dread. It was nearly unbearable watching this monster act as if he were a loving and concerned parent.

Neither of us said a word on the drive home. We parked in the driveway, got out of the car and remained silent the entire walk up the brick pathway to our front door. I wondered if he would sit down and talk to me or, better yet, acknowledge that the nightmare was over.

Much to my surprise, he unlocked the door and politely held it open for me. Just as I passed him and walked over the door's threshold, he punched me squarely in the back with everything he had. The pain shot through me like an ice pick piercing my spine. Terrified by the force of the blow and realizing that it was only the first of what was to come, the adrenalin shot through me and I bolted through the door. Entering the formal dining room on the right, I immediately found protection from the table situated between us. After he chased me around the table a few times, I escaped back out the front door.

I ran down the street looking for a place to hide. Fearful of being seen by any of the neighbors, I knew I had to avoid open areas. I entered the woods looking for cover. I immediately saw a large patch of overgrowth sufficient to conceal me. I burrowed into the brush and pushed away at the small branches to allow a partial view of my house beyond. With no thought of how long I would stay there or what my plan was, I shook and attempted to steady my breathing. When I saw my dad exit the house and enter his car, I let out a deep sigh of relief. This was just the break I needed. I assumed he was going to look for me or maybe he just took off, as he was prone to do when he got angry and I wasn't around to beat. Either way, I had a moment to reenter the house and get some supplies.

I know now that even though the brief intervention with Janice's parents wasn't fruitful, it gave me the courage I needed to finally get out; to get out for good. I ran back into the house to get some things and bumped into my sister, Nadine. I was surprised at her reaction when she saw me. To my utter amazement, she screamed, "Get out! Get the fuck out!" Then she began smashing her furniture on the floor. Being that she had the upstairs room with wood flooring, the large furniture crashing down made quite a bang. I was completely confused. I didn't know what my dad had told her while I was gone, but it was clear that she now saw me as an intruder in my own home. I immediately left and ran into the woods to take a shortcut to the main highway and hitchhiked to my friend Erika's.

Erika and her brother were latch-key kids. They lived with their single mother who was never home, so it was a good place to crash. Erika's room was upstairs in a converted attic. Posters of rock stars lined the walls and a queen-sized mattress sat on the rug in the middle of the floor. Her little brother, a cool, long-haired hippie kid around twelve hibernated down the steps in his own rock and roll retreat. Although I had been there several times to smoke out, I never saw their mom. By this time I was starting to wonder if they really had one.

A few minutes after I got to Erika's, I called home. I don't remember feeling overwhelmed by a desire to be responsible, nor was I the least bit concerned about my father's worrying. I suspect it was just out of habit that I called. I know now that calling was the wrong thing to do. When my dad answered the phone, I skipped over any pleasantries and simply stated, "I'm at Erika's house and I am not coming home." Not interested in his response, I quickly hung up. End of story—or so I thought.

Erika's phone rang at around 2 a.m. and she answered it. Still half asleep, she handed it to me and muttered "For you…" I was surprised to hear the sweet high-pitched voice of my Aunt Nora. Nora wasn't really my aunt; she was my dad's best friend's wife. She and her husband, Gus, spent so much time with our family that they had become honorary relatives. Aunt Nora was a cute old woman; short, chubby and sweet. She was an old fashioned gal, always making sure that my dad and Gus had whatever they needed to be comfortable and never daring to sit down with them. Gus worked with my dad at the Airline; they had worked together for years.

Before I could respond she said, "Lauri dear, the police are here at the house. We all know you have the gun and we are coming to get you." I was so accustomed to my family's insanity by this point that hearing this from her didn't trigger a major reaction from me. I do recall saying to myself, "At two in the morning?" I had no idea what my father was up to now, but I felt a certain sense of calm knowing he couldn't attack me if the police were there. Maybe we were going to talk about what happened and the authorities would help me. I felt relief in knowing that others were involved. The only part that still concerned me was "the gun." What the heck were they talking about? I guess I would find out.

A short while later, my aunt picked me up and drove me back to our house. We did not speak during the drive. It wasn't customary in those days for kids to speak to an adult about anything other than light conversation, so although questions ran around in my head, I sat quietly. I had no idea if she even knew what had happened over the past twenty-four hours or why I was staying with Erika. It was all so confusing.

As we drove, I thought about the call she had made to me earlier. I had no idea what was going on, but I played out several different scenarios in my head. The one thing I was pretty certain about was that she probably wasn't referring to my dad's BB gun. Even if I had taken the BB gun, I seriously doubt doing so would have compelled the police to come to my house or even warrant a visit from my Aunt Nora in the middle of the night. I knew the handgun my dad kept under his pillow was the gun Aunt Nora was referring to. Knowing little about guns, I only knew that it was black, small and looked like a police type gun. I assumed that it was dangerous and could kill someone.

When we arrived, I could hear the hushed sound of men's voices coming from the kitchen. My aunt escorted me in into the kitchen without a word and directed me to sit down by pointing to a chair. There were two policemen sitting at the table with my dad. The police questioned me about the missing gun, but never mentioned anything about what happened yesterday. As the policemen talked, it became clear they were indeed referring to my dad's handgun and, although I had no information for them, it also became clear that everybody thought I had taken it.

The police asked questions like, "When did you leave the house? Where did you go? Did you take anything with you?" Although I answered their questions directly and honestly, I also made no mention of why I left the house or of my dad's abuse. I gave clear and direct answers without offering additional information. With my dad sitting right across from me, I did what was expected; cover up the abuse. In the few times I accidentally glanced over toward my dad, the expression on his face spoke volumes. His lips were stiff the same way they were right before he would explode. I knew not to talk. It was our family secret.

On this particular night, I truly believe that if one of the police officers had taken me aside first and questioned me alone, not knowing how much they already knew, I probably would have revealed that something was "wrong." I say that because today it seems like the authorities have a better handle on this type of occurrence. But back in the 70's, the parents ruled the world. As far as they were concerned, kids had no voice. I am glad this has changed. Had it been that way then, my whole life may have gone down a different path.

With my dad, Aunt Nora and I sitting there getting nowhere, one of the policemen excused me and told me I could go to bed. I heard them quietly talking a while longer and soon after the front door opened and closed. I looked out my bedroom window and watched as the police car drove away.

A bit spooked by the police and fearing what my father might do next, I lay in bed unable to fall asleep. I was comforted by the sound of my aunt's voice. Knowing she was still in the house provided me some assurance that the beast wouldn't roar anytime soon. Suddenly, the house got quiet. I stared at my bedroom door waiting for God knows what to happen. Was he coming? I could not believe I was back in the house again; my journey to freedom at Erika's had been a short one. Just then, a shadow appeared outside my door. Luckily it was the short shadow of my Aunt Nora. Thank God she was still there. She quietly approached my bed, bent down next to me and whispered, "Lauri dear, I just saw your dad and Nadine take the gun out of the oven. It's clear that they hid the gun, but, if you tell anyone, your dad will lose his job at the Airlines."

Even though I hated my dad and often wished I knew of a hit kid at school that would off him for a few days worth of lunch money, in my core I still dreamed that one day he would love me. I had changed everything about me in order to gain my dad's love and acceptance. It was a constant battle to figure out what I thought he might want me to be. I had transitioned from being quiet— when I was a small child in my own world of sucking cookies, to thinking that maybe if I was smarter—I worked really hard on my math in 3rd grade thinking it might help, but it had no effect. Then I thought maybe if I was funnier, and although I didn't have the wit of my classmate Jerry, I was moderately funny, but my dad never paid attention and certainly never laughed. Lastly, I thought maybe my dad wanted a boy. To accommodate this thought, I had cut off my long brown hair, wore men's work boots, and fought all of the time. A small version of my dad.

I knew at that moment I would never tell. I hadn't worked so hard at gaining his acceptance to throw in the towel now. If I told on him, he would certainly never love me. And maybe, just maybe, this was the final act of loyalty he needed to see that I was on his team. Even with the police involved, I protected him. This certainly had to buy me some points. On the one hand, I wished he would just go away or die and on the other hand, I longed for him to accept me. I guess I wasn't really committed to how it ended, just that it ended. That night I simply looked at Aunt Nora and sleepily said, "OK, I won't tell."

9

THE NEXT MORNING I WAS WOKEN BY A POLICE OFFICER STANDING at the doorway to my bedroom. He very nicely asked me to get dressed, closed the door and waited just outside. I had no idea what was going on. Were they taking my dad away? Had they investigated and found out what really happened? I rushed to get dressed and find out. Finally something was going to happen.

Once I was dressed, he escorted me down the long hallway and out the front door, down the brick path and onto the gravel driveway toward a waiting police car. Without any explanation, he opened the back door and gently guided me in. As if the night before hadn't been baffling enough, now I really had no clue what was going on. The officer and my dad stood a few feet away from the car speaking very quietly and then my dad retreated into the house and the officer got in the driver's seat. He started the car, paused for a second, then turned toward me and said, "Bazooka?" I sat frozen and stared at him blankly, he reached out, handed me a piece of Bazooka, grinned slightly and then slowly drove off. This would be the last time I would ever see my home.

Silently we drove—for what seemed too long—questions pouring in my head like rain on a stormy night, going by too fast to actually process. A silent intensity that electrified the hairs on the small of my neck. I desperately needed him to say something, anything to break the silence. But nothing came. I just stared out of the car window in a world of my own. Is this safety? Is he rescuing me? From the looks of the conversation with my dad, I feared not. But where was I going? I was scared to death.

About twenty minutes later, the officer slowed the car and initiated the blinker. As he turned, a large gothic steel gate slid into my view. Perched up on my seat wanting to know where I was going and fearing all along, I strained to see. Beyond the gate was a large breadth of land. It was void of life with parched brown leaves covering the ground like a blanket of gloom and black lifeless trees scattered throughout. As I looked ahead, all I could see was a long, winding road covered with spider cracks and pit holes, revealing a combination of its age and its frequency of use.

As we drove further, I saw the dull red brick structure with steel bars sealing the windows. My hand clenched the armrest of the car door so hard that my fingernails created an imprint in the cushion. The ongoing silence was deafening, increasing my level of panic. The longer it went on, the more it seemed like I was sanctioning what was happening. The painful knot in my throat felt like a large rubber cork on a carbonated bottle; as the pressure grew, I fought back the tears. My body had long since become a shelter to house the horror of my father's abuse, and although I had felt the pressure in my throat on many days, on this day I was unsure of my ability to contain it.

The car stopped at the front of the building. The officer retrieved the hand-set from his radio and uttered a few words that had no meaning to me, but it was clear that he was announcing our arrival. He silently exited the car without a gesture or a word. In a military like fashion, he opened my door and escorted me up the large cement steps that met the massive steel doors at the building's entrance.

As we slowly climbed the steps, the pressure mounted. When we reached the top step, I stood frozen, unable to breathe. At a quick glance, I might have appeared compliant, but one look into my eyes would have exposed my swelling terror. I eluded all eye contact. In a few moments I would learn that these doors and the bars on the windows above, which ordinarily serve to protect those inside, were actually meant to protect the outside world from the residents within.

A large man opened the door, thanked the officer and motioned me inside. When he shut the door and engaged the lock, the loud clang of steel vibrated through my bones and echoed down the long, cold corridor ahead. In spite of the fact that I never spoke two words to that officer, I suddenly felt abandoned by his absence.

Without as much as a word, the large man escorted me down the endless corridor. I was startled as several men rushed up to a small window on the unit door to our left. With their vulgar breath steaming up the fogged glass, they fought to view the female specimen that had just entered their territory. The infusion of their voices howling vulgarities possessed a sick, perverted tone similar to that of a gang of cannibals viewing a fresh corpse. As if acknowledging acceptance of a gift, they fought for a clear, unobstructed view. We could not have walked fast enough. Violated and exposed, the pounding of my heart battled within my chest.

As we disappeared from their view, their howls faded and new noises erupted. The most prevalent of all was a woman's voice, long cries with irregular pitches. I could not determine if the sound was representative of someone in pain, or someone in despair. As my imagination raced, my terror grew. The man guiding me showed absolutely no response to the woman's cries.

I would later learn that the sound I was hearing was Stormy. A twenty-three year old deaf, dumb girl with a mangled body, abandoned at birth. Left in a basket on the cement steps on a stormy day, the nurses named her Stormy and accepted her as their own. The loud moaning sound was her only form of communication. Stormy was missing four fingers from her right hand. She had lost them one day when a nurse failed to notice her holding the steel door-frame to support her broken body. The weight of the large door closing severed her fingers instantly. Moaning and rocking back and forth in a world of her own, the hospital workers no longer heard her cries. Silent to their ears, she was completely alone. In a short time, I too would fail to hear her.

The vastness of the corridor served to amplify the sounds that were closest to us. The volume was so magnified and the echo so ominous, that chills shot up my spine. The further we walked the more the frightening sounds dissipated. When it finally quieted down, the only remaining sound was the clicking of the man's large shoes and the patter of the rubber soles on my sneakers as they hit the floor.

Finally we stopped; we had reached our destination. A steel door matching every other door we had seen along the way. The man retrieved a large ring of keys from his belt. He disengaged the lock, opened the steel door and guided me to what looked like an office. An older man sat behind a desk. He asked me to be seated as he ruffled through his papers before looking up at me. The judgment in his eyes was undeniable.

While I remember very little about the remainder of that meeting, I will never forget the moment he told me that this place was an institution for the mentally ill and that I would be staying indefinitely. I jumped up from my seat and exploded in a violent rage. I had been quietly boiling for several hours, but hearing those words set me off like a tornado. I tore up that office, throwing any loose items I could get my hands on. The cork finally blew and I was completely uncontrollable. I don't remember leaving that room or much of what happened after. But I can definitely say, in hindsight that was probably not the best response when trying to prove you are not crazy. Needless to say, I was staying.

I stayed in the institution for the next several months. My bed was the first in a long row of twenty or more beds that filled the ward. It resembled a prison infirmary I had seen on TV, even down to the detail of the bars on the windows. At the far end of the room was a locked door, which provided nighttime access to nurses entering the building from outside. To the immediate right of my bed was another door that led to the nurse's office and the solitary room.

The solitary room was a small cell with bars on the windows, a twin bed frame and a dirty striped mattress. Like the unit doors, the solitary room had a small Plexiglas window for the nurses to view the inhabitants. I initially had no insight into the actual use for this room, but once I did, I would never again peer into it voluntarily.

Restraints were always used in the solitary room. Although I have no memory of the actual events that resulted in me being sent there, I will always remember the struggle. Dressed in only my underclothing, several aides would wrestle me into submission. Once I was thoroughly exhausted, the aides would forcibly put me in a straight jacket. They would toss my restrained body onto that nasty little mattress and, while one man held me down, the others secured the pieces of cloth extending from the jacket's arms to the bars on both sides of the bed. With my arms firmly secured across my body and onto the frame of the bed, I would lie there, unable to move and open to the view of anyone caring to peer in through the foggy window. As the hours passed, I would scream to God.

The kind of God that would let a baby girl come into this world to be beaten by a man several times her size. The kind of God that would allow a fourteen-year-old child to be tied to a bed in a ward for the criminally insane. The kind of God that would not end the life of someone that so desperately wanted out. I would scream, *"I hate you! Just let me fucking die! I hate you! I fucking hate you!"* Several hours later, sometimes the next day, they would release me. By the time they came back in, I was in a world of my own. A steady stare straight ahead, avoiding all eye contact, throat sore and emotionless. I had retreated completely within.

When not in the solitary room, I slept in the back unit for mentally disabled adults. Although the institution clearly housed adults, there were three other children that I knew of there. They had all resided there long enough to be completely numb to the surroundings. Maritza was a 15-year-old Puerto Rican girl who was very street smart and extremely violent. Maritza had no family to speak of and was weathered well beyond her years in both appearance and cynicism. Daylene was 16 or 17 and was dating an older man named Sam who brought her gifts regularly, and then there was Tracey. Tracey was a schizophrenic pyromaniac who had witnessed her mother kill both her father and stepfather. Sworn to secrecy by her mother, she basically snapped when she witnessed the second murder. Tracey slept in the front of the ward with the more impacted adults. I didn't find out about Tracey's life until later in my stay, but I will never forget my initial interaction with her.

Tracey came right up to me on my very first day at Central. She was a chubby girl with short black hair cut like a boy's. She spoke very fast and punctuated each sentence with a giggle. She said, "Hi, my name's Tracey. I like fire, do you like fire? *Hee hee.*" I said, "It's Ok. Why?" Without any regard to my answer, she went on, "I like the colors in fire. Do you like the colors in fire? *Hee hee.*" I said, "Well, I guess I do, but I don't know that I ever really looked at the colors in a fire." She stared at me for a long beat and then said, "Beautiful colors in a fire. I could light a fire for you, you know? I have matches. Do you want to see a fire? *Hee hee.*"

I wondered if she was serious or just seriously whacked. Would this girl actually start a fire because I told her I wanted to see one? There was only one way to tell. I needed to know who I was dealing with here. The sooner I identified my comrades the better off I would be. While I doubted she would actually act on it, I also thought if she did "why the hell not?" I wasn't actually lighting the fire, so all would be well. It would probably cause quite a stir and I would be an innocent observer… sort of. So, I said, "Sure, I'd love to see a fire." Without so much as a word, she shuffled away…giggling. I knew she wouldn't actually do it. These people were crazy.

About forty-five minutes later, I heard screaming coming from the front ward. The beds at Central were separated by curtains the way they are in emergency rooms. Tracey had lit one of the curtains on fire and it quickly went up in flames. When I ran into the room, the staff was rushing towards the fire and Tracey was standing in the corner, giggling. I was quite impressed that she actually did it. Interesting girl, that Tracey. Very interesting. At least now it was confirmed, given her mental state, and lack of friends, if I told Tracey to do something, there was a good chance she would follow through. Although I had no immediate plans, it was just good information to have.

By the end of my first day, I knew that not only did Tracey fit the bill, but the rest of the inhabitants in our unit suffered from some level of permanent brain damage as well. All except me, Daylene and Maritza. I can clearly say without question that Daylene, Maritza and I were disturbed, but the disturbance came as a result of abuse, rather than brain abnormalities. Today I know we were suffering from Post Traumatic Stress Disorder.

We were all in the same boat. We were locked behind the doors in a ward for the criminally insane with no one to advocate for us. We had one thing in common; given the state of our life thus far, we trusted no one. We were loners. It is in a situation such as this that one might see the advantage of having made a friend along the way. In here, there was no one to call. The noisiest of the patients slept in the front of the ward and Tracey, Daylene and I slept among the quiet crew. As if suffering from the results of a lobotomy, they did not talk, nor did they function on their own. They were completely dependent on the nurses. Although lobotomies and shock treatment were prevalent not only at Central, but also at the partnering institutions (Kings Park and Pilgrim State) it is my understanding that this type of therapy started in or around 1946 and was discontinued a few years prior to my arrival in 1976. I had no idea how long my roommates had resided there. Bottom line, with the exception of us kids, it was quiet in the back ward.

As far as I was concerned this was a direct sentence from God. And although I was done with him, it seemed like he wouldn't let go of me. Daylene had a small record player and a bunch of 45's near her bed. It was all she had in the way of belongings and she protected them with her life. The nurses allowed her to use the record player at certain times during the day. During my first few days, she started playing a song that was popular at the time, David Soul's *Don't Give up on Us Baby* over and over again. The words reverberated in my head. For years I had used music as an outlet for my emotions. I could often be found in the front of the basement at home listening to music. When I was small it was The Jacksons, Helen Ready and the Carpenters, but as life progressed, it became Aerosmith and Led Zeppelin.

Although my relationship with God was finished, it seemed like everywhere I went I heard those words *"Don't Give up on Us Baby."* As if specifically meant for me to hear, the first notes of that song would set me off every time. I couldn't escape. I was losing my mind. As if God himself was pleading for my attention, my response was an out of control rage that would land me back in the solitary room, tied to the bed again. Once the song ended permanently, so did my communications with God. I was done. It would be years before I would talk to God again.

Every morning, the nurses would wake the residents and help them to get dressed and cleaned for the day. That is, all except Maritza, Dayleen and me; the three of us were apparently the only ones capable of taking care of our most basic needs. The medicine call came next. The medicine given to each patient differed based on his or her behavior during the week. While the meds had all sorts of complex pharmaceutical names, the process of doling them out was quite simple. If you were down, you got uppers and, if you were up, along came the downers. Regardless of your state of mind, everyone was required to take something.

Following medicine, the nurses would escort us out of the ward and down the corridor for breakfast. Mandated to stay together, we walked slowly to compensate for those needing assistance to keep pace. This was no ordinary bunch. We'd often be required to stop and wait as a nurse retrieved one of the more impaired patients walking in the wrong direction. Sooner or later, we would arrive at the kitchen. It was a cafeteria style set up. Patients proceeded single file and sat down rocking in their chairs and moaning, while the nurses retrieved their food. The drill was to grab a tray off the stack and roll it along metal bars as kitchen workers filled our plates with a bland variety of mystery meals. They could mix almost anything with instant mashed potatoes and come up with a whole new recipe. The moaning, barking and screaming during meal time made the dining experience frightening and intolerable.

Several patients needed to be spoon fed by the nurses. Although a few of them had the ability to feed themselves, the majority sat in wheelchairs moaning or hunched over tables with food dripping from their mouths. Those who did feed themselves chewed with their mouths open, often dropping food from their mouths back onto their plates. It was an absolute freak show. I was completely nauseated by the smell, the sounds and the images surrounding me. As a result, I rarely had an appetite. Although I steadfastly maintained that I wasn't sick in the head, hardly a day passed when I didn't find myself sick to my stomach.

Upon returning to the unit, most patients were assisted into chairs in the day room where they would spend the remainder of that day staring off into some unknown world, rocking and moaning. They would leave their chairs only to eat, sleep or be assisted to the restroom. The majority wore large diapers. The chairs were encased in plastic coating for easy cleaning; it reduced the amount of work for the nurses. With nothing to do, all the residents, including the children, were given five cigarettes per day.

On weekdays, Maritza, Daylene and I were bused to "school" with three boys who were confined to the men's ward. The boys were not normal. Kenny had a small body and a large head and had a habit of saying strange, off-the-wall, disgusting things. Even more revolting, many times when we were being dropped off he would yell, "I love you Lauri!" There was a large boy who had supposedly killed someone and a Rastafarian boy with long dreads who only spoke a lot about weed. I think he was the closest to being normal, but not quite there. The school, located in a nondescript building on the grounds, was basically a small room with nothing inside but a handful of old desks and chairs and a single ashtray to be shared by all present. Each day we were provided pencils and a few sheets of basic level math and English. The instructor would hand the assignments out and remain quiet as we worked. We smoked our cigarettes, passing the small ashtray around and completed the mindless exercises as expected. Upon completion, we'd file back onto the bus and return to Central.

During my time at the institution, I had become overtly preoccupied with killing myself. It was clear to me at this point that my family didn't want me; after all they devised a plan to put me away. By this time I was in total agreement with them; I truly believed I was worthless. There wasn't even a tiny piece of me that believed, even for a minute, that I had any right to continue to live or that anyone should love me. I hated myself. I had no reason to live. In my short life I had heard people speak of a spiritual awakening. My experience at Central was quite the opposite. Over the course of my time there, I experienced a spiritual deadening that would rule my life for the next ten years. Nothing mattered. I had nothing left inside me. I was done. My Pepper was gone, Poppy was dead and God had brought down the final bang of the gavel with a loud boom. "Sentence the witch to hell!"

Anything I could find with a sharp edge was collected and hidden for the final exit out. When I finally put the plan into action, I was caught in the bathroom with the sharp piece of a record protruding out of my pale thin arm. Back in the solitary room, drugged into submission, I awoke to the arching of the stiff canvas straight jacket restraining my limbs. I was useless, I couldn't even take my own friggin' life.

My father came to visit sometimes on the weekend and on occasion brought Nadine along. The two people who conspired to hide the abuse by getting rid of me would show up like caring family members coming to visit an ill child. Neither of them realized I knew about the hiding of the gun and setting me up, but that only made matters worse. The hypocrisy was inexcusable. The visits went down the same way each time. They'd wait in the corridor by the entrance to my unit with a Whopper, fries and vanilla shake from Burger King. My father would tell me to eat it and I would.

While I had absolutely no interest in seeing either of them ever again, I did, oddly enough, look forward to their arrival. I wanted the food. Although I generally had no appetite and detested eating in the institution's kitchen, I'd instantly become ravenous when the scent of that Whopper hit my nose. It was normal food and, a far cry better than the nightmarish experience of eating with the others in the kitchen. Alone in the visitor's area, I could eat without being nauseated by the freak show. I ate feverishly while being non-responsive to their presence, which was fine with them because there was nothing to talk about. I made sure to thank my father for the food and give him the customary I love you and hug to secure my next burger.

One day my father showed up with a large can of chocolate-flavored, powdered protein. It was the stuff you'd drink after mixing it with milk if you wanted to gain weight. I had lost a good deal of weight and was clearly in an unhealthy state, my dad had a meeting with the hospital staff to let them know I had been diagnosed with anorexia in the past. He told them I was a "problem eater" and had a history of not being hungry. He instructed them to give me this drink on a regular basis.

I found the whole thing quite bizarre because, in spite of my dad's proclamation, I wasn't the least bit anorexic. Probably as a result of my allergy to formula as a baby, I loved food. I could never get enough, and although you couldn't tell from my slim frame, eating was always one of my favorite hobbies. I was certainly never anorexic, and bulimia was never a problem either. I loved the feeling of a full stomach. It was just another one of my dad's crazy ideas to deflect the attention off himself and back onto me.

From there on out when my dad would visit, after I finished my Whopper, he would lead me into the small nurse's office, retrieve the protein drink and insist that I drink it in front of him. It was all a show for the staff, and I am sure as far as he was concerned it worked like a charm. The staff was aware of "my problem." I really didn't care. My dad's insanity had eluded all reasonable thought long before that day, so I had no problem drinking it. Not only did it taste good, drinking it got me away from the other residents and out of the kitchen.

My dad had learned about the disease of anorexia when Nadine was diagnosed and he was simply using it now as a way to avoid feeling guilty about my weight loss. It was easier for him to place the blame on me than to acknowledge it as being directly related to his abuse and being committed to a ward for the criminally insane at the age of fourteen.

The only other visitors I had while at Central were my best friend Lacey and my little sister, Alyssa. Both visited one time and that was one time too many for both of them.

For some reason I will never understand, my dad brought Lacey to visit one day. I will never forget the tragic moment when Lacey passed through the steel doors as she entered the main corridor. At the time, the door to the men's ward was partially ajar because a male nurse was on his way out. The howling and perversion that I experienced when I first arrived was multiplied because the men were pushing and pulling on the door to gain access to Lacey. To make matters worse, some of them were not fully clothed. Even dressed, they scared me to death, but Lacey was terrified. The clincher was when the kid with the oversized head who stood closest to the front in just his boxer shorts yelled, "I love you, Lauri!"

I don't think there are any words that can adequately describe how humiliated and embarrassed I was. Not only was Lacey already understandably in a state of shock, she was now probably under the impression that this nut job was my boyfriend. I knew right then that neither she nor any of my friends from school would ever perceive me as a normal person again. Lacey had now seen what I'd become. As far as she could tell, I was no different than the rest of the patients here. I was officially a mental defect. We didn't talk because there was nothing to say. What could I say after that? "So how's school?" or "What's been going on?" My head was screaming! LEAVE! LEAVE! I needed them to leave NOW! A few moments later, my father said, "Well, I think I'll head out." All I could think was LEAVE LACEY! GET OUT! And they did.

I don't remember Alyssa's visit at all. Four years younger than me, she must have been nine or ten at the time. I didn't even know she had come to Central until recently. She confided in me that my father had brought her to see me. She said they directed her and my dad to a room and, when they entered, I was tied to a bed. She immediately started crying and screaming. According to her, my dad grabbed her firmly by the arm and dragged her out saying, "I told you there would be no crying!" And they left.

To this day, whenever I think about Alyssa being forced to see me that way, it breaks my heart. She was so little and fragile and had already been exposed to so much. Her innocence was taken from her at such a young age. As strange as it may seem, I feel more empathy for Alyssa having gone through the experience of seeing me than I do for my own experience of actually being tied up. As far as I was concerned, I had become hardened and was able to handle it. But Alyssa was innocent and ill-prepared and stood no chance.

Due to the significant amount of psych medication I was taking, my memory of most things that happened during my stay is vague at best. But I know that I never saw or heard from my mom while I was there. It wasn't until many years later that I found out why.

One day the director approached me and informed me that I would be leaving and to pack my things. That was all the information he offered. Nothing was said as to why, how or where I'd be going. While I was initially elated by the news, fear of the unknown quickly overcame me. I momentarily panicked when I thought I might be getting sent back to live with my father. I thought about how deranged these people were. My father had deceived everyone successfully thus far, so it was a valid concern. My things packed, I paced and smoked. If I wasn't going back to my father's, where the hell was I going? At least from home, I could hitchhike somewhere else. To one of my friends—somewhere—but if I was going somewhere else, where was it? Where were they taking me now? What if it is worse than this place? Had I been that bad that they were maybe sending me somewhere worse? What if my dad wanted me really gone? My mind raced with one tragic possibility after another. Within a short amount of time I was an emotional wreck and had a headache from holding back the tears.

Just about the time I thought they must have forgotten about me, a male counselor from who knows where arrived to get me. As I had become accustomed to doing, we drove in silence. I had no idea who he was or where he was taking me. Paralyzed with fear, I sat quietly and tried to focus on two things. I am out of Central Islip, and if they take me somewhere bad, I can hitchhike out, if it's not a lock down. Of course I had no idea where I'd hitch to, but as with most "kid thoughts" the plan doesn't get much further than immediate need. And mine was just to get out.

For fear of being thought of as crazy and alienated by all of mankind, I never talked about my stay at Central Islip Mental Institution again. Nonetheless, I would be haunted for years by the sounds, the sights and smells that I encountered while there. I will never forget the moaning and rocking patients, being tied to a bed, or eating among the animals in the kitchen. While I may have looked different than those I was leaving behind, I had been forever changed, both emotionally and mentally, as a result of my time there. No matter how hard I try to block it out, Central Islip will be a part of me for the rest of my life. Like an Auschwitz survivor who forever feels a connection to her camp mates, I will always know that I am one of them, a mental defect. Stormy and the others, who sat there day after day in a world of their own, will most likely die just as they were when I left and nobody on the outside will ever know or care. Although I had escaped the hell, I will never forget those I left behind or disassociate myself from the pain I know they are still enduring. I may have moved on, but they will forever be with me.

10

EVENTUALLY, WE TURNED INTO A DRIVEWAY AND HEADED TOWARD A large colonial house. A small sign we passed identified this place as Stony Brook, New York. The house was beautiful and grand on the outside, but as I would soon come to discover, strange and disparate on the inside.

As we entered the front door, we nearly smacked into a regulation-sized pool table, inconveniently placed in the entryway. I followed the man as he made his way around to the left of the table and ventured up the narrow stairway. It was obvious that he was used to this. I could hear voices echoing throughout the big house. The voices clashed with dialogue blaring from a distant television set above. I felt oddly transparent as people walked right by us without even acknowledging our presence. Apparently, we had either become invisible or nobody passing had any interest in who we were or why we were in their house. I remember thinking that something wasn't right in this place.

At the top of the stairway there was an office no larger than a walk-in closet. There were two desks pushed up against each other with a large pile of files atop the one most visible from the stairway. There was an African-American man in his early 30's sitting on a swivel chair behind one of the desks and a Caucasian woman in her late 30's to early 40's sitting behind the other. As we approached, they stopped talking and acknowledged our presence.

The woman instructed us to be patient. She told my escort that he could leave and suggested I make myself comfortable in the next room. I walked into what felt like a large den with a weathered old sectional couch and a TV in the middle. There was a newer looking blue velvet couch nestled against the wall to my right and a big easy chair covered in green leather just ahead. The blue velvet couch, flower sectional and green easy chair seemed an odd combination for one room. At best, this was interior design by necessity, not by plan.

An African-American girl with light skin was huddled in a ball on the sectional couch transfixed on the TV. Either engrossed or oblivious, she too failed to acknowledge our presence. She appeared to be around 15. It was obvious from her lack of response that she had found comfort in her own world by shutting out those around her. She didn't appear to even know I was there.

I sat down quietly on the lone blue couch by the far wall hoping to remain unnoticed and thereby avoid any unnecessary communication. As had become my standard operating procedure wherever I was in a new environment, I immediately assessed my surroundings. As I learned with respect to my father's mood and whereabouts, speedy assessment was always a good asset.

To my immediate right, there was a long hallway leading to what I assumed were bedrooms. In the 40 minutes or so that I sat on the couch there was a continual stream of people going by. Some of them were adolescents and some were older. They seemed to be just as unrelated as the furniture, in their skin color, age and mood. As diverse as the people seemed to be, they shared the commonality of a lack of communication.

Although several teens and young adults passed in front of me as I sat on the couch in the communal area, no one attempted to speak to me. That was a good thing. Having just erupted from One Flew over the Cuckoo's nest, I was still affected by the meds, the trauma and the experience. Silence was good.

A while later, the woman from the office approached me and escorted me to a room with two beds. I was told to put my things away; this would be where I was staying. I sat on my bed for the next few hours staring at the wall. I did not want to exit the room for fear of communication and I did not want to fall asleep, as it would make me vulnerable in an unknown environment. I would never again leave myself vulnerable. From this point forward in life, my head was always in a state of "don't fuck with me or else."

The next few days were spent coming down from the medicine at the ward. Although I had convinced myself that I was fierce and dangerous and not to be messed with, at this point I was just over 5 feet tall and less than 85 pounds. My skin was pale and my ability to interact on a social level was greatly impaired. I had absolutely no desire to socialize with anyone and just wanted to be left alone. I have almost no memory of the first few weeks at this home. That is, with the exception of my roommate.

My roommate at my new home was a fifteen-year-old free spirit named Azalea. Azalea seemed to travel on a different plane than most. With long flowing brown hair, a halter top, bohemian style hippie skirt to her ankles and a comfortable pair of moccasin style fringe boots, she was unique. I can honestly say that I had not met anyone like her before.

She was beautiful and exciting and had no problem carrying the conversation when she noted my impaired ability to reciprocate. She possessed an intense spirit that was innately and powerfully free. A drifter spirit that traveled through life without a care in the world. Although she was only fifteen, she possessed the fortitude of an ancient warrior.

Azalea spent the first few nights explaining her family's mission to me. She educated me on the great honor and devotion they had for the Grateful Dead and the integrity and commitment of "the family" to attend every show. Although she also spoke of "the family" I didn't get the feeling they were fully related, but more of a group of travelers that would be eternally related by their shared mission.

I was amazed by the extent of her knowledge on the band, the culture and her strong commitment to the followers. She told me that she and her parents belonged to the family since she was just a few years old. Although she was not physically with her parents, she clearly explained that once separated, it was her duty to allow them to continue on the path to the Dead. Like a soldier left at the barracks to guard the supplies as the other soldiers went out to the front line, she felt as though her acceptance of being left behind strengthened the Grateful Dead family. Allowing them to continue on was the highest honor she could offer them.

Although she was residing at the home now, she always gave the impression her spirit was with "the family." I would continue to learn about the music of the band, the culture and the importance of freeing your mind and spirit through the use of LSD. Although I had no exposure to taking acid up to this point, she promised sometime in the next few days, she would take me with her on her regular trip to the Stony Brook College to meet a man named Fred who would provide us with some of the best tabs to allow us to free our minds. She explained, "Soon you too will be free Lauri!" I had a great amount of respect for Azalea. I was envious of her courage, strength and spirit. The more I got to know her, the more I wanted to be her. Her uninhibited beauty was unforgettable.

I quickly learned that I was not her only fan. Billy, an oversized bear of a kid who stood over 6'2" and a smaller skinny kid named Paul were by her side whenever she left the house. They too were mesmerized by her. I was clearly the newest member of the worship Azalea crew.

Billy had extensive life experiences and was prone to talk about the death of his best friend. He told us that his friend overdosed on acid while listening to the song "Dust in the Wind." While I believe his friend died as a result of a drug overdose, in retrospect, I find it suspect that "Dust in the Wind" was spinning when it happened. Paul had no stories, but always tagged along for the day's excursions and recreational drug use. Desperate to do anything to alter his reality, he just wanted to get high.

By this time in my life, I fancied myself a professional thief. I had become pretty good at shoplifting small items from the local store near my family's home, without getting caught. I believed I was blessed with an unusual amount of skill. In short order, I discovered that my new crew from Stony Brook made me look like an amateur. These kids meant business.

On one occasion, we decided to go to the local mall and steal a bunch of Levis. The plan was to wear oversized jackets, stash a few pair of color corduroys underneath and walk right out. That day, I wore a large letterman jacket that one of Nadine's previous party friends gave me. It had *Centerport,* our hometown, embroidered in big letters on the back. It was a common practice for kids in New York to wear jackets with the name of their hometown prominently displayed somewhere on either the front or the back. It was a territorial kind of thing, the way gang members proudly wear different colors these days to represent, identify and affiliate. Although it was meant for a high school boy and I probably looked like a nine year old in it, I loved that jacket because I felt tough whenever I wore it. I was part of something.

I left the mall alone that day while the other kids continued loading up their jackets. Once outside, I immediately noticed a man with a walkie talkie in his hand approaching me very quickly. As he grabbed my arm, the snaps on my Centerport jacket popped open and four pairs of corduroy pants fell to the ground. My heart was pounding like a jackhammer. He held onto my arm tightly while communicating with someone on the other end of his radio. I was scared to death. He was clearly excited as he spoke loudly in some sort of code. I knew it was over. What happened next blew my mind.

Billy and Azalea walked casually out of the mall's glass doors and looked directly at me while I was being detained. Although I expected them to keep on walking to the parking lot, they came running toward me instead. Billy yelled, "Get the Fuck off of her," grabbed the walkie talkie from the guard's hand and smashed it on the ground. Much to my surprise, he then freed my arm from the guard's grasp and screamed for everyone to run. Twenty minutes after we arrived at our planned meeting spot, Billy showed up unharmed. As a result of the whole experience, I developed a deep sense of admiration for both Billy and Azalea. They were like Bonnie and Clyde, only better. They were unstoppable.

Over the next few days, they trained me to join them in their most lucrative scam. Stealing money at the train station sounded big-time to an amateur like me. They had figured out that most travelers tend to carry a good deal of cash for things like food and taxis. And they explained that miraculously, the train tracks ran alongside the college field where Fred lived. Best of all, they had been doing this successfully for weeks with nothing even resembling a close call. Given their enthusiasm and the draw of potential danger, I was all in! Now that Billy had already protected me once, I had no thought of getting caught. I was ready to rock.

The next day we went to the train station for the first time. We sat in the bushes watching people come and go, and after a bit, agreed that we would only hit old ladies. As tough as we thought we were, Azalea and I were both quite frail and wanted to make sure we didn't get into any situations we couldn't handle. The simple plan was as follows: Azalea and I would each snatch a purse and then run as fast as we could. Billy would try to detain the attackee by pretending to help, allowing us time to get away. Pretending to run off to catch us, he would disappear into the distance and join us for celebratory drugs.

Because we had to strike when the station was scarcely populated to avoid getting caught, we only managed to get one purse. We made it to the college field safely and ducked into the bushes. Oddly, when Billy arrived, he told us to swap jackets with each other. New to the game, I asked no questions and did as instructed. We took the bills out of the purse, ditched it in the bushes and walked calmly across the field toward Fred's dorm room.

Barely five minutes later, Billy calmly and quietly let on. "Don't look back, but there's a cop coming." Sure enough, there were headlights from a rapidly approaching car, headed straight for us. The car was driving on the grassy plain of the college field. I knew this was the end. My heart was pounding. Billy said, "Act calm."

Moments later, the police car approached and the officer lowered his window. "Have you kids seen a large white man in a blue jacket?" We all said "no" simultaneously and he said, "thank you" and continued on his way. Just as Billy had anticipated, we escaped because we had changed jackets. Billy was a God. The next few weeks were all about finding new and exciting ways to steal money so that we could return to Fred's for more acid.

Azalea and crew are the first people with which I ever felt a bond. I never mentioned to any of them where I had been previously. Neither my dad nor Central. Too embarrassed to share where I had come from, in fear of being alienated as crazy, I never talked about it. Like a malfunctioning animal released from a test lab, I looked like the others, dressed like the others, but I knew deep down inside, I was different.

While we were having a good time, it wasn't problem-free. There were other kids in the house and one, in particular, stands out in my memory. Rachel, a 15-year-old red head was an ass kisser to the staff. She had threatened to tell on us every time she found out about anything we had done. We decided to teach her a lesson. We lined her bed with rose petals and a laid a large steak knife next to a note in the middle. It said, *"You will die tonight."* We actually talked about killing her and the various methods of doing so. I would like to think I wouldn't have followed through with our threats, but I am not sure I wouldn't have gone along with the others. That is how powerful the bond was that I felt with the group that had become my only family. She must have known something about us that we didn't know about ourselves because she was gone the next day.

> *Sometimes the light's all shining on me*
> *Other times I can barely see*
> *Lately it occurs to me*
> *What a long strange trip it's been (Grateful Dead—1970)*

Counselors were available at Stony Brook, but they never seemed to interact with us. As improbable as it may seem, I can only recall a single experience with a counselor during my entire stay there. Carlton, an African-American in his mid thirties, asked me to go to the local dock with him to check out the ocean. He drove a beautiful, white Cadillac and loved listening to Otis Redding and the Commodores. Although we didn't say much the entire time, I always appreciated Carlton for showing a legitimate interest in me. He didn't ask me any questions and he didn't try anything weird. I was perplexed by the whole experience and thought about it for years afterward. I couldn't reconcile in my mind why anybody, let alone a man, would want to spend time with me without expecting something in return. At some level, I felt that he actually cared. But I couldn't understand why.

One night when we returned home from the mall I was summoned to the office. I thought I was hearing things when they told me that my mom was on the phone. I hadn't heard from her the entire time I was at Central and, as a form of self-preservation I suppose, I assumed I never would never hear from her again. Believing she was out of my life for good, I had blocked my whole family from my mind.

When I picked up the phone, my mom was crying. She explained that she had been trying to find me and just continued to weep. A flow of feelings rushed through me like a tidal wave. I would not allow it. I swallowed the emotions back, closed my eyes tight and just repeated to myself, *don't cry, do not cry*...I could not break, not now, not in front of the only people who mattered to me. I would not allow myself to be washed over by the flood of emotions that threatened my present state of numbness. I was silent. She explained that she was working on getting us a place to live and that my sisters and I would be coming to California soon. She closed by saying, "I will send for you." And then I heard a click. I felt nauseous inside. I was devastated by that one short call. When I got off of the phone, my head was throbbing. I needed a nap.

In later conversations, my mom clarified a lot of things that had confused me up until that time. She told me that when she left my father to move to California she had no money, so it took longer than anticipated. Although she had started working almost immediately as an insurance agent, she was only paid a small base salary, plus commission. It took her a while to save enough money to rent a suitable apartment for us. In the meantime, she called a few times a week to check in. Whenever she phoned, my father and sister Nadine would tell her that I wasn't home or was outside playing. After a few months, it dawned on her that she hadn't spoken to me in a long time and she began to wonder if something was up. After all, she knew better than anyone just how crazy and unpredictable my father was.

Rightfully assuming he had done something to me, she called the police to see if they were aware of anything. She was relieved to discover they had no information about me. Still concerned, she called my Aunt Nora who, for whatever reason, professed no knowledge of my situation. Eventually, she contacted my long time pediatrician, Dr. Bergenstein, who told her that he had gotten word from an Asian doctor at Central Islip that I had been admitted. She called the institution several times before reaching someone who could confirm my residence. The staff member she spoke to also outlined the procedure she needed to follow in order to obtain my release. I had no idea that she was the one responsible for my release from the asylum. Lastly, she explained that my staying at Stonybrook was a temporary plan to allow her time to get an apartment. Within a few days I was shipped to California.

11

I DON'T RECALL MUCH ABOUT THE FLIGHT TO LOS ANGELES International Airport or my arrival there, but I do recall seeing my mom as I exited the plane. Although we hadn't seen each other for quite some time, it was far from a joyous reunion. She gave me what became customary for my mom in the following years; something that my sister Alyssa and I refer to as "air kisses." Grabbing both shoulders, she aligns her head alongside the recipient, and kisses the air. Having never remembered being kissed by her before in any way, I was rigid and completely uncomfortable. We both avoided direct eye contact and said very little as we walked to the baggage carrousel.

As we drove south on the 405 freeway, I sat silently staring out of the window while *"You are my Shining Star"* played on the radio. We didn't talk to one another the entire drive. I soaked in the surroundings. The palm trees, the warm air and the music draped over me like a warm comfortable blanket. I resisted the temptation to feel at peace. As the horror of my life hummed loudly below the surface, I wasn't about to buy into a happy-ever-after ending. I knew in my heart that an airline flight across the country couldn't possibly be enough to dispel the hell I had just lived through.

As had often been the case in my life, silence spoke volumes during that drive. The tension in the car was palpable and the vibe was awkward at best. My mother only recently revealed how she felt that day. She told me she was in shock when she first saw me. She was awash in feelings of guilt and remorse. She said I looked like a scared and frail animal; thin, pale and devoid of even the most basic emotions. I was unable to make eye contact, let alone communicate. I was guarded, distant and unable to touch her. She said she had never felt the kind of guilt she felt that day. It was more than she could handle. She couldn't look me in the eyes that day or for many days to come. She wasn't mentally ready to address what had happened to me so she never asked about it. Although she's now able to talk about some of the things that transpired, thirty years passed before I first asked her if she wanted to hear about my time at Central Islip. Her eyes welled up with tears and she simply said, "No." I understood. She was suffering enough without knowing the horror that I had endured.

As we pulled off of the freeway into a small neighborhood, we passed a Seven Eleven, some tennis courts and two girls on roller-skates. Eventually, we turned into a parking lot surrounded by lush green landscaping with a row of shrubs providing a short wall around the complex. A small wooden sign read "The Lillywoods." Once parked, we grabbed my bags and set out for the next place I'd call home.

My mom opened the door allowing me inside first. I stepped into a very small living room decorated with a nondescript couch and a solitary chair. Just beyond, I could see a small bar that led to a tiny kitchen. My sisters had arrived before me. The three of us would make camp in the living room pending my mom finding us a home. The apartment complex only allowed adults, so we were told to stay out of sight. If anyone asked, we were told to say that we were visiting. The place we were staying at was my mom's boyfriend's. Although I had met him in New York, I did not know that he was her "boyfriend." Now in his apartment, I was clear on why we moved to California. That being said, I was just glad we were out of my dad's house.

In no time, my mom got some money together and moved us into a newer three bedroom duplex in Irvine, California. It was basically two houses attached with a plain wooden front and very little detail.

Inside, there was a small family room to the left and a very small kitchen straight ahead. There was muted brown shag carpet and freshly painted off-white walls. To the right, there was a dining room with a glass table and a stairway at one end. At the top of the stairs there were two small rooms to the right, one large room to the left and a bathroom straight ahead. Alyssa and I shared one of the small rooms while Nadine took the other. Of course, my mom got the master suite. There were new bedroom sets in the otherwise plain rooms and, while it was certainly much less than we had in Centerport, nobody ever complained. It was safe.

Although my life appeared to be getting better, I still had secrets. The memories from the past few months haunted me, a quiet stirring voice ever present...*you are different, no one wants you...*The abuser that I thought I left behind was now inside of me. That constant voice would not only ensure that I never forgot how much I hated myself, it would also serve to alienate anyone who ever tried to get close to me or show me love. The acceptance of love would conflict with my core belief; that I was worthless. Without that belief, I was nonexistent because it was all I knew. I was glad to have left my life in New York, but I felt like an alien in California. The bottom line was that I didn't fit anywhere.

A few days after our arrival, Nadine suggested we go to the beach. She had met a guy at the liquor store down the street who told her that the pier was "the" place to hang out. We had never hung out before and wouldn't do so again, but being new to the neighborhood; we were momentarily dependent upon each other. Having nothing in common and completely revolted by everything about each other, we hitchhiked down to the beach. It was on this night that the culture shock became clearly apparent. I headed out in my usual boy wear and Nadine on the other hand, dressed to impress, with a skirt and boots.

I hadn't anticipated total culture shock, but that's exactly what we found in our new town. Walking along the boardwalk shortly after arriving, we encountered a group of kids. Out of the blue, one of the boys said, "Hey, how's it going?" We looked at each other quizzically, wondering if he was talking to us. Knowing we didn't know him, neither of us responded. And then a cute blond surfer looking girl said 'hi.' That was when we knew for sure we weren't in Kansas anymore.

Where we grew up, you didn't even make eye contact with somebody unless he or she was in your social circle. Initiating eye contact or conversation generally indicated a desire to fight. No stranger ever said hi or asked how you were doing. I recall a few occasions when a simple glance at a group of kids brought on a fight. It would start with, "What are you looking at?" in a thick NY accent. I learned to walk with my head down unless I wanted to stir something up. There were fights every day at school, at the bus stop or at the designated fighting ring in the field after school.

By the end of the night, Nadine and I had concluded that people from California were strange. They asked *how* you were without even knowing *who* you were. Very strange, indeed.

We met some boys at the beach that night who had just moved to California from Michigan. Experiencing culture shock in common, we immediately bonded. They smoked a lot of pot and obsessed about the band KISS. They played KISS albums, wore KISS tee shirts and talked incessantly about KISS. I believe that in some alternate reality mindset, they believed they were KISS. Ladies and gentlemen, I give you the new KISS; Jeremy, Matt, and Dane. Matt went by the nickname Bush on account of his large, unruly Afro, while Dane might as well have been nicknamed Vain. Apparently, he came to California hoping to get discovered, but, with no notable skills to speak of, relied on his trendy name to attract attention and spent most of his time in front of the mirror. Bush became my best friend and Jeremy had a crush on me from the start. A short time later, he became my boyfriend.

Considering that Jeremy was my boyfriend, he knew very little about me. We rarely spoke. He was a decent guy with a big heart, but I was generally nervous around him. I wasn't used to the "dating" thing. I had acted like a boy for so long that I had difficulty transitioning to the female role. I was pretty sure he wanted the boy role. Kissing was about all I could handle. I had no interest in sex and he never pushed me. Kissing and taking about KISS was just fine for both of us.

The guys rented a motel room on a weekly basis, and we spent the majority of our time smoking pot there. For the next few months, the Michigan crew would pick me up in an old brown, rusty Plymouth and take me to the motel. While the guys smoked a lot of pot and talked about KISS constantly, I just smoked a lot of pot. I figured they must also have been selling pot because work was not in their dialog.

A few weeks after moving into our new digs, my mom befriended the next-door neighbor. Turns out, she had a daughter my age named Karlee and both moms thought it would be a good idea for us to spend time together before school started.

Karlee and I hit it off immediately, but I didn't care for her friends at all. They were obsessed with their appearance, wore expensive clothes, carried their parent's credit cards and dated older boys. I had nothing in common with those girls, but I liked Karlee a lot so I did my best to accept her crew.

12

IT WASN'T LONG BEFORE KARLEE AND HER PALS LET ME KNOW ABOUT their plan to hitchhike to the Colorado River before school started. I was excited by their invitation and even more so when they told me it was a non-stop party filled with music and sunshine. Being new to the parental approval game, I brazenly asked my mom if I could hitchhike to the Colorado River. While I can't recall her exact response, it was something like, "Hell no! Are you an idiot, or what?" To this day I don't know why I even bothered asking. I was only 15 years old and I wanted her approval to hitchhike to another state with teenagers, but at the time, in my teenager mind, it seemed like a reasonable question. Needless to say, I did it anyway.

Karlee, two of her rich girl friends and I left for the Colorado River the very next day. It was quite an adventure. We met a lot of nice people along the way who took us as far as they could, dropped us off and gave us directions to our next landmark. While I thought we were incredibly lucky at the time, today I understand a whole lot better why three young female hitchhikers never had to spend a lot of time waiting to get picked up. As soon as our thumbs would go up, the next car would pull over. Easy as pie. With zero driving experience and no insight into where we were going, we ended up there. We thought that to get to the Colorado River, we needed to go to Colorado. Much to our surprise, we learned that it went through Arizona as well and that was much closer. Although we got there, it had nothing to do with my help, the only states I remembered from Geography were the boot of Texas, the long leg of Florida and New York. Oh yeah, and California on the left side. Between the three of us, with plenty of luck and determination, we somehow made it.

When we finally arrived at the River, it was just as Karlee described it. A giant party was in full swing. There were vans and tents everywhere with thousands of people smoking pot and drinking beer while music blared from hundreds of speakers competing for air time. Just as we had hoped, it was completely out of control. Everyone was having a blast and, as far as I was concerned, we had made it to heaven.

We spent our first night partying until we crashed. Everybody was so friendly. Perfect strangers instantly transformed into good friends. Like typical teenagers, we hadn't thought about food or any other necessities before hitting the road. We did, of course, remember to bring along our make-up and bathing suits. We slept on the ground without sleeping bags or blankets, wherever there was an available spot. Nobody cared and nothing mattered. A good time was all we were after and that was in ample supply. We partied through the first day with enthusiasm. Day two was a different story entirely.

Tired from the long journey and slightly disoriented from some serious partying, I was woken by the sound of loud music and the scent of good pot wafting through the air. As I gathered my thoughts and remembered where I was, an unfamiliar sense of tranquility washed over me. A teenager's heaven. I felt safe and secure. Seeing as we had arrived at around 6 p.m. the night before, we were surprised to find it nearing 110 degrees. Much too excited to complain, we devised a simple strategy to cope with the heat. The plan was to spend most of the day in the water drinking cold beer. It was a perfect plan for a perfect day.

Unfortunately, the day didn't go as planned. As I walked out of the river and headed for my towel, one of Karlee's friends started screaming at me. She caught me completely off guard as she yelled, "You stupid bitch. Look what you've done." Acting a little over dramatic for my taste, she grabbed her bathing suit from the back of the chair and pointed to where I had dropped water on it. At first, I thought she was kidding, but she continued ranting and raving. I stared at her in total disbelief and then said, "What the fuck, isn't a bathing suit supposed to get wet?" She made the mistake of responding by getting up in my face. So I hit her. We went at it until a few people from the crowd pulled us apart. I had kneed her in the face, so she was bleeding pretty good and I had scratches on my neck and face and a swollen eye. As I quickly bolted from the "scene of the crime," I was pretty sure that I wouldn't be traveling with Karlee and her friends any longer.

I walked away, alone. Just moments later a man who appeared to be in his late 20's approached me. He was rough looking, awkward and unattractive. He told me he had witnessed the altercation and asked if I was okay. He invited me to join him at his camp for a while so I could relax, but I declined. He said he would give me a cold beer to press against my eye to relieve some of the swelling. Given that I was alone without a plan and he seemed genuinely concerned, I eventually agreed. I left what few belongings I had with me and followed him empty handed.

We walked to a nearby clearing that was surrounded by vans. A handful of beanbag chairs were scattered around the remains of a burned out fire. Music was erupting from one of the vans. When I looked over toward the music, I noticed a few young guys lying on more beanbag chairs inside. Their outstretched bodies barely moved, giving me the impression that they had either passed out cold or were comatose. Eventually they moved just enough to alert an onlooker that they were still alive.

The man who had invited me over handed me a beer and crawled into the van to retrieve a joint from one of the living dead. He sat down, lit the joint and extended his arm out of the van to offer me some. He tilted his head to the side a few times, motioning for me to join him in the van. I did. After the joint made the rounds a few times, the van appeared as if it were breathing. Although no one was actually driving it, it was alive. Something wasn't right.

As I looked around, I noticed a planet resembling the sun coming out of one of the other vans. The voices became distorted and my breathing seemed louder than usual. The music got louder and softer and then louder again as if it were playing out of a boom box situated on the rotating blade of a helicopter. The joint came my way again but I passed. "There's something wrong with this pot," I said. One of the zombies looked in my eyes, laughed and said, "Relax. Its fine. It's just good pot." I said I didn't want anymore, but he insisted. Not wanting to be ostracized, I took one more hit. That was last memory I have of being in the van.

The next thing I knew it was night time. I was lying on a grassy dirt area next to the van with a dirty white blanket on top of me. Still in my bathing suit, I woke to a cold hand touching my stomach.

A moment later my eyes cleared and I realized that the dirty, awkward man that had brought me to the van was lying next to me and his hand was tugging at my suit bottom. "I want to be with you." Panicking I said, "Please no, I've gotta go...Please don't...I've gotta go...Please let me go... I have to get out of here...Please let me go... Let me go..."

I was afraid to scream; afraid to do anything that would make him angry, as I fought to free myself from him. With his smelly, hot body wrestling beside mine, he struggled to rip off my suit. His large dirty hands fumbled with the elastic on my suit as I squirmed about in a wild panic trying to prevent him from undressing me. I struggled to hold my bathing suit bottom up with my left hand while pushing my body as hard as I could with my right to free myself from him. His sour hot breath and sweat drenched my face. His large hands clasped on my shoulders and I absorbed the weight of his body as he pulled himself on top of my small frame. His left hand clenched around my neck in a chokehold, as his right hand continued to tear the damp bathing suit from my body. Suddenly a sharp pain shot inside of me and his sour breath and sweat drenched what remained of my clothes and engulfed my body. Like a knife piercing me, the pain tore through me over and over again. The surge of disgust was unbearable. His strong hand was like a vice on my small hip. As I fought to dig my heel into ground, the blanket slid beneath me. Unable to gain control, I was completely immobile. I struggled right up until the moment I realized there was nothing left to save. Finally, I gave in. I then had a thought I will never forget. *"Well now at least you know how to have sex Lauri…"*

He released his large hand from my neck and rolled off me. My suit bottom snapped back on my leg, drenched with sweat and blood. I lay perfectly still, dirty and silent.

I wanted to scream and cry, but I couldn't. There was nothing there. I was dirty. *You have no reason to cry Lauri…, you deserved what you got, you shouldn't have left home. It is your fault for being stupid…you deserve it…you could have stopped him and you didn't…you let him do it…*

The pig sprawled next to me, motionless as a rock. I squeezed my eyes and willed for him to get up. Just a few feet of leeway and maybe I could outrun him. With all of the people around us, I could surely find safety in another camp. Being right next to him, I had no chance at all. I was shocked when his large hand reached over and grabbed my arm. He literally dragged me onto my feet. Pulling me so fast that I couldn't catch my footing, he dragged me to his car, opened the passenger door and pushed me in. He threw the dirty white blanket on top of me and told me to hide the blood from the others, or else. I did as I was ordered.

He said, "I will take you home now." He started the car and began to drive. I thought about jumping, but he was going too fast. I just kept saying to myself, *"Just sit still and he will take you home; it won't be much longer, you will be home…PLEASE take me home…"* I had never before longed to be home, but on this particular day, I couldn't have wanted anything more.

The freeway drive was quiet except for the hum of the large engine and the wind. He dared not look at me as his large hand again yanked the blanket and tore it from my body. He grabbed my torn suit bottom and his large dirty hands began to violate my small frame again. He kept repeating, "Sit still and I won't hurt you. Sit still and I won't hurt you." He continued to violate me on and off throughout the long ride. The thought of jumping from the car was ever present, but with bare feet and no clothes to protect my body from the fall, I knew I didn't stand a chance.

By the time he pulled off the highway several hours later, the sun had been up for quite some time, and I was in a complete state of numbness, far, far away. All the time that he violated me throughout the long ride, my only escape was to check out mentally. And I had. As he suddenly jerked off the highway, I was catapulted back.

A quick survey revealed that I was still far from home. We were in a lower-class rural neighborhood with dirt where grass should have been and garbage scattered throughout. Bars covered the front windows of each home.

I assumed he was looking for a gas station or a convenience store. All I could think about was jumping from the car as soon as he stopped, or maybe I would see someone, a cop, anyone. As he veered down a small side road, thoughts ran wild in my head. Maybe he knew people around here or maybe he was going to buy pot. I didn't say a word because I didn't want that pig to think that any part of this was in any way less than revolting. I doubt that I could have spoken coherently anyway, due to the state of shock I was experiencing. Silence was the only thing I had left.

Suddenly, he pulled the wheel to the left turning his large old car into the driveway of a small rundown white-shingled house. There were piles of garbage lining the sides of the house, the front yard consisted of a straw-like yellow lawn, and a rickety old ripped screen door, partially ajar. The screen door banged open and shut with the wind at the top of the front steps. He jammed the car into park and ordered me to get out. Again, not wanting to incite more trouble, I did as I was told. Clearly riled, he yanked open the screen door and motioned for me to go inside.

The moment we entered, I saw an old lady sitting on the couch looking at photographs. I silently screamed, *Thank God, I'm finally safe! There's no way he'll touch me in front of her.* She glanced up at the man and, without saying a word, returned to her photographs. It was as though I was invisible. He grabbed my arm in a slightly less aggressive manner than before and escorted me right past her into what appeared to be the master bedroom. He motioned for me to sit on the bed while he tossed things around in the closet, obviously looking for something. I sat silently wondering if that woman was his mother. I assumed this was where he lived. Although I was still terrified, I found some comfort in the fact that he had left the bedroom door open.

From the corner of my eye, I watched his every move. Without looking at me, he made his way from the closet to the bedroom door. With his hand on the knob, he turned toward me and then slammed the door shut. I nearly jumped out of my skin. I could see he was angry and now I could see what he had retrieved from the closet: rope.

He grabbed my right arm and pushed himself on top of me. As he pushed his body up against my face, I screamed, "Stop!" over and over. He didn't. While I continued pleading with him, he tied each of my limbs to the poles of the bed. I flashed back to the moment when I accepted the fact that my mother was no longer coming to my aid when my father beat me.

Sadly, I realized right then that the woman in the other room wasn't coming to help me either. Whenever I think back about that night, I thank God that I remember nothing after he tied me up. I know the details of that night are somewhere in my mind, but I pray that they never surface.

The next thing I recall, I was sitting in his car staring blankly out the window while he drove, the hum of the car now resounding through me. I was in a trance. After a few familiar landmarks, I realized we were by my home. Then he spoke. "Where is your house?" I lied and had him drop me off about half a mile away. He pulled over to the side and I got out. I stood there barefoot and shivering in the cold night air, wearing only my stained and torn bathing suit. With sharp rocks poking at my bare feet, I watched as he drove away. As soon as he turned the corner, I ran as fast as I could. Although my feet were bloodied from the stones, I didn't stop until I arrived at the front door of my house. Fearing that he had followed me, and praying no one was home, I fumbled with my key in a state of sheer panic. Eventually, I made it inside. I was grateful to find the house empty. I was in no shape to respond to an interrogation about where I had been or what I had done.

I never cried again about the events that happened on that trip to the Colorado River. It was so far buried within me that I consciously forgot about most of the horror. On the other hand, I'll never forget the moment I said to myself, *well, at least I now know how to have sex.* Or the exact moment when I felt that I gave in. At some level, I believed that I must have allowed it.

I HAVE SINCE COME TO REALIZE THAT MANY RAPE VICTIMS OR victims of incest have had similar experiences where they "gave in" to the abuser. I clearly know now that although many of us gave in for different reasons, some gave in because we knew our pleas were pointless. Others gave in to their father to protect their little sisters from being attacked. And some even gave in so their moms wouldn't hear them and be mad. Regardless of the reasons we eventually gave in, we were raped.

Grown men are NEVER allowed to attack children. You are not responsible for not stopping it. They are deranged and sick for ever starting it. If you still question it after reading this, stop reading for a moment. Search your mind for a child that you know now that is about the same age that you were when you were raped. Someone you care about. Ready? Good. Now picture the same man attacking that child. How angry does it make you? Do you want to protect the child? Pretend for a minute that you love yourself as much as you love that child. Now how do you feel? Sad? Disconnected?

If you're anything like I was, you are sad and disconnected, because you just realized how much you don't love yourself. I urge you to seek therapeutic help so that someone can work with you to forgive yourself. The child inside of you needs your love and acceptance in order to heal.

I never told anyone about what happened that day; it would be thirteen years before I would mention it in light conversation to my therapist. The moment she said it was rape, I immediately saw how obvious it was. Denial is a great form of self-preservation which allows people to retain sanity when conditions are fixed and unchangeable.

I QUIETLY GRABBED SOME CLEAN PAJAMAS AND MADE MY WAY TO THE shower. I felt dirty and needed to cleanse myself of his stench. As the water ran over me, I felt an overwhelming pressure swelling in my chest. I shut my eyes tightly and fought back a storm of emotions. I shook violently until I nearly collapsed. Crouched down on the shower floor, I wrapped my arms tightly around my folded legs and wept. The sounds of the shower muffled the sounds of my sobs. Although he was gone, the nightmare was far from over. In an effort to gain control of my emotions, I quickly reminded myself that I had brought this nightmare on and I need to straighten up. After a few deep breaths, I blinked the tears out of my eyes, got out of the shower and dried myself off. *Stop being a baby. He is gone now. You are home.*

Thank God the house was quiet when I crept out of the bathroom. Luckily, everyone was gone. My mom would have been furious if she had seen me in this condition. I was in no shape to fight with her. My head was pounding. I crawled into my bed and lay there wondering if that monster had followed me home. Although I had seen him drive away, he may have turned around while I was running. I was terrified. I trembled until I fell asleep. I stayed in bed paralyzed until the next day.

As I slowly walked down the stairs the next morning, I saw my mom in the kitchen. She glanced at me, but turned away without saying a word. The fact that I had a swollen eye and was covered in bruises was not unusual and did not even warrant a comment. She was obviously furious and I was getting the silent treatment as a result. Had I been given the opportunity to choose my form of punishment, the silent treatment would have been at the top of my list. I was so messed up inside that I couldn't handle being questioned or getting screamed at. Silence is truly golden.

A few days later, Karlee returned home from the river. We never again discussed what happened after I left her and her friends.

My mother didn't speak to me for the next few weeks. Every now and again she'd give me what I referred to as the "dead eye," a mean stare accompanied by invisible daggers filled with guilt. Words were unnecessary, the look itself was enough.

As if she believed the "dead eye" wasn't enough to get her point across, she also went out of her way to keep her distance from me. From what I could tell, she never understood that treating me as she did provided me the freedom I so highly coveted. No talking meant no questions about what I was doing, where I was going or when I'd be coming home. The perfect level of parental supervision for a teenager hell bent on consuming as many drugs and as much alcohol as possible.

Two full weeks passed before she finally spoke to me. It was bordering on 4 a.m. when I came home from a night of serious partying. Assuming she'd be asleep as usual, I thought it'd be no problem to slip in quietly and crawl into bed. Not only was I sure she'd never know what time I came in, I had come to believe she no longer cared anyway.

I attempted to open the door as quietly as possible. To my horror, the hinges, apparently in need of some WD-40, refused to cooperate. The squeaking disturbed the silence like a security alarm announcing an intruder. As the door widened, I noticed the light from the porch streaming through the window into the living room. After a few gentle steps forward, I recognized the shadow of my mom's silhouette looming on the far wall. I composed myself and entered. Once inside, I saw the expression on her face and knew that a storm was brewing.

She stood a few feet beyond the door with her arms crossed tightly on her chest. She was crying and yelling. "You don't give a shit about me!" Before I could respond, she slapped me hard across the face. She was in one of those shaky, took too many pills and didn't sleep angry type moods.

Because of my father's abuse, anytime someone physically hurt me I exploded like a bomb. Each time she swung at me, I hit back. Although I was somewhat constrained with my mom, out of guilt, it was still bad. Nadine came running down the stairs and pushed me. It was clear that she wanted in this fight. I had no problem taking the full force of my anger out on Nadine. I was fueled up with rage from my mom hitting me and there was no better person to take it out on than "daddy's girl."

She grabbed a handful of my hair and I shoved her to the ground and held her there, while punching her in the ribs. My mom called 911.

Minutes later, two male officers knocked on the door. They told all of us to sit down and questioned us about the altercation. Without explanation, they turned their attention toward me. They wanted to know about my decision to hitchhike to The River and, suddenly to my surprise, changed tack, asking if they could search my room. *Why the heck would they want to search my room?* They invited me to observe them as they searched and too scared to object, I had little choice but to sit back and watch them. An indescribable shock erupted in my gut when they removed a bag of weed from my sock drawer. Up until that moment, I had forgotten that I told my boyfriend, Jeremy, that I would stash it for him. Bad idea.

13

THE OFFICER TOOK A FEW STEPS BACK AND COMMENCED READING me my rights. My heart was pounding as the words screamed in my head. "You have the right to remain silent. Anything you say may and will be used against you…" Without skipping a beat, he walked behind me, joined my wrists together and cuffed me.

After a short ride in the police car, I was admitted into Juvenile Hall. The policeman handed me off to a large woman just inside the steel door. The sound of jingling keys and large metal doors banging shut instantly resurrected the buried memories of the asylum. That familiar feeling of terror rose to the surface as we entered the girls' unit. It was clear almost immediately that the majority of the inmates were gay. Not only were they gay, they were all massive, tough and angry as hell. I was seriously outweighed and outnumbered. The woman escorting me barked, "Hands in your pockets!" I complied.

We stopped at a large glass room with toilets and showers. The room was adjacent to a TV area with three couches in it. There were six identically clothed inmates watching television. I could feel their attention shift our way as we entered.

Either unaware or unconcerned that other girls had a clear view of us, the woman ordered, "Take your clothes off." An avalanche of indescribable feelings rushed over me with an intensity that I could barely contain. As I undressed, the girls howled and laughed from the other room. One of the girls shouted, "Take it off," while another yelled, "I'll shove my fist up your ass, bitch!" A counselor close by commanded, "Shut it down or you'll be in your rooms." I felt a sense of weakness in my knees. Chills pierced through to my bones. I did all I could to block their presence from my mind.

I quickly learned that this fish tank room was used by all the inmates. Whether showering or using the toilet, you were completely on display to anyone hanging out in the TV area. While I assumed the room had been designed that way in order to provide counselors at the control desk a full view of the bathroom, it was unnecessarily invasive for those inside. Although the other girls seemed fairly immune to it, they were either just playing cool or had been conditioned to this way of living over time. I have always had issues with public restrooms, but with people sitting on a couch watching you, it was seriously disturbing.

I was given a stack of clothes and then told to shower. My wardrobe consisted of a large pair of white underwear, white tube socks, an over-sized pair of blue jeans, (I was told the smaller ones go quickly) a button down shirt and stiff cotton pajamas. As I got dressed, I was told that no belts were allowed to prevent suicide attempts. Walking past those girls in the TV area, wearing pants three sizes too big for my tiny body, only intensified the feelings I had of being a wimp. No matter how hard I tried, I couldn't access the tough girl image I was so accustomed to projecting.

The woman, who had walked with me to the glass enclosed bathroom, escorted me down a long brick hallway with large metal doors lining both sides. We stopped at the third door. She unlocked it with a key from her enormous key ring. Inside the cell there were two metal framed twin beds. Each bed had a thin plastic mattress sitting on top of the springs and a thick plastic pillow. "I'll be back in a while with sheets," she said as the door slammed behind her. Although it was cold, I was thankful to be isolated from those girls in the TV area. I slept the rest of that day straight through to the next morning. I woke up from time to time from the chill and it would hit me again. I was in jail. I cried until my head ached. What was in store for me? In the morning I awoke from a bang! The steel doors all shot open simultaneously in one loud swoop.

A loud voice from beyond yelled, "Burns…medical!" *Was I supposed to go out? Did she say Burns?* I peered out of the door to see a large woman waiting by the entry to the unit with dangling keys. "Come on!" she yelled. Holding open one of the steel doors as I approached, she barked, "Hands in your pockets, Burns. Follow me!" We made our way down a long corridor passing through several identical units. As we walked, I quickly discovered that there was a direct correlation between making eye contact with other kids in those units and getting verbally assaulted. Generally a fast learner when my ass is on the line, I made it a habit to either look straight ahead or down at the ground for some time to come.

Eventually, we stopped at a door marked MEDICAL UNIT. My escort unlocked the door and waved her hand as a signal for me to enter the room. *"I'll be back when you're done,"* she said. She shut the door firmly and engaged the lock from the outside. The room was nearly barren with a cement floor, brick walls, locked metal cabinets and a steel table bolted to the floor. The only item in the room that wasn't secured to the floor or walls was an old fashioned scale sitting beside the wall. The place was cold and, unlike most other doctor's offices I'd been in, there was no comfortable place to sit and nothing to do or see. There was a window that looked out onto an empty field with patches of brown grass. The window pane was infused with chicken wire and encased with large metal bars.

I was very apprehensive at first. *What were they going to do?* I had certainly seen and heard enough about jail to warrant being worried. After 20 minutes or so, I moved from an anxious state to being aggravated. Anger has always been a more comfortable and familiar state for me than fear anyway.

By this point in my life, I had spent a great deal of time waiting in the offices of doctors, psychiatrists, psychologists and medical practitioners. Doctors like to schedule appointments centuries before the time they are actually ready to see you. This serves as a leveler to let you know who is in charge and, of course, to remind us of the years they spent in medical school. The problem here was that unlike other doctor's offices, there was nothing to do in this room. Normally I could fiddle with something or go through the doctor's drawers to see what kind of interesting tools they have, but in this case, there was nothing. There were no magazines and when I got bold enough to investigate, I confirmed that the drawers and cabinets, like everything else in prison, were locked.

As the time went by, I started to think maybe they had forgotten about me. Maybe the lady brought me here and forgot to tell anyone. I could stay in here forever, unnoticed. Or at least until the next kid needed a doctor visit. But, maybe there was more than one room? I began to panic. Then I came up with a plan. I began to make as much noise as I could without causing trouble, a little pang with my foot now and again on the thin metal cabinets as a reminder that *hey*, there *is a live person in here.*

A few decades later, I heard the familiar sound of keys. Thank God the locks were disengaging. As quickly as the relief came, it was replaced with the feeling of apprehension that had existed prior to the annoyance. A man entered the room. He made no acknowledgement of my presence, spoke no words and made no eye contact. He set a manila file folder on the metal counter, flipped it open, pointed and said, "On the scale please." He performed the usual procedures without a sound.

After ascertaining my height and weight and checking my blood pressure, he jotted down each of his findings in the opened file. He then drew blood abruptly and walked out of the room. Aside from the few directives he gave me during the exam, he didn't speak to me at all. Shortly after he left, the female counselor returned and escorted me back to the unit. She asked me if I wanted to watch TV, but I declined. Going to my frigid little box of a room to lie by myself on my bed seemed like a much better idea. The last thing I wanted to do at this point was to get in to a fight with one of the Amazon dykes.

I was summoned back to the medical unit later that afternoon. This time the doctor showed up very quickly. He set the file down in the same location he had during my last visit and looked at me. After a long pause that nearly paralyzed me, he matter-of-factly said, "I have the results from your blood work. It seems you have a venereal disease that we can treat today with a shot." He paused briefly, shook his head from side to side and in the most judgmental tone he could summon spat out, "And you know you're pregnant, right?"

By the time the word "*no*" fell out of my mouth, I was miles away. The room started spinning and memories of my experiences at The River flooded in. While those horrible thoughts raced through my head, I heard the doctor's voice echo as if from another dimension, "Do you have a boyfriend?" I mumbled "yes" in a kind of knee jerk response to his question. I was in shock. The automatic pilot in me had taken over the controls. It was as if I wasn't completely present in the room. Again, I heard the doctor's reverberating echo say, "I'll treat you today for the venereal disease, but you better tell your boyfriend." I didn't respond. I couldn't. He continued, "Also we'll also have to inform your parents about your pregnancy."

The only boy I had dated was Jeremy, but since he and I had never had sex, I knew I wouldn't have to tell him about the venereal disease. But what about the pregnancy? I had the rapist's baby inside of me. I was sure if I told my mom, she'd kill me. I also knew if I told Jeremy, he'd break up with me. I needed a plan.

Mustering up all manipulation and exit strategies I could devise, I settled on a plan. I decided that my only way out was to have sex with Jeremy as quickly as possible and then announce to everyone that I was pregnant. Everybody would assume that Jeremy was responsible. While I had no desire to repeat that painful act, it was the best my 15-year-old brain could come up with. I just needed to figure out when I was going to be able to see Jeremy again and how I was going to get the deed done.

As I lay in my bed that day, I could feel the dirty man growing inside of me. I made a conscious attempt to deny the existence of my body and the evil inside of it. I hit my stomach, trying to make it go away. I was cursed and wanted to die. I lay in my bed crying until I fell asleep, refusing both dinner and breakfast. I had no appetite, but even more repugnant was the thought that I would be feeding a part of the rapist inside of me.

I was taken to court the next morning and held in a cold cell with three long metal benches around the perimeter. There were twelve girls in the cell with me that morning. Due to the limited talk, I had to assume most of them, like me, were new to this. We sat in silence nervously waiting for our names to be called. Around noon, a lady entered the room with brown bags for each of us containing an apple and a bologna sandwich. We ate and then resumed waiting, and waiting.

When my name was finally called, a police officer escorted me to the courtroom. This was the first of many appearances before the judge. Upon entering, the officer pointed to a seat next to a man dressed in a business suit. I sat where instructed, but the man failed to acknowledge my presence. I wondered if I was invisible. Then the judge said, *"Burns, Lauri, case number $#%# #$#* #*%&^ #*&^% (&^%. $#%# #$#* #*%&^ #*&^%* . They spoke in a language consisting of numbers and codes intended as a secret code for those with degrees and long black capes. Finally, I heard the only words that made any sense. *"You have been charged with blah, blah, blah. Do you understand the charges against you?"* I sat there like a stone statue. The man in the business suit said, "Do you understand that you have been charged with possession of marijuana?" I said, "Yes." He turned and interpreted, "Yes we do." The judge continued with his official ruling. The man in the suit said," Thank you your honor." And it was over. The officer signaled for me to stand up, approached me from behind and escorted me back to my cell. Excluding the lengthy wait, the entire process took about five minutes.

Although the court had released me to my mom's custody, I quickly realized I was not going home. My mom, who had shown up with a girlfriend I had never met before, informed me that she was not ready for me to come home yet. She told me that I would be going to a "home" for a while so I could get some help. While I wondered what kind of help I'd be getting, I didn't have any real aversion to the idea of not going home. Partly because I was still coming down from the shock of everything I had just experienced. And I couldn't focus on anything other than the fact that I was pregnant. I wanted to know if they had told her. I was hoping they hadn't. What a nightmare that would be.

After signing me out of juvenile hall, my mom turned me over to yet another man. This man drove me in an unmarked car to a large house in Garden Grove. The basketball hoop in the driveway might have given the impression that this was a normal home, but it wasn't. The garage had been converted into an office and the adults coming and going were counselors, not parents.

It was called the Our Star Home for Abused Children. My being sent here was particularly strange because I was sure that no one knew about what had happened with my father. I was asked all sorts of questions, but none were ever about that, thank God. Since this was a house for abused children and I was a child living there, either they were out of places for me to go, or they suspected something, but no one asked.

My stay at Our Star was short lived. Although no one had mentioned the pregnancy, I was surprised to learn that an appointment had been made at the "clinic" for an abortion. Thinking it best to avoid anything that might further expose my condition, I just went with the plan. I hoped that as long as I went with the plan, no one would ask how I got that way.

I don't remember anything about the abortion. I must have blocked most of the experience from my mind, but I do remember the hours following the procedure. Upon returning from the clinic, I was told to go my room and rest until dinner. Tired and uncomfortable, I was pleased to be alone. I proceeded to the small room they had assigned to me. It was simply furnished with a twin bed, a rocking chair and a dresser. Just as I entered my room, I noticed a small Asian girl trailing closely behind me. She followed me in without an invitation.

When I sat on my bed, she plopped down on the rocking chair adjacent to me. Before I could process why she was following me, she began talking. Curious about who I was, and why I was there, she began shooting questions at me like bullets from an automatic weapon. "Where are you from? Why are you here? What did you do at the hospital today?" All I wanted to do was crawl into my bed and go to sleep until the medicine wore off, but she clearly had other ideas.

I opened my mouth to answer one of her questions and felt as though my jaw was pulling to the right. At first I thought the medication I had been given was playing tricks with my head, but then she said, "*You look weird.*" I told her that my jaw felt funny. Just as I began describing the feeling, my jaw locked up completely. I lifted my hand to touch it, and then everything went black.

The next thing I knew I was lying on my back with a couple of paramedics directly above me. They were rubbing some sort of sticky ointment on my chest while telling me that I had been having seizures as a result of an allergic reaction to the anesthesia I was given during the procedure. They instructed me to never allow anybody to give me that particular type of anesthetic again. One of the paramedics gave me an injection and told me I would be fine. Before walking out the door, he turned and said, "You are lucky to be alive, young lady." I wanted to feel that, I really did. But sadly, I knew I didn't. I just nodded and smiled.

Less than forty eight hours later, I bolted from Our Star. I was in the TV area and noticed that there were no counselors around. Without any forethought, I simply walked out of the front door. I figured if I was walking casually and got caught, I could always say I was just going for a walk.

When I reached the main road, I stuck my thumb out as I had become accustomed to doing. I rarely worried about who picked me up. Even though I felt tough and dangerous, I'm sure that most of the people who picked me up were kind to me because I looked frail and in need of protection. All in all, I was lucky.

My first goal was to go to Jeremy's apartment. I knew if my mom ever questioned him about the pregnancy and I hadn't had sex with him, this would expose the rape and my mom would blame me. I had to have sex with him as soon as possible. A few weeks later, I could tell him he had gotten me pregnant and I had had an abortion. Hopefully by the time this came to light, no one would remember the exact date and the stories would sync up. This was the best plan I could come up with.

I made it to Jeremy's, spent the night and accomplished my goal. The experience was not only extremely painful and awkward, but it felt unnatural at best. The circumstances surrounding the event didn't help. I had never really seen a man's body and I attempted to appear unaffected, but it was very weird. The bottom line was, I got it over with and my tracks were covered. I was not interested in pursuing intimacy again anytime soon. This was strictly unfinished business.

I am sure my perception of sex was largely affected by that first experience at the river. Jeremy and I never actually broke up, but instead just drifted away from each other due to my instability, lack of permanent residence and failure to bond.

After leaving Jeremy's house, with nowhere else to go, I returned home. My mom decided to give me one more chance. Although my mom was there for me that day and throughout my life to rescue me from myself, I never noticed. For years, I would only remember when she screamed at me or hit me. It wasn't until I was an adult that I would look back and see how she fought for me, over and over again.

14

SCHOOL WAS STARTING SOON AND I ALREADY KNEW THIS WAS GOING to be trouble for me. I recognized almost immediately after moving to our new home that there was a notable difference in the attire and demeanor of the kids. I was different. They seemed overly happy, friendly and outgoing. I was quietly cunning, deceitful and manipulative. I didn't want what they had, unless it was alcohol, cigarettes or weed.

The girls I had met were accustomed to wearing fashionable brand-named clothing, going to hair salons and having several pairs of shoes. I dressed in preparation for a potential fight. My attire was loose fitting and worn with protection in mind. As the first day of school crept closer, my fear intensified. My mom must have also noticed the obvious gap because she took my sisters and me shopping for school clothes. She even talked me into some more "girly" outfits. Although they were not expensive or fashionable, I thought she might be right. If I have to go to school here, I should try not to be an outcast.

On the first day of school, I walked with my sister, Nadine. I was wearing a recently acquired skirt and a long sweater. I felt like a raccoon in an Easter bunny suit. The other girls seemed to be waltzing down the street in their designer clothes and done up hair. I, on the other hand, was trying desperately to integrate my best *don't fuck with me walk* with my new flowered skirt and knitted sweater. My stomach ached. I felt like an imposter. Even worse, I was positive that everybody saw through me.

When we were three quarters of the way across the parking lot approaching the quad, I saw a group of kids over to the right. They were huddled by the back stairs of the school and a cloud of smoke hung slightly over their heads. My sister Nadine seemed to spot them simultaneously and said, "Hey, how about if we go over there first?" It was music to my ears! After a few minutes of socialization in what we later referred to as "the smoke pit," Nadine suggested we hang out there today and officially start school tomorrow. I couldn't have agreed more. Within minutes, I felt at home. These kids felt familiar. I could sense their quest for survival. I had found my people. Although I'm pretty sure Nadine went to class the following day, I never made it past the smoke pit. I loved it there. It was as far as my feet would take me.

I quickly befriended two girls, Kitty and Beth. Kitty was an average-looking girl who knew everything about everything. She hung around a lot of older druggies who rented a house nearby. They smoked a lot of pot, took a good deal of acid and mushrooms and listened to bands like Led Zeppelin and Pink Floyd. Beth, on the other hand, was a beautiful young girl who came from a wealthy family and dressed like the bulk of trendy girls at school. I never understood why she hung out at the smoke pit. She clearly didn't fit the part.

Kitty, Beth and I met at the smoke pit every day like clockwork to hang out, smoke and talk. When the actual students went to class we would walk through the field, go to the store or just find a place to kick back and avoid the school patrol. A few days into school, Kitty told me that she and Beth had a wrong to right, but I was sworn to secrecy. I was interested before I even knew what it was. Kitty told me that someone had messed with them and they had the perfect plan to get these people back. They explained the details to me—the location of the house, their normal hours of departure and the items in the house that they were interested in taking. I was definitely in.

The next day we set out to break into the house of the enemy. Kitty was supposed to knock on the door to confirm that no one was home. If someone answered, she would ask for John and when they informed her that she had the wrong house, she would apologize and walk away. If no one answered, we were clear.

Kitty knocked. No one answered. We unlatched the gate and went into the backyard, expecting to break a window. Much to our surprise, the window was open, with just the screen securing it. We pulled out the screen and Kitty jumped up, wiggled through and unlocked the back door for us. We took a few dollars, some alcohol and we found cigarettes. We also took jewelry. We had no idea why we were taking jewelry, but we all agreed it was standard procedure for thieves on TV to take jewelry. We split up the jewelry and took it home for safe-keeping.

When we got back to school we decided we should put the money to good use. We agreed on pizza to celebrate our success. During our celebration feast, we acknowledged our hidden talent for thievery and decided it would be best not to waste it. We would be foolish to just sit around at the smoke pit when there are so many empty houses containing alcohol and money. We decided to hit a new neighborhood each day and knock on doors looking for empty houses. For the next few weeks we would meet at school, smoke for a while, find a house or two to burglarize and end up at the party house.

We became less and less careful over time. One day we arrived at a house that was actually locked. Even the gate was locked. It was secured with a thick padlock. Being rebellious teenagers, the fact that it was locked only made us more determined to get in. Sure any burglar could get a screen off, but to break into a locked house, now that took skill. Feeling confident in our newly acquired talent, we were up to the test. Noting the height of the fence and the sprinkler pipe running alongside the edge of the house, I knew with a bit of determination, I could do it. I also knew that this would earn me respect amongst the team.

With little more thought, I wrapped my hands around the top edge of the fence, placed my foot on the pipe and lunged to the top of the fence. With another breath, I jumped down on the other side. The plan was to enter the house and let the girls in. When my feet hit the ground, I heard a distant but familiar sound: the pitter patter of large dog feet quickly hitting the ground. When I turned to see the face of the angry beast, I flew back over the fence! Let's just say, although it took me two separate moves to get in the yard, I hoisted myself out of the yard in one quick, *run for your f*** ing life* second. We laughed about it later.

One day we broke into a house that was different than any we had seen yet. I dropped in through the sink window and as I plopped on to the floor, I immediately noticed the scarcity of the surroundings. The appliances and furnishings looked to be quite a bit older than what we were used to seeing in the area. I let the girls in through the back slider and we continued to explore. We entered the master bedroom together. The white doily on the weathered wood dresser and the picture of the elderly couple erected on top affected each one of us. The bedspread and pictures all looked like antiques. The jewelry in the drawer was carefully packed into fancy little boxes. Knowing the old lady in the picture probably packed these things herself, we knew we couldn't go through with it.

We looked at each other with mutual sadness. We agreed almost instantly that we wouldn't feel right stealing anything. Although we did agree that we had to take something just because we broke in, we all agreed it would be something that wouldn't cause them harm. It was unanimous. We took a box of pork sausages out of the freezer and left.

We continued burglarizing homes for the next few months. Each day was a new adventure. But it all came to a sudden halt the day I returned home from "school" to find a man and woman sitting in my living room talking to my mom. When I walked through the apartment door my mom said, "Lauri, please come in the living room for a minute." I had no idea who these people were, but I can tell you they looked serious. Both dressed in dark suits; neither was smiling.

My mom introduced them as detectives and told me they wanted to ask me some questions. She lifted her head as if to say, have a seat. It was at that moment that my heart took on a life of its own. Battling my rib cage, I could feel it thundering beneath my t-shirt. I was positive anyone sitting within reasonable distance could see it. The voice in my head was so loud, I was sure they could hear it. *Lauri...look natural... smile...your mouth is too tight...for cripes sakes...do something with your arms...you look scared...relax...try to relax...*I did everything I could to look natural, but it was useless.

The man informed me that they were there to ask me about some recent burglaries in the area. Although I remained silent, my heart pounded even more vigorously. I had no idea what to say, so I said nothing. The woman broke the awkward silence in the room when she said, "Lauri, we're investigating some recent burglaries in the area and we're wondering if you might know anything that could help us." I tried to keep it short to conceal my nervousness. "No, I don't know anything about any burglaries." The man reached for a piece of paper that was sitting on the table in front of him. As he opened it, he said, "Before you got home, your mom let us take a look around your room. We found this note." Having no idea what the paper was, I listened intently as he read. "Dear Kitty, do you want to do some burglaries today? Blah…blah…blah…Love, Lauri." He turned it around to reveal a picture of a big heart that I had drawn at the bottom. He wanted to make sure I knew just how obvious the evidence was.

I immediately realized the gravity of my present circumstances. The room started to close in on me. Although they were still talking, I was not listening. It was a do or die situation; they had proof! I need to get away now! I jumped up and bolted for the door, but the lady grabbed my arm. I kicked her and tried to punch her in the stomach. The man immediately caught my other arm and forced it up behind my back, pushed me down on the ground and handcuffed me. "You have the right to remain silent…" Everything became a blur.

I later learned that my mom had gone into my sock drawer to put my laundry away and discovered a large mound of jewelry. When she took it to the jewelry store to get it appraised, she almost got arrested.

15

WITHIN A FEW HOURS, I WAS BACK IN THE SHOWER AT "JUVIE" AS the regulars referred to it. While hardly jumping for joy, I was grateful that I had arrived at a time when the other inmates were in their rooms for the silverware count. The silverware count takes place after each meal and is intended to ensure that none of the kids steal eating utensils to use as a weapon or a tool for committing suicide. Surprisingly, given the circumstances, I actually felt lucky at that moment.

I also felt fortunate this time around to have a much nicer woman escorting me through the arrival procedure. Although it was the same routine, it seemed easier. I guess it is like that with anything. The tragedy of the situation is dulled with each repetition. A shower, a pair of oversized blue jeans, white underwear, white socks and sheets—I knew the drill.

The woman unlocked the door to my cell and I went in. The thump of the lock being engaged from the outside echoed. I wrapped my sheet around the thin plastic mattress and went to sleep. The next morning, all of the cell doors were unlocked electronically with the familiar bang and a staff member shouted, "breakfast" from the control booth in the distance. The word reverberated off the cement walls and echoed around the unit for an unusually long time. I rubbed my eyes and regained consciousness enough to register that I was in jail, again. Breakfast was optional. If you didn't come out, you didn't eat. I passed.

The following morning, I was taken to court. The judge's decision that morning would dramatically impact my life for at least the next three years. Seated at his elevated bench, he looked down at me with obvious disdain and mandated that I become a ward of the court. Simply stated, the judge and the court system would be my parents for the foreseeable future. When I wasn't living in some sort of facility, juvenile hall would be my home. Given my propensity to run, this was a recipe for disaster.

For the next few months and what would actually become years, my life was a revolving door. Arrest…shower…medical exam…Then the judge would say, "Burns, Lauri—$#%# #$#* #*%&^ #*&^%." I would be at a new group home and then I would run. My average stay was just under a few weeks, so although I have memories of many places, the memories are very disjointed. My file was marked SR and AWOL. Suicide risk and absent without leave for running away.

Every time I ran away, I got caught almost immediately. It seems like I couldn't last more than a day or two out in the world without being arrested again. I could never figure out how they would see me walking down the street and know to stop me. I mean, there are kids all over the place, right? Did I look suspicious? I had the repetitive thought that the police must have had my picture in their cars. To this day I cannot say for sure that they didn't. Maybe if I dramatically altered my appearance, they wouldn't catch me. I decided to go to the beach to sunbathe for several hours. Attempting to change my skin tone, I also tied my hair back in tight braids. Confident that anyone who saw me would think I was mulatto or Hispanic, I headed into town. I was walking down the main boulevard just mere minutes later when the police car pulled over. Within 30 minutes I was on my way back to juvie. Frankly, I am still baffled.

I was in and out of juvenile hall so many times that very little of what happened during those stays is crystallized in my memory. The number of times I had run away began to have a direct impact on how long it would take them to place me in a new home again. The judge would set the next pre-placement review for 45 days out and since no place would take me; I would still be in juvie when that date came up. I became accustomed to the life. I had some really good roommates and I picked up a job. I mopped the hallways after dinner. Although my intention was simply to be out of the room while everyone else was locked up, the routine was actually therapeutic for me. I also learned to draw while in the hall. With several hours locked alone in a room with a pencil and paper, I drew until I got good at it.

Group home placements were no longer than six months in most cases anyway. The powers that be decided they didn't want kids to bond to the people in any given place because they eventually would have to move out. They realized the insanity of this thinking many years later, but the outcome of this era was a bunch of messed up, abused kids, with an inability to bond.

I continued to live my life isolated from humanity. I was intensely guarded and repulsed by closeness with another human. Although I had boyfriends over the next few years, relationships never lasted. I was getting locked up regularly, which meant a new city and a new life. The guys I was dating never knew what happened to me. I would just disappear. There was no way for minors to make phone calls and I always thought it was silly to write. I mean, what do you say? "Hey nice knowing you, but I am in juvie now and won't be seeing you again." What was the point? It simplified things. I never had to break up. I just left. It also served to reinforce my strong belief that people and relationships are temporary. Don't get attached. Getting attached guaranteed eventual abandonment. Once Pepper was taken from my life, intimacy and vulnerability were yanked from my vocabulary. I was forever on my own. I learned that it is best to leave first. The abrupt breakups actually infused me with a sense of independence, control and power.

Given my propensity for moving on, most of the people that I met along the way came and went too quickly to remember. I did have some very cool roommates and met two particular adults that had a positive influence on me.

Karen was a unit staff member who stopped in my room every now and again just to say hello. With no subversive motive, she'd always show up with a chocolate bar or some other kind of candy for me. She told me that she came by specifically to see how I was doing and generally hung around for about five minutes or so. Karen acted like she really cared about me and I got the feeling that she truly did. Although I didn't understand her motives, I grew to like her.

There was also my psychiatrist, Dr. Limner. Lord knows I had been to see enough of these guys over the years to be tainted, but Dr. Limner was different. Where most doctors would question my activities on the outs, Dr. Limner said nothing.

Whenever I was in juvie for a long period of time, we had regular visits. Most of the time I would go to his office, but on more than one occasion when the unit was on lockdown, he came to see me. He would always come with a checkerboard in tow. He would lay the board on the bed and we would play. Little or no words needed to be spoken. I always appreciated the time he took to spend with me, and the fact that he didn't interrogate me. His quiet nature afforded me a small amount of self-respect.

Being a regular at juvenile hall had both its benefits and drawbacks. While I made a handful of friends, I also made my fair share of enemies. Riley, Fran and Ella, and anyone they happened to be dating, went into the friend column. Riley was a tough, stocky chick with short, dirty blonde hair. She was prone to violent outbursts and had a sizable scar on her chin as proof. She was also rough around the edges and much more butch than the others. Riley was completely one-hundred percent gay.

Fran was a very tired, overdeveloped 15-year-old girl who seemed to have lived several lives already. She knew everything there was to know about juvie and the system, but was too tired to educate anyone else. She clearly had made up her mind to do the bulk of her time there sitting on her ass in front of the TV. Although Fran had been in and out many times, she wreaked so much havoc that it was nearly impossible for her to get placed in an outside home, but she worked the system like a pro to get her needs met. Being afforded special privileges, she was able to stay out of her cell later than the other inmates and was permitted to use better quality shampoo and soap than the rest of us. Even so, life was far from rosy for her. While the facility sanctioned family visits a few nights each week, no one ever came to see her, or Riley.

Ella, on the other hand, was a beautiful girl. Her mother was Asian and her father was Caucasian. She had long black hair, beautiful big round eyes and the sweetest little voice you could imagine. Ella was Riley's girlfriend. Ella was a walking paradox. The innocence that she exuded was a facade to hide the anger that simmered beneath. I always wondered if this was an asset or a liability. Her inability to sustain the innocent act for long was a liability. She was too cute to scare anyone and too angry to be nurtured. Ella's mother visited often. Each time she visited, they would fight. The result would range from self-injurious behaviors to violence toward the staff, or simply sleeping until delivered out of a depression. Ella's mom was soft-spoken and would often retreat silently when the visit went bad. We were all surprised when Ella returned home to live with her mom, time after time.

I would never go so far as to say I enjoyed juvie. I hated it. Waking up day after day to remember that I was in jail and that I had no idea where I would be going next was completely gut-wrenching. I lacked control over everything; where I would sit, when I would sleep, when I would eat. I had lost the ability to make any choices for myself. The only thing I could have possibly had any control over was my attitude and even that was way far out of my reach.

During one of my early stays, my mom and my probation officer devised a plan to implement upon my release. They decided it would serve me best to live at my mom's, (while still being a ward of the court) attend continuation school and get a part-time job. As far as they were concerned, I had too much free time on my hands. This, they proclaimed, was my problem. A job, they went on to say, was the solution.

The school referred my mom to the duplication office. The duplication office was responsible for creating and disseminating all the school materials for the entire district. It was housed in an old elementary school that had been converted into an office with a printing press, collating machines and binding equipment. Edwina, a short German woman with a heavy accent, ran the shop. She was a serious, no-nonsense and demanding woman in her mid to late 50's. Her stern German dialect made every request sound like a command. Marie, the only other employee, was a frail black woman in her late 20's. She was very quiet and served under Edwina's rule obediently and without question. This made for an interesting mix once I joined on.

I was told to show up at work after school every day. My mom bought me a moped so I could get there and back on my own. Although not related, things at home started deteriorating after just a few days on the job. My mom and the probation officer quickly decided that they had made a mistake and it would be best if they found a group home alternative just in case. They told me I'd be staying there until they came up with a suitable alternative. I had moved so much by this point that the news had little effect on me. I assumed they would just tell me when it was time.

Much to my surprise, I did fairly well at the duplication office. It was a quiet place except for the hum and drum of the machines sucking in, sorting and printing, And Marie was so submissive and kind that I couldn't help but work well under her rule. I enjoyed helping her. It was quite a change for me. She would spend a good deal of time with me showing me how to operate the machines. I enjoyed her company and respected her knowledge and humble nature. As the days went on, I felt empowered. I was actually learning how to use the machines unsupervised. For once, I was doing something good.

About a week later, feeling a bit guilty with all she had taught me, I confided in Marie that I probably wouldn't be working in the duplication office much longer. I felt terribly embarrassed when she asked why. How do you explain this? I just told her my mom and I weren't getting along. She asked where I would be going. I explained that sometimes I live in other places. She had such a sad look in her eyes when I told her that people were looking for someplace and I would let her know when as soon as I found out. I didn't want to leave her in a bind. While my instincts about people were legitimately suspect, I could tell she looked sincerely concerned. She was very thoughtful about the manner in which she responded. Clearly aware that I was uncomfortable discussing the situation; she smoothly shifted the focus of our conversation to the new collator.

When I showed up at work the next day, Edwina called me into her small office. She said that Marie had told her about my situation. I was mortified. What could she possibly want to say to me? Fire me? What would happen now that she knew the "good girl" thing was just an act? Much to my surprise, she offered to let me stay at her home. She told me that she and her family had an extra room and she insisted that I come and stay with them. I was completely blown away by her offer. It felt strange that she would do something like that after knowing me such a short time. She had no reason to trust me. Maybe I had gone too far with the compliance at work thing. They really thought I was a "normal" kid. Now what? I couldn't help but think that my obedience in the duplication office was deceptive. I felt guilty. They had no idea what I was capable of.

I was not accustomed to anyone reaching out to me without expecting something in return. She asked for my probation officer's number and told me she would handle the arrangements. I gave it to her and, with no further discussion, she dismissed me and I went back to work. I was seriously conflicted about the situation. The whole thing sounded weird and uncomfortable, but I felt I had to accept because I didn't want to hurt her feelings.

Arriving at her house was unbearably strange. When she introduced me to her husband and son, I felt like "the dirty little homeless girl." I assumed they knew my mom didn't want me and the fact that they didn't know why was even worse. How could I explain what had happened up until this point in my life? I lived it and I couldn't make sense of it. I just knew that if they knew the real me, they wouldn't want me. I was a traitor. I couldn't bear that they felt sorry for me. I couldn't stop my head from racing. I told myself over and over again that it would only be a matter of time before these people learned who I really was. Although they welcomed me with open arms, I felt sick to my stomach.

Edwina told me to grab my small suitcase and follow her upstairs.

She opened the door to the first room at the top of the stairs and allowed me to enter first. It was an elegant room with refinished antique furniture, a large oak framed bed and matching end tables. The bed was covered with a beautiful flower patterned comforter and the matching pillows sat perfectly in place. It looked like grandma's room in an upscale house.

As I set my bag down, Edwina said in her thick German accent, "Settle in and come downstairs. We'll be having dinner soon." After she left, I sat on the bed, afraid to go downstairs. I didn't know how to act or what to say. I knew they were waiting for me, but I just froze. Even though I was certain that they were downstairs trying to figure out what was keeping me; I sat on the bed for over an hour. The more time that passed, the harder it was to go down. Unintentionally, I was already distancing myself from them.

A few moments later, I was startled by a loud knock on the door. Before I could respond, Edwina's stern voice announced, "Dinner is now." The emphasis on the word "now" transformed the simple statement into a command. Knowing I had no alternative, I stood up from the bed and sheepishly managed my way down to the dining room. Without a word, Edwina pointed to my designated seat. As I pulled my chair out to sit down, the sound of the legs scraping the floor's surface reinforced my feelings of being completely out of place. For God sakes, I couldn't even sit down at the dinner table without ruining the dining room floor! I was sure I would never be able to measure up around this place.

Although we were all seated, everyone remained perfectly still. I wondered why nobody was eating and tried to imagine what they were waiting for. Just then, Edwina's husband asked, "Who would like to say the prayer tonight?" I panicked. I thought for sure he would say, "How about our new guest?" I would have had a nervous breakdown on the spot. I didn't have a clue about prayers. What prayer? A Hebrew prayer? The one for the wine or the bread? Certainly not the Chanukah prayer! It was heating up by the second! My arm-pits began to sweat and my mouth was sucked dry of all moisture. I was a wreck. The only prayer I could think of was *God please help me to get back to the room upstairs!*

Luckily, within seconds the dad started with "Heavenly Father, thank you for this..." Just as the short prayer ended, they began what I later learned was a customary Catholic ritual. Sweating profusely, I tried to follow along as they each touched their forehead, chest, left shoulder and then right shoulder. They moved so quickly, I didn't stand a chance! By the time I touched my forehead they were done with the whole salute. I turned my head tap into a scratch to cover up my inadequacy with the routine. Sealing my fate for the night, I lost my appetite.

After dinner, Edwina suggested that we move to the living room to watch TV. Against all impulse to run back to my room, I did as I was told. Afraid to utter a word, I sat silently for several hours watching the news with her husband. I anxiously waited for permission to go upstairs. I still remember the sense of relief I felt when I heard Edwina finally say, "OK, time for bed." I couldn't have gotten out of that chair fast enough. As I started up the stairs, she said, "While you're staying here, you'll get up when I get up and we'll eat breakfast together. Then, you'll go to work with me and stay there until school begins. After school, you'll come back to work and we'll close up the shop together." She clearly wasn't throwing this plan out for discussion purposes. This was how it was going to be.

The next morning, Edwina entered my room at 4:30 a.m. I assumed I had died and gone to hell. She couldn't possibly be waking me up. It was still the middle of the night, for cripes sakes. I wrapped the blanket around me and started to doze back off. Then in a stern, thick commanding voice she said, "Get up and shower, it's time for work!" I HAD died and gone to hell.

We were almost two weeks into the routine when Edwina called me into her shop office. She said she was disappointed in me. I had failed to make my bed. For cripes sake, at 4:30 in the morning, I couldn't even see my bed, let alone make it. I can assure you none of my friends were getting up that early for work. She said that I needed to abide by her rules. She was not happy with my choice of friends or my weekends at the beach. She forbade me from going out with my friends and insisted I focus on school and work instead. It was also clear that I was to make my bed every day. When asked if I understood, I said, "Yes." Without any further discussion, she summarily dismissed me from her office.

When I returned to the duplication office after school that day, a large burly man in his early to mid-30's was standing just inside the entrance. Even from a distance, it was evident that he spent most of his free time shooting steroids. As I walked up, I noticed my probation officer speaking with Edwina in her office. Just then, the large man said, "Put your hands behind your back." Although I had grown accustomed to hearing those words, I was shocked to be hearing them now. I was thoroughly confused. What could I possibly have done this time?

I stood handcuffed, waiting for an explanation. The longer I stood the more embarrassed and out of control I felt. Marie was in there; what was she thinking I did? She tried not to look at me. She was probably embarrassed for me. I stood outside like a stray dog having been caught by animal control. A few minutes passed before my probation officer approached me with Edwina following just a few steps behind, crying. Then Edwina blurted out, "I didn't know this would happen. I only called to tell you that she wasn't cleaning her room." Apparently, she had called my probation officer to complain about my room being untidy. Although she had only sought some suggestions from her, my probation officer determined that my behavior constituted a failure to comply with the new house rules. As such, she said, I had violated the terms of my probation and would therefore be returning to juvenile hall. I remember the look on Edwina's face. She was filled with guilt and totally devastated. I actually felt sorry for her. I know when she made that call; the poor lady had no idea who she was dealing with. My probation officer hated me. The lady never actually spoke to me like a person. She never asked me questions. She only constantly reminded me what a failure I was. As we drove away, she started in again.

A FEW DAYS LATER, AS I WAS BEING ESCORTED INTO THE COURTROOM handcuffed, I was horrified to see Edwina and her husband. I was so embarrassed. I looked like a washed up rat. My hair was ridiculously frizzed, I had no makeup and the jail wear was not helping. Although they sat far across the room, I was sure they could see who I really was now. After the proceedings, my attorney explained that they came in hopes of getting me back, but after learning more they decided I was too much for them to take on. I was sure it was because of how I looked, inside and out. Worthless.

I never spoke to Edwina again. Although it didn't work out, I will never forget her. *A quiet stirring inside…someone cares…*

16

THE ONLY GROUP HOME I EVER LASTED IN WAS LESS THAN TEN MILES from my mom's. It was brand new and had space for six girls when it opened its doors. For some reason, our unit was picked to fill the available spots. This meant that Riley, Fran and I would be moving into a home together for the first time. We couldn't have imagined a better plan. The wicked old woman that ran the joint was named Wanda. Her name couldn't have been more fitting. Wanda clearly had a disdain for our type. Even when reprimanding us, she didn't make eye contact. She avoided us at all costs. I don't know what Wanda envisioned when she offered to run a house with six girls, but clearly she had no idea what she was in for.

Riley, Fran and I all went to different schools. I don't know why this was, other than the variance in our educational needs. I started school at Mount Vista Continuation. I found continuation school to be a fascinating element of life.

The continuation school campus is surrounded by a fence with economical buildings set up to convince outsiders that education is taking place. When the gate opens in the morning, a few hundred connoisseurs of some of the best skunk weed in town leisurely drag their feet toward the school barrier. Like brainless zombies, they close in on the complex as if being drawn by an unexplainable force. Continuation schools have the perfect balance of kids selling drugs and interested customers. Everyone on campus is aware of the selection of drugs available and who to get it from. There is no hiding or segregation from the general population like at my old school. At Continuation school, the entire school is the smoke pit. All are welcome. I don't know about Riley or Fran, but I really enjoyed going to school.

Other than Wanda, the remainder of the group home staff was mostly comprised of college students who generally hung around watching TV and, on occasion, told us when to eat and when to go to bed. We were afforded no privileges at Gisler. We were required to take the bus home immediately after school and could not eat, sleep or watch TV without permission. Once in a while, we were authorized to walk to the store. On these trips it was customary for Fran and Riley to stop at the graveyard to make out. Riley and Fran were only together when Ella wasn't around. It was a relationship of convenience. It was routine for Fran to sneak into our room at night to do the deed with Riley. It didn't bother me much; I would just roll over in the other direction to give them their privacy. There was a certain feeling of triumph that we could get away with something and even if I wasn't directly involved, I was on "lookout." I must say, after just a short period of time of being exposed to my new life, I was unusually comfortable with girls dating girls. It felt safe. Although I was never interested in girls, guys were still a mystery to me. Unfortunately, it didn't take long for our newfound home to take a turn for the worse.

The old lady who ran the house informed us one Friday that we were taking a trip to Bakersfield over the weekend. I didn't know where Bakersfield was, but I assumed we were going on a vacation or, at the very least, a field trip of sorts. We loaded into her old, blue van the following morning and took off. There were two benches behind the driver's seat with windows lining both sides. It was about 92 degrees out when we left and the lady refused to use the air conditioning declaring that the van got better gas mileage when it was off. After about 45 minutes of sweating in the back of the van, we literally would have sold our clothes and given the money to the old crow to turn the air on.

After shedding a few pounds of sweat, the mobile sauna arrived in Bakersfield. At that point, it was clear that this was no vacation. Bakersfield was not a city of choice, but more a city of circumstance. Out of money, hiding from the cops or having run out of retirement money before your life ended—this was your destiny. The old van pulled in front of a small tan house and we went inside. We were told to sit on the couch. Wanda spoke to the lady in the adjoining room. Within a few minutes, there was some sort of money exchange and then we left on our journey back to our group home. Little did I know I would never actually get there.

The ride home was more of the same with one small difference. About an hour into the drive home, I needed to go to the bathroom. I asked the lady if we could stop so I could use a restroom and, to my surprise, she said, "No." She told me she wasn't going to stop and that I could use the bathroom when we got back. I waited as long as I could and then asked her again if she would please stop for a minute. Again, she said no. I remember saying to myself, "Are you f*...g kidding me?" Although I was seething mad, I did my best to contain myself. A few minutes later, I completely lost it. I screamed, "I need to go to the f*...g bathroom!" Without turning her head toward me, she shouted, "Go in the bucket if you need to." She shoved the old blue bucket we used to wash the van back my way and tapped the ash of her cigarette out of the window. Now out of control, I exploded and screamed, "You better watch your back you old witch. I may just come in your room and stab you one night." Morphed from a line in an old movie I had seen, it did not have the desired effect here. Suddenly, there was silence. Clearly, my threat did not sit well with her. Although I had no history of stabbing anyone, she took me quite seriously. She stopped the van, turned toward me and said, "That is it young lady. I'm calling the police right now." While I knew I had messed up big time, all I could think about was how happy I was that she had stopped at a gas station so I could pee. With little thought of what had occurred, I jumped out and ran for the head. When I exited the bathroom, I noticed that she was still on the payphone. I walked beyond the building, out of sight, crossed the street and stuck my thumb out. On the road again. Within four hours, I was arrested again.

It was at this time that I learned my mom was actually paying for my stay at juvenile hall. Turns out it was costing her $54 a day for every day I had spent there! I couldn't believe it. She was paying for this? I would have gladly taken $50 and made myself disappear. She came to court this time and said she would give this thing one more try at home. She couldn't afford the bill anymore.

I went back to my mom's and continued to attend school at Mount Vista. Now accustomed to returning to the group home every day promptly after school, I pretty much kept to myself. That was until Savannah came along. I don't know how I had missed her before, but once I noticed her, it seemed like she was everywhere.

17

SAVANNAH STOOD OUT FROM THE REST OF THE KIDS. SHE HAD LONG, flowing brown hair past the middle of her back and beautiful green eyes. She wore oversized men's shirts that looked as though they were borrowed from some biker she slept with the night before and carried a leather hippie purse with suede tassels. She had an aura of maturity and independence about her that separated her from the kids. While I never saw her buy or do drugs, it was clear that she did. You could tell just from looking at Savannah that she had been places. The moment I spotted her, I knew I wanted to go places with her.

One day an old Pontiac pulled into the school's parking lot to pick her up. Smoke poured from the exhaust and Janice Joplin screamed through the speakers. A longhaired biker type jumped out of the front seat and got into the back to allow Savannah to sit up front. She jumped in the car with her knight in shining armor, slammed the door shut and they tore off into the sunset. I watched, mesmerized as the music faded into the distance. *"Freedom is just another word for nothing left to lose..."*

I desperately wanted to know her and I needed a plan. I had a met a coke dealer a few months earlier who lived down by the beach. He clearly took a liking to me, but I was only interested in the goods he had to offer. He offered and I indulged. Much to my surprise, I didn't like cocaine at all. It made me talk incessantly about things nobody found interesting. While my initial experience with cocaine was not a good one, I knew it was just the ticket I needed to get in with Savannah. I figured I'd go to his house and flirt my way into a free quarter gram and bring it to school. The next day, I arrived at school with the goods in tow. Savannah was settled in on her usual bench, when I went in for the kill. "Hey, do you wanna do some coke?"

Savannah seemed less than enthusiastic when I offered her the coke. She mumbled something about going into the bathroom to do it. As we began to walk, she turned back my way and said, "Hey, go get a cup of water first and bring a cigarette, but don't light it." As I hurried to gather the things requested of me, I was feeling uncontrollably elated. A few moments later, I walked into the bathroom.

There were four girls in the bathroom and Savannah was standing near the sink. She glanced my way, gave me a nod and then pulled a pocketknife from her purse. When she flipped it open, all of the other girls dispersed. Word around school the next day was that they thought we were going to stab them.

Savannah motioned for me to accompany her into one of the stalls. As I stepped in, she swung the door shut and secured it. She pulled a small suede pouch from her purse, untied the little string securing it and extracted an oddly bent spoon and needle. She looked at me and said, "I'm gonna shoot up. You want to?"

My first thought was, *well, I've been trying to kill myself for quite some time*...and then I thought... *if I live, I might like it. So, what have I got to lose? Maybe, just maybe, this is just what I need.*

Without skipping a beat, I said, "Yes." She told me to tie something around my arm and to turn my head if the needle grossed me out. I watched her every move like a student observing her master. She was exceptionally precise with every detail of the preparation. I was extremely impressed. My mouth was dry and my heart was pounding. Savannah poured the coke into the spoon and used the needle to extract a small amount of water from the cup. With the cigarette she had requested, she pulled the filter apart, rolled a small ball in between her fingers and dropped it in the spoon. She used the ball to mix up the potion she was preparing. She really seemed to know exactly what she was doing.

Satisfied, that the preparation was complete, she asked if I was ready. Unable to speak, I nodded my head and then turned to the side to avoid seeing the injection. I grimaced as I felt the needle pierce my skin. I hoped she knew what she was doing, but it was clearly too late to turn back.

Her large green eyes stared straight into mine as she gently withdrew the needle from my vein. I felt as though fumes from an exhaust pipe were pumping into my mouth from my abdomen. A high piercing tone rang in my ears as a feeling of euphoria enveloped my entire being. My knees weakened slightly as the tone slowly faded. My body fell limp against the cold metal stall. I shut out the world around me and retreated inward. I was totally at peace. I had *arrived*. As Savannah continued to stare at me, her mouth turned up into a small grin and her beautiful eyes pierced me with comfort. Without saying a word, it was as if she had said, "There, there child, now isn't that better…?" I was comforted. She then turned her attention back to the spoon to prepare the rest for herself.

Savannah and I became inseparable from that moment forward. When we weren't taking drugs, our days were spent figuring out how to get more money. For various reasons, we spent a good deal of time at the beach. Our primary coke connection was there and there was also a very reputable jewelry store that we could rely on to buy stolen jewelry from us. Although I never burglarized another house, both Savannah and I had a knack for picking up things wherever we went. The employees at that store never questioned us about the source of the goods. They simply looked at the stuff through a magnifying glass, weighed it and made us an offer. We spent a lot of time stealing jewelry, selling jewelry and going over to the dealer's to pick up more cocaine. Cocaine and cannabinol were our drugs of choice. Although not your typical high school teenagers, we were like two peas in a pod. I worshiped her.

Savannah often talked about her boyfriend, Rick, who she usually referred to as her "old man." She clearly had a great deal of respect and admiration for him even though he evidently had another girlfriend, Katrina. According to Savannah, the other girlfriend was an older woman who lived in a nearby trailer park. She said that she appreciated the fact that Rick and Katrina had a long history together and wasn't jealous of her because she knew in her heart that Rick loved them both. The zinger was that she and Katrina were intimate on occasion as well. She claimed to love her also. While I found the whole idea interesting in a wild hippie kind of way, I was also a bit creeped out. In an effort to avoid appearing uncool, I just smiled and nodded.

There was more. Savannah lived with her mom, stepfather and two older brothers in a modest three-bedroom condo in a mediocre part of town. She had a small room to herself while her older brothers shared a larger one down the hall. Her parents went to work every day, and by all accounts, led an ordinary life in a relatively normal household. Her younger brother Judd was an intravenous drug user and a member of a notorious motorcycle club. Now here's the clincher: Savannah and her family were white supremacists and I was a Jew…and we were best friends. Everyone, including Savannah and I failed to notice. Clearly the drugs took on a higher priority.

Sleepovers at Savannah's were dramatically different than they were elsewhere. In retrospect, I think it's nothing short of a miracle that I'm still alive to talk about them. After changing into our nightgowns, we'd go downstairs to chat with her parents about school. A little while later, we'd grab a snack and say good night. Back upstairs, we'd both squeeze into her twin bed and talk quietly while waiting to hear her parents close their bedroom door. Once assured they had fallen asleep, we'd climb out of bed and sneak into her brother's room. Judd was always waiting for us and had good coke and a permanent kit. A permanent kit is a glass needle in a custom case. While that may sound like a good thing, it was very large, which made shooting up problematic with my small kid veins, but we felt honored to be accepted by him.

A moment of clarity came one night while standing in the hall saying goodnight to Savannah's mom. It was as if I was standing above myself looking down on the hypocrisy of the situation. Here we were, two girls about sixteen years of age, dressed in flowered gowns with delicate lacing, chatting about school tomorrow. Just a few feet behind us, Savannah's brother was sitting in his room impatiently anticipating our arrival. Savannah's loving mom, the innocent gowns and the lure of danger lurking at our backs merged together and stirred a thought inside of me: *something is not right here.* Then as quickly as it came, it slipped away.

Although Savannah and I spent a good deal of time together, she would often go away with her old man for days at a time. It was imperative that during the downtimes I branch out and meet other people so that I could continue to use in her absence.

When Savannah wasn't around, I spent most of my time hanging out with a bunch of guys down by the beach. They lived in a party house that was rented by an older lady. They were "punkers" between the ages of 17 and 25. They wore black leather jackets, slim black pants and had big safety pins sticking out of various places. They all wore hair gel that forced their hair in a messy sort of upright position. They liked bands like the Buzzcocks, the Dead Kennedy's and the Sex Pistols and enjoyed slamming into each other or banging against the walls. We had nothing in common aside from our mutual interest in cocaine. The lady who actually paid the rent at the place was in a wheelchair from a car accident. Apparently she had received a large settlement and had no problem paying for everything in exchange for having lots of parties and people around her. One of the draws for me was that she was a diabetic, which meant she had needles. Much to my surprise, she had no problem donating them for our purpose.

While hanging out at the party house, I met two other people that would dramatically impact my life. One was a nine-year-old girl named Lauren and the other was a guy named "Binky Bill."

It was hard to believe that Lauren was only nine. She bore the striking features of a sophisticated woman way beyond her years. With her thick blond hair and bangs blown straight up, blue eye shadow, little leather boots and red lipstick, she fit right in with our crowd. Lauren and her little brother, an eleven-year-old mini punk rocker, were always around and were pseudo-adopted by the punkers. I was intrigued with Lauren for a variety of reasons and felt connected to her. When the guys were blasting music and doing their punk rock thing, Lauren and I would sit on the couch and talk for hours. She told me all about her wonderful life, her cool mom and the great parties they had at their house. It turns out her mom was a Playboy Bunny when she was younger; she was chauffeured around in limos, hung out with famous people and even made the centerfold. Lauren told me all about their adventures with rich people, great parties and the adult things that she had experienced. At the end of each of our talks, she always said, "I can't wait for you to meet my mom!" Although she always suggested that I just show up one day to meet her, I felt uncomfortable just showing up. It was too weird.

One evening before sundown, Lauren arrived at the party house. Now having a keen sense that I was not going to come to her house alone, she said, "My mom is having a party at our house tonight. I am going to come and get you. I want you to meet her." I agreed, but as the time got closer, I became more and more apprehensive. Would her mom think it was strange that a sixteen-year-old was spending so much time with a nine-year-old? Although Lauren was years beyond her time, I thought her mom might have a different view. Lauren came to get me around 8 p.m. that evening.

As we walked through the door of her home, I was accosted by music blaring through the speakers. *It was David Bowie's "Space Oddity." Feeling like I was on Mars already, it was surreal.* "The pounding of the base shook my insides and lifted my awareness. As I listened to the words of the song, I felt like I was entering another planet. There were adults scattered around everywhere. Drinks were flowing, ashtrays were packed and a mound of coke with several parallel lines sat along the glass table. The coke, like a bowl of Doritos, just sat there…as if placed there by the host to make the guests more comfortable. Everyone appeared to be more into their conversations than the free coke. Very strange.

Before I could take in the enormity of the situation, Lauren tugged at my hand and pulled me across the room. As we weaved through the room, the adults did not acknowledge our presence at all. It was as if we didn't exist. To tell you the truth, at this point I was feeling much closer to Lauren's age than I ever had before. She stopped abruptly at a small black leather couch with two men, one on each end, and a woman in the middle. Although there were men hovering around the perimeter attempting to get within earshot, the men on the couch had the woman's full attention. Like the others, fully engaged in their conversation, they didn't notice us.

Directly in front of us was Lauren's mom. An older, more mature version of Lauren, her beauty was undeniable. She was a stunning woman in her mid 30's with a Marilyn Monroe air about her that drew men to her. She was laughing, chatting and smoking and the men were obviously hypnotized by her presence. As we stood there waiting, my nervousness intensified. I felt like I was meeting a movie star. Lauren interrupted their chatter and said, "Mom, this is the girl I told you about." She immediately turned her full attention to me. "Hi, you must be Lauri, I have heard so much about you! So glad Lauren brought you by. My name is Sue."

I think Sue was intrigued with me in the same way that I was intrigued with her and Lauren. I don't remember much of what we spoke about that night, but I can assure you it wasn't anything substantial. One of the items of discussion was my habitual fighting. A few weeks prior, while hanging around at the beach, another girl had attempted to steal my moped, and she actually did get away with it for a few days. I was able to track her down through some friends to a party. I dragged her out into the street, beat her up and took my moped back. Sue had heard about the incident and was impressed.

At the end of a long meaningless discussion with Sue, she spoke under her breath and muttered, "When these people clear out; I have some secret stash just for you and me." From that day on, it became customary for Sue to grab me during a party, drag me off into the bathroom and pour "our secret stash" on the counter. When we initially entered the bathroom, Sue was excited and friendly, but shortly after she experienced what I can only describe as a mental shift. The Sue I knew would completely disappear and she became a strange, nervous creature. An ugly, deranged darkness, equally as powerful as her attraction and beauty, enveloped her when she was alone with cocaine. Huddled over and small, she removed her shoes and crept around the cold tile floor on the tips of her toes with her hands pulled up like a rooster, afraid to touch anything. The first time I saw her like this I was petrified. I said, "Sue are you okay? Are you okay?" She looked me straight in the eyes and very quietly whispered in my ear, "Check the shower..."

I thought, *Oh my God! Is someone in the shower?! Someone bad? Were they waiting here for her before we got here?* I too was now scared. As I quietly grasped the edge of the shower curtain, I slowly drew it back and peered around the corner. Now as paranoid as Sue, I was quite relieved to find it empty. Just a shower, bar of soap, bottle of shampoo and a towel, whew! Nothing there, that was weird. I took a deep breath and smiled; how crazy are we? Regaining my senses, I turned and happily reported, "Sue, there is no one in the shower."

Much to my surprise, the report did not help. Her creeping accelerated, and as if in small circles, she crept around and around in a state of confusion, avoiding all touch. There was nothing I could do to calm her down. I quickly realized that the more I spoke or made noise, the worse she got. Finally she stopped, grabbed my shoulders, glared straight into my eyes with a look of panic, put her lips by my ears and whispered as quietly as she could..."Check the shower."

Having known that it has only been mere moments since the last time I checked the shower, the door had not opened and there was no other form of entry into the room, I was highly confident the shower was empty. But Sue was petrified. To make matters worse, she had the coke. Sue always kept the bindle in her pocket. She would retrieve it from her pocket, dump some out and fold it back up several times while we were in the bathroom. When preoccupied with invisible people, she was unable to focus on the coke. I quickly learned that my intermittent shower checks helped to accelerate her ability to dish out more coke. I continued to check the shower several times as requested in order to secure my ongoing cocaine supply. Sue and I remained friends and engaged in this activity for several years to follow. Although I grew older and she moved several times, the routine never changed. The more time I spent with her, the clearer it was to me that drugs can cause irreparable brain damage.

I always thought if I ever get weird like that I would quit immediately. I could never understand why she didn't. In my kid mind I thought maybe everyone has like a cookie in their brain. The cookie would represent a person's sanity. Each time you use coke, a small part of the cookie crumbles off. After years of using, when you are old like Lauren's mom, your cookie has completely crumbled and you need to stop. I thought if my cookie crumbled, I certainly would take note and stop. Being a teenager at the time and having a short-lived addiction at this point, I was still quite normal. Nothing to worry about, yet.

The only thing worse than Sue's deterioration was the reaction it caused in Lauren. While Lauren was a self-assured little spitfire the majority of the time, on nights when her mom would use heavily, Lauren's mental state would deteriorate as well. Although Sue never allowed Lauren to enter the bathroom while she was using, Lauren seemed to be very aware of the frightened creature that possessed her mom beyond the bathroom wall.

Still at the party after all the guests had left and the sun had come up, we finally exited the bathroom. The silence in the house was deafening. The house was littered with dirty glasses, ashtrays overflowing with cigarette butts and dirty dishes everywhere. In the midst of the silence, I heard the sound of someone weeping. I followed the sound to Lauren's small room.

Huddled in a ball on her bed crying, Lauren wept. "What is the matter with my mom?! Why is she doing this? What is the matter with her!?" Not knowing what to do or say, I just sat on her bed. For the first time I was exposed to the little nine year old girl beneath the makeup and hair. Seeing her red faced, hair straight with sweat, frail and afraid, I put my hand on Lauren's back and repeated, "She will be fine…your mom will be fine. It will just take some time." "Will you stay with me?" she asked. "Yes," I replied.

I felt like a traitor, trapped between what I was, and what I had become. Lauren represented everything I was as a child and her mom represented not only my addiction, but what I was to become and worse.

As time went on, I would spend many nights there. In the bathroom till the coke was gone, and in the bedroom with Lauren until she calmed down. Many times she had school the next day. Awake with fear, sleep would not come. I couldn't imagine being expected to go to school after a night like this. The insanity was that although I still had my mental capabilities, I was also part of the badness. I clearly had no idea who I was.

Over the next few months, I was a true vagabond. I stayed at the party house, Lauren and Sue's house or wherever I could have the best chance of getting and using more coke. I also spent a good deal of time at Binky Bill's.

About six months after meeting Sue, I met Binky Bill at the beach one day. His real name was Bill. Binky was another term for syringe. Bill was a real coke junkie. He must have had rich parents, because he very rarely left the room in the small apartment, but always paid rent and usually had money for coke. He was nineteen. Lacking daily care, his hair had grown into a large frizzy mop. He had no interests, no aspirations and no wants, except for coke. Sitting on a dirty mattress in his small dark room with the curtains drawn, he waited.

It was in the room with Bill that I began experiencing the kinds of paranoid delusions I had witnessed in Sue. I started to hear voices. In the beginning, I heard people; they were always whispering and they were on the other side of his closed bedroom door. They were talking so quietly I couldn't make out the words, but I knew one thing for sure. They wanted to get me. Simultaneous with the onset of the voices, I lost the ability to talk. As if that wasn't enough, much like the allergy incident at the group home, my jaw pulled and locked to the left side, and my hand began to spasm. Voluntarily opening and closing at a fast pace, I had lost control of it.

The combination of my inability to talk, my jaw being out of alignment and my hand freaked out anyone within sight of me. Within a few months of onset, these symptoms worsened and my tongue would begin to swell as well. In a state of complete and utter helplessness, my body reacted as if I was suffering from a severe case of Multiple Sclerosis. With my first shot of cocaine on any given day, all of the symptoms would simultaneously erupt. It wasn't until almost an hour after my last shot that my body would begin to return to a normal state.

Every time I knew coke was coming, I told myself that I would not get weird this time. This time it would be different. I felt aware, relaxed and normal. I was sure there was no way I would lose control again. I was in complete denial that my ability to control my mental or physical state would never return again.

It was almost expected for anyone new around me to attempt to try and help me. They were clearly alarmed by my behavior. Unfortunately that only fueled my paranoid thoughts that they were in cahoots with the people outside of the door…

They would say, "Lauri, calm down." Just the sound of a full volume voice would shoot me into instantaneous panic. Didn't they know that the people outside were listening?

Now they know we are here…they can hear us…they may have guns…They are going to kill us…We are dead meat. I had to get away from anyone who was talking to me. They were giving up my spot.

Then it got worse.

Maybe they are on the same team with the people outside of the door. They are trying to tell them where I am. The more they would talk to me, the more accelerated my symptoms would become and the faster I would walk to try and get away from them. If you can imagine a person chasing me around a small room while my body went in to spasm and my eyes glared with panic, you may be able to get a clear picture of the massive deterioration I was experiencing.

You're probably thinking, *what about the cookie?* Didn't I notice it was crumbling? Why didn't I stop? What I didn't know when I initially thought about the cookie is that by the time the onset of the symptoms occur, I would have completely lost the ability to make a choice to use or not to use. It was too late. I took the drugs, and then they took me. I was gone.

Over the next year or so my drug use took on a whole new dimension. I remember one day in particular when I had a little bit of coke left over from that morning and decided to go to my mom's to shoot up. By this time, my mom had moved to a new area and I was not allowed in the house. In fact, my sister was instructed that if she saw me, she was to call the police.

I stood on the doorstep, covered the peephole with my finger and knocked. My little sister opened the door, saw me and attempted to slam it shut. Too late, I already had my foot in. With my thick Dr. Marten boots, she could not close the door. I forced my way past her and proceeded to the bathroom. I knew the police would take at least ten minutes and I only needed five to do my thing. A few minutes after forcing my way in, I bolted out of the bathroom and out of the front door of the house. Hiding from "them," I quickly took cover behind a tree. Like a paranoid schizophrenic, I had lost it.

Over the next few years, I slept where ever I could crash and got arrested a lot. None of the group homes wanted me anymore. Occasionally my mom would let me sleep there, but this was short-lived. My old bedroom became her work office. Her patience had worn thin.

One day on my way down to the beach, with no money and no plan, I ran into Karlee, my old friend from the river. With little or nothing in common, our conversation was limited. In a few brief minutes she told me she was getting ready to take the GED exam and went on to say that if she passed it, she would effectively graduate high school. I thought "interesting," and not much else. In my mind I wasn't going to live to be eighteen, and with my out-of-control drug use, I had no thoughts about school. No more school, she reiterated. She begged me to go with her. She said she would sign me up and drive, she was just scared to go alone. Not knowing how to say no, I agreed. At seventeen years of age and with nothing else on my schedule, what else did I have to do?

The test lasted all day and was grueling to say the least. For the life of me, I couldn't understand how or why I agreed to this torture. I remember how happy I was when the teacher shouted, "Pencils down." We slid our test sheets down to the left, stood up and left. What the hell was I thinking? Well, I felt like I had done something good for Karlee. She was a mess.

It was about six months later when visiting the school to look for Savannah that the attendance lady said, "Congratulations Lauri!" I asked, "For what?" "Your GED," she said. Although I thought she was whacked out of her mind, I went in the office and verified. Much to my surprise, Karlee had failed and I had passed. The only way I could even begin to account for it was my love of English and math. Even though I hadn't seen anything substantial since fifth grade, I guess I had a knack for it.

I will never forget my last trip to juvie or my last group home. They had really had it with me. It just so happens that this time I was on lockdown. It was my first and luckily my last time on lockdown until released. When a girl in the unit began to badger me at dinner, I stood up on the long dinner table suited for twenty kids and ran down the middle, food flying and all and jumped on her. Locked in my cell for days, I was bored into another century when the door popped open and they yelled, "Burns! Release!"

There stood my mom and a man. They said they found a great place for me. By this time, I really didn't care where they were taking me. I would be leaving as soon as I got there anyway. We got in the car and we drove, and drove, and drove. It quickly became apparent to me why it was "so good": it was on another planet!

We drove endless miles through desert and nothingness and finally turned down a long dirt path leading up to a cluster of large houses. There was a lot of dirt, horses and nothingness for as far as the eye could see.

We walked in through the sliding glass door of what appeared to be the main house and found ourselves standing in the kitchen. I vividly recall being awestruck by the enormous wooden dining table and the amount of place settings on it. I remember feeling terrified at the thought of eating meals at a table with so many strangers. Before I could fully process my fear, a man walked up and introduced himself. Then he looked at me and said, "Let me show you to your room."

Escorting me through the door to the small room, he suggested that I rest while he finished the paperwork with my mom and probation officer. Although I thought the orientation was rather brief, I took him up on his offer. There were two twin beds inside and a partially open window providing a slight breeze. I lay down on the bed and waited. About thirty minutes later, I saw my mom and my PO get in the car and leave. I remember feeling saddened by the fact that they didn't even bother to say good-bye.

As soon as their car was out of sight, I climbed out the window of my room, ran down the hill to the main road and stuck my thumb out. The first car stopped and I got in. I didn't think about it for years to come. But my poor mom just drove several hours to take me to a place she thought would keep me safe and I was probably in the car behind her as she got back on the freeway.

Aside from being in the desert, I had no idea where I was. After catching several rides, I got out at a gas station and started collect-calling people. A bit short on true friends, the second person I called was a guy I had met at one of my group homes. I had gotten the name of the city I was in from one of the gas station attendants and couldn't have been more relieved to find out that the guy on the phone actually knew where it was. He said it was pretty far, but he knew somebody that lived around there who might be willing to help me. He told me he'd call me back on the payphone.

An ex-boss of his drove out and got me. By the time he got me, he had been briefed about my situation from my friend. I was surprised when he offered to help me out by letting me stay with his family in exchange for babysitting their son. While I immediately agreed, I cringed when he told me he lived in "Bakersfield." *Oh no,* I thought, *not again*...but my life was such a mess, at that moment Bakersfield sounded like heaven. Just get away from everyone and everything.

It was a tiny two-bedroom house with a kitchen about the size of a walk in closet. There was no air conditioning and their only means of battling the unbearable heat was a small oscillating fan in the living room. Although food was scarce, there was always enough beer to satisfy an alcoholic. The parents slept in one room while I slept in the other and Trevor, their son, slept in the living room. In spite of the obvious shortcomings, I was happy to be out on my own.

Trevor was a little seven-year-old terror. I immediately took a liking to him; he was a handful. Nevertheless, I was content sitting around smoking, watching soap operas, and hanging out with Trevor and his best friend Javier (known as "Silver Tooth" due to his lack of teeth and silver cap replacements).

After a few weeks at the sweat box, my friend who hooked me up there called to tell me that my PO was looking for me. When I told Trevor's parents, his dad suggested I call her and remind her that I was going to turn eighteen years old in two months. He thought if I told her that I was in a safe place and working and promised to stay put at least until my birthday, she would probably back off. Surprisingly, she was so tired of chasing me around; she agreed to put my file away for the next couple of months if I stayed out of trouble. I did as I promised and I walked out of that house a free woman the day I turned eighteen. Finally out of the system! They no longer have my number and I will never have to go to jail again! Or so I thought…

18

WHEN I TURNED 18, I RETURNED TO THE BEACH AREA AND PICKED up right where I left off. Things quickly spiraled downward. Within a few months I was worse than ever. While people had moved around, gone to jail and gotten out, their addictions remained constant. I slept wherever I ended up at night and shot drugs around the clock. The only thing that mattered to me during that time in my life was cocaine.

Around that time, there were brief periods when I felt death closing in on me. My skin was void of all color, I had no desire to eat, and my mental state had deteriorated so much that it had taken a toll on my soul. I could feel evil lurking regularly. Sometimes when I would get desperate I would think of calling my mom. Not knowing what to say, I wouldn't. Lord knows I couldn't possibly ask for help.

I was walking down the street one day after just leaving an apartment where I had spent the last few days. I was there with two older men and I had no idea where I met them or how I got there. While they didn't appear to have any sexual interest in me, they did have a lot of money and a whole bunch of cocaine. The normal routine for junkies is to put cocaine in a spoon. These guys had so much coke, they poured it into a drinking glass, filled it to the rim with water and used the mixture to load syringes around the clock.

In a short time, I was hiding behind the closet door sweating and grinding my jaw. The smallest noise was amplified, tossing me into a world of unimaginable terror. After about five hours of hiding in the closet, I was able to relax enough to sit down. Two or three more hours passed before I'd muster enough courage to walk out of the closet and rejoin the men. Caught in their own spiral, neither noticed I was gone, or that I had returned to the room. I believe I was very close to death when I left that afternoon.

The sunlight stung my eyes as I opened the door. The sound of birds singing and children playing revolted against my dark state of being and intensified the evil I had just emerged from. I was an anomaly. I didn't belong here. I could feel death hovering within me. I was terrified. I had to get out.

While I can't say for sure that it was my plan, I walked until I arrived at my mom's house. As luck would have it, the garage was open and inside was a door leading directly into the house. Now eighteen and off probation, I no longer ran the risk of anybody inside calling the police upon seeing me. The most they could do was kick me out. One thing that was consistent about my mom is that she would never wake me if I was sleeping. Whether I crept in or was invited, if she saw me sleeping, she would wait until I woke up to talk. I don't know if it was because of my violent nature or her motherly instinct—it just was. With no one in sight, I sneaked up to the office and went to sleep on the small bed. I awoke the next morning and went downstairs. Hardly excited by my presence, my mom approached me and bluntly asked, "What's your plan?"

I knew I had to get out or I would die. I had a long time to think about it while walking to my mom's house the day before. The thought occurred to me that I could go to New York. I never got to say goodbye to any one from school. Although I didn't have any "close" friends, I felt the need to return to counter any rumors that I was crazy. After all, the last time anyone saw me I was in the crazy house. More importantly, no one shot up in New York. They just used social acid, mescaline, pot and alcohol. It would be a good chance to clean up my life. Much to my surprise, she quickly agreed. She said, "Your father's in New York and it's about time he took some responsibility in this. Let him try and help you now."

19

I HAD NOT SEEN MY DAD IN YEARS BUT I KNEW THAT IF HE LIFTED ONE hand towards me, I would fight back hard, or to put it more directly, I would kill him. I was a kid when I left, but now I was older, both physically and emotionally and the resentment toward the man who had beaten me and had me locked up had grown. I thought, "You put one finger on me and you had better be ready for a fight. You will never hit me again and get away with it." Although I still didn't amount to as much as 100 lbs., like a ticking bomb, I knew I would blow. I had a feeling that when he saw my tough exterior, he wouldn't be dumb enough to try anything.

I spotted him immediately as I walked through the airport gate. Although I hadn't seen him since my last Whopper delivery at Central Islip, he obviously saw no need for pleasantries. When I approached him, he avoided eye contact and said firmly and directly, "We need to go to baggage."

I followed him to baggage and eventually to his car. We did not speak at all. As he entered the car beside me and shut his door, the sense of close confinement was almost unbearable. As the smell of his cologne hit my nose, my body revolted and my stomach turned with nausea. Stiff and disconnected, I stared out of the window. My entire body tensed as I replayed over and over in my mind what I would do if he hit me.

The music on the radio provided a buffer, but it was not enough to calm my nerves. My head ached. On the exterior I attempted to appear normal, but under the surface the fury grew. This was the longest drive of my life. When we approached my hometown he broke the silence.

"I rented you a room in a house. We will stop for food. You will get a job." I said nothing.

We stopped at a grocery store. He grabbed OJ, milk, bologna, bread, mayo, eggs, cereal and hot dogs and put them on the counter. He paid and we returned to the car. He drove me to a small house just outside of town. I exited the car and followed him to the door. He knocked. An older lady in her 60's answered. "I am the man who called about the room. I am dropping my daughter Lauri off. I will pay for the first month as agreed. I bought her some food. Can we put it inside?" The lady replied, "Yes." He handed her a check, put the two sacks on the kitchen counter, looked at me and said, "OK, I am going to go." I nodded.

The whole encounter should have been obvious to anyone within close proximity. The short sentences, the lack of interconnectivity between father and daughter and the robotic nature with which I interacted with him told all. Something was clearly wrong. It was several minutes after his departure before I could breathe deeply again. Even in a house with complete strangers, alone in a city I no longer knew, I knew I would be okay. Thank God, I was on my own again.

With little to say, and probably sensing she had just received the "bad seed" the lady rattled some keys and showed me to my room. Then she simply turned and walked away. I dropped my bags in my room. The house was silent. After a few minutes of standing there looking around I knew I needed to get out. Much like the feeling I had with every other "new" room I had ever been walked into, I felt an urge to be free. Even as an adult completely on my own, the new room felt like confinement. I used the bathroom to freshen up and ventured out to explore my new environment. I walked out the front door, back to the main road and hitchhiked in the general direction of my hometown.

I quickly located some people I knew. They were the "popular kids" from my seventh grade class. I found them in a local bar down by the docks. In California the popular kids were the cheerleaders and the football players, but in New York the popular kids were the ones who partied first and had sex first. The popular girls were always the ones who were the most sexually developed. I clearly was never one of the popular kids. When I had left New York at thirteen, I was completely flat-chested, emulated a boy and was a social misfit. They had no idea who I was and that was good.

To them, I was the new girl from California who talked and dressed differently and although I still had no chest, my long brown hair and thin tan body made up for it. I still felt like the outcast crazy girl on the inside, but I played it off like I had been places, and clearly I had.

These kids were into partying, but no one was into shooting up. The scene was alcohol and acid. This was good. I was pleasantly surprised to learn that the drinking age in New York was eighteen and the bars stayed open until 4 a.m. I couldn't have landed in a better place.

Everyplace I went was pretty much the same. A long bar with a lot of round wooden stools and a pool table. Due to my level of insecurity and need to relax, I drank Jack Daniels to take the edge off and ran the pool table all night to avoid communication. Thanks to my time in Stony Brook, I was a pool shark. Pool was a good ice breaker in any bar. By the end of my first week, I had the routine down. Go to the bar, get drunk and play pool until four, then go to the local diner for breakfast and return to the bar at six a.m. Every few days I'd go to the old lady's house, rest for a while and pick up where I left off.

After just a few weeks of being in New York, I ran into Burt. Burt was one of the popular kids from my old school. I never so much as spoke to Burt, but I remembered the first time I saw him. It was the middle of the school year. The teacher interrupted the class to introduce the "new kid." With long, almost white blond hair just past his shoulders and oversized work boots, he fell into his chair and kicked his awkwardly large boots out in front of the small desk. Within minutes he was slumped over like he was prepping for a long nap. He was done and unexcited about life at thirteen years of age. I could relate. I had an instant crush on him.

It was obvious the first night I saw Burt in the bar that he was interested in me. Fortunately, as sad as it was, he had no idea who I was. This was a good thing. I don't know how interested he would have been if he realized that I was the former "boy-girl" from class. So all was well and after a few bar dates Burt and I slept together to consummate our relationship. Being only eighteen and having never seen a "normal" relationship modeled, I had no idea there was anything to a relationship besides the sex. That relationship lasted about one month. What started off as exciting, grew boring very quickly.

I pretty much replaced my drug habit with guys and drinking. I went from one guy to another with little or no thought. Although I always had a "boyfriend" the term of the relationships got shorter and shorter. In no time I lost interest in the old school kids and returned to the people I had associated with in my days with Savannah, the bikers. I began hanging out at a bar inhabited by a biker club called the Pagans. Although they pretty much ran the place, unaffiliated bikers frequented as well. It was a tiny hole in the wall with a pool table, and a good size parking lot for motorcycles.

The next few weeks were glorious: sleep, bar, sleep, bar, sleep, bar. It didn't take long to be thrown out of the old people's house. Although my dad sent another check, they were justifiably upset about my late schedule. The lady told me that my dad was going to be there at three that afternoon and that he had said I'd better be waiting.

My dad drove up right before 3 p.m., thanked the lady and apologized. Without a word, I followed him. I had no idea what was going to happen now. Was he going to send me back to California? When I got in the car he said, "I rented you a very cheap small room with some older girls. This better not happen again."

I had no idea what he meant. What better not happen again? And what should happen then? I really had nothing to go on. Throughout my life, adults rarely ever told me what to do. I don't mean in a *get a job* kind of way, I mean really what to do. I heard an awful lot about what *"not"* to do. I had no idea how to get a job, about interviews, how to talk to people, or even why and how to go to college. It was a big blank spot. I was clueless. I assumed when he said this better not happen again, he meant coming in late and waking people up. Although I could swear I had been quiet from the start and assumed it was easy rent for the old folks since I was never there, I knew they didn't trust me in their house and frankly I knew I didn't fit in there. The bottom line is, if there were adults there, I didn't fit in.

The next house was down by the beach. The beach in New York is very different from the beach in California. Most of the houses down by the beach were low-rent as opposed to California's pricey beach properties. The beach water was dark brown and still. No waves. It was more like a huge dirty pond. But it was all we had, so we accepted it. The only "real" beach we had in New York was Fire Island, hours from where we lived.

The room my dad had rented was the attic of a small house. The two girls who lived there were both in their late twenties. Vicky was in charge of the place. She was a very tall, big-boned girl with long, ash-brown hair. Vicky was a very serious girl. She was extremely straight-laced and direct. She had a lot of rules and expectations. After dispensing the rules to me, she rarely spoke to me again. The moment I met her I could tell from the look in her eyes she was not impressed.

Patsy, on the other hand, was more my style. She was a single mom and very friendly. She had a little boy, and although she was still dating the daddy, there were issues that prevented them from being together.

My new home was a two bedroom, one story house with a ladder leaning on the wall in the living room that was the entryway to my room. After climbing a few steps up, I was able to reach the latch that released the small door that provided entry to the attic. At the top of the ladder I could grab the sides of the frame and lift myself up into the room. I could stand erect in the entryway, but in order to move around I had to crouch. The room was shaped like the roof. The tallest part was by the entrance and the sides sloped down. My bed was off to the side next to a small window with a little wooden dresser next to it. The ceiling over my bed was just over four feet. The window next to my bed was parallel with the tree tops. Like living in a tree, the leaves and twisted branches brushed up against the window and sparkles of sunlight glared through. I loved this place. It felt safe. I loved the forest, which reminded me of when I was a child and I was able to venture out alone into the woods. This felt free. I liked the seclusion. This was just the level of aloneness I needed to not feel trapped. Most of all, I liked it because it felt like a closet. As a kid, I always felt safe in the closet.

Although I didn't spend much time with my roommates, I quickly realized that Patsy and I had more in common than I originally thought. We both liked to get high. The only difference was, I went out to the bar every night, and being a single mom, she stayed home and drank with her friends. It didn't take long to notice that Vicky wasn't really impressed with Patsy either. Patsy and I bonded. Vicky walked through occasionally and glared at us.

Many nights, on my way out, I would smoke a joint or have a drink with Patsy in preparation for the night. Patsy had access to Nitrous Oxide. I don't know where she got it, but it was normal at the house for a bunch of hippies to be sitting around sharing a mask connected to a large tank. It appeared to be the same stuff they gave me at the dentist's office. But unlike the monitored dentist dosage, we could increase our intake levels unconditionally. It was a strange head-thumping, closed-in acoustic high. I wasn't crazy about it, but it was better than nothing. It also felt cool to be using with the "older" crowd.

About a week after my arrival, my dad called to inform me that he was coming to get me the following day to take me to my Uncle Gus's. My dad was always short on words. I said okay and we hung up.

It wasn't until I was standing on the doorstep and the large wooden door opened that it hit me. This was my Aunt Nora's house. The last time I had seen my Aunt Nora was the night of the gun. Feelings were coming at me like knives from all directions. She knew...Or did she? She left that night after the police. Did she know they came back the next morning? Did she know I was in the insane asylum? Or did she think I went to California? She certainly knew about the gun. When she opened the door and looked at me, it was as if nothing had happened. "Oh Lauri," she said. "It is so nice to see you. Oh my, look how you've grown. You look just like your mother. Come on in dear." My Uncle Gus, a mild mannered guy, quiet and harmless, was standing just beyond her. He said, "Come on in, come downstairs and sit."

Was it me that was crazy or them? I wasn't sure if Gus ever knew most of what had transpired. But my dad and Nora? When the truth is denied on so many levels and the deception is coming from everywhere, you really begin to question your own sanity.

Although my Aunt Nora was involved, her lack of response led me to believe she didn't know what happened to me that next day. Maybe she was innocent. But I would never know for sure. It was all so confusing. Since they were acting like nothing happened, so did I. Lord knows I was used to that. Deny reality at all levels. The only part of me that couldn't deny it was my gut. I did my best to appear normal and unaffected.

After a few minutes of sitting while my dad and Gus talked shop about the airlines, my dad said, "OK then, let's go to the garage. Gus and I have something to show you."

As we stood on the driveway, my dad lifted the garage door. In the middle of the garage floor sat a Honda 360 motorcycle with purple sparkles all over it and extended forks. It was a crazy looking thing. My dad said, "You have one hour to learn to ride this. If you can't you will get a moped and that's final."

It hit me so fast, I couldn't figure it out. What did he want? Had he wired it so that I would get killed on it? What motive did he have? Most dads would buy their daughter a car. Why a bike? I flashed back to Frances Higgenbottom, a kid I knew when I was about eleven. This kid had a crazy dirt bike and at the time I was so jealous! It was tiny but could easily do 40 mph and we would go screaming around a small dirt field on it. I pleaded every Chanukah, "I want a dirt bike, please; nothing else, just one small dirt bike." Is that what this was about? Frances Higgenbottom's dirt bike? For cripes sakes, I was a kid then. Although I couldn't assess my father's motive for the bike, I suspected even more strongly that he had always wanted a boy.

While I didn't know how to ride a bike this size, one thing was abundantly clear. Riding around on a moped would surely get me beat up. My dad firmly said, "I will drive you to a parking lot." I was petrified, but there seemed to be little choice.

My dad sat on the bike and told me to get on, motioning toward the back. As I slid on, I was immediately aware that I was touching him. I was paralyzed with disgust. My body froze and I shut down mentally.

When we arrived at the local parking lot he told me to get on front. He quickly reviewed the gears and the brakes and then slid to the back position on the bike. This was even more horrifying. Now he was holding onto me. What choice did I have? In a panic to end this interaction as soon as humanly possible, after a few stalls and near drops, I was able to drive it. Once I mastered the gears, it was like a very big moped. He then drove me back to Gus's and sent me on my way. My first car was a bike.

I will never know why he bought the bike, but within a few days it was the best thing in my life. At the time there was no helmet law. Jeans, biker boots and a wife beater with my hair flying in the wind, I was completely free. Being a teenager, I had no fear and a complete lack of responsibility. I would drink at the bar all night and head out on my bike without a second thought.

I had a few near misses. One night after leaving the bar, I was obviously not paying attention and was almost broadsided by a large car barreling down the road. Another night I was traveling with a bunch of bikers and I was falling behind. I accelerated to catch up. As I sped around a corner I noticed they were all stopped at a red light a short distance ahead. Traveling at too fast a speed with limiting stopping distance, I hit both brakes and screeching along, I slid sideways with my foot skidding on the ground to keep from going down. Finally the bike stopped in the full upright position. My heart was pounding out of my chest and all I could think of was how stupid that looked. With the guys all looking back my way now, I winked and nodded once as if I meant to do that. What a hot mess.

Now that I had a ride, my biggest problem was money. I quickly ran out of bologna and hot dogs. I was able to land a job for about a week at a telephone solicitation place. They sold trash-can sized tins of tar to people for roofing. Can you imagine? Why would anyone want to buy a four-foot can of tar from a telephone solicitor? Believe or not, in my one week of employment, I sold two cans. I felt horrible about it. I don't know if it was my tardiness or my presentation, but I was let go just days after starting.

I quickly moved into plan B. Although my dad was sending me $40 every two weeks, I needed that money for gas and cigarettes. I found a good market down by the dock that I could steal food from. It was a small market with a deli. I would go to the deli counter and ask for a half-pound of roast beef and Swiss cheese. Then I would simply slide them under my jacket and walk out. I figured that nobody would think that someone was going to steal fresh cold cuts. I also didn't think there is a record of how much meat was cut on a given day. I now realize that the amount on the scale is probably checked with the register, but I had no idea back then. I had never really gone food shopping and paid for it. My life skills were limited.

Besides the roast beef, I did not steal while in was in New York other than being loosely involved in a burglary. I say loosely because it was not my idea, my job or my intent, but I was driving around with a few people from the bar one day and one of them announced that they would be stopping at an old friend's house. I guess they were in a feud of sorts, and the guy owed him. We stopped at the house and waited out front while the guy went in. There were four of us in the car; me, another girl, the driver and the guy that was now in the house.

When he returned to the car, he dumped a mound of jewelry on the seat. He informed all of us that we could each have one thing. I chose a ring. It was a large diamond ring. That was the last I saw of those people. It is my understanding that about two weeks later, the other girl entered a local jewelry store attempting to sell the remaining jewelry using her real ID. I know this because the detectives showed up at my house one day while I was out and informed Patsy of the situation. The girl had been arrested, and in order to get out, she gave the names and descriptions of everyone that was in the car. She also knew where I lived because they had dropped me off. For weeks the detectives would show up daily at the house like clockwork, and ask for me. Due to my crazy lifestyle, they always missed me.

Wanting to keep my life interesting, I hung out at different places every night. I was always jumping between the pubs down by the docks, the biker bars and the occasional house party. One night while out at the biker bar, I met *him*. He was beautiful. Although we slept together for the next few months, I never knew his last name. They called him "Push Rod." I thought the name referred to a motorcycle part, now I realize that it was more because he was such a slut.

I later learned that his name was Nate. Nate lived with another guy in a small hole-in-the-wall room behind a bar. He was hot and mysterious. He was about six feet tall with long, light brown hair and glasses. He was remarkably sexy and the glasses made him look smart. He was older than the kids from my usual crowd. I think he was at least twenty-five. Nate knew a lot about a lot, but the only thing I can distinctly remember is what he told me about his brother. Nate's brother was a junkie. Nate was adamant that he was firmly against shooting up or anyone engaged in it. That stuck with me.

As planned, I was able to avoid the needle almost the entire time in New York, until one very unlucky night. I was at a bar by myself and I saw a girl whom I knew from the docks. She was a happy, homeless chick who lived on the streets, or more exactly in the park. She had made a nice little nest for herself in a beautiful park by the Centerport docks. She and I had smoked out a few different times and it became customary for her to share my stolen roast beef and cheese.

That night, she spotted me in the bar. Excited to see me, she quickly approached me and introduced me to her friend Otto. Otto was engaged in conversation, but halted momentarily to acknowledge my presence. With nothing else to do following the brief introduction, I just stood there listening. Otto was talking to another guy about having drugs and needing a needle. After a few more minutes they announced that they were leaving. They said they were off to shoot up and asked if either of us would like to join them. I immediately agreed to go. By God, it had been way too long since I had shot up. And even though I knew that this was a genuinely bad idea, the overriding voice in my head said "*just this one time won't hurt.*" At that moment nothing else mattered. Otto, the junkie guy and I headed out.

We loaded into the cab of a U-Haul truck and began driving through a small neighborhood looking for the drug man's house. After about twenty-five minutes, the truck sputtered and the junkie guy stopped and announced, "Crap, we are out of gas!" After a little bitching and a few "are you kiddings?" Otto said, "Fine, I will be back with some gas." He grabbed a red plastic jug and disappeared into the darkness.

After a few moments of small talk, the junkie and I sat silent. I had actually started to drift to sleep when I was startled awake by a knock on the window and the blinding strobe of a flashlight. It was the police. Although shaken at first, I remembered Otto had the drugs, so this was not going to be a problem. The police asked us to get out of the truck. We did. As expected, they asked the driver for his driver's license and registration. He gave the police officer his driver's license, but explained that this was a rented truck.

When the policeman started to question the purpose of the truck, the junkie guy got visibly nervous. The officer than proceeded to the back of the truck, shined his flashlight on the lock and said, "Open it." The junkie stupidly replied, "I don't have the key." Then the officer turned to me. "Where is the key?" I tried to explain that I didn't know, and furthermore, that I didn't even know this guy whom I am sitting in a U-haul truck with in the middle of the night. The police officer seemed to think that was very amusing.

I continued to try to convince the officer that I was really here with my friend and he went to get gas. This story did not fare well. After handcuffing the junkie for failure to comply, the cop discovered the key to the lock. The police officer unlocked the padlock and pulled the sliding door up. I stood there in shock as he exposed thousands of cartons of cigarettes. The officer got in the truck and inspected the cargo. Within an hour we were booked and jailed for smuggling cigarettes into the United States.

As I sat in the police investigation room, with a bright light on me, being questioned by several different men and giving the same answer,

I began to see the insanity of my situation. My alibi was *I don't know the guy?* Although true, I knew I was in trouble. A while later, a large, old black man entered and calmly announced, "Well you might as well make yourself comfortable. Seems your buddy here refuses to talk until his attorney is present. His attorney is on vacation 'til Tuesday. Let's lock 'em up."

I opted for the offer to make one phone call. I figured if you get it, you might as well use it. As I stood there, I realized I had no one to call. I certainly wasn't going to call my dad and Nate didn't possess a phone. Clearly, the only people with a phone number that I knew off-hand were my roommates in the attic house. Luckily Patsy answered. I quickly explained the situation and thankfully she believed me. Her brother was an attorney and she said, "I will see if I can help."

After twenty-four stressful hours of sharing a cell with a girl who had escaped from the loony bin, I was shackled to a small group of women and taken to court. Our hands and feet were shackled to each other with chains. I was scared to death. The whole lot of us stood up in front of the judge and he went down the line. I guess they figured it was easier to process us in an assembly line fashion than to break down the locks binding us.

It went something like this…$#%# #$#* #*%&^ #*&^% (&^%. And then we were escorted out. Before we even left the courthouse, my roommate's brother showed up. He asked me to sign something and I did and I was released. I think I signed a paper saying that I would return to court at a future date. I never returned.

The last encounter I had with Nate was that same day. He came to the attic house to see me after he heard what had happened. We spent some time talking, but I noticed an unusual nervous energy about him. A few hours later, he kissed me and rode off on his motorcycle in a cloud of dust. I later noticed that he had stolen the diamond ring from the burglary that was sitting on my desk. That was the last time I ever saw Nate.

I was kicked out of the attic house for not paying rent. For the next few weeks, I went from place to place partying and crashing out with not much of a care for where I ended up. To add to my instability, my motorcycle's shifter lever was stripped due to improper gear changes. Experiencing a serious lack of cash, I had been shoving small items (nails and metal) into the open area to create friction. My motorcycle, like my life, was falling apart.

That night at the bar, I met Dallas. Dallas was a nice guy. He had long brown hair, always nicely brushed and tied back in a ponytail. He was clean cut and well mannered and had a job. Clearly not my type, but I was drawn to him. Dallas and his dad were fishermen. They got up early every morning and worked at the docks all day. Although Dallas was much too tame for me, he didn't know me, which made him a great option. I only went out with Dallas for about two weeks. During the time we dated, I stayed at his house with him and his dad. His dad did not have a problem with me being there. He figured that if Dallas wanted me there, I could stay. Dallas and his dad would wake up before God every morning, drink coffee, read the paper and head out to the docks to fish. I would sleep in of course.

I don't know how or when exactly it happened, but one morning I woke up, went downstairs and fixed some coffee and lingered in the living room. With nothing else to do, I went through the albums and picked one I liked. Stevie Nicks. I threw it on the player and stood at the window just thinking, not about anything in particular, just taking it all in. Landslide, by Stevie Nicks soothed me as I stared out into the woods beyond the house. *And I saw my reflection in the snow covered hills...well maybe the landslide will bring you down...*I placed my hand on my belly and started to rub it. As soon as my hand hit my belly, I knew...something was wrong...my stomach...it had a bump. The room literally started to spin. The music seemed to surround me...*I've been afraid of changing...I built my life around you...*Not only have I never had much of a stomach, I hadn't eaten regularly in months. I was instantly jolted into reality. I was with child....*the landslide will bring you down...*

Unable to think clearly, but somehow knowing there was a tiny baby in my belly, I began to panic. The tears poured out of my eyes uncontrollably. I shook. I sat on the couch and covered my eyes with my hands, dropped my head in my lap and wept uncontrollably. My body shook and I rocked back and forth...*think...think*...What am I going to do? A baby? Maybe I'm not pregnant, maybe it's something else. But I knew. I can't have a baby! I can't kill my baby with an abortion! My baby...I have a baby...*I have a family*...

It was so much more than I was capable of. So much more than I could handle right now—so much more than I could ever handle... This can't be right. This must be some kind of a dream. I can't be pregnant? Not now. Not here. How? And I wept because I knew I would love this child...I wept because I had a family...someone to love...someone who would never leave me...a real family...The thing I had always wanted...a family, a beautiful baby...and this baby would be mine, only mine...I would have a family...someone who would never leave me...

As I flashed back to Central Islip and being alone, I knew I never had to be alone again. I had to have this baby. I wanted the baby more than anything, but at the same moment, I heard myself say the word "baby" in my head and I knew it was just a dream. I don't know what to do with a baby. I have nothing. I have less than nothing. How? Is this a dream? Can I be a mother?

> *Oh, mirror in the sky, what is love, Can the child within my heart rise above*
> *Can I sail through the changing ocean tides, Can I handle the seasons of my life,* and the *Landslide brings you down....*

The cloud of confusion was so intense I lost the ability to sort one thought from the next. The feelings were barreling in; fear, panic, happiness, shock and then as quickly as the confusion hit me, it was whisked away. *OK, Lauri straighten up, you need to think this through, quickly*. I wiped the tears from my face and processed. I needed to come up with a plan and this time it had better be a good one.

I ran the possibilities through my mind. If I told Dallas, he was such a normal guy; he would probably marry me. I can't get married, for cripes sakes. Realizing he was too good for me, he would break up with me, *then he would want his baby*. He would almost certainly find a nice girl to marry and then they would take my baby. I knew I couldn't let that happen. I could never tell. I had to leave now.

I went to the kitchen and phoned my mother and I told her I needed to come home. I pleaded that I had nowhere to live and no food. My mom was so used to my tough exterior that on the few occasions when I exhibited genuine dramatic crying, she was so stunned by the personality change that she complied. I have rarely had such desperate need that I was willing to wimp out at this level, but this day was an exception. I had already decided to give it whatever it takes and as a last resort threatening suicide was something I could pull out of the hat. I needed to get out. I had my mom's buy-in within a few minutes.

She instructed me to phone my dad immediately and insist that he get me a standby ticket home and call her back. I did. My dad was more than agreeable, and I am sure happy to be rid of me. I grabbed my bags and my father picked me up within a few hours. He dropped me at the airport. No words were spoken during the ride. The silence was the final nail in the coffin. Neither of us had any interest in discussing what went wrong on my move to New York. It was obvious. As expected by all, I had failed again. Only it was much worse than they knew. I was in deeper than ever. The only consolation was that I was the only one who knew. I never said goodbye to Dallas. I left while he was at work.

20

ARRIVING AT MY MOM'S HOUSE WAS DEPRESSING. I WAS SUCH A failure. My mom and I had not spoken one word on the way home and the moment we got there, I went in the office that used to be my room, closed the door and lay down on the bed. I certainly was not ready to have "the conversation" and I desperately needed to sleep. As usual, I had no real plan to address the problem, but I was sure about what I was not going to do: terminate the baby. The best plan I could come up with at this moment was to sleep and shut the world out.

When I awoke in the morning, my mom yelled for me from her room across the hall, "Tell me your plan, you can't stay here." At this point I thought if she knew I was pregnant, I might gain some sympathy, so with no practical communication skills to speak of, and afraid to look at her in the eyes, I yelled back, "I am pregnaaaannnt!"

After an awkward silence, she appeared at my bedroom door "You're getting an abortion!" Not wanting to escalate any further, but needing to state my position, in the smallest voice, I replied, "I am keeping the baby."

The screaming began immediately. "You cannot have a baby! You can't even take care of yourself! Over my dead body you will bring a baby into this world. You are an idiot Lauri Burns. Now you go and get yourself pregnant! You can't do anything right! You are getting an abortion and that is it!" She stomped back to her room and slammed the door shut.

This is the point where the inner self-hatred talk usually begins and suicide becomes an option. But now it was different. I had someone else to think about. I shut the door and cried myself back to sleep. I didn't know what I was going to do. I just knew what I was not going to do and that was to kill my baby. The overriding thought in my mind was, "Lauri, you were responsible for getting pregnant, now you will be responsible for having the baby. You cannot take a child's life just because you were too lazy to get birth control." Escaping through sleep would make it all stop, for now.

For the next few days, I stayed at my mom's and the only talking that occurred was my mom's pleas for me to give up the baby. I ignored her and for once did not say much back. I lasted one week, listening to my mom cry, scream and make demands. She informed me clearly that if I were to have the baby, she would never see it or have anything to do with me again. Although scary, I knew I had to choose the baby. The only reprieve from the constant yelling and pleading was when my mom went to work. She would leave the house like a normal working person in the morning and revive the conversation when she returned at night.

One day she came home from work and something was different. She entered my room and told me that a lady that she knew from work would like to speak with me about my "situation." She went on to say, "She will be calling this evening." She said, "She can help you." I had no idea what kind of help she had in mind and I certainly was not interested in talking to one of my "mom's friends." This whole thing reeked of the kind of deceit that I had come to expect from adults. I assumed it was one more way to get me to get rid of my baby. Maybe now she had found someone to adopt my baby. I had no response to my mom's new information because if I responded positively, it meant I was in agreement and if I responded negatively, it would make my mom scream again and I couldn't endure another breakdown.

About seven that evening, the phone rang. After just a few seconds, my mom yelled, "Lauri, the phone. Take it in my room." The phone was on the bed in her room and although she appeared to be out of sight, it was obvious that she was just around the corner, close enough by to eavesdrop on my portion of the conversation. Knowing I could hang it up at any time, I reluctantly picked it up.

"Hello…?"

"Hi Lauri, my name is Ginger, and I think I can help you."

After speaking with the lady for just a few moments, I realized that my mom had told everyone at work about what a mess I was; that I had come home pregnant and she needed help in getting me to an abortion clinic. Unfortunately for her, the coworker that she chose to plead her case with was an active antiabortionist. When not at work or home, Ginger spent the majority of her off hours parading around with picket signs of dead babies in front of abortion clinics trying to get young girls to change their minds.

Ginger said, "I want you to come here. I don't have much room. I have six kids of my own and my husband in a small condo, but you can stay on the couch and I will help you with your pregnancy." I felt empowered that someone actually agreed with me and shocked at the possibility that not only could I keep the baby, but someone actually wanted to help me. It was more than I could have imagined. I don't know what that lady said to my mother that day, but it must have been harsh. My mom never mentioned abortion again. That afternoon my mother took me to Ginger's house with a small suitcase.

The last thing she said was, "You and Ginger will deal with it." I had the feeling that Ginger and my mom would never see eye to eye again. I later learned they had been good friends at work for years. My mom's intent to send me to the abortion clinic had struck such a chord with Ginger that I don't think it could ever be repaired. Going forward there was a permanent wedge between Ginger and my mom.

Knowing my mom is not one to give in to opposing views, I was really surprised that she even had me call Ginger. I later realized it was probably the lesser of two evils. Being known at work as "the baby killer" would not have been good for business.

We exited the freeway and immediately pulled into what looked like an apartment complex protected from the main road by a large cement wall. The perimeter of the complex consisted of guest parking spots and the fronts of garages as far as you could see. We stopped in the front of a garage. My mom exited the car and said, "Grab your things." We entered through the fence and knocked on a sliding glass door. Ginger opened the door with a loud friendly, "Come on in!" She very quickly introduced herself and told me to put my bag next to the couch. Ginger and my mom exchanged greetings and within minutes my mom was gone. Ginger was a fifty-one-year-old Catholic woman with six kids; the youngest was six-month-old Mason. I think he was a surprise because her oldest was already grown up and out of the house.

Ginger insisted that I do something during the day. She told me there was a college close by and I could take classes there. She spent a good deal of time talking to me about what I wanted to do for a living and questioning me on my interests. Until this time, I had never had anyone talk to me about these kinds of things, so the thought of my future had never crossed my mind.

The only other occasion I was asked a question like this was in the fifth grade at Bellerose Elementary School in New York. We were in the lunch room and out of the blue a conversation broke out among the kids about what we wanted to be when we grew up. After a bit of chatter, one of the kids looked over and asked me, "What do you want to be?" I spent a moment thinking about it and responded confidently, "A hippie." All of the other kids started to laugh and one of them said, "You mean you want yellow teeth?" I immediately flashed back to a memory of me and my neighbor Jenny sitting on her front porch with her Victrola listening to the Beatles...

> *The song was about a girl named Jude.*
> *Much like me, she was in pain.*
> *But she seemed to have an answer.*
> *I needed the answer...*

I asked Jenny what this song was about. She responded, "Jude is a junkie." I didn't know what a junkie was, but I didn't want to seem stupid so I said nothing. I just figured Jude was some kind of a hippie. The only thing I knew was that I wanted to be free like Jude. When I answered the question at the lunch table, I was remembering how free Jude was in the song and I knew that above all, I wanted to be free.

Finally I responded, "No, not with a yellow teeth, a different kind of hippie, one with a tooth brush." They continued to laugh about dirty hippies and I just retreated into my mind, thinking about freedom.

The next day Ginger picked up a class schedule on her way home and brought it to me. Although I had never before thought about going back to school, I found myself excited at the possibility. I was immediately drawn to the portion of the schedule focused on psychology.

I told Ginger that I wanted to help children who have been abused. I met with a lady at the college to discuss classes and ideas and decided I wanted to be an expert witness in child abuse cases. I wanted to start taking classes that would help me to achieve that goal. I started with two classes, Human Development and Child Development because I knew one thing clearly: I wanted to stop kids from being abused.

Although I was introverted and uncomfortable with the other students at school, I was absolutely in awe of my teacher. He had me captivated from the moment I entered the class until the bell rang. His presentation of the material, combined with a witty sense of humor and animated teaching style, kept me spellbound. I thought, if this is what college is about, I am in. I put everything I had into my work. At some level I was uncertain if my motivation was a desire to do well or to gain acceptance from my teacher. It didn't matter. I was on a roll. He was a retired Harlem Globe Trotter gone PhD. He was fabulous.

Until this time, authority figures in my life were associated with punishment. This man represented the possibility of significant change. The chance to do something worthwhile. The chance to help someone else...

Since Ginger worked during the day, my mom let me take the moped from the garage to get to school and back. This seemed like a good idea at first, and lord knows I pushed for it, but in hindsight it may have been the antecedent to what happened next.

One weekend after I completed my homework, I decided to go to the beach on my moped. Unable to find anyone to hang with, I decided to go by Binky Bill's apartment to see if he still lived there. My intention was not to use, I just wanted to say hello. I was surprised to see that he still lived there. He answered the door as usual, anticipating the arrival of new drugs. At first he was excited to see me, thinking maybe I had brought something. When I revealed my new life of pregnancy and school, he was visibly let down and became increasingly distant. There were long spaces of silence as I struggled to fill the uncomfortable space with words. I could feel the darkness in the air like a heavy black drape of evil. His room was dark and stagnant, the dirty drapes hung lifeless and the bent spoon on the table called to me. I had to get out. After about fifteen minutes of awkwardness, Bill told me he knew where Lauren and her mom lived now. With that information, I left and headed out. Although similarly uncomfortable upon my arrival at Lauren's, I was pleased to find out that Lauren's mother Sue was also pregnant. This was good. I didn't stay long, promised to keep in touch and left that night, without using.

A few days later, I returned to Lauren's to find her mom using. I was visibly disturbed. Before I could even process what I was feeling, Sue informed me that the baby was still so small that the drugs wouldn't even affect it. She said the drugs were not in that part of her body. The baby was in a protected area, that it had its own separate system, kind of like a space capsule. It would not be affected at all. Furthermore, she added that she had used during her other pregnancies and the babies all turned out just fine.

With the drugs and needle right in front of me, and the new information from Sue, it was as if I had no defense. The monster turned on like it had never left. It was as if I had two voices in my head. The one that knew better was overpowered by the old familiar voice that said, *Yes, do it. It won't hurt. Look at Sue, she's fine. She's had lots of babies. You deserve it, just do it, it will be fine. Sue is fine.* The louder voice consumed me. Rational thought had little chance with the screaming monster in my head. My heart began to pound and my hands trembled. I needed it. I needed to do it before I became reasonable again. I needed to do it now. The monster continued to scream *Just do it! Just do it! Sue is fine. She wouldn't tell you to do something that would hurt you. She is fine. Everyone is here if something happens, just do it. Stop thinking and just do it! She's right, the baby isn't even real yet. You'll be fine.*

I will never forget the feeling of death that consumed me as the needle popped through my skin and the drug enveloped my consciousness. The innocence and spiritual state that surrounded my pregnant little body was never as clearly felt until the moment it was crushed with an undeniable darkness that enveloped my being and the innocent baby within.

The fear, guilt, despair and darkness crashed through me like a dark intruder crashing into a baby's room in the middle of the night. I wanted to die. Death was all around me. The darkness surrounded the baby and I felt cold. I felt as though the devil was alive within me. My hand nervously opened and closed. My jaw began moving from left to right and my teeth scraped against each other with an audible grinding noise. The screaming of the monster within pierced my ears, locking out all other noise and I was unable to speak. Alone in the bathroom, paranoia leapt in and the voices and shadows of the darkness came alive. I stepped into the bathtub and pulled the shower curtain closed as I crouched on the floor, shaking, sweating and hiding from the approaching darkness as the voices drew closer.

It was two hours before I could open the door to face other humans, but I was still not normal. My jaw remained slightly locked to the side, I was feeling intense demoralization and I kept my head hung low with my eyes fixed to the ground. I made my way to the door without being noticed. As I walked out, the bright sun sent a chill through my skin and stung my eyes, as if able to pierce through my evil soul. The sunlight illuminated the darkness within me as if even light was repelled by me. I started my moped and drove, my heart racing and the darkness chasing my back. My heart was thumping loudly through my head. The bright world threatened my safety. I had to get home.

When I arrived at Ginger's, my jaw was still pulling to the side and my hand was out of control. I had still not regained the ability to speak. I was only capable of whispering. I was horrified to see that the entire family was still up and terrified that they may notice me. I quickly walked in, waved and went straight to the bathroom. I hated myself.

I felt as if I was bringing the devil into their blessed house and God knew. My baby was surely dead.

I stayed in the bathroom weeping silently until I was able to speak, which was at least an hour later. Although you would think this would have been enough to never go near a drug again, this cycle would continue on and off for the next month. The monster was unleashed. During the week, I would go to school and on the weekends, I would go to the beach.

At this point, I was on AFDC, otherwise known as welfare. Ginger had helped me to get food stamps and welfare so that she could afford me. I used my AFDC money to get drugs. Ginger also took me to the doctor regularly. The doctor would always say everything was going just fine with the pregnancy and that I looked great. I became more and more confident that Sue was right. The baby had a different blood supply.

One day Ginger approached me. Although she never confronted me about the drugs, and I am not sure if she knew specifically what was going on, she knew something was very wrong with me. I was gone all the time and was always coming home late at night. My behavior must have been somewhat erratic. She told me that it was becoming too difficult for me to stay with her, but that she made arrangements for a great place for unwed moms close to school. She said she knew several girls that had lived there and loved it, but then dropped the news. I would not be able to bring the moped. The girls in the facility used the bus. This would prove to be a short-term saving grace.

In short order, we were packed and in the car destined for my new home. Ginger drove me to a place for unwed mothers called Casa Mesa. It was a very large, historical house run by nuns. Upon our arrival, I was introduced to the lady that ran the facility and was escorted upstairs to my room. It was a small room with two twin beds and a window that overlooked the roof of the house next door, which was also owned by Casa Mesa. I had my room to myself due to a low occupancy rate at the time. Being a Jew in a home ran by nuns was quite awkward, but at this point, I would take whatever I could get.

21

I**T WENT WELL FOR THE FIRST FEW WEEKS. A**LTHOUGH I WAS introverted when it came to getting to know the people, I went along for rides to go food shopping and sat in the TV room with the others at night. I was provided bus vouchers to get to school. At this point, I was not doing well in school due to the changes, but I continued to go anyway. It had been two weeks by the time I noticed that I hadn't shot up. Because of the rules and location, I was unable to go down to the beach and visit my friends, and frankly I was glad.

One of the girls in the house told me about the Casa Mesa apartments next door and explained to me that if we did well, we could stay and live there. I didn't know that this was what I wanted, but I listened.

One evening I was stunned to return from school to see my teacher sitting in the living room. I was horrified. I had no idea what he was doing there, but evidently, he made a habit of volunteering at Casa Mesa. I felt embarrassed and ashamed that he knew I was homeless and unwed. I was humiliated. My only hope was that he didn't recognize me because of the large size of the class. I only saw him the one time and to this day, I am not sure if he remembered me, as he never said a word about it.

I only lasted at Casa Mesa for just over a month.

I had made friends with an older girl in the apartments who was shooting up. She was twenty six and had twin baby boys. The experience at Ginger's was still fresh enough in my mind that I had no desire to use. Although I chose not to use when she offered it, I also didn't report her activity. I was suspect by association. I understood their reasoning.

That whole honor among thieves thing got me in trouble on more than one occasion, but everyone knows it is totally unacceptable to be a narc.

The only person I could think to call was my mom. I told her there had been some trouble and I needed to move. After the usual 'you're an idiot' speech, she told me she thought her cleaning lady needed someone to watch her kids. She called her, and within a few minutes, it was done. I could stay at Beatrice's and babysit her four kids while she and her husband worked. I would be offered free room and board in exchange for sitting. I had no other options or plans. This also meant I would have to give up my classes at school, but having a place to stay took priority. Beatrice had been my mom's cleaning lady for years. She was a heavy-set white woman whom I didn't really know at all. Exchanging pleasantries when she arrived to clean the house was the extent of our familiarity.

I was surprised to learn that Beatrice lived only two blocks from my mom's house in a roomy, one story home. She had four kids; two boys and two girls who all seemed to have a lot of energy and a husband who was quiet and a bit strange. Beatrice was a chatty woman who seemed very happy most of the time. From what I gathered, both she and her husband grew up in Idaho, the home of the potatoes, where they met, fell in love and got married.

The entire family ate dinner together every night. The dinners consisted of mostly kid friendly foods like hot dogs, chicken nuggets, and mac & cheese due to the level of activity, the number of mouths, and the amount of cleanup. The kids were not allowed to drink soda. I quickly learned that Beatrice's family was Mormon. Up until this point in my life I had only been exposed to a few religions other than Judaism, but even with the little exposure I had, I knew they all had one thing in common: Rules. The strange thing was, unlike other religions that had rules about sex and important stuff, the only rule I was aware of from Beatrice was abstinence from caffeine. Although I wasn't interested in religion, I thought if you had to pick one, this was a natural choice given the options. Almost anyone could pull off God, juices, and milk.

Tami, Tommy, Tasha and Todd were dirty, hyper-active little kids who would watch TV, snack and fight with each other throughout the day. I liked them all. They also attached to me fairly quickly. Tommy was a baby—just learning to walk; Tami was around 9; Todd was 13 and Tasha was 12 and the most mature of the crew. I have no idea why everyone's name began with an T. Like the Mormon religion, it was a mystery.

One day while watching TV with the gang, the two girls were wrestling and then began to simulate what looked like a sex reenactment. I was horrified. I immediately thought about my child abuse classes and specifically the information about kids who have been abused exhibiting similar behavior with others. I remembered the part where they talked about secrecy around abuse, the threats of the abuser and the inherent 'no communication' rules. I also remembered interviews with children in the book where they said they felt safe enough to talk about it with certain people.

I directed the girls to stop what they were doing immediately and called them over to the couch where I was sitting. I asked them where they had learned those things and what it meant. After ten minutes of very uncomfortable non-responsive interactions, I decided my time in class had warped my thinking. I dismissed the incident completely, chalking it up to my being paranoid. It was just child play and these kids were perfectly normal. I clearly saw how my classes on child abuse and my own history could make me see abuse in even the most normal situations. I needed to take life a bit less seriously and understand that not everyone is being abused.

The other weird thing that happened during my stay at their house was the day the dad approached me in the kitchen. He said, "I want to show you something." He came over to me with a very dorky looking fabric doll. It was a rag doll of an older man with a shaggy head of hair and a beard, sort of Ernie & Bert like... I smiled and said, "That is funny." Just as the words came out of my mouth, he lifted the doll's long shirt and exposed a long fabric penis with fake hair around it. He laughed loudly as he exposed the doll's parts and said, "Isn't that funny?" My smile drifted immediately and feeling uncomfortable I said "interesting" and left the room. From that day forward, I thought he was strange, and creepy, and made sure I was never around him alone again.

Now that I was living so close to my mom and my stomach was getting bigger, she started to change her attitude about the baby. She actually offered to go to Lamaze classes with me so that she could be my coach. I couldn't believe it. In addition, she and her new boyfriend offered to help me to buy a car. My luck was starting to turn.

My mom always has a boyfriend, just not the same one. From the time she left my dad to relocate to California, there have been many boyfriends. She was looking for the "right" one. Unfortunately she found something wrong with all of them. I didn't really know her new boyfriend, but he seemed nice. He was extremely friendly and a single parent to boot. We had something in common. He was divorced and had a ten year old son. Although I was never comfortable with the succession of boyfriends, it was refreshing when a nice one came along. He spoke to me about real stuff and smiled at me when he talked. My mom told me he was a Christian. I didn't really have an understanding of what that meant; only that he wasn't Jewish.

It was always difficult for my mom when her boyfriends would acknowledge me. It was clearly uncomfortable for her. In an effort to gain the man's acceptance, she would try to be cordial and friendly to me as well. This was very difficult and uncomfortable for both of us after all we had been through. The worst part was when she would put on the "loving mom" act. My skin would crawl from the deception and confusion. Although my mom was physically there through my whole childhood, she was never emotionally present. We never hugged, touched, exchanged I love you's or had real conversations. I knew at a very real level she was uncomfortable in this act and it was tough for me to watch it.

My mom and her boyfriend picked me up one day and took me to look at a car. It was an old Audi in pretty good condition. I didn't care about the specifics. It would be "my car." My mom agreed to purchase it with the agreement that I would pay her back. I knew it was her boyfriend who had driven this effort and I was very grateful. I was sure my mom had told him all of the trouble I was in and he certainly knew I was pregnant, but he still treated me like a normal kid. Although I couldn't figure out why, I knew he really liked me.

Now that I had a car, I was able to get around much easier. I was hooked in with a local doctor for my maternity care and was able to get prenatal pills with my welfare money and things seemed to be moving along quite nicely. On one doctor visit, the doctor informed me that my baby was definitely a boy. He had determined this by the heart-beat and by the position of the baby in my body. I had always wanted a baby girl and had actually been relating to the baby in my body as if it was a girl. I had no thought that it would be a boy, but after a good deal of processing and coming to acceptance, I decided to name him Joshua.

By this time, I was doing well at not visiting my friends at the beach. I saw no problem with bars though. I loved going to the local biker bar and playing pool. One of the guys there told me that beer is actually good for the baby because it contains wheat and barley. As long as I didn't get wrecked, it was completely safe. The Silver Nickel was my favorite spot. It was a rectangular shaped wood shed with a small bar, six chairs, a juke box and a small pool table. There was a small parking lot in the front on the main road and a large parking lot in the back. On a good night, both lots were packed with motorcycles. There was never a need for fake ID. Any girl that looked half way decent was able to stay. Sometimes I would get hassled when there was a woman tending bar, but I became a regular in very short order.

I loved the place. The bar consisted of mostly MMA members (Modified Motorcycle Association) and a club called the KLAN. The MMA guys, although serious bikers, didn't really seem to have a bone to pick with anyone. They were mostly about protecting motorcyclist's rights. The KLAN, on the other hand, always had some sort of drama going on. Once in a while they held MMA meetings at the bar. I felt important when they let me stay for the meetings. The KLAN meetings were always offsite at one of the member's homes. Only members were allowed to go. There were also occasional red and whites (Hells Angels) hanging out around the bar, but we never heard about their meetings. Bottom line, they were all very nice people and I felt honored that they allowed me to be part of their crew. The fact that they liked me, made me feel important and validated.

The bikers all went by nicknames. The names were usually chosen by the other members of their club and usually had something to do with the person's attributes. The people I was closest to were Drifter, Warlock, Sleezy Steve and Stumper. Stumper was a guy who lost his leg in a riding accident, continued to ride and then lost his other leg. Unable to break his bond with the freedom of riding, he designed and rode a custom trike with hand controls. Drifter was a lady around 40 years old with long brown hair, a laid-back attitude and a heavy addiction to shooting up. If it weren't for her love for speed, she would have had a beautiful smile. Brown and rotted from the drug's impact, she had already lost a few and the others were on their way out. Drifter had a heart of gold. As scary as she may have looked, she was one of the nicest people I knew. She took me under her wing immediately, and was someone I could always go to for advice. Warlock was a shy guy, with frizzy dirty blond hair who was fairly straight-laced. He had a full time job at a local machine shop and a regular life, or so it seemed.

Drifter and Warlock were married at a biker bar on a beautiful day. They were married by bikers, amongst bikers, and then we all drank. The day of their wedding, I celebrated by getting my first tattoo. I sat in the backseat of my car while a member of the KLAN tattooed a motorcycle wheel with clouds erupting from it and a big HD (for Harley Davidson) on my right shoulder blade. It was glorious. *Until I looked at it in the daylight a few days later.* Let's just say it's better to tattoo when *not drinking.* But what the heck, I rarely looked at my back anyway, and now I was officially white biker trash. I actually belonged somewhere. All was perfect.

The only person I met at the Silver Nickel who, like me, did not have a biker nickname was Autumn. Lacking motorcycles and club affiliation, Autumn and I were just handarounds. Autumn was a sweet looking girl about my age with black hair just past her shoulders and a cute shape. We became friends immediately, but as time went on, our friendship had more to do with drugs than anything else. Autumn was from out of state. She arrived with no local friends and never spoke of family, only that she had always wanted to hitch to California and when she was old enough, she did. Lacking a job or money, Autumn crashed at one of the biker's houses on most nights and when she wasn't able to, she would have a biker drop her off at Beatrice's and sleep over with me. Autumn didn't pursue a job, but like many of the others, she worked the carnival when it was in town. It was a good source of funds and they didn't require much paperwork to start.

I didn't realize how much Autumn and I had in common until about two months into our friendship. Not knowing if she could trust me or not, she was very private at first. By the time she exposed her true colors, she had her hooks in me. I loved her just for who she was. A young girl with the self assurance to stick out her thumb and travel miles in the pursuit of her dreams, never looking back. She was a part of me.

I could never explain how it happened but throughout my life, like a magnet, I was always drawn to the same people over and over. Like scattered survivors from a mutual war, our similar tragedies drew us together like long lost family. I can always tell who my people are by the way I feel when I meet them. Unexplainably familiar and at home.

The day Autumn showed up to Beatrice's with drugs, it was on. Stating that she needed to show me something in private, I told the kids I would be back. We left the TV room and went into my bedroom for privacy. Before I could ask her what it was, she dug into her pocket, pulled out a small white bindle and threw it on my nightstand. She proudly announced, "I have almost a gram and I have a needle." The moment I saw it, I knew I was gone. Completely conflicted, I had to have it and had to make it go away. My hands began to sweat and my heart pounded. I felt like I was going to throw up. Not only was I now six months pregnant, but the baby was moving inside of me. From that day forward it was crystal clear to me. When I see drugs, I lose the ability to make a choice. The monster, the addict in me, battling against any logical thought always proved to be an unfair fight. The moment the monster turned on, it was over. I stood no chance.

The enormous glow of love that surrounded my young pregnant body was in danger and I did not possess the power to protect it. With no God and no moral beliefs, the voice took over. *YOU WILL GO FIRST. AUTUMN CAN WAIT. DO NOT CHANGE YOUR MIND, GO NOW! And the final thought. Sue was right. Her baby is fine. You need this.*

The moment the prick of the sharp needle broke through my soft skin, it was over. As the drug entered my veins, the darkness engulfed my entire being and I began to tremble with terror. Like a small, deranged animal, I found refuge behind a small nightstand and crouched down behind it as if being hunted.

Covered in sweat, cowering behind the small dresser, I pulled at my limbs, for fear of being captured. Unable to completely conceal myself behind the tiny barrier of the dresser wall, I struggled. My small feet extending past the edge of the dresser, I frantically shifted back and forth to tuck them beneath me. I could feel Autumn's eyes on me, staring at me in horror, but it didn't matter. She didn't understand. "They" were coming. I could feel them. As I looked down to hide my head from the hunters and avoid Autumn's stare, it hit me: My big soft stomach was completed hard, frozen stiff! *MY BABY! MY BABY ISN'T MOVING!" MY BABY!* All movement of the baby had seized. My soft stomach had instantly hardened.

It was at that moment that the sounds of the hunters dissipated and were replaced by the voice of a larger power. Instilling shame, disgust, shock and remorse, it spoke to me. It cursed me to hell for the evil witch that I was. *You killed your baby! You are a witch! It would be too good to let you die; you never deserved the baby, so we took it from you!* I knew the voice was telling the truth, I knew it would come and take my baby. I always knew it would come.

I sat on the floor shuddering with my arms wrapped around my legs, rocking quickly back and forth. Autumn moved into my face and grabbed my cheeks. When her eyes were looking directly into mine, she felt the terror. I saw it as her eyes widened and her hands shook. "Stop sugar, stop. You will be okay, you will be okay. You are just high. Your baby is fine. Calm down honey, calm down. Please baby calm down."

Although Autumn continued to get in my face, her words were futile. While she clearly felt my state of panic, she had no way of knowing the loss of a presence, the loss of a life. The black hole that filled my entire being. I was a murderer. The intensity of the drugs ringing throughout my head also rang in the tiny little child that existed in my womb. It was more than I could bear.

How did I do this? How could I believe the lies that Sue told me? Was I so stupid? Did I really believe this? I killed my baby. In a state of complete denial and now unwilling to accept this outcome, I shot to a standing position and began pushing on my belly. *Maybe if I push, and the baby feels it, it will kick back. Maybe it is sleeping.* "Please God, tell me I didn't kill my baby. Please God. Please God!!!! Please tell me I didn't kill my baby!" I knew that sometimes if I poked at my belly, the baby would kick back. But I was pushing and prodding and there was nothing. Cold and still. Sitting on the bed with my head in my lap, I wept. Autumn was in the other corner, her back up against the wall. Small tears fell from her eyes. The room was silent.

Twenty minutes passed, I curled up in the fetal position on my bed and I stared at the wall. My eyes stuck wide open as if toothpicks held them open to force me to look at my evil self. When I first felt the flurry, I knew it wasn't real. The powerful one reminding me of what I had lost, but then it happened again. I shot into an upright position and placed my hand firmly over my stomach. Something moved! It was real! My baby was alive! As I looked over to tell Autumn, I saw that she was emptying the remainder of the bindle into the spoon. She said, "This is the last of it. I assume you don't want it."

My body and mind were completely worn out from the massive outburst of remorse and horror that had enveloped me, but now I was starting to feel semi-normal again and I didn't want to miss my last chance. I said, " I want it." *The baby is moving. I am fine. Sue was right. I was wrong. I have nothing to worry about.*

For the next month, I unsuccessfully fought my urge to pick up, and used cocaine every time that Autumn showed up. The horror that I was killing my baby, the sobbing and pleading with God, the self hatred and then the realization that my baby was still alive. This was a roller-coaster that I would experience over and over again. I was completely void of the capability of saying no, even when it meant threatening the life of my baby that I loved so much. The level of self-loathing that I had become accustomed to as a small child intensified every time that I was unable to say no.

A few weeks later my water broke. I phoned my mom per our instructions at our Lamaze class. Although we had only attended two classes and never really discussed much about it, I knew the drill: Call her up, go to the hospital and she will help me with my breathing. I had opted for natural childbirth because I didn't want the baby to be affected by drugs when she was being born. Amazingly enough, this very irrational thought process was never overridden by the thought that I was using much more dangerous drugs all along. On good days, when I wasn't using, I clearly thought the best thing to do for the baby was natural birth.

When we arrived, they wheeled me into a private room while my mom headed to the admitting room to fill out the paperwork. When the nurse came in, she told me to remove my clothes and put on a gown so that they could hook me up to the monitor. I immediately realized that I couldn't. There is a huge slit up the back. I explained to the nurse, "My mom is my coach. I want this to go as well as possible, but if I wear that gown and she comes in and sees the huge motorcycle wheel tattoo on my back, she is going to start screaming at me. I can't do this today, not today."

The nurse immediately understood my dilemma. She returned shortly after with a large rectangle of bandage gauze and some tape. She taped the bandage over my tattoo and kindly said, "That ought to take care of it." My mom came in shortly after and never asked about the large bandage.

The 12 hours of natural childbirth was more than I could ever have imagined and much more than I could endure. About 30 minutes into it, I began the pleas that would occur for the next eleven and a half hours. "*Please* give me some pain killers! Please! It hurts too much!" The pleas were answered with a firm, but adamant, "No. You signed the papers with your doctor and we can't change it now." Natural childbirth? What was I thinking? I would have stayed pregnant the rest of my life to stop the pain. It was a long night.

My mom had forgotten her breathing coach thing and was flopped on the chair next to me trying to sleep. Each time the pains came, I screamed out and each time I did, she got more upset with me. Her sympathetic response was, "Please stop the noise. I have to work tomorrow and at this rate I am going to be up all night!" By the time they pushed me into the delivery room and the baby came out, I was so exhausted, I barely responded when they said, "You have a beautiful baby girl!"

The next day, I was lying in my hospital bed when they brought in a baby wrapped in a white blanket like a burrito, with thick black hair on its head and thick side burns. It looked a lot like "Ernie" of Ernie & Bert. I thought, *"Are you kidding?* It must have been *all the drugs. It looks like the hair on a full-grown man!"*

Luckily, the nurse walked right past me and handed the boy to the thick haired Hispanic lady next to me. Twenty minutes later, they brought in another baby. The most beautiful baby I had ever seen in my life. She was a tiny little angel. All of her tiny little features and hands were beautiful. I was in awe. This perfect little angel came out of me? I was able to hold her and I didn't want to let her go. Every time they came to get her, I worried, would they carry her okay, would they feed her? Are they keeping her warm? For the first time in my life, I genuinely bonded with another life.

Shortly after giving birth and meeting my child, a lady came to my room and asked me for the birth certificate name. My sisters, my mom and her boyfriend were all visiting the hospital. Mom and her boyfriend were off looking at the baby, but my sisters were with me.

Months ago, I had thought Rhiannon from the Fleetwood Mac

song would be a good girl name and I liked Joshua for a boy. Since I had thought it was a boy all along, I hadn't thought more about girl's names. When I blurted out Rhiannon, my sister was quick to inform me that the Rhiannon song was about a witch. Having spent my entire life thinking that God was punishing me for being a witch in a past life, I said, "Hmmm not a good way to start". Thinking mostly about boy's names up until this point, I was stumped. One of the two ladies I shared a room with was in a similar situation. She thought she was having a girl and ended up with a boy (not Ernie's mom, the other lady). She told me her top ten list for girl's names. When she said Madison, I knew that was it. I would tell the nurse as soon as she returned. I would name my perfect baby Madison.

My mom and her boyfriend returned before the nurse. I told them that the baby's name would be Madison. My mom was a bit set back and said, "I thought we would name her after a relative." Suddenly my mom had gone from not wanting to have anything to do with the baby to wanting to name her. Much to my surprise, her boyfriend also wanted to weigh in! Suddenly there was a slew of names being tossed around that certainly would not fit. For instance, my mom said, "What about naming her after my dad, Phillip, by calling her Phillis?" As much as I cared for my grandfather, I didn't think so. Her boyfriend suggested Ray after one of his relatives. After much bartering on the possibilities and insistence that it must be a girl name, we decided that just using the P from Philip counted for something, and we could shove Ray in there somewhere, if it was spelled correctly, sort of a semi middle name. The end result; Madison Rae Phoenix, the most beautiful little angel my eyes had ever seen.

22

I COULD NEVER HAVE IMAGINED THE INTENSITY OF EMOTION THAT having my own daughter would bring to my life until it actually happened. I realized almost at the onset that I was scared all the time. Scared that something would happen to her. Scared that she was going to get sick. Scared that she would die. I knew I didn't deserve her. I knew that eventually she would be taken from me.

The day I brought her home to Beatrice's house, my paranoia was obvious. The moment the door opened, the children darted in from outside with their sticky little dirty hands and runny noses wanting to see the baby. They circled around her and started to breathe on her. I was petrified.

I told them that the baby and I were tired and we would need to sleep. They could see her later. I immediately dashed her into the room and closed the door for protection. I could not let her be exposed to the germs. I was sure something would happen to her.

My small room had a tiny bassinette arranged at the end of the bed. I pulled it up next to me and aligned it with my pillow so that I could see her at all times. It was difficult for me to fall asleep right from the start. I had learned about Sudden Infant Death Syndrome, or SIDS, a sickness where small babies just stop breathing for no reason, in my child development class. I knew I didn't deserve such a beautiful gift, so I was sure God would take my baby one night through SIDS.

Madie would fall asleep and I would watch her tummy—up and down, up and down and then still. In a state of panic, I would wake her up. She would begin to cry. In an effort to calm her, I would give her the tiny little bottle of milk, sing to her and rock her back to sleep.

I had made up a song that I would sing to her: *Mommy's little princess, mommy's little baby, mommies little angel, mommy's little baby girl.* I would sing it lower and lower and then start to hum it until she fell asleep. After a while, when she fell into a deep sleep, I would lay her in her bassinette and I would watch her. Up and down, up and down and then still. In a state of panic, I would wake her up.

After doing this insane repetition several hours, I would finally doze off from pure exhaustion. In the middle of the night I would wake up in a state of panic and look at her belly. Convinced that it was not moving and that God had killed her, I would wake her up. She would start crying again and I would sing her back to sleep, over and over again. For the first six months of her life this is what we did. She was a gift that I knew I didn't deserve and being that God hated me, I knew she would be taken from me.

Although Autumn still came over, seeing the baby affected her. She didn't bring anything by anymore. That is for a while.

Madie was about four months old when Autumn brought drugs over again. This would be the start of a nightmare of drug addiction as a mom that would haunt me forever. Autumn would get the drugs, bring them back and we would close the door to my little room and shoot up.

I realized almost immediately that Madie had a strong reaction to my using. She would scream as soon as I picked her up. It took me a few times to realize that she was unaccustomed to my accelerated heart beat. It was more than I could bear. The heartbreak of knowing that my baby child could feel the evil within me was coupled with the fierce craving that could not be quelled. We would set Madie in the mechanical swinging chair for hours. Even then, she could feel it and would cry. Her screaming sent me through the roof with guilt, horror, paranoia and a level of self-hatred that cannot be described. And yet, I could not stop.

Although Beatrice never mentioned anything specific, it was obvious that they knew something was wrong. She noticed the silent hours spent in the room with Autumn, hearing only occasional whispers behind the door. She worried about my refusal to come out of the room when requested during these silent hours.

I could feel the evil and death all around me. The mortifying, sinful corruption that surrounded my beautiful perfect baby. It wasn't long before I too couldn't live with myself anymore. I knew I had to get out of here. I had to stop. I had to get away from Autumn, away from everyone.

I told Beatrice that I was going to try to find an apartment or a room to rent. I told her it was too much with the baby and watching all of the kids. She agreed. Although nothing was spoken between us about my use, it was at this point that Beatrice made several comments about taking care of my baby for me, if I ever needed a break or just someone to watch her. If I ever thought it was too much, she said, they would be more than willing to adopt her. I thought it was nice that they loved my baby that much, but were they crazy? I would never give her up. She was all I had.

Oblivious to all this insanity, my mom's boyfriend at the time suggested I move to his house and watch his eleven year old son while he went to work. I loved that idea. Although this only lasted for a few weeks, during this time I did not shoot up. I spent most days at home with Madie and his son, and at night I would go to the Silver Nickel to play pool.

It wasn't long before I met Toby. Toby was a beautiful biker from the Midwest who had moved out here with just his motorcycle to make a new life for himself. He wore a leather jacket, flannel work shirts, Levis and chaps, and had the most adorable twenty-five-year-old baby face and the most beautiful blue eyes you ever saw. He had a nice trailer close by and wanted to make a family with Madie and me. Although my mom and her boyfriend did not agree with or understand my thinking, we left with everything packed into my little car following the exhaust cloud of Toby's beautiful Harley Davidson, on our way to our new life.

Toby, Madie and I lived in a small oval trailer with two round porthole windows. It was a tiny little place, but we were happy. Toby worked construction for a local company, digging ditches. Although he was always dirty when he arrived home, I didn't mind. He was wonderful: A soft-spoken individual who didn't drink more than a beer or two when he did drink and was strictly opposed to drug use, besides marijuana. Marijuana never really counted as a drug in our world. It was a natural herb meant to bring all of the beauty of the world to the eyes of the smoker and forge relationships with friends. There was no harm with weed. Every day, Toby would go to work and Madie and I would hang around the trailer or go on errands anxiously awaiting Toby's return.

It wasn't long before I started to become acquainted with our neighbors at the trailer park. Up until this point I was fortunate to be completely oblivious to the kind of devil's den we were living in, but I was about to find out.

Bo was a normal looking, nice guy who lived with his girlfriend in a lavish trailer one row over on the left end. His trailer had an entry-way, a large kitchen, a large living room and two or three bedrooms. He was the king of the trailer park. The place was beautifully decorated with expensive furniture, artwork and massive fish aquariums. I would soon learn that Bo supplied not only the entire trailer park, but also others beyond the park, with some of the best cocaine in town.

Dane and his twin brothers, all in their late twenties lived three rows back on the right end with their mom in a two-room trailer a bit larger than the one I lived in with Toby. Their mother was a very ancient, chubby woman who only spoke if she was screaming orders out the door. Otherwise she never moved from the chair, where she was permanently transfixed on the TV. She reminded me of the lady in "Throw Mamma from the Train" in personality and appearance.

All three of the boys were hopelessly addicted to crank, a form of speed. Conveniently enough in the backsplash of their trailer, way up over the rooftops, was a sign from a local automotive store beyond the park. It read "THE CRANKBROTHERS, a transmission shop, which would eventually become their handle to anyone who knew them.

It was from the crank brothers that I learned about dumpster diving. Although I never did it myself, they would go out at sundown to begin the hunt. Like clockwork, by dawn, the crank brothers would return to the park with a vast collection of treasures. The treasures ranged from jewelry to car parts to toasters and more.

There was also a guy named John who lived in an old school bus that looked like the Partridge family gone wrong. He sold acid, spoke in riddles and did a great impression of Jim on Taxi. He even looked like him a little. Lastly, there was the circus freak, a tall man with ears four times too big for his emaciated head, who circled the park endlessly on his bicycle. He was a permanent fixture. Relentlessly, he rode round and round, like the large hand on a clock. The crank brothers told me later that he too was a speed freak. I could never figure out how and when he used because I never saw him stop.

It wasn't long before it was on. My welfare checks were going straight from my hands to Bo's. Even if I ran out of money, he would front me. He knew that I feared him and that I would constantly need more. When Toby was at work, I sank into the pits of hell, but I made sure to stop hours before he got home. Although there were some close calls, he never knew. Madie and I were locked in the small trailer with my mental state quickly deteriorating.

One day Toby came home from work early to surprise me. Madie was fast asleep in the room and I was hiding in the tiny trailer bathroom behind the door, paranoid schizophrenic, jaw locked permanently to the left, hand opening and closing in a strange repetition that screamed of abnormality and the absence of normal brain function. I don't know who was more horrified when he walked in. The sheer demoralization that I felt when he saw me was so immense that the realization only caused me to accelerate my mental depreciation. For the next few months, I was never sober long enough to fully comprehend the monster that I had become. I never fully understood the level at which I had destroyed this beautiful, loving man.

Toby didn't give up. He put all he could into trying to help me to get off of the drugs. He made rules and restrictions and handled all of the money. The day he came home and the piggy bank was devoid of all bills and coins, he knew he had to get me out of the park. He rented a small two bedroom apartment for us across town. Madie's crib was in our room and we planned on renting out the other room.

Although Toby was planning on joining us, he only needed a few minutes away from me to realize that my addiction was far beyond his power to rectify. A few days later, in the wee morning hours, a beautiful, redheaded girl from the Silver Nickel bar left flowers on his trailer steps and he was gone. He deserved better and we both knew it.

I was nineteen and a single mom with no job and no friends. The thought of stopping the addiction never entered my mind. Instead, I made a clear and conscious decision that I would limit my drug use to the nighttime to protect Madie from the evil spirits. I would only let the monster out when she was sleeping.

During the day, I would smoke cigarettes and drink beer like a normal person. At night, the monster would come alive. As a result of my tragic childhood, I made a commitment that I would never hit my daughter. Because of the absence of love in my childhood, I would constantly tell her how much I loved her, how beautiful she was and how much she meant to me. I would do everything the opposite of what my parents had done—except the addiction part, of course. For some reason I failed to notice that.

I also remembered a good deal of the information from my child development classes. I knew about the Golden Rule of Parenting, "Ignore bad behavior, reward good behavior." I knew the impact of positive words and hugs, time-outs instead of hitting, never say "you're wrong" or "your bad" just say "you made a bad choice today." And most of all, I always remembered that it was never good to tell a child to lie. I learned that a life of dishonesty and keeping sick secrets would destroy a child. I swore I would never lie to her. That created quite a dilemma for us over time. I loved and hugged on my daughter every chance I could, and at the same time, I had her surrounded by criminals and drugs on a regular basis. The insanity of the situation would have been laughable, had it not been so tragic.

23

SHORTLY AFTER MOVING TO THE NEW PLACE, I MET A MAN WHO
would have a huge impact on my life in many ways, but at the time, I
was just plain intrigued. The new apartment was close to the local 7-11.
Although I still had the car, it was more convenient to just walk around
the block. It was there that I met Gabriel, dark-skinned and sleeved
with tattoos. He looked like an old tribal Indian with a beautiful black
braid almost to his waist and a smile that could melt mountains. "Hello
darling! I was thinking maybe you could help me out. You see, I am
making a tattoo gun, but I need a battery. If you could help me out,
I would be glad to help you with a tattoo!" Although I didn't want a
tattoo, I was very interested in how you could make a tattoo gun with
a pen, a small battery and some guitar string! Within a few minutes we
were back at my house and I was learning the tricks of the trade. Gabriel
was amazing to me. Due to our age difference, I wasn't attracted to him
in a romantic kind of way, but he very quickly became my life mentor.
He had a world of life experiences and his wisdom drew me to him.

For the next few months, I would tattoo whoever would let me.
I specialized in disappearing tattoos. Evidently I never pushed hard
enough, so although it looked great that first day, within three months
or so your tattoo would be gone. Needless to say, I didn't get a lot of
referrals or repeat customers.

Gabriel was a tree trimmer by trade—that is, when he wasn't in
prison. He lived in a motel around the corner with his mom and his
nieces, who were two and six. Gabriel had two sisters and two brothers,
although one brother had died. Gabriel and all of his siblings were
heroin addicts. Gabriel's older brother and sister were rats, in protective

custody when in jail and we didn't associate with them for that precise reason. I learned about rats, up front and personal, when I was arrested on Christmas day.

With Gabriel came a plethora of other prison-bound guys that I immediately took to. For the first time in my life, I felt protected. Their tattooed bodies, worn faces and passionate hearts drew me in. I loved these guys and I loved being seen with them. I was small and insignificant in their presence and I felt honored that they took me under their wing. Their protection of Madie and me was undeniable. Now no one would mess with me. I felt powerful.

Alvin was Gabriel's best friend. He was also a tree trimmer and more of a drunk than a heroin addict, but he would indulge anytime Gabriel brought some dope around. Up until this point, my drink was always Jack Daniels, straight up, whether at the bar or at home. Gabriel introduced me to Seagrams 7. He always had a pint in his back pocket. He said, "The first gulp has a bit of a bite, but after that, it's smooth as silk!" Although I only really indulged in hard liquor when I didn't have drugs, it was always interesting when I drank to excess. I sipped Seagram's throughout the day, but when I really drank, I liked to fight. Although it didn't happen often, I could usually find some drunk hitting his girlfriend in the parking lot of the bar. I would fly into the middle (all 98 lbs of me) and I would let the tough biker know he was a fucking wimp and that he was going to have to deal with me if he didn't back off! Amazingly enough, I was only beaten up once. I think the remainder of the guys I threatened were probably humored back to tranquility.

During my first few weeks of hanging out with Gabriel and friends, I tried heroin. The experience was horrible. I threw up all over the place. I was euphoric in a sickening kind of way, and then I fell asleep. I remember thinking, if this is what Dorothy and the Tin man were feeling in the poppy field, I would have cancelled the trip to the Wizard. I didn't get it. It made me sick, much too friendly, in a joyful everything is perfect kind of way, and ended with me passing out. I didn't like being this nice or this sick. I had to stay on my toes. I couldn't understand how anyone would like this shit.

Gabriel and his friends were over a lot. For a while I rented my extra room to Gabriel in exchange for drugs. We also had a detached garage in the alley that I rented to Gabriel's friend, Danny. Danny made himself a nice home in the garage. He threw a mattress on the floor, hung a boom box on the wall and carpeted with an old rug he found in a trash bin. I never actually paid rent with the money I collected from them. In fact, all of my bills went in the bill drawer and never saw the light of day. My routine quickly became to stay at a place until the legal eviction process finally forced me out. My thought was—why spend good drug money on bills? I had friends pay the rent for the first few months in exchange for staying at the pad and I started dealing weed as a side job. This arrangement helped pay for drugs and made me more useful in our little crew.

Although a junkie himself, Gabriel was not happy with the effect the coke had on me. He used to say, "You gotta stop using that shit, it's making you crazy." He and I both knew I couldn't stop. It was a repetitive cycle of people coming in and out of my apartment. The regulars were Gabriel, his friends and the teenagers that stopped by to pick up weed. One thing about Gabriel and his friends—they never bragged. I had met a lot of people who bragged about their crimes and drug use. Gabriel and his friends never discussed prison or any of the crimes they committed. I always knew they were of a different status than most and although that would be alarming to normal people, I was drawn to it.

There was a certain honor within the crew and they had protected, not violated me. I had lived in a beautiful home with manicured lawns and "normal people" but nothing was normal about it. At least here, I understood the rules.

There was also my need for danger. I had lived on the edge for so long, I wasn't sure I knew how to live any other way.

24

IT WAS DURING THIS PERIOD THAT MY SISTER NADINE CALLED ME. Both of my sisters were drug addicts as well. My sister Nadine was a DJ at a local disco. Her job was to dance in a glass cone in the middle of the dance floor and change records. She had long black hair, was tan, model thin and wore cute little dresses with very high heels. Her purpose in life was to find the richest guy with the most cocaine and cohabitate. My little sister Alyssa was a punk rocker. Her hair never stayed the same for more than a month, pink, blue, white, never a dull hair day. Alyssa partied with high school kids and Nadine and her rich friends freebased cocaine.

Although I spoke to Nadine from time to time, we never liked each other. The gun experience and the mixed feelings about my dad kept us alienated. I always felt robotic around her. One day, Nadine phoned my apartment and told me that she wanted me to go with her somewhere close by and it was very important. She told me it was less than a mile from my house and she really needed me to go. Having nothing better to do, and figuring there might be something in it for me, I agreed.

She brought me to a little building that was right next to the Silver Nickel bar. Although I had been next to the place many nights, I had never really noticed it. It looked like an old wooden shack with a big triangle on the door. When I first saw it, I thought, *some strange cult?* When I went inside, my suspicion was confirmed.

There was a hippie-looking guy sitting behind a candle in a dimly lit room speaking in an almost inaudible tone about love and unity. At first I thought Charles Manson had escaped. Like a bird on a perch, he was twisted up Indian style on a square fringed mat, hiding under a thick patterned, wool poncho. His long, greasy, brown hair was tied back in a ponytail and he had a thin, wiry beard with hairs sticking out in all directions like the branches of a dying tree struggling to survive. In a trance-like state with his eyes softly shut, he muttered some final words about drugs and love. Chills shot up my spine as the whole group joined in on some sort of trance and the room fell silent.

Before I could process the realization that my sister had joined this cult, the craziness started again. Now they were circling the room with unified chanting and identifying themselves as part of this drug love group, Sissy Addict, Jane Addict, Thomas Addict, Nadine Addict. Then it got to me.

With no idea what to say, and knowing that my sister had brought me here to show me her life, and knowing I didn't belong, I blurted out, "Lauri…and my sister is an addict." The room erupted with a flow of quiet chuckles. I couldn't figure out what the freaks thought was so funny. Did they think I was one of them? They had no idea who I was. Hell, I was only shooting up at night. Real addicts can't stop during the day. They were clearly just looking at everyone as addicts at this point. Their organized self-deception was disturbing, but I didn't take it personally. They could stay in their little room chanting to each other while I went back to real life. On the drive home Nadine asked me what I thought. I told her that her new friends seemed "nice" and left it at that. I was glad to get home.

One night Gabriel came into the apartment in a rush. He had some guys with him. They were running in and out carrying bags. Although I didn't know much about these guys, it was evident that they had been in prison together at some point. I knew from my experiences with Gabriel that when a new guy showed up, sleeved with tattoos and a long thick mustache, that I had never seen before, he was from prison.

On his way back out, Gabriel yelled, "Keep the doors closed!" Alvin had been in the house prior to their arrival. While these guys were running in and out, Alvin started to open the bags. The bags were filled with silver the size of real bricks and coins. Our heads were spinning. Rushing in and out loading up more bags. Gabriel finally stopped and handed something to Alvin. "Here is some dope. It is very strong. Do *not* use a full balloon." Alvin was a pig when it came to drugs. A few minutes later I heard Gabriel yell from the bathroom, "Shit! Alvin! I told him not to do the whole thing!" This was my first experience with a drug overdose. It all happened so fast, that I reacted like a trained ER room technician. Emotionless and focused on the problem I did whatever they told me to.

From the rushed conversation amongst the guys, I was immediately aware that we only had a limited amount of time to revive him. Gabriel yelled at him, smacked him, put him in a cold shower and stuffed ice down his pants. It was no use. He was not coming back. His face was blue and he was turning red from being punched. Gabriel immediately explained that we needed to come up with a plan.

He said, "At this point, we have a load of stolen money in the house and cannot take any heat." We all agreed that we had to dispose of Alvin's body. We could not risk the alternative. There was talk of a local dumpster. This was the point in my life where I clearly realized that death was expected in our lifestyle. I will never forget the casual nature with which they discussed the disposal of the body. Alvin, Gabriel's best friend? There was no sorrow, just panic and planning. I knew from this point forward that if I was going to play this game, I would need to accept the consequences. Death was clearly one of them. It seemed that everyone else present knew this already. On that day I realized the consequences on a much deeper level. From that day forward, when people died, we accepted it. There were no funerals to be attended for us. Death was just the final move in this dangerous game.

I was jolted back to reality with a moan coming from the bathroom. It was Alvin. "Man that was some good shit." I now know this was a fairly normal reaction for a heroin addict en route back from final departure. I was shook up, to say the very least. For cripes sakes, we almost threw Alvin away. Clearly, he had no idea that he had just been granted life again. Reacting as if he just sucked a good hit of weed, he was oblivious.

I continued to frequent the trailer park. On most nights I would make as many as fifteen trips. I would always go for a quarter gram of coke. I never purchased more than a quarter of coke in my life. I always told myself, *I will just do one quarter.* This was my rationalization to myself and to others that were trying to stop me. Anyone who knew how I got when I was loaded would try to talk me out of going. I made a conscious effort every time I went to the park to avoid bumping into Toby. I was deteriorating quickly and didn't want to face who I was to him or who I was becoming.

One night while at the park, the more verbal of the crank brothers yelled, "I love you Lauri!" Soon you will be mine, Lauri!" Before I knew it, he was stockpiling the best of the night's dumpster-diving prizes for me. He was a shy guy up close, but from a distance, he was a charmer. It wasn't long before we were an item.

25

OUR SCHEDULES WORKED OUT PERFECTLY. BY THE TIME I WAS well into my insanity for the night, he was out collecting treasures for me. We would meet up in the morning, when everything was normal again, and he would bring me a new toaster or an old piece of jewelry. I didn't care what it was, just the fact that he took the time to think about me enough to bring me something made me feel good.

One Christmas morning I awoke to the police. There was weed in the spare room, the house looked and reeked from the party the prior night and Madie was on the couch sucking on her bottle. The only other adult at the house was a girl named Lucy from down the street who spent a good deal of time partying at our apartment. She had a small baby girl about Madie's age named Kiki. She often helped me with Madie during the day in exchange for a playmate for her daughter and a drug and drinking partner for herself. Although she technically lived with her mom and step-dad, she spent most days at our apartment. On this particular morning she had fallen asleep on the couch and awoke to the police at the door.

Evidently, I had gotten a ticket while driving and never took care of it. I guess I ran a red light. I say I guess because I didn't give it much notice and promptly forgot about it. Not used to having a car, I had no idea what you do with tickets, and not liking court, I just ripped it up and threw it away. We were all woken to the loud knock at the door. As soon as I appeared at my bedroom door, they asked me to approach the door and started to read me my rights. I was stunned. I couldn't believe that these guys thought it was reasonable to arrest a single mom on Christmas morning. When I pleaded with them that it was Christmas morning and I was a single mom, they explained to me that this was the only good time to arrest people like me because for the most part, we were home. It was apparent that the outstanding warrant had more significance to them than my personal holiday plans. I went to jail for the first time in my adult life and I was mortified that my daughter, although under a year old, had to see me being arrested. I was lucky to have friends over from the night before to watch Madie or the situation could have turned out much worse.

When I was transported to the local jail awaiting a ride to the main jail, a detective came to speak with me about the drug dealers in the area. This was my first up close and personal experience with the "rat" squad I had learned from Gabriel. The detective talked specifically about Bo from the trailer park. He told me if I would work with them, they could help me to have my charge dismissed. Thanks to Gabriel's guidance, I denied any knowledge of his information about Bo and drug trafficking, and although he pressed me for a while more, I held my ground. Rats are outcasts; they are not to be tolerated. The scary thing is you really never know who is a rat and who isn't unless you get information from someone else. If you are using with them or picking up with them, or in any way involved with them, you never know when the police are going to show up. We avoided protective custody people at all cost.

I was very happy to see that, unlike juvenile hall, in jail you were allowed to smoke. That was a definite benefit. I was always able to see the lemonade through the lemons.

The most alarming thing that I noticed was that there was no one watching the inmates. Girls were being beat up and harassed with no intervention what-so-ever. I witnessed a pregnant girl being beaten to the point where she lost her baby. I was horrified. I realized very quickly that while I felt tough at times, I was surely a wimp in my new environment and had better lie low to avoid involving myself in anything other than reading and sleeping.

When I returned home from jail a few days later, I learned my mom had been by, picked up Madie from Lucy and decided she needed to intervene. With no other good plans, she decided I needed to get back in school, hang out with normal kids and stop doing drugs. She enrolled me in Business College, and decided I would be trained to be a Legal Secretary. The plan was for me to have a career working for an attorney. And to tell you the truth, it sounded like a great idea, at first.

By this point, my original car had broken down from lack of maintenance, so my mom gave me her old Toyota Corolla and told me I could pay her back when I finished school. The idea was for Lucy to watch my daughter during the day. It all seemed like the perfect plan. Much to my surprise, I did very well for the first month. I took to shorthand very quickly and I actually enjoyed learning. It was about thirty days into school that I got to know some of the other students. The first girls I met were Sharon and Jewel.

Jewel was a hippie with yellow teeth. The kind of person the kids in grade school were referring to when I said I aspired to be a hippie. Now I could see why they were laughing. No one in their right mind would actively pursue this. It really wasn't attractive. Jewel wore long hippie skirts, talked of world peace and smoked way too much pot and for some reason never shaved her arm pits or used deodorant. You could tell by her lack of boundaries and personal hygiene that she had seen better days. When Jewel wasn't at school, she traveled with her boyfriend, Dustin. Jewel and Dustin had matching teeth and he was completely marinated physically and mentally by his constant weed intake. They were a match made in heaven.

Sharon on the other hand was from a well-to-do family. She had the best of the best of everything. Her parents were very "normal," still married and supported her in every way. Sharon and her mom were very close. I was completely shocked the day that Sharon confided in me that she had a habit of shooting up coke. Again, like always, I was drawn to my people by some unseen mysterious magnet. Whether in the bar, at the store or at business school, we were destined to meet over and over again. They had different names and looked different, but on the inside, we were all the same: Wounded beyond repair and willing to take anything to make it feel better.

The first time we decided to skip lunch break and shoot up together, it was on. This was the beginning of our friendship and the end of my success at school. Although I continued to attend, I may not have done much worse if I hadn't attended at all.

The next few months were more of the same; shooting up, drug deals, robberies and deteriorating welfare checks. The lives of my friends were coming apart also. Although only in his early thirties, we knew Alvin was too far gone when he no longer recognized Gabriel. His eyes were yellow, his stomach was bloated and his memory erased, with the exception of the yearning for a drink from anyone who would provide it. When Gabriel handed his best friend Alvin a bottle of whisky and Alvin said, "Thank you Mister," we knew for sure he was gone. A few weeks later he died of cirrhosis of the liver.

Danny, the guy who lived in my garage, returned to prison and he too died of liver complications. It was also during this dark time that a customer of Bo's was brutally stabbed seventeen times on his trailer steps while picking up. They said she had burned the wrong people.

It wasn't long before it became impossible for me to engage in reality on any level. I vaguely remembered my mom stopping by just a few weeks prior. She was starting to check on us and informed me of a planned trip we would be making to Florida to visit her mom. My grandparents had moved down to Florida from New York just before my grandfather's death.

Although I remembered the date of the trip, what happened the night before impeded my ability to process the information. It was a Friday night. I was acutely aware that my mother would be dropping by the apartment to pick us up around seven the next morning, but at this point, that was several hours away. I still had time to pack. I figured; sit around, relax a bit, start packing around eight and go to bed early.

26

THAT NIGHT ONE OF THE GUYS FROM THE LOCAL BIKER BAR STOPPED by unexpectedly. I didn't know him very well and he was always a bit of a strange bird. Very shy and withdrawn, having had no real conversation with him, he had been by a few times to pick up weed. That night, he showed up at the door with a sandwich baggie of white powder. He claimed it was very potent coke, but he needed a needle. I was in. I had a rig on hand and no one else was around. I figured I would do it once or twice and then continue with my packing plan.

As I injected the first dose, I realized immediately that it had no effect. I told him nothing was happening. He said he was positive that it was me that was out of whack and not the stuff and he proceeded to inject himself. He said he definitely felt it. Frustrated and confused, I injected myself again and again and again. About twenty five minutes later, standing at my bedroom window, I was staring outside, completely frustrated by the claims that this crap was good. My arms were swollen from injecting myself and the stuff was fake. I felt absolutely nothing. The insane part was that having felt nothing, I continued to shoot up over and over again. *Maybe this time it will be different.* Having been from the same baggie, there was absolutely no logical reason that it would be different at all, but that didn't stop me.

All of a sudden, it hit me. A rocket of heat rushed through my body and my heart started to bang. It hit me like a sledgehammer. I knew what had happened and it was bad. I had shot up speed, otherwise known as crank. The bad part was at this point, I had shot up far beyond my limit and to make matters much worse, I had a paranoid-schizophrenic reaction to speed that made my cocaine outbursts look like child's play. A few seconds later I was gone.

It was six a.m. by the time I erupted from the trance. Having been in the bathroom tub for well over five hours at this point, my sweaty hand, sore from squeezing the large kitchen knife that protected me, I awaited the predator. Sure they would come any moment now, I had to be ready. Each time my hand tired, I reengaged my clasp around my weapon. I could not weaken, that was just what they wanted. In my weak moment, they would come and get me. When I heard the front door swing open and the loud voice echo through the apartment, my body froze. They were here.

When the bathroom door shot open I pushed the shower curtain aside and bolted out. Knife in hand, I was ready. Until I saw it was my mom. At the moment our eyes met, one thing was clear, the unknown predator was not only expected, but would have been preferred. When she saw my mental state, she started to scream. "OH MY GOD!!!"

"What is wrong with you, Lauri!!! What is wrong with you?! What is the matter with you?!"

With my jaw pulled to the right and the horror of my mom standing in front of me, I couldn't talk. I tried to whisper, but that made matters even worse. When I opened my disfigured mouth to speak and out came a whisper, she screamed, *"WHAT IS WRONG WITH YOU!?"* She went to grab for my shoulders, but I was gone before she could grab hold of me. Her loud voice had me in an elevated state of panic that accelerated each time she spoke. "You are supposed to be packed for Florida right now! We have a fucking plane to catch! *WHAT IS WRONG WITH YOU? WHAT THE FUCK IS WRONG WITH YOU?"*

With my jaw locked to the side, my hand clenching and my tongue swollen like a large kitchen sponge that no longer fit in my mouth, I was catapulted into a spiraling state of panic. Like a frail bird in a tin cage, petrified by a fierce approaching Rottweiler, my mother's voice shook every part of my brittle body and sent damaging vibrations through the refuge that had protected me just moments before. In a state of terror, my body reacted instantly. *TOO LOUD! TOO LOUD!*

TOOOOO LOOOOUD!!! Darting out the front door, knife in hand, hunched over like a primal being looking for cover, I was catapulted into another dimension. My only thought was escaping the noise of her loud, screeching voice that continued to shake the depths of my being. *RUN, RUN, RUN... RUN for your life! GET OUT!*

I RAN and RAN and RAN and RAN until the sound of her voice diminished to that of a distant cry. I found cover under a thick area of brush that provided sufficient camouflage to hide me from others and still allow me enough visibility to watch for any oncoming danger. Hunched over, completely drenched with sweat, knife in hand, I was planted in the middle of a cluster of small bushes that surrounded the lush gardens of a neighboring apartment building.

The protective cover of the green garden shrubs was not sufficient to shield the sharp rays of the sun that pierced my eyes. The contrast from the safe, warm, dark shelter of the bathroom tub to the hot rays of the sun grew more apparent by the moment. The bright sunlight propelled against the darkness that grew within me and I knew it was only a matter of minutes before I would have to return to my safe harbor. But not a moment before the screaming stopped.

My mother didn't realize that the ongoing yelling, intended to bring me back, was actually the very thing keeping me away. Between the sunlight and the activity of the surroundings, cars, birds and kids playing, I was close to cardiac arrest by the time the screaming finally subsided. Thirty minutes later I was able to dart from one parked car to another to make it back to the apartment. As I crept back in, I could see she had the baby and my bags fully packed. The large kitchen knife was in my back pocket, sharp end up. I attempted to hide the presence of the knife in an effort to not alert my mom of my dangerous state, but needing it close enough in the event a predator appeared unexpectedly. My mother was temporarily out of sight, but before I could make it back to the tub, she exited the bedroom and intercepted my path. She avoided direct eye contact and firmly muttered four simple words. "Get in the car." Not wanting to expose myself to sunlight again or cause her to raise her voice again, I sheepishly complied.

Drenched in sweat, with blood stains running down the sleeves of my shirt, my jaw still locked to the side and experiencing involuntary hand movements, I crept outside and crawled into the car. I slumped down in my seat to avoid being seen. I knew they were out there and the chances they saw me getting into the car were good. With a clear shot of my head, in seconds they could fire against me. I was a still target. Crouching below the view of the window, I dared not peek. Then I thought that although they could not see me now, it was not out of the question that one had already seen me and would appear at the window without notice. That thought sent my heart racing again. I knew this was a possibility, but long-term exposure of my head to the outside world was equally dangerous. As the moments passed, I calmed myself by saying, "They didn't see you or they would be here by now." Moments later, with my keen sense of hearing, I could sense their bodies slithering on the sides of the cars like snakes on the small hot pebbles, ready to bolt up and shoot me. Not only could I hear them, I could feel them. Every noise, oncoming cars, planes and human voices caused my heart to skip a beat. I just knew that the noise was "them." They were coming for me. The sound of a helicopter approached and I realized almost immediately that from a helicopter, with their special heat sensors, they could see me and shoot me even from the sky...

BANG! The car door opened in the back. The noise was my mom, putting in Madie's car seat. *Although my body remained where it was, the voice in my head said, "Sit up! Sit up! Or she is going to start yelling again! Sit up!"*

When she entered the driver's side of the car, I was sitting up the best I could manage. The knife was wedged in between my seat and the door and my hand was clenched on the door handle. My face was turned toward my window to keep her from seeing my eyes. When she started the car, she was silent, but as we approached the first light, she began to talk, something about, "I can't believe you..." As soon as the words hit the air, I opened the car door as if to jump. Unable to talk or communicate, it was my only method of letting her know that I couldn't handle noise. She screamed, "What are you doing?" I shot her a look. I have to believe she could see the terror in my eyes, for she stopped immediately and the remainder of the drive to the airport was quiet. No talking. No noises. By the time we got to the airport, my paranoia was reduced to a manageable level. I had lost the primate posture and I was able to stand up straight. I was still unable to talk and saw many people watching me, but I decided by this time, *if they kill me, they kill me. There is nothing I can do about it.* But I insisted on being far away from my mom and Madie so that they would not get shot in the crossfire. I followed them from a safe distance. My mom noted my distance upon our arrival, but said nothing. Occasionally looking back to see if I was still there, she went along with it. I spent the majority of the time on the plane in the safe shelter of the cabin bathroom. Coming out occasionally to release it for other people in need, I returned as soon as it was available again.

Due to the amount of speed I had shot, I spent the next three days awake at my aunt's house hiding in her backyard suffering from intense paranoia. My mom's entire family was there. They were all speechless when they observed my condition. Everyone, that is, except my Uncle. My uncle, who is an avid pot smoker, approached me in the yard on the second day and said something to me that was meant to communicate to me how horrified they were. I was completely unable to process the information, and have no idea what he said. I only knew that he was the messenger of the family, sent to deliver a message of disgust. Unable to process what he said, he was successful in delivering the theme. You are a huge disappointment.

There was no amount of demoralization from the others that could exceed the current state of demoralization I was already experiencing. With involuntary body twitching, inability to speak, a contorted face, hiding in the bushes of my aunt's yard, the others took turns looking out of the bay window over the sink to view me. Like an animal in a cage, I could do nothing more than allow myself to be watched. I stayed awake for the entire trip and spoke to no one. The majority of the trip was spent in the back yard or in locked rooms away from others, unable to communicate.

My mom and I never discussed this. A few days later, we were preparing to return home and I was just beginning to return to normal. Having spent over six hours in the bathroom the day before, the drug's effect on me was now just beginning to dissipate. My mom, now having experienced what I was like when I got high, was more detached from me than ever. I am sure she wanted nothing more than to just drop me off and return to her safe life, but unfortunately it was not over yet.

Upon our return home from my complete breakdown at my aunt's house, my mom noticed my car was gone. Naturally, she wanted to know where it was. I explained that Sharon had driven me home from school the week prior so I had left it at school. My mom was adamant that I explain why I would leave my car and get in Sharon's. I had no answers. The reality of the situation was that we had left at lunch time to shoot up, and due to my compromised mental state, I was unable to return to school to pick up my car.

Unwilling to accept my story, she insisted on driving me to my school at that very moment to retrieve it. When we arrived at the car, it was sitting alone in an old automotive parking lot. We had parked it away from the school so that it wouldn't get towed. As I stepped out of my mom's car, even in the distance, I could see that something was wrong. The hood appeared to be unlatched. "Get out and get your car," she yelled! "And close the hood!" As I pulled the hood up to identify what had happened to the latch, I was horrified to discover the guts were gone! The engine had been stolen? The transmission? Being a girl, I don't really know what was gone, but the best way to describe it is, "the big parts in the middle." All of them.

Under the hood, where there had been a bunch of big metal car stuff prior, now there was nothing. The death walk back to my mom's car to inform her was a slow one. I have since realized that it is a lot of work to pull an engine, a transmission or any major car part. To this day, I don't know how they did it, but they obviously have some skillful criminals in that town. For the next few weeks, my mom paid Sharon to pick me up, having no idea that we were actively engaged in drug use together.

27

ONE MORNING WHILE I WAS WAITING FOR LUCY AND GETTING ready for school, Dane entered the apartment. I had not seen him since before Florida. It was obvious that he was in a drug-crazed state. He was looking for something. He was running through the apartment looking inside of things and under things. I told him he needed to leave. He went crazy, yelling and screaming and eventually he poured my jewelry box into the toilet and attempted to flush it. In an attempt to return the favor, I took the last of his weed that he had thrown on the table and attempted to flush it. The next few minutes went by very quickly. He grabbed me and began to wrestle me down to the ground, all the while screaming, "Don't you ever throw out my drugs! I will kill you!"

Within what seemed like seconds, the situation escalated to a frightening level. He had taken a hold of my neck. With his hands firmly clasped around my neck, he began to squeeze. In a dire effort to escape, I kicked him as hard as humanly possible in the jackpot. Although that worked to free his hands from my neck, it also served to increase his anger. The baby was screaming and my thoughts were crashing upon each other, until there was black.

With one strong push, I broke free from his grasp, and ran into the kitchen. He followed just inches behind me attempting to grab me. I reached for the closest sharp knife I could find. He screamed, "ARE YOU GOING TO STAB ME BITCH? YOU GOING TO KILL ME?" I looked at him, knife in hand and said, "YOU WANT TO KILL ME? I WILL HELP DO IT FOR YOU, FUCKER!"

In a moment of complete insanity, I turned my left arm over and plunged the knife straight down into the exposed underside of my arm, directly on top of the vein. Much to my surprise when I pulled it out, blood shot up like a fountain. In my rage and desperation at that moment, I never thought about the consequence of stabbing myself, but the power of the blood erupting from my arms scared the hell out of me. A dark trickle would have been dramatic and soothing, but this water fountain, blood eruption thing made me instantly faint. When I looked at Dane, his whole mood had changed from rage to sheer panic! He cried, "Get something quick! Get something to stop the blood! Help!"

The next thing I knew there was an ambulance and paramedics present. Dane remained at the house with Madie until Lucy picked her up. When I was at the hospital I recall being truly disturbed by the doctor's repeated questioning. I didn't know if he was absent-minded or just trying to drive me crazy, but he kept on saying, "So tell me again how this happened." As if I hadn't been through enough. He was wearing me down. I kept on repeating the same story. "I was in the bathroom when the mirror broke and a shard of glass went into my arm." Lord knows, I didn't want him to think I was stupid or weak enough to get beaten up by my 'boyfriend.'

It wasn't until I returned to Lucy's later that day to pick up the baby that I looked in the mirror for the first time and saw the distinct bruises on my neck from where Dane's hands had tried to squeeze the life from me. How naïve was I to think the doctor believed the mirror story anyway? He must have thought I was truly insane telling this story while he gazed at my bruised neck. Oh well, I would never see him again.

Well into the process of eviction from my apartment, a boyfriend trying to kill me, a drug habit that threatened my life and being the sole parent responsible for Madie, Lucy and I decided it best to get some help. After a few phone calls, I was accepted to a shelter that housed abused women and children. The facility was full with a long waiting list, but they put me up in a motel pending an opening and gave me some food stamps. They also instructed me to get a restraining order as soon as possible and to take someone with me if I had to get anything out of the house. Dane realized that it was just a matter of time before Gabriel and his friends got wind of what had happened, so he went into hiding anyway.

Lucy lent me some of the welfare money she had saved, and we rented a U-haul. We didn't have much: An old ripped couch, a crib, a mattress, a small broken TV with a clothes hanger for an antenna and an old used fridge. But it was ours. With the help of a few teenagers from the street, I quickly lugged our furniture and clothes into the U-Haul truck and left. Although I had never driven a U Haul before, I was confident that being a master motorcyclist and a good driver, even on drugs, I would have no problem driving this truck. It was merely a big car.

As a side note, for anyone planning to rent a U-Haul, remember to pay attention to signs that refer to height when driving through businesses. After loading up our goods on the way to the storage area, and having not eaten all day, I decided to stop to get a taco from Jack in the Box with .92 cents I had in my purse. Both the girl at the drive-up register and I were shocked into another dimension as I drove the truck confidently up to the window and it almost smacked her little booth right off the side of the building. The top of the truck far exceeded the height of the awning that protected the drive-up window. Who reads that stuff anyway? As soon as she collected herself, she politely said, "Next time you might think about walking in," and handed me my taco.

Madie and I arrived at the motel within a few hours. As I entered the small stark room, an intense smell of disinfectant hit my nose. My gut rebounded as memories of distant places flashed in my mind and then disappeared before I could fully process them.

The room had two twin beds with flowered nylon bedspreads, a TV and a bathroom. The devastation of recent events was exacerbated by the sense of isolation of the motel. The sound of freeway traffic and warm air hit my back as I stood at the door. I was alone. I closed the door and picked up my beautiful baby girl and rocked her gently in my arms as I sang her song, *Mommies little princess…mommies little baby girl. . .* And then I cried. Through my clouded eyes, I began to see my reflection in the long mirror on the wall. As my vision cleared, the large hand prints on my neck stood out as a symbol of what I had become. How would I protect my perfect little angel if I can't even protect myself? So small, so alone. At nineteen, I felt old beyond my years, but at this moment I felt dangerously frail.

I sat up all night. I had to figure a way out. I had to be strong. I had to be more for Madie. Having missed school now for several weeks, and certain that I had already been kicked out, I thought maybe I could use this recent situation to gain sympathy and they would let me back in. Then I could get a job and be a better mom. I would never let this happen again. I was devastated. We had nothing. The small life I had built up was completely gone. I was horrified that I could do this to Madie. I had to fix it.

I called the school and told them of my state. I was living in a motel with my child after being beaten. They said they would allow me to come to school with Madie in tow for a few days if I could assure them that she would be quiet while I was in class. Madie was always a good baby, so I thought if I could get a few bottles and bring her little plastic car seat, she would be fine. I could continue to do my school work and she would sleep and drink her milk. For the next few days, I was determined that if I did nothing else, I would go to school.

With no money or car, I stood on the freeway on ramp with Madie on my hip, her small bed handle hanging from my shoulder and my thumb erected, hoping to hitch a ride to school. People were much more willing to pick up a young girl with a child and, although I knew it wasn't the best idea, it was all I had left. Each day that I had to hitchhike to school with my little angel on my hip, my fear increased.

A few days later, we were picked up by an old lady, destined for the women's shelter. It was a huge institution with long corridors filled with bedrooms. The steel doors and large brick walls were similar to many of the institutions I had been in, but this time it was different.

The love in the eyes of the people there exuded enough warmth to hide the bleak exterior. In each room there were two bunk beds, allowing a minimum of four people per room. If you had enough children, you could have your own room. If you only had one, you shared a room. The large structure was flowing with movement all day with women with broken bones and broken lives, struggling to put the pieces back together. Their smiles and strength hid the broken hearts, bandages and bruised faces from the children. Like a crystal ball, the children each looked into the eyes of their mother to affirm their safety. Breaking only at darkness, after the children were asleep, to weep silently in their pillows, they would shield the children from the shadows.

Although we had classes and education while we were there, I learned more from the strength of the women around me: some good, some not so good. Madie and I shared a room with a lady named Joanna and her fifteen year old daughter, Andie. Joanna had been repeatedly beaten by a man she had been with for years. This wasn't the first time he beat her and it wouldn't be the last. She was a repeat visitor at the shelter. "It's the drugs that are making him crazy," she said. If only you *really* knew him."

Joanna was on something called Methadone maintenance. She and her boyfriend had been heroin addicts for years. When the habit became more than they could support, they were assisted by the state. About four years before, when they began maintenance, they would pick up small bottles of medicine once a week from a clinic. Although I understood the concept, I didn't fully comprehend why the state would give out drugs, but I didn't ask any questions. I just listened. Joanna seemed to know a lot more about life that I did, so I would sit quietly and soak it in.

Joanna explained that they used to let her take the medicine home, but one night when she and her boyfriend went out to a movie, her daughter, Andie and a friend drank their Methadone. Andie's friend died. She went on to say that Methadone is poison to people who are not addicted. She explained that after the death of Andie's friend, they make her pick up her doses and ingest them at the clinic. Regardless of the bad choices I had seen in others and made for myself, I would always wonder why the death of a child did little but change the method of delivery.

I could not continue school during my stay at the shelter. It was important that the abuser never know where we were, so we pretty much had to say goodbye to our old lives for the safety of the abused and our children. That being said, all of us did it for the safety of our children, not ourselves.

Unlike many of the others who would repeatedly return to the abuser, I was thankful for once that I had an inability to bond. I had no thought of ever returning to Dane. I was very focused on the fact that I had no life plans at all. That realization, along with the knowledge that my beautiful little baby looked to me each day with hope and love in her eyes, created more guilt for me than I could absorb. She was so hopeful and full of love. The love and confidence in her eyes screamed, *MY MOMMY WILL TAKE CARE OF ME!* The fact that I had no plan shook my very being. I was supposed to be her anchor, but instead I was pulling her down with me like a brick. The love I returned to her felt like a lie. I slept a lot to avoid thinking.

During my time at the shelter, I had a good deal of time to reflect on my life. I thought of the good people and the bad people that I had chosen and I decided I needed to get some of my old friends back. When I received my first welfare check at the center, I cashed it, and determined to make my life better, I called 411 and located Bush at his parent's house. Having only talked to him a handful of times since I was a kid, it was as if we never stopped communicating. We picked up right where we left off. I told him about what had happened to me—not the shooting up part, just the baby and the beating. For the next few weeks Bush would call the pay phone at the center to check in on me. His calls made me feel protected and gave me hope.

Part of the program at the shelter was designed to put some of our welfare checks aside in savings, after doling out a bit of pocket money, to prepare for our new lives. After just a few months, Madie and I were able to rent a nice apartment in a big complex. As a parting gift, the shelter gave us a beautiful set of living room furniture that had been recently donated. It was fabulous; better than anything I ever had!

I was also surprised to learn that they had secured me a job. I was to work at the apartments as a maintenance person in exchange for a reduction in rent. I liked this, as it was kind of a butch, tomboy way to make a living. It was right up my alley. I couldn't have been happier. It looked like I would be able to provide a life for Madie after all. I could look into her eyes confidently, and although she was still a baby, I could tell her things were going to be okay, and mean it.

To add to this run of new good luck, I was able to buy a car from the Ugly Duckling Car Rental agency that I found in the classified Ads for $300. Let's just say, if Ugly Duckling didn't want it, it was *not a looker*, but it got me from point A to point B.

The rust color matched the rust around the frame, a hole in the trunk provided access to the car through the back seat in case I lost my keys, and when the ignition failed, I was able to start it by climbing underneath the car and hitting the starter with a screwdriver to create a spark. This part was almost a feature for me because it enhanced my tomboy attitude. Although I had really no idea of how or why it worked, I acted as if I did. The ability to start my car with a screwdriver and a car part, made me feel like a mechanic and I loved it. All quirks aside, I loved that car!

A few weeks after having the car, the outside mirror fell off the side. I didn't mind. I kept it in my purse as a make-up mirror. For some reason I felt cool pulling a car part out of my purse to check out my make-up. Looking back I realize it was very white trash kind of move. Who knew?

Jewel and Dustin also stopped by once in a while and Bush called regularly to see how we were. We had a nice one-bedroom apartment with a playground and a swimming pool right outside of our back sliding door. Madie had her crib from storage and I had my bed. This was more than we could have ever hoped for.

Although I was thankful for everything the shelter did for us, I was unable to maintain the job. My job was to drive around on a golf cart and fix up apartments to prepare them to be rented. This included taking off the face plates from the walls, painting the place and performing a commercial style cleaning routine on the joint. This just wasn't my gig. Although I thought I looked great in my wife beater and torn jeans, I got more paint on me and on the carpet than I did on the walls and my ratio of hours to apartments was not good. I hated the cleaning part. The dirt grossed me out and made me itchy. By mutual agreement, they increased my rent and I stopped working for them. Eventually the white paint came out of my hair.

I remember how excited I was the day Savannah called. It turns out that Savannah was pregnant at the same time I was and she had given birth to a little boy. When Savannah first came over, I immediately knew she had changed. Her little boy was beautiful and I saw her immense love for him. She loved being a mom and her whole world revolved around her baby. Much to my surprise, she had even cut down on shooting up and switched to a more mellow drug. She called it "wack." It was a cigarette soaked in angel dust. She pulled it out of her purse and put it in the fridge. She said, "It just kind of mellows you out…doesn't make you act weird, and it's pretty cheap." She told me it was fairly popular in the neighborhood in La Puente and we could try it after the kids went to sleep. I thought little of it; it was just interesting.

That night after the kids went to sleep, Savannah pulled the vial out of the fridge and showed me how to use it. The vial was about two inches full of a clear liquid. We dipped our cigarettes in it and waited for them to dry. As soon as they dried, we lit them and smoked. The best way to describe the feeling was a sensation of slow motion with trailing vision and the sound of large helicopters in my ears. I felt very robotic. It was interesting, but the more we smoked it, the spacier I got. Somehow I knew if I kept on using it, I would be lacking several brain cells in very short order. Savannah continued to come over from time to time with tattooed guys and wack. I always thought about how nice it was for her to come all the way over. I knew she cared about me.

Before I knew it, I had a new boyfriend. His apartment was directly above mine. He was my age, had a normal job and wasn't a drug addict, with the exception of some social beer and weed. Since I had not been shooting up, I also appeared to be slightly normal. Much like the rest of my life, it was not long-lived. The week of Valentine's Day, he and I got into a big fight about god knows what and broke up.

When Jewel and Dustin stopped by the next day, they suggested a weekend trip to Catalina to get away and clear my mind. I had no job or responsibilities and my mom could watch Madie, so it sounded great. All except the money part. They suggested bringing someone with money. Before I knew it, Bush was recruited.

Catalina is a little island about twenty-two miles off the coast from where we live. There is a ferry that goes back and forth on a regular basis taking cars and people to and from the island. As close as it was, it was the perfect "getaway place" and it was within Bush's budget at less than $20 a ferry ride. I had never been there, but I had heard about it from the beach. They had scuba, snorkeling and lots of bars. It sounded like the perfect resolution to a crazy week.

When we arrived in Catalina we realized that we needed reservations, especially because it was a Holiday weekend. None of us were old enough or worldly enough to have thought of this in advance, so we were stuck. With our heads in our hands, sitting on the curb, we decided on desperate measures. We would beg. With a little desperation and some premeditated tears, Jewel and I we were able to rent the maid's quarters on the roof of a small motel.

As we climbed the narrow stairway that was marked "roof access" we were wondering what we had gotten ourselves into. When we pushed the roof door open, we were immediately accosted by the bright sun and a small circle of Hispanic men drinking. Not appreciating our bold entrance on their little get-together, they muttered a few unfriendly words in Spanish and continued drinking. We looked around and wondered if we had gone the wrong way. Toward the back of the roof, there was a large shack made of metal and wood. Although we highly doubted this was a room, we were surprised to see that our key fit the door. The dark square room was just large enough to accommodate the full size mattress bed that lay on the floor, leaving just a narrow walkway in front. The window was covered with an old sheet and there was a small can for an ashtray on the sill. We could certainly make this work. It beat being outside through the night.

We decided that since we were staying two nights, Bush and I would sleep on the bed the first night. Dustin and Jewel would lie in the pathway with a blanket and we would switch the second night.

That night in bed, Bush began to tell me that he had been in love with me since we were young. He said that he never told me because I was dating Jeremy, but I was all he ever wanted and he was deeply in love with me. He reached over to kiss me. Although flattered, I was also disturbed. Hell, I had just broken up with my boyfriend and Bush was like a brother to me! I told him I loved him, but not like that. He got very upset and began ranting about how I always chose losers and how I can't accept a nice guy who really loves me. Suddenly he jumped up and screamed, "No one wants me here! I am going out to sleep with the wild boars!" Our tin door opened and slammed shut as he stormed out.

It was obvious that he was not coming back anytime soon and although the lights were off, given the volume of the recent argument, I knew Jewel and Dustin were both wide awake. I said, "Why don't you guys take the bed and I will take the floor. I won't sleep."

They agreed. Within minutes they were doing the wild thing on the bed. I found this very awkward and weird, especially on the heels of the recent fight and the fact that I was still crying, but I tried to ignore it. A few minutes later, Jewel said, "Lauri. Do you want to join us?" I was horrified. What do I say to that? Hmm... let's see... continue to cry or have an orgy with the yellow tooth hippie people? Are you freaking kidding me? Disgusting! Attempting to be polite, I simply responded, *"No thank you."* Funny how, given the absurdity of the situation, I still chose to answer politely. I mean really. It would have been equally polite if they had asked, "Lauri, do you mind if while you are crying on the floor, we have dirty nasty sex just a few feet away from you?"

A few minutes later, again, "Lauri, we want you to join us." At this point I had been covering my ears trying to block out the noises so that I could cry in peace. I quickly responded again, "No really, not interested." After a while I finally blocked them out and started to doze off.

I was propelled back to consciousness when I felt Dustin grabbing my legs and Jewel grabbing my arms. Before I realized what was happening, they had torn down the curtain sheets from the windows, ripped it into shreds and threw me on the bed. As I struggled against them, they worked as a team to tear off my long tank top and panties and secure my limbs with the curtain sheets. They wrapped the long strips around my ankles and my wrists. One by one, they worked to create a slip-knot that would tighten if I pulled. Which I did. Within seconds I was completely immobile. Still not aware of exactly what they were thinking, I laughed. "OK, you guys, you win. Now please let me go. You saw what just happened. I am *really* not in the mood for playing. Come on you guys, now."

They exchanged a wordless glance and Dustin climbed on top of me. As he did Jewel closed in on my face as if to kiss me. Are you kidding? "There is no fucking way!" Still thinking maybe this was some kind of friendly hippie activity that I was not familiar with, I squirmed from side to side to avoid letting Dustin penetrate me. I turned my head toward the wall to keep Jewel's dirty mouth away from mine, still saying, "Really you guys, stop, I am not into this."

It did not take long to become acutely aware of just how serious they were. Jewel held my body and put her face on my breasts as Dustin violated me. I was horrified and panicked. My wiggling, screaming and crying, *"LET ME GO! GET OFF OF ME! STOP! STOP! STOP! STOP!!!!"* had no affect on them.

The feeling of her mouth on my body and him inside of me was horrifying. The repulsion shot intense pressure through my head. My raw throat stung from the vibration of my screams. *"LET ME GO! GET OFF OF ME!!!! STOP!!!! STOP!!!! STOP!!!! STOP!!!! STOP!!!! STOP!!!! STOP!!!! Please stop..."*

As I fought to free myself, the bonds became unbearably tight. After several hours my body was limp and lifeless. In a state of disgust and final exhaustion, I mentally drifted away from the room and could no longer feel their presence. I was numb to their touches. I was completely quiet. In a state of complete disconnect, with all defenses down, this would be the first time I would climax sexually. I would never forgive myself. With no energy left to fight, my body responded without my permission. I was horrified. As with the experience at the river, I blamed myself. Shortly after the sun rose, I was awakened as he untied me and kissed me on the cheek. My arms and ankles were purple and swollen from the restraints and I stared at the ceiling as involuntary tears rolled down my cheek.

When Bush finally returned Jewel and Dustin were asleep on the floor and I was curled up in the corner of the bed alone, fully clothed and wrapped tightly in the blanket for protection. My sweats covered my swollen arms and ankles. I would not tell him what happened. Although my eyes were swollen, I knew he thought I was crying over our fight. That was fine.

That was until Dustin woke and blurted out, "Feel special Bush! She wouldn't have sex with you, but she had sex with both of us. She's a real angel…" I said nothing. I was sure he thought I was a whore. The only defense I had was the purple bruises that marked my wrists and ankles, but not wanting to talk about it or ever think about it again, I covered my wrists with my sweats and we never spoke of it again. I didn't know that this was rape until many years later because I always remembered when my body responded and I convinced myself that at some level I must have wanted it, or that wouldn't have happened. They speak of shutting things out of your mind, a sort of forgetting. This one went into that category until many years later. I completely forgot it happened. The only obvious residual affect was the urgent need to get as high as possible when I returned home.

My most influential neighbor was a black man who lived upstairs with his wife and his son, Jamal. Although his wife seemed very normal, "Booker" would come home on payday, and the apartment would get dark. Booker was a serious free-baser. He would spend his entire paycheck on freebase and then attempt to steal money from his wife's purse. I never interacted with Booker until the day Savannah showed up and suggested we buy some of his coke. That was when it started all over again. Savannah and her white supremacist friends would come over with wack and money and we would pick up from Booker. Before I knew it, I was addicted again. Hiding behind things with a kitchen knife, sweating, paranoid and crazy. Again, I was spending my whole welfare check on coke and I couldn't pay rent. Over and over again, I would destroy my life. I cannot explain why, other than to say, I was building memories I wanted to forget. The drugs were the only reprieve I had. I could forget everything. For a few hours, like Azalea put it, I could free my mind.

In an effort to keep Madie fed, I rented out my living room to a guy and his girlfriend. They drank a lot, but did not use serious drugs. I also rented the space above my carport. It was a four by eight foot box that I rented to a homeless guy for $50 a month. I thought he was renting it to store his belongings, but was surprised to find out, he was sleeping in it when he crawled out one morning.. C'est la vie. It was far enough away from the apartment that I never saw him except on payday. I continued as much as I could to shoot up only at night so that Madie would not be affected during the day. At this point, she was almost a year old, but very aware. Although she wasn't speaking much, her emotional state shifted along with my state of intoxication. Even though she never saw me shoot up, my addiction was severely affecting our lives.

On her one-year birthday, when I got my check, I took her out and bought party hats, invitations, cups and plates. She was so excited! When we got home, Booker showed up and I got high. For the next few days I was on a long binge that would keep me isolated in a dark room, curtains drawn and unable to speak. I was unable to communicate at all, so the invitations remained in the bag. On her birthday, we sat alone at a table with party hats and plates. I will never forget the sadness. I was a failure as her mother and even if she didn't know, I knew. I deserved only to die and I knew it.

The last time I ever saw Savannah was a few months later. She rushed in to tell me to grab my things, we were going to Vegas and that she was getting married! I was shocked. I told her I had no one to watch Madie. She quickly brought me up to speed. Her mom had died of cancer and her step dad kicked her out. She and her son had been living in her car when she met this rich biker guy. She explained, "He is not the best looking guy, but he loves us and will take care of us." She told me he bought her a house and they have a nanny who will watch the kids. She ended by saying there was a limo waiting outside.

When we arrived in Vegas, I met her husband. He was slightly over three-hundred pounds and a serious drug-dealing biker. Her husband brought his whole biker following with him and two kilos of coke to keep them happy. Although they were into doing cocaine, they were adamant about "no junkies." Savannah explained that she was never going to shoot up again. She said they were very serious about their business and they saw junkies as weak and a definite threat. I couldn't believe it. The girl that was so into it—the one that got me hooked—was quitting? Just like that? There was no way. It was just a matter of time. Especially with the unlimited coke supply that she had access to now.

The day we arrived, he gave us two-thousand dollars and sent us to the mall for wedding attire. Savannah bought a white leather skirt and some white sequined pumps and I got a black leather skirt and some leopard sequined pumps. When we arrived back in the room, her fiancé laid out some coke and told us to do it. I had no interest in snorting coke and I politely said, "No thanks." But Savannah insisted that it was very strong and I would definitely like it, so I tried it. Now when I say he laid it out, I do not mean in a line. He poured about a quarter cup of coke on the table in a pile. He gave me large straw and said, "Put your nose down in it."

I immediately realized I was in trouble when a massive amount of coke went into my nostrils. My ears immediately turned on like stereo speakers!. Savannah saw what happened and said, "Oh no!" It was more than any person should ever do in one snort. I ran to the bathroom and attempted to blow, blow, blow my nose out! Quickly! My heart was pounding like a railroad engine and my jaw was starting to go round and round and now my hand. I was in trouble. Locked in the bathroom for the next two hours unable to speak, it was a problem, or should I say, I was a problem. As Savannah pounded on the door, I was only able to mutter, "*Tooooo muchhhh...*" She returned about an hour later with a handful of Valium and I took it.

At the wedding the next morning, I was unable to stand up. Her new husband gave me two-hundred dollars and said, "Catch a plane home. We never want to see you again." I felt like a piece of dirt. I was being terminated for being a loser from a group of drug-addict bikers. Could it be any worse?

As I walked out of the hotel, I decided to make a bad situation better. I would hitchhike home and save the money. This was a great plan. Although upset about what happened, I was also glad that I had just made some money.

My first ride took me for about an hour and dropped me off in the middle of the desert. I quickly realized that hitchhiking alone in the middle of the desert at night was not the best plan. *Do you know there are no streetlights in the desert?* Standing on the side of a dirt road, so dark that I couldn't even see my hands, I came to the realization that there are rattle snakes in the desert. In this blackness I wouldn't even know if I was standing next to one. Furthermore, now that I had walked a few feet, I didn't know if I was on the dirt or on the road. Every few minutes I would see a small light approaching and wait, hoping they didn't hit me as they flew by. The 18 wheelers, in particular, flew by like the speed of light, *whoooosh*. Most of them never even saw me. I was just a speck in the darkness. The ones that did see me, and attempted to stop, were light years ahead of me by the time the brakes were able to bring their gigantic rig to a halt. Only a few were willing to wait for me to run up to them. I slept in their bed shelves and smoked their cigarettes all of the way back to Elsinore to pick up Madie and return home on the bus. With no money and a rapidly growing drug habit, I returned home to find we had been evicted again.

With limited time left at my apartment, things were getting stressful. My new roommate and his girlfriend started fighting a lot. One day, while in my bedroom, I heard screaming. I ran into the living room to find Madie crying. I rushed over to her to see what was wrong.

She had been sitting on the floor playing when I left the room just minutes prior. Now she remained in the exact same spot, but now she crying, or more accurately at this point, she was screaming. With no other logical explanation, I assumed she was feeling traumatized by the yelling. I picked her up and rocked her, but it didn't help. When I attempted to put her down, she screamed more. For the life of me, I couldn't figure out what was wrong. Finally, I saw it. Her leg had been clearly broken. I could see the bump where her bone had been severed. Horrified, I started to scream and not knowing what to do, I phoned 911.

We were brought to the hospital and she was x-rayed and given a cast up to her thigh. When the doctor asked, I told him what I knew, which was only that my roommates got into a fight, she started crying and when I tried to pick her up, she started screaming. And that was it. I later found out that when my roommate's girlfriend smacked him, he fell directly onto Madie. For the life of me, I couldn't figure out why they didn't tell me. I was sure from his response when we returned from the hospital that he had no idea he broke her leg. He was horrified. I have to assume they were scared to tell me what really happened before. I was just relieved that she was now okay. The next day Madie and I went food shopping with the money from Savannah's biker husband and returned home to find a social worker at my door.

She told me that a neighbor had reported the yelling and the broken leg as a possible child abuse case. I explained what had happened with my roommate and his girlfriend. I also told her that I was very informed on child abuse from my classes and loved my daughter immensely and would never hit her. She thanked me for my time and left. I felt glad that there were people like that. I was not upset that she came, but instead happy that there were people who protected kids. I was even thankful for my neighbors, whoever they were, because they too were out to protect kids. I never saw the hypocrisy of my situation.

28

WITH NOWHERE TO GO, WE MOVED IN WITH A GUY FOR A FEW weeks and then I called my mother. She let me stay at her house for one week while we figured out a solution. She made it clear that Madie was the only reason she would even go that far. I understood. By the next day, she had found me a job and a place to live. There was an ad in the Pennysaver from a single dad who was a fireman in Lake Forest with two small children who needed a live-in nanny. My mom answered the ad and set the whole thing up. Madie and I would be moving to Lake Forest the next day. He was a nice man and handsome for his age. He had two children, a boy around nine and a little girl around six. They were adorable. My job was to wake up and walk them to the YMCA for camp and pick them up at the end of the day.

When a few of my friends stopped by to visit, we drank some Boones Farm-like stuff that was in the fridge. I was sure their dad wouldn't mind. The label said Dom Pérignon. Now I know, not like Boones Farm after all. Live and learn. Anyway, Madie and I were moving again.

After calling all of my resources, I was able to get a place to stay from Bush. Bush was working for a telemarketing company. He had been doing this for years. He had a great radio type voice and could come up with tricky sayings very quickly to close a deal. He sold everything over the phone; timeshares, film, loans, and he was working some deal for a telemarketing place where he was managing their office. Bush rented a motel room for us about twenty minutes north of my hometown. Bush, Madie and I stayed in a small room. He continued to profess his love for me, but never approached me physically again for fear of rejection.

By this point, Bush knew clearly about my downfall with shooting up and was determined that if nothing else, he would prove he loved me by getting me to turn my life around. Our new health plan started off the next morning with an Egg McMuffin for each of us and a membership to the gym. Bush was confident that my new way of life would steer me in the right direction. He was insistent that he would not let me use again. Although we bought a membership, we never actually saw the inside of the gym.

Two days of drinking and hanging out at the motel and Bush returned home with a bindle of coke from work and a speech. His speech was about moderate drug use, snorting only occasionally. I guess one of the guys at work had been getting him high for the past few days and he was now to the point where he couldn't stop. He had to frame the deviation from the prior suggested path with a new crafty speech. As I mentioned, he was a master with words. It actually sounded good. Unfortunately, the sight of the coke had turned the monster inside of me back on. I had to have it. I was fine if it wasn't around me, but the minute I saw it, I was gone. It was at this point that I knew I could convince him to let me slam. I knew he would have to use the rest of the coke because the cravings where on and given the choice of flushing it or both using how we wanted to, he would fold. I had an old needle in my stuff that was bent and the numbers were worn off, but given the circumstances it would probably work. I was surprised to see that not only did I convince him to let me use, he wanted to try it. I felt guilty, but now that that dope was here I had to have it and this was the only way. Due to his sensible nature, I knew he would not do it again. Not knowing how to do it himself, I had to inject him. Given the choice of neither of us shooting up, or helping Bush to shoot up for the first time, there was nothing to think about. After we came down that night, we were both upset about our choice and decided to get back in to the healthy life. Bush called his boss and said he didn't want to work at this office anymore due to the drugs. His boss transferred him to my hometown. This was perfect. We were able to rent a two bedroom upstairs apartment in an area that I knew.

Bush, Madie and I stayed at the apartment for a few weeks before the argument. Although Bush never put pressure on me again for a relationship, he was clear on this particular day that he intended for us to be a family. He professed his love for Madie and me and reiterated his intention to care for us. I can see clearly now as I look back that Bush was a nice guy with a good sense of humor and personality and all of his cards were on the table. A relationship with Bush would have proven way too intimate for me because he knew me better than anyone else. I needed to be with the dark, mysterious type. Being "real" with someone completely grossed me out. It felt disgusting and I felt too exposed. After his fair share of rejection, Bush decided that if he couldn't have me, he didn't want to live with me. He told me to find a roommate. He said he would pay for the first two months and then he left.

Now, not only was I back in my hometown, but I was only a few miles from the trailer park again. The roommate I found was my dealer Bo's older brother, Damien. I found out after he moved in that Damien was a distributor for Bo. This was good and bad. Good, due to the fact that I only had to leave my room to pick up; bad, in that I only had to leave my room to pick up.

After only a few months in my new apartment, I could feel the darkness closing in. Damien was much older than me. I think he was probably close to forty. Although he didn't do coke himself, he was heavily addicted to speed. He was extremely unattractive and perverted. He was also one of the scariest men I had ever met, up until that point. I often wondered if Damien was his given name or he had inherited it, due to the persistent presence of evil that he possessed. Everything about him was scary, but since he had the drugs, he always had people over, mostly girls. In need of a fix, they ignored the rest. I think it made him feel important. In actuality, the only thing important to anyone was the drugs. He spoke of death incessantly and had girls as young as fourteen in his room to exchange sexual favors for coke. He would speak about it afterwards in a graphic, repulsive manner and then laugh. Even though it was obvious that we were all repulsed by his nasty tales, no one was willing to confront him for fear of losing access to the drugs. Then one day I saw his evilness truly materialize.

Madie and I had picked up a small kitten. She was grey and white and fluffy and we both loved her. One night Damien came out of his room, picked up the kitten, opened the sliding glass door and said, "Watch this." Before I could reach him, he catapulted this tiny helpless kitten into the next building and crushed it. Before I could even process the horror of what I had just witnessed, he quickly turned and grabbed Madie, who was sitting close to the door and said, "*NEXT!*" I let out a piercing scream as he swung her small frame around in a circle as if to throw her off, and then he gently put her down. He walked away laughing as I sat trembling. From that day forward I was petrified of him. I knew I couldn't kill him, but I needed him to go away. I asked him to move, but that only pissed him off. He stopped paying rent and installed a deadlock on his bedroom door.

Over the next few months we had a constant flow of visitors. One of our usual customers was a white hooker from the Mexican side of town who lived with her sugar daddy in a trailer park. Her name was Cherry. Cherry had completely given up on life. She would show up on our doorstep a few times a week in a dirty night gown, robe and slippers, with no regard for the part of world that operated "normally." She left her trailer solely for the purpose of making money or picking up.

With no regard for time of day or night, if she had money, she was there. If we were asleep, she would throw rocks at the window until we woke up. Oftentimes her jaw was locked shut from the amount of cocaine she had ingested and she was unable to speak. Looking over her shoulder for night ghosts, she would reach her jittery hand in the crack of the door with a roll of money and wordlessly Damien would return a bindle and close the door.

There was also a constant flow of young girls.

I was surprised the day my little sister Alyssa showed up. Although she had come with friends to visit me, they were very excited to find out my roommate dealt coke. Alyssa's punker friends were Zena and Mona. Zena was a beautiful girl with powder white skin, large blue eyes and green and purple hair. Mona was Zena's sidekick and they were inseparable. Alyssa informed me that her new friends wanted to buy some coke and that she wanted to try shooting up with them. I was horrified! She followed the request by telling me that I was the only one she would allow to inject her. The more I insisted that I could never, and would never do this, challenging her to look at the way I was deteriorating, the more adamant she became that either I do it, or she would go somewhere else and have it done and maybe die. She insisted that if she did it with me, I would be able to protect her. After a very heated conversation, she turned to leave in search of a needle. In fear that something might happen to her, I reluctantly agreed.

I was revolted at the thought, but I didn't know what else to do. Now I was taking my baby sister's life in my hands. What had I become? Luckily she only did it occasionally after that day, and unlike me, she never became a junkie. At some level, that made it easier for me. It was only a few months later that her friend Zena died of an overdose. She was sixteen.

Before I knew it there was another notice on my door. I stayed for the customary three month period before they put the locks on the door. I was forever grateful the day Damien died while driving drunk. It gave me a great sense of relief. Madie and I were safe now. I have never wished for someone to die. But I was terrified of him. To me, he represented everything that was evil. At this point I was twenty years old and people were dying all around me. Danny, Gabriel's friend who rented out my garage had died in prison. Alvin died of cirrhosis and now Zena and Damien. As I learned with Alvin way back when, we knew the price when we enrolled in the game. Death was always a part of our lives.

Now, having to move, with no ideas, and almost out of options, I ventured out one day to look for Cherry. I thought maybe she could help. Having survived for years with nothing and a vicious drug habit, Cherry knew things. When she wasn't completely out of her mind, she told tales of people and places from the past. The girl had been around and she knew stuff, survival type stuff. Although Cherry was white as day, she always hung out in a Mexican neighborhood, at Mexican speaking bars and spoke fluent Spanish. Her favorite bar was just over a mile from our apartment. Leaving Madie with one of the neighbor ladies to babysit, I walked down the street in pursuit of Cherry.

The first thing I noticed was that Cherry was not at the bar. The second thing I noticed was that I was the only chick at the bar. Filled with Hispanic men, looking like they were on lunch break from their construction jobs, the bar got quiet and several of the guys were staring at me. I don't know if it was because I was white or simply because I was female. Feeling uncomfortable and out of place, I turned to walk away. Before I could cross the parking lot a girl whom I hadn't noticed erupted out of the barroom door and shouted, "Hey! What are you doing here lady?"

This was the first time I laid eyes on Ramona. Ramona was a Mexican girl with long black hair and chipped front teeth who spoke broken English and walked like a man. I said, "*Oh, just lookin' for someone.*" She said, "*Come here pretty lady, maybe you found her.*" I was flushed with embarrassment and intrigued at the same time. We began to talk. Ramona quickly became my sidekick. My life at the apartments ended at the same time as my car. The old duckling died, but my new life with Ramona had just begun. After just days of knowing each other, Ramona suggested Madie and I move in with her and her "husband" and her two kids. She lived about ten minutes inland from the beach in a lower class Hispanic neighborhood in a small apartment house. As confusing as it was, Ramona preferred women, but also had a husband with whom she had borne two children. Ramona loved her kids and stayed with her husband because he supported them and kept them safe. Ramona had a great dislike for men and a passion for beautiful women. She didn't care for cocaine, but she had an ongoing romance with heroin.

At this point of my life, I could see how cocaine was taking everything from me. It not only controlled all of my money, but it was destroying my ability to be a mom. Madie was always able to sense when I was on a binge and the guilt afterwards was enough to make me near suicidal with remorse.

It was a vicious cycle of shooting up, losing control of my body and mind in a dark hell, coming out, knowing that I had spent everything and fully aware of the evil that I was bringing to my daughter's innocent life, wanting to die, swearing to do better and then shooting up again.

Ramona explained to me that we could pick up some of the best heroin for just ten dollars a balloon at the very bar where I had been looking for Cherry. A bit concerned about the use of heroin, I hesitated. I knew it was her life, but I wasn't sure it was for me. In the best broken English words she could muster, she said "Relax baby, don't be crazy. Just relax. I will show you the good life."

Ramona was right. Not only would the heroin help me to stop doing coke, it was a cheaper high. Even if it made me throw up, I could get sick and then go to sleep. The switch from coke to heroin became a fabulous detox/savings plan for me. Throw up, sleep and save. It was a move in the right direction.

Although Ramona had a crush on me, we never had a thing. I loved her young spirit and her ways reminded me of my sisters in juvie, but even if I was going gay, she wasn't my type. Even so, she was captivating.

Ramona and I spent many days hitchhiking from her house to the bar to pick up and back again. During those times she would tell me stories about her life in Mexico when she was a little girl and the wonderful life she had there. Although her mother had died when she was very young, she always spoke of her dad and his enormous strength. She reminisced about their night rides through the village on donkeys with no lights other than the illumination from the thick blanket of stars that watched over them for protection. Ramona's love for heroin was synonymous to the way she felt about her father, completely safe and at peace. I never asked her about her hatred for men, but I had to assume someone had hurt her. She was under constant protection with her dark clothes and an even darker demeanor.

I did heroin a few times a week. Forgetting my detox/savings plan completely in very short order, I started mixing the heroin with coke. It helped to take the edge off and greatly reduced the paranoia. Although it sounded like a miracle cure, my ability to measure correctly failed miserably in very short order. I would use all the heroin and be left with only coke, doomed into hiding, in an attempt to escape the night ghosts. Ramona hated it when I did coke. She insisted I stay away from the coke and stay "good" on heroin.

Ramona's dealer, Paco was a short Mexican guy who didn't speak a word of English, but through Ramona managed to tell me that he liked me. Paco began to show up regularly at Ramona's house. He would deliberately wait until after Ramona's husband left for work to drop in. He made a habit of bringing free heroin for me to prove his love. I was not using heroin daily since I was still more interested in coke, so I would share it with Ramona. After her morning shot, Ramona would cook up Mexican food like her grandmother taught her. She made burritos that tasted like they fell straight from heaven. All was well. After a few weeks, I was so grateful for Paco's generosity, I became his "girlfriend." This was the first and only relationship I had with a person who spoke no English. Due to the fact that my Spanish was limited to ordering a taco or picking up heroin, we had no disputes.

My relationships were clearly based on meeting basic survival needs and accessibility to drugs. I had no clue how to really bond with anyone, but I genuinely loved the people in my life to the extent that my limited capabilities allowed.

I remember the first night Ramona showed up at my bedroom door in the middle of the night asking if she could sleep in my bed. By this point I knew her enough to know she wouldn't hit on me and also knew that she didn't like sex with her husband. She felt safer around me. Of course, I let her sleep next to me. Her husband took issue with this arrangement. And after just a few occurrences, he insisted that I move.

With no plan in mind, again, a Spanish kid named Manuel from the bar offered up his place with his grandma just twenty minutes north. Since I had no real attachment to Paco, I thought, *What the heck?*

There were a number of people from Manuel's extended family already living in the house, so Madie, Manuel and I slept on a dirty mattress in the garage. When Madie would fall asleep, Manuel would make sexual demands on me. I was mortified, but I had nowhere else to go and his grandma was feeding Madie, so I knew I had to do it. When it was done, I would go inside and wash off and attempt to forget it.

At this point, I was no longer receiving my welfare checks. In order to receive a check, I needed to have a permanent address. I had switched homes so much over the past few months that my welfare check had been sent to Ramona's house and then returned. After several calls from Manuel's house phone I was able to arrange a day and time to go to social services to pick up my checks. Manuel's mom gave us a ride. With two checks in hand and the horror of the occurrences on the garage floor on my mind, I knew I had to get out. If I began having my checks sent to Manuel's, I would be stuck. I needed a new address.

I took the bus to Gabriel's mom's motel in the hopes that he was out of prison. Gabriel and his siblings, when not in prison, would use their mom's motel room as a sanctuary. They would stop to take a break, devise a new plan, get money from their mom, or simply use the bathroom to shoot up. Although she didn't approve of her kids' lifestyle choices, she had long ago lost any hope of ever changing them. She sat in her big chair in a state of complete submission, her purse clutched to her hip to protect what little of her social security check remained.

Although the constant moves might seem alarming at this point, I was completely confident in my ability to secure a new plan. I always lived one day at a time, even one hour at a time. I always knew if all else failed, all that I needed was a new plan. Even more surprising was my mental and emotional state. I was always calmest in the midst of the storm. Not knowing what was next, where I would end up, or with whom, I was completely at peace. Just as confining as it was to be under another person's control, there was a freedom in not knowing where I was going next.

Their motel was located on a busy boulevard lined with cheap motels, buses and homelessness and everything that went with it. When I arrived, Gabriel's mom was sitting in her large recliner watching game shows and the door was wide open. I quickly determined that Gabriel's mother and two nieces were there, but no Gabriel.

I really liked Gabriel's mom and he told me that she was fond of Madie and I as well. I could feel it. She never judged. In addition to her love and acceptance, I will never forget her meatballs, they were to die for. Although the whole family looked Hispanic, with the exception of Gabriel who looked like an Indian, their true ethnicity was Italian and if there was ever a dispute, 'the truth was in the meatballs.'

When I arrived that day with Madie in tow, his mom just blurted out, "Not here...they left a few hours ago...don't know when they'll be back, but you're welcome to come in and wait." I am sure she never really wanted to know where her kids were...Either way, the "Price is Right" was apparently a safe escape. She always invited us to sit and wait, but I could never spend more than a few minutes there. I didn't do well with socializing. I always felt weird sitting there in silence and I ran out of stuff to say very quickly. After a few minutes of small talk, I would start to feel uncomfortable and be on my way. On this particular day, I sat down and luckily, within a few seconds, a car pulled up.

It turned out to be Mandy and Lexie. Mandy was the natural mother of the children in the room. Lexie and Mandy were inseparable when they happened to be out of jail at the same time. They were longtime "using" friends. Lexie was a pretty, thin girl who drove a new Mercedes and wore furs. I never really understood the furs, a little over the top especially in sunny Southern California, but Lexie had money and she wanted everyone to know it. The story was that she had been a dancer in Japan for a while and had made a lot of money.

Mandy and Lexie wordlessly walked straight past us and headed for the bathroom. Obviously, they had scored and needed to fix. I figured I would wait for a bit. It was futile to attempt to share some of their drugs. They were ruthless; you could never get into their supply. This was a good thing given my present living situation and Madie's presence. I had to stay focused. I would need to stay drug free until I figured this thing out.

The overriding issue at this point was what they were using. If they were using Heroin they would be out in about fifteen minutes. If they were using Coke, it was a whole 'nother Oprah (*as I like to say for a bigger issue*). While I manifested my cocaine paranoia in odd ways, Mandy played out her coke high in a strangely different way. She would think she had worms under her skin and she would try to pick them out. Her whole body was covered with scabbed sores.

If they had coke, they would be in the bathroom for several hours while Mandy stared into the mirror picking at her face. In that case, I would have to come up with a plan B. A few minutes later they erupted from the bathroom very relaxed. I was in luck; it was heroin. As they walked out, Mandy gave me a nod to direct me to go outside with them. They would normally smoke and talk out in front of the room to avoid having her mom hear. Not that she would say anything, she had long since blocked them out, but more out of general respect.

As soon as we got outside, I revealed my situation to them. Not the gory details, just the headlines. "Madic and I need a place to stay." Lexie suggested a motel called Shady Acres. It was just across town. They had weekly rentals and she said she knew some people that had stayed there. The majority of the people we knew were living on public assistance of some sort, so she said she thought the rates were cheap. That was all I needed to hear, Plan A was already coming together!

29

MADIE AND I LEFT GABRIEL'S MOM'S PLACE ON A MISSION. WE took the bus to the Shady Acres motel. Before we even entered the office, I could see the place was run-down. The little office had all of the basic necessities; a counter, a phone and a couch, but it looked more like a homeless shelter than a motel. That was okay though; at this point anything would do.

I hit the small bell on the counter and an old lady who looked to be right around 140-years-old emerged from the back room. She was very grouchy and very direct. "What do you want?" I told her we were looking for a room. She snarled at me and asked, "Is it just you two?" I replied, "Yes." She said, "Cause you know if you are hiding a guy and you sneak him in, it is more money. I am not up for any tricks, I will kick you right out...no refund." After 15 or 20 other disclaimers she added, "I have one room in the back...nothing fancy. If you want it, you take it "as is"...$130 per week. Pay on time or leave immediately before I change the locks."

The price was good. With my two welfare checks, I could pay for two weeks upfront. When we arrived at the room I immediately noticed the window next to the door was broken. There was a crack straight down, but the glass was still intact. The slightest nudge would have finished the job, but for now, it was still in place. I found it interesting that they hadn't fixed it, but from the looks of the place they didn't do much fixing. I was okay with it because it was summertime and the glass was still keeping the bugs out. This must have been the "as is" part. It was a different matter when she opened the door...My initial reaction was "fear." It was a stark room, with dirty brown carpet. Actually it was more like a thick blanket. It was flat, torn in many places and stained with what smelled like beer and cigarettes. The room had a queen size bed. The lady walked in ahead of me and continued to rattle off the rules, as I followed closely behind her. When I plopped down on the bed to test it and it didn't bounce back, I immediately realized I should have braced myself better. It was hard as a rock and felt like it was held together by a large rubber band that had lost all elasticity. My butt instantly hit bottom, "plunk." Embarrassed by the sound and my sore butt, I turned my attention back to the old lady. Now crossing the room, she was quickly reciting the "dos and don'ts" of the place. She stood in front of the bathroom next to the small sink. On the sink there was a small grill looking thing with a black wire going into the electrical socket. "And this is where you will cook your meals...you must always make sure you have turned off the grill when complete... lord knows we can't afford a fire here. Any sign of irresponsibility and you will be out." She pointed to a small refrigerator that sat on the floor. "You can easily fit enough food for a week in here. Should stay cold enough to keep your milk good."

When the initial reaction wore off, I started to feel better. We had a place. It wasn't the best place, but it was our very own place. Our own place...

The motel consisted of two very long buildings with rooms on both sides. There was a fenced-in pool in the middle of the cement parking lot with some folding chairs sitting around it. It reminded me of the kind of pool you would see in an institution. It seemed like it was mainly there so that they could advertise the "Motel with weekly rates and pool!" The pool water was off-green in color and the cement around it was covered in small spider cracks. The only vegetation consisted of a small planter with a tree in it that appeared to serve as the primary ashtray for smokers at the pool.

The other residents were all partiers. When the sun went down, the doors opened and the volume cranked up. There was alcohol and drugs everywhere. The locals consisted of mostly welfare families, truck drivers and bikers. Up until now, I had always been hesitant of interacting with "normal people." Wherever I was, they were always there. They were the working class of America. They went to sleep every night, worked during the day, ate dinner with their families and spoke about politics and current events. I avoided "normal people" at all costs due to the lack of commonality and shared knowledge. They spoke a whole different language. I was scared to death to engage in conversation with them. I had absolutely no insight into politics and certainly nothing to chat about that they would understand. After years of being on the lookout for "them" for once I could finally relax. Shady Acres had no "normal people" living there.

My new neighbors were carnie bikers (bikers that worked at the carnival when it came into town), welfare families and junkies. My initial introduction was to the four carnies that shared a room around the other side of the motel; two guys, a child and an older woman. The cutest of the bunch, Kevin, saw me outside and invited me in to meet the others. He was about my age with a slim frame and freckles and beautiful strawberry blond hair tied in a neat braid down his back.

Ralph was the oldest of the gang. He was about 45 with dark curly hair and a limp. He was the dad of the small girl that lived with them. Even though I thought he seemed way too old to have a kid, I quickly deduced that if you can still do the deed, you can still have a kid.

Jessica was six years old with long dirty blond hair that was always tied in a braid down her back, like Kevin's. Kevin was her buddy and it was clear the moment I met them that she was very suspicious of any women trying to get near him. I am sure the matching hairdos was something she had requested. Although she was quiet most of the time, you could tell that her little wheels were always turning. Clutching either her dad's leg or Kevin's hand at all times, it was clear she was afraid. But I could never quite figure out what it was that she feared.

The last of the crew was an older lady who rarely spoke. She seemed to be the Ralph's mate and, although there was no apparent romance, they slept in the same bed. Kevin and Jessica slept on sleeping bags on the floor of the room. It was an odd arrangement, but they were making the best of the space they had and sharing rent.

I found Jessica to be an interesting kid in more ways than one. In addition to her quiet nature, she seemed to have more of a natural bond with the guys than with the women, which was uncommon for little girls. She rarely spoke to us women and took little interest in "girly things." She had an obvious distrust for most women. Not knowing if it was something left over from her natural mother, or an event that occurred afterwards, I couldn't help but wonder.

Being that I had not experienced a healthy bond with anyone until I gave birth to Madie, I was very familiar with the kind of walls we build around ourselves for the purpose of protection. I can't say that I never bonded, that would not be true. Up until that point in life, I had formed several unhealthy bonds. It started in grade school with the "smokers bond" and continued into group homes with the "stealing bond" and then in high school with the "junkie bond." Anytime I was engaged with other humans injecting drugs, there was an unspoken bond. Words, no words, white, black, male or female...with junkies, the bond was there and could be felt by all. For intravenous drug users, the process of shooting up is even more bonding than sex; as a matter of fact, it often replaces it.

Not knowing the specifics, I completely accepted Jessica's avoidance of women, as I am sure she had her reasons. Shooting her a smile and a wink occasionally, I felt close to her just knowing we had both survived "something."

After shooting up with this crew for a few weeks, Kevin and I started to mess around. We spent a lot of time together, but we never really communicated much. Then again, no one in our world communicated much unless it was in regards to the next drug score.

After a few weeks, I knew all of the junkies living in and around the motel. My resources for scoring were greatly increased. In addition to Kevin's crew, there was a man on the other side of the motel that worked a normal job. He had a habitual "after work" heroin habit, which was unusual in this world, but worked great for me. It was customary for him to bring me with him when he went to pick up. He liked the company and I liked the drugs.

The strangest of all of the residents at the hotel was the old lady who lived above me. She and her husband were severely addicted to heroin. The only time I ever saw them was when he OD'ed. This occurred more often than reasonable by any stretch of the imagination. They were not sociable or friendly, but from the first time I saved his life, they seemed dependent on me…

It was about five o'clock at night when I heard the heavy footsteps of someone running down the plank in front of our motel room doors screaming, "Help! Help! My husband needs help!" Being the only person around at the time, I jumped off my bed, grabbed Madie and ran out in a panic. "What?" I asked. "What happened?" She shrieked, "I think he is dead. He shot up too much!" With Madie tightly clutched to my hip, I followed her quickly to her room. When we arrived, her husband was lying on their bed, his skin was completely blue and he looked like he wasn't breathing.

I was immediately mentally transported back to the event with Alvin in our Joann Street apartment. On instant autopilot mode and without much thought, I yelled, "ICE! We need ice!" She had a cooler on the floor and opened it up. I shouted, "We need to get ice in his pants NOW! And if that doesn't work, we need to get him in the shower!" We shoved ice on every area of his skin we could get to, starting with his underwear, and I smacked him around like Gabriel and his friend had done to Alvin.

Within a few minutes, his color returned and he woke up! It was a miracle! It worked! The lady was so thankful that she gave me enough of her supply to make my sickness go away for the rest of the day. I saved a life, and I was well, it couldn't have worked out better. But unfortunately, things didn't remain this way.

Much to my surprise, over my remaining time at the motel, which was just a few months—he died three more times. I don't know if this was normal for him to do, whether he had passed through some imaginary door where you just die all of the time, or whether knowing I could help him kept him from limiting his use. Regardless, it happened too many times. The next two times I helped him, it was the same. By the third time, things had changed. Due to the amount of access to drugs at Shady Acres, I was more addicted than ever. Not only was it more accessible than ever, but due to the number of guys that thought they might have a run at me, most of the time, it was free. Being the only young woman left at the motel with a full set of teeth, I had my share of drugs, when it was available. When it wasn't, I was different. You would think being aware of the changes in my personality would have been alarming enough for me to stop, but for reasons that I will never fully comprehend, the thought of stopping never entered my mind.

I will never forget the last time I helped them. The lady came running down to get me as usual and said, "Can you please help my husband? He is dying!" Without as much as a glance in her direction or any sign of a reaction, I quickly recalled the last time I helped him. When he started breathing again, she said "thanks" and looked away without as much as an offer of drugs. When I asked her if she had anything, she nodded her head towards the sink at an empty spoon. With a dry cotton in the spoon she said, "If you add water, you can probably get something out of it." Having no other drugs, I did as she suggested. It wasn't even enough to make the fierce aching in my bones subside.

Feeling used and taken advantage of, I would not let this happen again. Now it was different. Still sitting on my bed, watching TV, with no sign of reaction, in a small voice I said, "If I save him, what will you give me?" She quickly responded, "I am sorry, I don't have any left." And I responded by saying, "then I guess he will die" and continued to watch TV.

I was changing.

I will never know what happened to him. What I will never forget, though, was the hardening of my heart. It was cold. But knowing this didn't change it. Heroin had become my lover, my friend and my God and I would do whatever I had to do to get more; no exceptions, even if meant the loss of a human life. The only human that I would never sacrifice for drugs, was Madie. For Madie, I would do anything

I needed to do. At least that was what I thought then. I had greatly underestimated the power the drugs had over me. I took the drugs, and the drugs took me.

People around me continued to die, but it was different now. The message of someone dying seemed to take on a much more casual tone. As if we were soldiers on an active war field, we began to think of it as an accepted part our mission. When Drifter and Warlock split up, she left the apartment they shared and moved just few motels down the street from me. From time to time I would go by to visit. Drifter was a strong brave woman, but the last time I saw her, she was broken and thin. They say she died of cancer. I am not sure, but I know one thing, like all of the other friends and acquaintances who died, there was no talk of a funeral. We had no time in our day for anything other than getting more drugs. The time it took to get to a funeral home, be sick at the service and stand around in the hot sun was too much. If you died, you died.

The news of friends passing away was always present in conversation. Although the news sometimes invoked surprise, it was mostly surprise that we didn't know, not that we were surprised that they died. We were all walking on a thin line between life and death. We knew it and we accepted it.

30

I WILL NEVER FORGET THE DAY MY WELFARE CHECK CAME AND THE man around the corner scored me some black tar heroin. Since this was more potent than our usual stuff—he suggested I get more. This very rarely happened for me, since I had always been a one day at a time person. My pattern was always to score just enough for the day. I knew if I had more, whether planned for the next day or not, the temptation would get to me and I would use it all in one day, whether I needed it or not. This was my only way to moderate my usage. Knowing the man was right, I took his advice with self control and moderation in mind.

Much to my surprise, I was able to do it. The next day I woke up, injected myself and the sickness subsided. Although my addiction still had not reached its full potential, it was customary for me to wake up with a dull pain coming from my bones and a stuffy nose. Since I was feeling good now and it was a beautiful summer day outside, I thought it would be a good idea to lie out by the pool. I could get a tan and Madie could play with her feet in the water on the pool stairs and we could relax. Committed to my plan of relaxation, I grabbed a few of her dolls and we headed down to the pool. Although my ability to properly mother was significantly handicapped by my addiction, I loved my daughter with every fiber of my being. Even though you'd think I was a horrible mom simply by virtue of being a heroin addict, I did my very best when it came to Madie.

A product of my child development classes and teachings at the battered women's shelter, I was a walking oxymoron. Albeit I hung around with crazy looking people, and did crazy things, I did my best to let Madie know at all times how much I loved her. Hugging and kissing her constantly, I never hit her or yelled at her and was sure to tell her how beautiful she was and how much I loved her several times a day. I didn't shoot up in front of her and I made sure that anyone smoking drugs never did it in her immediate area. All that said, that day at the pool, the heroin won.

I sat with her for the first few minutes on the stairs of the pool and then decided I wanted a smoke. I pulled the lounge chair next to the ashtray plant and smoked while watching Madie play. I must have nodded out, but I was unsure for how long. When I opened my eyes, the pool scene slowly appeared as I adjusted my eyes to the bright sun.

As I slowly lifted my head, I realized it was silent. Like a shot through my heart, every cell of my body exploded as I reengaged to see Madie floating in the pool, face down! *FUCK! NO! NO! NO! SCREAMING, YELLING, FLYING AS FAST AS MY LIMBS WOULD CARRY ME! I THREW MY BODY INTO THE POOL AND PULLED HER BODY OUT AND ONTO THE CEMENT! AS I TURNED OVER HER BODY, SHE STARTED TO COUGH! SHE MUST HAVE JUST SLIPPED IN! WHAT KIND OF MOTHER WAS I? MADIE ALMOST DIED!!!*

I had been visited by the angel of death, who had decided to give me one more chance. In a state of complete hysteria, I wrapped my arms around her and held her as I tightly as I could. I was shivering with fear and shock. I held her so tight she could barely move. I rushed back to our room, wrapped her in warm blankets and rocked her tightly in my arms, violently weeping. I clearly saw what the problem was and decided that I would never go back to the pool again. Although I sat there for hours rocking and singing to her and crying, I knew as soon as the guys showed up with more heroin, I would be okay. I would inject myself, it would hit my stomach with a soothing warmth and then I would feel every muscle in my body fall limp. Ok again.

I had lived the life of an addict for so long that I knew no other way. Every day was exactly like the one before: fixing before the sickness was too much to stand and then surviving another day to repeat that day. The monster had been unleashed so long ago that this seemed normal to me. The spiral downward came in such small increments that it virtually went unnoticed.

Later that week I went over to my mom's during the day to let my little sister Alyssa know where I was living. I thought maybe she'd want to visit sometime. Being that it was midday and several hours away from the time I would be able to score again, I needed to do something with myself. Knowing that Madie would enjoy the walk and the visit with Alyssa, off we went. When I arrived, I found Alyssa watching TV with three punk-rocker type guys. There were two skin-head type kids and the third was a cute James Dean looking character. Overly comfortable, with their feet on the table, ashtray on the couch, their heads thrown back in a semi sleepy state, they made little movement when we entered.

As was customary for us on a visit, we entered in the front door, headed straight for the kitchen to get Madie a snack and then plopped down on the living room couch. Having not spoken to Alyssa in more than a few months now, she quickly brought me up to speed. They were just getting into heroin in the past few weeks and they were starting to feel sick. Brandt (Mr. James Dean) had a normal job at a butcher shop a few days a week, but had no money currently. One of the punker looking guys had a few places in mind where he thought he could rob some crap, but not during the day. Lastly she added, "Brandt has a car." They were brainstorming on how they could get some dope without money and thus far coming up empty. Knowing I was older and knew a wider range of people, they requested my brainstorming assistance.

The only actual heroin dealer that I knew personally was Gabriel's dealer, "One-eyed Pepe." He lived in Santa Ana. Santa Ana is one of the most prevalent towns in Orange County for picking up drugs. Infested with gangs, drug dealers and crime, it is frequented day and night by junkies looking for a fix. Pepe lived in a dark shack in the back of his mom's house and he had only one eye; hence the name "One-eyed Pepe." Gabriel gave me the run down the first time he took me there. They had done a lot of time together in prison and they owed each other "favors." He never divulged the details of these favors, but my understanding was that they would do whatever was needed, no questions asked, no exceptions. Pepe was an old Mexican guy around fifty. He was always happy to see Gabriel and always very pleasant to me. When Gabriel brought me to Pepe's a few years back, he introduced me with, "Pepe, this is my girl; you take care of her." That being said, I didn't feel comfortable calling on any favors without Gabriel being with me. At some weird level I honored the relationship between the two of them and didn't want to make any promises to Pepe that I couldn't fulfill, which included paying him back. The other thing I clearly knew was that I could never take these young white kids to Pepe's house. He would not like it.

We had to think of another plan. In my mind, there were still a few possibilities. One was to drive through the known gang neighborhood and the other was Buena Clinton. The gang neighborhood was good for wack but not so great on heroin. Buena Clinton, on the other hand, was a kingdom to heroin addicts; kind of like what West Hollywood is to gays. It was a shopping mall of heroin dealers.

This heroin haven was about twenty minutes away in Santa Ana. The small neighborhood had one street providing access in and one street providing access out. The only bad thing about this was once you were in, if the cops blocked the entrances, it was impossible to get out. The cops were all over Buena Clinton. A few times a day they would drive through with paddy wagons and sticks, beating and arresting people. This was the only time I ever saw this kind of violence inflicted by the police. They would literally drive into the street, and people would scatter and the police would disburse and beat and grab as many as they could and throw them in the vans. Being a white girl in a Mexican neighborhood, with bruises and welts up and down my arm from shooting up, this was my worst nightmare. Luckily, the few times I saw this occur, I was in a car and the cops were on foot.

From the direction we headed into the neighborhood, the street providing access in was on the East side and was called Buena. The street providing access out on the West Side was called Clinton. As you entered through either street there were three streets running perpendicular that were fully populated with Hispanic guys selling heroin. As you drove down the street, you heard whistles erupting from every pore of the neighborhood. If you were interested, you would simply stop your car. Then they would rush up, grab the money, hand off the drugs and run off.

On any given day or night the streets of Buena Clinton were buzzing with activity. It was great for newbie's because you didn't have to know anyone to pick up. It was also the last house on the block if you didn't have a needle. In exchange for a damp cotton when you were done, you could find a junkie that would let you borrow his personal needle. This would have been alarming to me when I first starting using, knowing how many different people had used it and what kinds of diseases could be potentially passed around, but by this point, I thought *"Who cares if I die of AIDs ten years from now, I just want to get well now."* With no regard for my health or my future, I would use whatever I could.

Having considered our options, and knowing the boys had a car, I suggested we rob someone in Buena Clinton. It was a dangerous choice due to the number of guys that carried guns, but as usual, the more dangerous the plan, the more fun it sounded to me. Although I had never tried it before or for that matter even thought about it, the more I let my imagination run with it, the better this dangerous plan sounded. The tougher looking of the punker kids immediately wimped out and exclaimed, "Are you crazy? You'll get fucking shot!' I confirmed, "Yes, I am one crazy bitch, but you watch, I will get the dope and I won't share because you are too much of a pussy to help." This statement was necessary to set the pecking order within the pack and also to bring Brandt's attention over to me. How attractive is that?

I continued, "If anyone has a dollar, I can get drugs. I will rob a dealer in Buena Clinton by rolling it up and making it look like more. Who's in?" The room was dead silent and then Brandt, who hadn't spoken a word muttered quietly, "I am in." That was the moment I fell for him. The James Dean looking angel with a long thin trench coat and slicked back dark hair had won my vote. Leaving Alyssa and her punker friends to watch Madie while she snacked and watched cartoons, we were on our way.

Brandt and I, two skinny white kids, followed the plan and were ultimately chased by a mass of Mexican guys screaming, as we floored it out of the neighborhood. We returned with enough heroin for everyone. I felt like Bonnie and Clyde. I knew I had met my match; he was hot, shy and lived dangerously. In case you are wondering what happened to Kevin, if I forgot to mention the breakup before going into my story about Brandt, the answer is yes and no—I didn't forget to mention it, I forgot to breakup.

Strangely enough, when you're high all day, formalities like that tend to slip your mind. Although I felt momentarily guilty, I immediately, like I did with all feelings that attempted to crowd my mind, shot it away. With my welfare check coming, I spent the next week or so hanging around with Alyssa, Brandt and his friends doing drugs

By this time, I had spent so many days running around with Alyssa and her friends; I had failed to pay rent at Shady Acres. When I went back to the motel, there was a sign on the door. With no money remaining, I picked up the few things that remained and was on my way. With a welfare check coming in just a few days, we stayed with Brandt's friends and returned a few days later to retrieve it. I was able to rent a motel room on the main boulevard.

It was during this period that I realized the level I was willing to go to in order to get well. One morning, when I woke up extremely sick and Brandt had gone to work, I called over to Gabriel's hotel to see if someone could take me to pick up. His sister Mandy answered and told me she and Lexie were headed out to pick up and would gladly help me. Being just a few motels down the street, they made it to my place in no time. They told me they would be back within the hour. About four hours later, they finally pulled in to the motel parking lot. Mandy ran up to my door, told me they were in a rush, shoved a balloon in my hand and ran off. As I poured the balloon in my spoon, I quickly realized it was dirt. They had used the heroin and filled the balloon with dirt! I couldn't believe it! Someone I knew and trusted. By this time, I was too sick! This could not be happening to me. And then the drug addict part of my brain kicked in. If they used the heroin, it must have been in this balloon prior. Maybe if I heated up the dirt in the spoon I could cook out all of the impurities and any remaining heroin powder would still be there. So I did. I cooked and shot up the dirt. Within fifteen minutes I was paralyzed with pain. My head felt like a knife had gone directly through it and I was freezing. I spent the next ten hours freezing and shaking beneath my covers. I was lucky I didn't die. To this day, I do not know the implication of what could have happened to me that day. But I was now keenly aware that I was willing to kill myself to make the sickness go away. Things would only continue to get worse, much worse.

31

A LYSSA AND BRANDT'S FRIENDS WERE THE ONLY ONES WHO CALLED on our motel phone regularly. It was customary, given that we lived in such close proximity to each other, for most of my friends to just show up unannounced. Most drug addicts really don't work on a schedule and anything that cost money (like payphones) was out unless specifically for the potential gain of drugs, so the general rule was if you were in the neighborhood, you stopped by.

I was very surprised when just a few nights into my stay at the motel, I answered the phone to hear my sister Nadine's voice. "Hey Lauri, it's Nadine." She launched right into her reason for calling, "I have something you can do…"

I was still thinking, *How does she know where I am and why is she calling me?* Her chatter was like background music in my mind while I quickly tried to figure out how she had located me. I deduced that Alyssa must have told her. She must have called there and asked where I was. But why…? Then I tuned back in. "So I have this thing that I was supposed to do, but I can't do it. You can make a lot of money. The people are really nice." *I still had no idea what she was talking about or why she was calling me, but I heard the word money and I sharpened my listening skills.* I no longer cared how she found me.

"I had a job that some rich guy that I know set up. He is a good friend of mine and takes care of me, but I can't go. I told him maybe you would go. There is a lot of money in it, Lauri."

I heard money again, but was now skeptical; I thought this must be a trick. Lord knows I didn't trust Nadine, but now I also wondered, what kind of person gives away an opportunity to make a lot of money?

I knew there was a catch, but I hadn't figured out what it was yet. "Ok, what do I have to do?"

She said, "I have this friend Amir. He owns a restaurant. He is very rich, Lauri. He wanted me to come over there, but Donny (her buff boyfriend) won't let me. I told him I would see if my younger sister could come and he said good. You will make really good money. He's rich."

I somewhat skeptically asked, "Ok, so where do I have to go?" She said, "I am going to give you the number. Call the restaurant and ask for him. Just tell him you are Nadine's sister. He is really nice. He will send you a cab. You have to dress nice. It's a fancy place. Wear a dress."

I didn't own anything like that, but I instantly thought I could borrow something from one of the other girls at the motel. She asked, "So you can do it, right?" I said, "OK, if there's really money, I will call him." She practically begged, "Call him right now please," and we hung up.

Nadine and I were so opposite of each other that I still thought it was crazy that she was calling me. Nadine and her friends wore little mini-skirts, really high pumps and lots of jewelry and makeup. Her rich guy friends liked that. What was she thinking, sending me to see one of them? I knew one thing for sure. He would know immediately that I was not one of the prissy dress up girls, but maybe wearing a dress, I could semi pull it off. Although it was against everything I believed in to wear a dress, if there was money involved, it was worth a try. Even though it still didn't make sense, I went with it.

When I phoned the restaurant, I asked for Amir, the owner, as instructed. Within just a fraction of a minute, I heard the voice of man with a heavy Persian accent, "This is Amir." "Oh" I said, "Hi Amir, this is Nadine's sister, Lauri. She asked me to call you." He responded, "Lauri! How are you? So nice to hear from you! So your sister tells me that you're going to visit me here. I am looking forward to meeting you!" Before I could think of what to say next, he said "So where should I send the cab?"

In less than an hour a cab arrived outside of my motel door.

Wearing a borrowed dress from the girl next door, who also agreed to watch Madie, I walked out and got in. About thirty minutes later, the cab pulled off of the highway and into a large parking lot with a sign reading Sunset Cove at the Inn. She was right. It was a fancy place. I was very nervous. Socializing was definitely my biggest downfall.

Having no clue what this guy looked like, I told the taxi to wait and entered the hotel. To the left, there was an archway to a restaurant. The sound of Christmas music, clinking champagne glasses and the quiet mutter of old people was a constant hum. I was certainly out of my element.

I was sure anyone looking at me could tell from my rigid appearance and awkward mannerisms that I was completely freaked out. I asked the hostess if she could get Amir for me. A few seconds later, he appeared from around the corner. "Well, well, so you're Nadine's little sister! I am very pleased to meet you, my friend. Come, come, relax, I will have the girl pay the taxi and we will get to know each other."

Amir must have sensed my nervousness because he overcompensated in his welcome. He treated me as if we had been friends for years. Amir was a good looking Persian man in his mid-forties. As we entered the restaurant he took a hold of my hand and led me toward the back. As we were walking he continued to talk, "So this is my restaurant, and whatever you want, it is yours!"

Can you spell Scarface? A Persian Al Pacino he was...

The Christmas music was seeping out of the walls through hidden speakers. There was tinsel and decorative pine cones everywhere. He pushed through the big, swinging kitchen doors and we entered a kitchen in full swing. Men with large white chef hats were rushing around, chopping steaks and standing over hot grills, so focused on their jobs that they didn't even notice us.

He grabbed the big metal handle of a larger than life refrigerator and pulled it open. It was so huge we were able to walk right in. "In here I have lobsters and steaks that will make your mouth water; the best of everything my friend! You select what you want and when you return, we will go to my house, and I will personally cook it for you.

Then we will smoke Opium, and relax so we can get to know each other." I was still on the *when you return* part. Was I going somewhere? It sounded like it. I was surprised because I thought I was already there.

"Come, come my dear," he said. "I have everything set up for you." He took my hand and led me back outside of the restaurant and into the parking lot. He walked me up to a golden Mercedes. It must have been brand new because the sticker was still on the window. Then he handed me the keys and said, "I put the directions on the seat."

As he sat in the driver's seat and stretched to the glove compartment to rummage through a pile of papers, I was thinking, *Are you kidding? The freaking thing is brand new! I can't drive this!!!* But being this far in and not wanting to sound stupid, I said nothing. I just acted as if.

He helped me in and showed me a map that displayed the directions to a golf resort. He said, "I need you to drive to this place. My friends are waiting for you there. They are here for a doctor's convention. They are all very nice. They know you are coming." He explained that they might still be out golfing or back at the lounge, so the key to the room was on the car key chain. He said, "Just go in and wait. They will be there shortly. You will like them." Although I was nervous, I also felt honored to be trusted at this level. It made me feel important.

As I pulled away, the nervousness dissipated a bit—that is the portion of nervousness that was related to being with the Persian Pacino. The fear of driving this brand new car and going to some unknown place to meet strangers about God only knows what still remained. I drove like a granny, making sure that no harm would come to the car. That was all I needed; lord only knows if I scratched the car, I would probably end up in the trunk next to a river somewhere. Better to be overly cautious than river bound.

I had no idea what to expect, but the underlying thought in my head was that Nadine wouldn't send me somewhere dangerous. Or would she?

I felt weird all over; the rich people, the dress and the crazy unknown. Although I liked risky stuff most of the time, this seemed crazy even for me, and the silly dress wasn't helping.

When I arrived at the resort, there was a building with the designated address on it. I looked for the room number that matched my key and parked. Now, standing at the door, I froze. Should I knock? Should I just go in? For the next few minutes I just stood there. After what seemed like an abnormal period of time to be pacing back and forth on the other side of the door I realized, jeesh, they could be watching my lame ass from the peep hole, for cripes sakes, do something! So, I knocked. And I knocked.

When no one answered, I determined that the next and only logical step was to use the key. I inserted the key and with a turn to the right, the door opened and I entered the room. Although it was somewhat like a motel room, it was much different from the motel rooms I was accustomed to. The furnishings were dark wood and there were large leather chairs overlooking the lush, green golf course outside the window. Along one wall was a beautiful king size bed. The room was dead silent, but I still wasn't sure if I was alone. There was another door just ahead to the left that was slightly ajar. I slowly crept over to the far end of the room and peeked around the corner into what appeared to be the bathroom area. A bathroom almost the size of my motel room I might add. After a few seconds I confirmed the room was empty. I was alone.

Hmmm, now what? Well, he said wait. They will come soon. But then what? This was all too strange.

Looking around, I couldn't decide where to sit. To sit on the bed would be weird. Should I be standing up when they come in, since it isn't my place? Maybe I should be sitting on the chair? Either way, I should look relaxed and I was doing a very poor job of that at the moment. After much consideration, I thought that sitting on the chair looking out at the golf course was the best approach, and although I had to admit to myself that it would be highly unlikely under any circumstances that I would appear relaxed in any way, it was the best I could muster up.

I was only there for about five minutes when there was a soft knock on the door. Not knowing if this was the person I was waiting for or the resort staff, I approached the door with little thought other than that when someone knocks, you answer.

I opened the door to an older gentleman around sixty with a bright smile and a friendly demeanor. He reached out his hand to shake mine and said, "Hello, you must be Amir's friend." I said, "Yes, I am Lauri."

As if it was my hotel room, he asked, "May I come in?" Strange question. I thought he was staying there. It was at that moment that I realized there were no personal belongings in the room. No remnants of any lodgers. I invited him in.

As he walked into the room, he looked just as uncomfortable as I felt. He stepped in and looked around, similar to the way I did, and as quickly as he looked at the bed, he looked away as if its mere existence made him uncomfortable. He then turned his head to the left and gazed over at the large leather chairs by the window. He seemed equally uncomfortable with that for some reason. He quickly returned his gaze back to me and began to talk in a fast, fragmented, nervous tone.

"Young lady, I don't want you to take this wrong. I certainly appreciate Amir's gesture, but this is just not my sort of thing. I am grateful for the offer to be a guest at the resort, and the golf and food service are wonderful, but I am a doctor of high moral beliefs and I can pay you, but that is it. If you tell Amir that we did not do anything, he may be offended. Just tell him I said thank you."

He continued, "My dear you are so young, please consider the risks of what you are doing. I don't mean to preach or judge, just to tell you that there is a great deal of disease out there. I wouldn't want to see you catch AIDs. A mistake like this would be fatal. I realize I don't know you or what happened to you that put you in this position, but you are so young and I just don't want to see you get hurt or sick. You do not need to answer me or say anything, just please think about what I said later. I will send the other doctors in." He shook my hand, laid some money on the table and with a friendly smile, opened the door and gently shut it.

Now that was confusing! But thank God he didn't want to have sex with me...Not having fallen off the turnip truck yesterday, I knew that was the reason he was talking about AIDS. Man, that would have been awkward. Would he have told me if he did want to have sex? How much money do you get for that? My God, would I take off my clothes if he did? Would he take off my clothes? How much money would I get for that?

As I peered over at the table where he had left the money, the door slowly opened again. A younger man around fifty with a golf shirt, but a much more serious look on his face entered the room. He had his head down and his hand over his eyes, as if in a thinking posture. He closed the door and asked me to sit down. I sat on the bed. As quickly as I sat, I thought, *JESSSH!! Not the bed!!* Although my instinct was to get off of the bed as quickly as I sat, all that erupted from me was a small shudder of my shoulders, for I knew if I jumped back off, it would have been equally awkward.

I felt like a small child on that huge king size bed, my feet hanging over the edge, too short to touch the floor. What if he sits next to me, or worse? Is a person like me supposed to sit on the bed? I remained uncomfortable and frozen, not knowing what would happen next. I was a bag of nerves. He paced back and forth alongside of the bed mumbling. "I have talked to the other doctors and we are in agreement that this is not our sort of thing. At the same time, we would like to urge you to stop prostituting and find yourself a better life. You were lucky to meet nice guys who would never cheat on their wives or engage in this type of activity, but the health risk you are putting yourself in is not good. Will you promise me to take the money we are giving you, go home and think about what I told you?" In a small voice, I muttered, "I will."

He reached in his pocket, withdrew a small pile of bills and set them down next to me on the bed. He said, "The other doctor is resting in his room now and will not need to come in. You can leave a few minutes after I leave." He continued, "Take care of yourself and tell Amir we said thank you," and he exited the room.

For the first few seconds after the door shut, I sat frozen, thinking that the door may reopen. Maybe one of them forgot something and would be coming back. I then glanced next to my hand on the bed and saw the money. A hundred dollar bill? Are you kidding? I quickly counted six, $100 dollar bills! My God! And there was MORE on the table! I jumped off the bed to see what the other man left, and it was two more $100 bills! My freaking God! This is mine? Are you kidding? What should I do with it? I don't want to lose it! $800? Just like that? My God! My friends are not going to believe this!

I had my hand clutched around the money so hard that my knuckles were white. I couldn't believe that I had made so much money! It was a miracle! I was so distracted and elated that I left, almost forgetting to lock the door or take the key. I reentered the room, grabbed the key from the table overlooking the golf course, smiled, took a deep breath and thought, *Now that wasn't bad was it?* I left the room with a bit of a skip in my walk and locked the door.

As I jumped into the Mercedes, I realized I had to let go of the money to start the car and steer. I don't know if I ever had this kind of money in my hand at one time. I was scared to put it down, and although none of the windows were open, it was as if I thought it would magically disappear or fly away. I transferred the money from the right hand to the left and then decided that wasn't good either. My hand was clenched so tight it hurt. I decided I would put the money in the small purse that I had brought, and even though my mind was telling me that I might lose the purse, I didn't feel there was any other option. I slipped it in and set it on the passenger seat. All the way back to the restaurant, I was distracted by the purse. My eyes darted back and forth between the road and my purse, guarding it like a rare treasure.

My mind quickly considered all of the new possibilities. I could buy food, cigarettes, pay rent, buy Madie new dolls and still have money left over! This was like two freaking months worth of welfare checks! And I didn't have to do anything to get it! I had a permanent smile on my face.

When I reentered the restaurant, I could see that they were shutting down for the night. The light tingling sounds of wine glasses and silverware being cleaned erupted from the kitchen and replaced the sound of music that had existed prior. The quiet chatter of the handful of remaining customers was muffled by the sounds of change being counted behind the bar and chairs being placed on top of tables by the waiters. In the back of the restaurant I saw Amir sitting at a table reviewing small white forms.

I approached his table slowly. He was initially distracted with the process he was involved in and did not notice my presence. A waitress standing just behind Amir cleaning a table approached him and put her arm on his shoulder and motioned my way. "Your little lady has returned."

He jumped up a bit embarrassed and said, "Lauri! Come sit! Come my friend!" He yelled over to the bartender, "Please bring Lauri a drink!" He motioned to me, "What would you like?" Again, completely out of my element, I deduced that ordering a shot of Jack Daniels like I did at the biker bar was probably not appropriate. Not wanting to sit dumbfounded for too long, I looked at his glass, "I guess whatever you have." I immediate realized how stupid that sounded, but couldn't take it back…"Good choice!" he said. "Get the lady some of my wine." Inside of my head I thought, *Jeesh Lauri, what a retard. I can't wait to get home.*

Just a few minutes later, Amir said, "You know what, this can all wait until tomorrow. Let's go back to my home so I can cook you dinner and we can relax. I have some friends there and they are looking forward to meeting you. We will have a great night." Every time I thought I was feeling a little less nervous, it would start again. Friends? My God, what would I have in common with this guy's friends? And where would I put my purse? *Just act as if Lauri, Just act as if…*I couldn't wait to go home.

We drove to Amir's home, just minutes from the restaurant, in his small red sports car. The next few hours with Amir seemed like days because I was largely distracted with the location of my purse and the thought of returning home with a bundle of money.

Amir's condo was a small two bedroom place, but unlike the places I frequented, you could tell by the way it was decorated he was made of money. The walls were white as walls could be, with no handprints or dirt; all the way down to the floor as stark white as you could imagine. The art on the walls displayed bright dramatic colors with severe shapes and sizes. The kitchen was clean and had a very expensive looking wine rack, which sat beside a large knife holder. This was definitely a "grown up's" place.

There were three people in the living room sitting on a clustering of large black leather couches passing some strange smelling foil and sucking it through a straw. There was a lady in her early thirties in the kitchen opening a bottle of wine. After a few minutes I realized everyone was either high or drunk and I was finally able to relax. This was more my style. Although these clearly weren't my peers, their level of intoxication helped me to feel less watched and more at ease.

They introduced me to the drug on the foil, called Opium. I had heard of Opium, and thought it was supposed to be what heroin was made from and I assumed it was strong stuff. I smoked it with them for hours, and while Amir's guests kept on professing how good it was, I felt nothing. That was nothing other than effects of the wine I was drinking. The stuff looked like a large ball of dark caramel. Every so often, Amir would open a small safe and remove a large brick of the stuff. With a small knife from on top of the safe, he would cut off another piece for smoking. I didn't get the big deal about the opium, but I indulged anyway to be polite. After several hours and seeing that the sun was starting to come up outside, Amir said, "I better get you home." He called a cab and gave me $80 for the ride.

When I returned to the hotel, Brandt and Madie were both crashed out on the bed, the thick hotel curtains were drawn in the dark room and the TV was on with the volume turned so low it was barely audible. Finally, safe at home, I put my purse between the mattress and the box spring under my body for protection, lay down on the bed's edge and drifted to sleep, safe at last. In three days it would be Christmas and I had $800 in tow. We were rich!

Within 24 hours we had spent the money on food, cigarettes, beer, paid rent for a month, bought some toys and baby clothes for Madie at Kmart and shot up the rest doing speed balls, heroin and cocaine combined. The speed balls were always bad for me. I was never able to calculate correctly and always ended up being paranoid. I was horrified every time someone saw me like this; most of all Brandt. I knew he was in awe of my being older and street smart, but when I turned into a crouching sweating paranoid mental defect, it was hard to bounce back, and frankly, I wondered why anyone stayed after seeing me like that. I always thought if I had a movie of what I looked like, I would never use again. We couldn't spend good drug money on a camera, but the thought persisted.

The next morning I awoke with $15 left. Although I was devastated that I had spent all of that money, I was glad I had at least bought new toys for Madie and had food in our little fridge. Madie was sitting on the floor playing with her toys when I awoke. She was always such a happy baby, which was good and bad. The fact that she was always happy created a false perception that everything was okay. Since the time in the pool, for the most part I used only when she was asleep at night or being watched by someone else. I knew I needed to keep it away from her. I also never, ever used in front of her. I felt like she was safe because she was not near it. At the same time, we would drive with her in the car to pick up and leave her with other questionable people in the motel. Although they all looked fine to me, it is clear now that my perception was dramatically damaged by my drug use. What kind of normal people "live" in a motel?

I knew from the few times that she was around that when I was terrified and hid in the bathroom, she would cry incessantly, which would increase my paranoia and create a vicious cycle of trying to calm her, while hiding and being petrified by the screaming at the same time. I knew I should stop the coke completely, but when I drank or did heroin I always told myself that I wouldn't get paranoid this time. I always got paranoid.

Brandt never asked about that night. Wanting to close the door on any future conversation, I just told him I pulled off a good scam. Like Gabriel taught me, I learned to keep the details to myself. I think if

I had told him the truth, he would have thought I had actually done something for the money. I didn't need that kind of heat. Later that day, when Brandt went out, I started thinking. That wasn't a bad gig. Those men seemed very nice and the money was crazy good! Is that how much these girls get paid? That is crazy! If I made $800 a day, we would be rich. I could buy everything we ever needed and money would never be an issue again. I needed to know more and there was only one way to find out.

I opened the small hotel room drawer to expose the regulatory Gideon bible and a phone book. On this day those two books seemed like a crossroads: Sell your soul to the devil or pray about it.

Without another thought, I retrieved the phone book and quickly thumbed through it. What do they call those places? I looked up prostitutes and then thought how silly, who would call themselves prostitutes? I think that's illegal. I don't think they would list that in the phone book. Working girls? No. Hookers? No. Then I found it. Escorts. Hmmm. Although that sounded like a person who takes someone on a tour, I continued to read. *STAR Escorts, Beautiful Ladies, Professional Dating Service.* If it wasn't legal, how could it be listed? Maybe you just go on dates and don't do anything. I could do that!

I picked up the phone and dialed the number. A lady answered the phone, "Star Services!" I told her I was in need of a job and wanted to know if they needed anyone. She said, "Not really, but let me ask you some questions. How old are you? I replied, "Twenty." She asked, "What do you look like?" I said, "Thin with long, dark brown hair." Then she asked, "What kind of job are you looking for?" I said, "I am a mom and just need to make some money." She replied, "Well, since it is Christmas, we are getting a lot of calls. I'll tell you what. If you call me back in a few hours, I will see what I can do." Before we hung up, she asked for my name, driver's license number and address. She said, "I will check you out and if everything looks okay, we will talk more later." Then we hung up. It was all I could do not to call her right back. I was so excited that I couldn't relax.

Around four p.m. I dialed her number again. She said, "Ok, you look good. We will start you with one of our "regular customers. Guys we have known for a while so that we can see how you do. The next time you call me, I will give you a man's name and address. You will go to the address, but you will not close the door until you have seen his driver's license and collected the money. Once you get in, before you do anything else, you will call me and give me his driver's license number. We charge $150 per hour. Seventy-five goes to you and seventy-five to us. When you are finished, you will call me and then we will meet. At that time, you will give me the money and we can talk about you continuing to work with us. Sound good?" Mentally counting the money, I immediately said, "Yes, sounds very good."

I couldn't believe it. My luck was changing. I had just made $800 and now I was going to be making $75 per hour! My friends are going to be so jealous! I was on top of the world. I had a job.

I was instructed to continue to call in over the next few days to see if they had anything. Although I was excited, it had been almost 24 hours since I had any heroin, Brandt was gone and I had no money. I was hoping I could work that day and make some money. Sure I was concerned about what I would have to do for the money, but it was overridden by the fact that I was getting sicker by the hour and the symptoms had been worsening over the past few weeks. It would start with flu like symptoms, snuffy nose and weakness, then I would pass out and wake up with my bones aching like they were rotting from the inside out. On this particular night, Madie fell asleep around eight p.m. and I fell asleep right next to her. We both slept through the night. The next morning the loud ring of the motel phone jolted me back to life.

My motel was about three miles from my mom's house. My mom had told me a few weeks back that my dad had mentioned that he might visit. His route for the past few years had been from LaGuardia to LAX. We never really saw him anymore and my mom's only relationship to him was receiving the ongoing child support for my little sister Alyssa, so when she mentioned it, I just thought, *Yah, whatever. Not interested.*

But now my mom was on the phone, saying that my dad was coming today and he wanted to see Madie. I was not expecting the call, but I also was not surprised. My dad was always a last minute guy. Being an airline employee, he and the rest of our family always flew standby. Although that may mean nothing to the normal person, what it meant for me as a child was that without any prior notification, my family would say, "We are going on a trip, pack up." If the arrangement was that we were going to Florida, we would pack bathing suits, shorts and stuff. A few hours later we would be standing at the airport looking at the big chart of flights. A few muttered curse words would be exchanged between my parents and the plan was changed. We were going to...hmmm...let me see...well? There are still openings on flight 219, so okay, I guess San Francisco. We would arrive to fifty-degree weather with all of the wrong clothes. But this was how we traveled. To this day, my dad has a habit of calling in the morning to announce an appearance that evening. On this particular day, my dad was due to arrive in about six hours.

I was not interested in a friendly visit with my dad, but my mom was not up for a discussion. I guess being the recipient of his ongoing support; regardless of her true desires, she would comply with his request. I also think she was interested in showing off Madie. For a lady who was going to disown me for being pregnant, she was very attached to Madie, which was good. She told me she would be picking us up and there was no backing out. I asked her if she could just pick up Madie, but again she said no. It was not negotiable. "I am coming for both of you and you'd better be ready, Lauri Burns!" When she used my last name she was pissed. With no money and the sickness creeping in, curtains drawn and cartoons on for Madie, I hung up the phone and slept...and slept...and slept, until I heard a knock on the door. Let's just say, I was not in prime condition when my mom first set eyes on me. More than a day into the sickness, it was very obvious something was very wrong.

No words were spoken on the drive. My mother made baby sounds and cooing noises at Madie, but as expected, ignored me. When we pulled up to the house, I opened the door and saw that the living room had been decorated with the usual holiday decorations: An electronic menorah and the customary Christmas tree for Jews. I headed straight upstairs and into my old bedroom.

After leaving New York my mom became confused about religion and from year to year her faith would change depending on who she was dating or what new fad was going on. She never went full-bore Christian, but we starting having trees with Jewish colored bulbs. She drifted through Christian Science, Buddhism, Hinduism with Yoga, EST and some other kind of life scientist thing. Who could blame her? Between my dad and now me, and both of my druggie sisters, she was having a hard time touching ground.

The worst part was when she would land a Jewish guy, pull out the Hagadah (a Jewish prayer book) and demand we all do Passover. This was always interesting. I was the only one who remembered how to read Hebrew, so I would comply by reading the Hebrew portions. I had no idea what the words meant. My sisters and I all agreed this was heavily bordering on hypocrisy given the state of our lives, but we played along.

Anyway, heading into my old room and passing out immediately, I was awoken a bit later with something I would quickly become accustomed to, but on this night was new to me. I was shocked into reality when in a deep slumber I went to suck in air and found the trap door in my throat had closed. I panicked to suck in air, but it wouldn't come. From a totally relaxed state of sleep, I shot straight up in the bed and gasped frantically for air! Nothing! I grabbed my chest and with my mouth closed, I attempted to suck air through my nose, but it too was shut! Not knowing what was happening and more afraid by the second, I bolted out of my bedroom and into the bathroom and hit the cold tile floor. I don't know why I chose the bathroom floor—something about the cold tile. Maybe it would wake me up like the ice woke Alvin.

With my butt in the air and my cheek pressed on the cold tile, I panicked to breathe. As I weakened and my eyes began to roll back in my head, a small straw size hole opened up in my throat, allowing just a whisper of air. As I pulled to fill my lungs, it worsened. The more I struggled, the less I was able to breathe. I calmed myself enough to breathe in the pin hole of air available without fighting for more. The more I relaxed, the more oxygen I could take in through the tiny air space. Slowly, but surely, the pipe began to open up again. I now lay on the cold tile floor, my face and body wet from the flu and my eyes dripping with tears in a complete state of exhaustion.

I would soon learn that this attack would occur each and every time I was heroin sick, somewhere between the 24 and 48 hour mark. Whether by accident or a planned detox, somewhere in the midst of the first few days a choking attack would trigger a trap door in my throat to slam shut and block the oxygen. It was also at this point that a sweet "syrup-like" stench would emit from every pore of my skin and drench my body.

As my drenched skin hit the air, it chilled the moisture that covered me, sending a chill through my body. My bones ached fiercely as the poison seemed to rot me from the inside out. When I awoke a few minutes later, I pulled my now stuck cheek off the cold tile and quietly made my way back to my room; doing everything I could to avoid detection. I was fortunate that everyone was still downstairs watching TV. I lay back down, wrapped the blankets around my freezing body and created my own personal chamber of warmth, safe at last.

I was glad my dad hadn't arrived yet. I was in no condition for "social hour." I could hear Madie's voice downstairs. I wanted to be near her, if only for a second. The smell of her hair, the way she looked at me; just to be close to her made me feel important, like I mattered. I felt like I had a reason to be alive. I was not able to truly absorb love at any level, but she was all I had and she was pure, perfect and beautiful. She felt so alive and I felt so dead. She was the only connection I had to life. Clearly, I needed her more than she needed me.

Longing to be next to her, I wrapped my blanket around me like a human burrito and made my way down the stairway. Madie was sitting in front of the TV alone, in a trance-like state watching one of her favorite Disney movies. "There's mommy's little princess!" She looked right up and giggled. I saw my mother by the kitchen, but didn't make eye contact. I didn't want to read her eyes. I sat on the floor right next to Madie, and with our backs turned toward my mom, we watched TV.

When my mom returned to the room, I retreated upstairs again. I cannot explain the next course of events. A few minutes after returning to the bedroom, Alyssa appeared at the door. She said, "Mom said she doesn't want dad to see you like this. She gave me $20 to make you well. She said we should take her car and go pick up some heroin to make you better." She added, "We need to hurry back before dad gets here." I could not believe my ears. Are you freaking kidding me? Mom, gave us money to pick up heroin?

As confusing as it was and still is, I was ecstatic. Before she could get it out of her mouth, we were out the door and the exhaust of my mom's car filled the garage. I was going to get well again.

I don't remember actually getting well, but I clearly remember what happened after.

It was about six in the evening when we left to pick up. My dad was due to arrive in the next hour. Alyssa took me to one-eyed Pepe's and, as was protocol, she waited outside while I went into the old shack in the dirt yard and picked up. I only shot up in Pepe's shack on rare occasions. Drug use on Pepe's property was strictly prohibited, but being a friend of Gabriel's and very sick, Pepe made an exception. Pepe had a permanent kit, like Savannah's brother when I was young, a glass tube with a big needle. I had to let him do it for me; it was too big for me to manage. By this time, my veins were covered with blue and green bruises, scabs and scar tissue. What was left of my damaged small veins was very hard to get, even with a small needle. If I missed, I would remain sick for several hours; if I hit a vein, I would be well instantly. I desperately needed to get well and he was nice enough to help.

After returning to the car, Alyssa informed me that she wanted to get high too. We had no money left, but Alyssa knew I could always come up with a plan. At this point, I had no qualms about telling Alyssa about the adventure Nadine sent me on, how I made $800 dollars in a few hours and how I looked in the yellow pages and found a place that I could get more money from. Although you'd think she would be concerned, she wasn't. To Alyssa I was always her "tough" older sister. Having fought for years, hanging out with parolees and in awe of my ranking in the drug world, she always put me on a pedestal. She thought if anyone can pull it off, it was Lauri. Although she would never engage in such activities, she had faith in me. We decided that we would call STAR right now and see if they had anything. For all we knew, we had a Christmas present waiting for us.

Not having cell phones in those days, we stopped at a pay phone at the local gas station and called STAR. The same lady that I had spoken to last time answered the phone again, "STAR Service." "Hi, this is Lauri, the girl that called yesterday. I am just checking back in."

She said, "Well as it turns out, the only existing customers that I had tonight requested specific girls. But, being Christmas week, we are getting a good deal of new customers. I'll tell you what, I wanted to start you off with a regular, but if you're up for it, I will start you off with someone new. The most important thing is to make sure that you get the money and the driver's license before going in. The regular customers know the routine. If you get one that doesn't comply, do not go in." I agreed. She gave me a name and an address and we hung up. Although I wasn't wearing a dress, I figured I had to make do with what I had. Having dressed to see my dad, I had on white jeans, heels and long silky blue shirt. It would have to do.

Luckily my mom's car was loaded with a Thomas Guide for her insurance business, so with the assistance of the map, Alyssa got us there. We finally located the house. It was on a dark, winding road in a pretty nice neighborhood about twenty minutes south from where we started. We both sat outside staring at the house, petrified. It was a one-story home, with green grass and a small cement walkway that led from the driveway to the door. There was a big wooden front door with a huge knocker at the end of the walkway. The part of the house that we could see looked pitch black inside, like it was shut down for the night. There were windows on both sides of the front door, but they were infused with stained glass so that nothing could be seen beyond them. The only light in the house emanated from beyond the foggy colored glass.

In order to prepare for the unknown, we discussed the game plan.

Our discussion went something like this: "It's probably safe; it is in a nice neighborhood...It looks like a nice house...would a killer call a service and give his address? Probably not, so either way, I should only be one hour. If it goes over an hour, knock, NO DON'T KNOCK. If I am in trouble then you may get pulled in too! I could get delayed for a bit, not knowing how this goes, if it goes over two hours..."

"Alyssa barked, "WHAT? TWO HOURS?!" "OK...OK...relax!" I responded. "You're not the one having to do anything! Just stay in the car, I will be back in an hour. Maybe a bit more if I have to do stuff with money and a driver's license."

I could see she was still very apprehensive. I was freaking out as well. In complete frustration, I barked "I DON'T KNOW! Shit! I will give you a signal if I am going over the time. Or if you feel like I am in trouble, I mean *REALLY* feel like I am in trouble, go call someone. Not mom! Anyone else...Not mom."

I walked up to the door and knocked. Listening intently to see if I could hear anyone approaching, I heard a weird swishhhh sound growing louder at it approached the door. Someone was home.

When the door swung open an old man in a wheelchair sat before me. He looked like he was in his early fifties with long wiry grey hair that resembled Albert Einstein. Like an old wicked tree, the hair flew simultaneously in every direction possible, as if each strand was committed to traveling a very different path. His eyes were squinted and his mouth was twisted in a snarl, as if he dared not smile. He pulled the door fully open, quickly swung his wheelchair backwards and growled, "Hurry, get in, before the heat gets out." As he spun around to shut the door, he did a 180 in his chair and swished into the living room beyond. "Sit on the couch," he growled.

My survival skills from living with my dad instantly kicked in. I needed to rapidly scan the situation to determine my level of safety. As we entered the living room, I did a quick analysis for escape purposes. The room was noticeably barren. An uncomfortable looking black leather couch to the left and a small table to the right. That was it. One thing hit me instantly. No escape route other than the front door.

Following orders, I walked over; my little purse clutched close to my side and sat down. Still not fully aware of what I was dealing with, I continued to observe both the man and my surroundings.

He was wearing Levis, with a red bandana that tied his legs to the chair. Well, this was good. At least I could outrun him, but then again, he was fairly quick on those wheels as he spun around and flew in from the door. He was wearing a long sleeve flannel shirt and the wrists were unbuttoned and hung open. The muscles in his arms confirmed that he had been this way for quite some time. His unbuttoned sleeves were the only part of him that appeared relaxed. The room was empty with the exception of some electrical parts and tools on the table and an old wooden bookshelf with a few books sitting atop. There was no artwork on the white walls and the floor was dull old cement with no coverings. There were no Christmas decorations.

No Christmas decorations? It was Christmas Eve and there was nothing to commemorate the event. As I recalled driving up, there were lights on every house, except this one. Dark and lifeless, with the exception of the light emitting from the window, there was nothing. What kind of person doesn't celebrate Christmas? For that matter, it was Christmas Eve and he was alone. The whole thing was strange and unsettling. Something was wrong with him. He was angry and alone, but why? His face was hard and firm and his eyes were penetrating as he inspected me.

"What is your name?" he barked. Without much thought, I blurted out, "Lauri." *Oh shit....I gave him my real name! What are you thinking Lauri? You don't give your real name! For cripes sakes, you say Candy... Trixie...Mercedes, but certainly not Lauri! Great Going!* It was at that moment that the lady's voice invaded my head. "Do not go in until you have checked his driver's license and gotten the money." This is especially important with new customers." CRAP! I was really screwing this whole thing up! I have to ask for the money *now*? My God, the last thing I wanted to do was upset this guy, but I knew I had to do it. If I didn't, I could get fired. I couldn't take that risk. In a meek quiet voice, I said, "I am supposed to get your driver's license and some money."

"Yeah, yeah!" he snarled as he retrieved a wallet from the backpack sitting on top of the small table across from us. He pulled his driver's license out and flashed it. "See! Here is your money!" I felt awkward shoving his money in my purse, but I did it.

I also told him that I needed to call the service with his license number. He growled, "Oh Jesus, I don't want people knowing who I am, I thought this was a private place!" Not knowing how to respond I just sat tongue-tied. "Fine!" he exclaimed.

He pointed to a phone on the desk in the middle of the computer parts. I got up and walked over. He remained sitting in front of the couch. I made the call quickly to avoid any further upset. I wanted to reach out to the person at the other end and say "Is this guy normal?" I knew I couldn't because he was right there.

"STAR Escort Service!" I explained that I was told to call. The lady that answered knew the drill. "Ok, tell me the number at the top…and the expiration date…Did you get money? Great." And she hung up.

I placed the receiver back on the hook and returned to the couch. Not knowing how to proceed, I just sat there waiting for him to give me a pointer. He seemed to flinch as if uncomfortable; too much silence. In an attempt to lighten the tense moment, I thought I could try to make conversation.

I thought what the heck, I need to know what I am dealing with here. I might as well see what I can find out. "No Christmas tree?" I asked. "No!" he growled. Not willing to give in this quickly and needing to know what I was dealing with, I continued. "Doesn't your family celebrate Christmas?" "I don't have a family and Christmas is for fools!"

CRAP! Did he kill his family? Where were they? This was not good! He was visibly angry, and from the depth of the lines in his face, I could tell he had been angry for a long time. I needed to figure this out quickly! You have to face this head on! You have to know what you are dealing with Lauri! Let him know you're not afraid (or at least make him think so) or God only knows what will happen to you! Be bold now! Show him who he is dealing with! "So, how did you get in a wheelchair?" *That's right sister, come out with it!*

"Got shot in the war!" he barked. *Oh, shit, this was not good! He was crazy! I quickly flashed back to the crazy guys who escaped from the VA hospital in Centerport and hid in the woods for weeks. Having continual flashbacks of the war, they always had weapons! I mean look at Rambo for cripes sake! That guy could kill like ten cops with a sharpened stick. I knew I was in trouble. He definitely had guns. Everyone that fought in Nam had guns. No wonder it's so bare around here—he is ready for war!*

Shit, he may be in a flashback right now and he may think I am the enemy. This guy has killed people! Where are the guns? Does he have one on him? I wonder if he ever killed a girl before, here? At his house! Did he kill his family? Crap! Alyssa. Fuck, she is never going to believe this. This guy is crazy!

OK, I had to get this over with and get back to the car as quickly as I could. I needed to give him what he wants and get out. I mustered up the most calm I could, "So what do you want to do?" "I am paralyzed from the waist down" he barked, I can't have sex! Just talk to me!" *Okay, the "no sex" part is good…but what the hell do I say?* "SOOO, do you live here alone?" "Yes."

"How many rooms is it?" *Still trying to figure out if I was safe and where the guns were.* He said, "Three, go look if you want." *Great! I can do an inspection. Maybe I will see the guns. Oh no, now I get it. He is going to trap me in a room. I better do what he says so that I don't appear scared. That would be the worst thing I could do!*

As I got up, he remained stationed where he was. I went down the hallway and moved from room to room. Each room revealed the same cold bareness as the last. The kitchen was old and stark, nothing on the counters with the exception of an old silver tea pot. Off to the left was a room with a TV and a couch. The TV was from around the 1920's and looked like something out of the Jetsons. I was sure it didn't work. The next room was a guest room. Surprisingly enough this one looked like a normal room with a flowered bedspread and wood furniture, probably where he lured young girls in before he killed them *Shit! Keep moving!*

The last room was bare of furniture, but had a few boxes and a wooden chest on the floor. *This was it! I knew it! Where the war guns were!* I quickly spun around to see his chair at the entry of the hall.

"Very nice!" I exclaimed. And flew back to my seat on the couch. As I walked past him, I felt shivers up my spine. *He could pull a gun on me right now and I would be helpless to do anything about it.* He rolled in behind me and snarled, "Want wine?" *Wine? No real booze?* Having experienced this at Amir's too, I figured this must be what old people drink. "Ok," I replied.

He rolled into the other room, returned with a bottle and we drank in silence. *Maybe he doesn't want to talk anymore.* I didn't want to upset him. I just sat. "How old are you?" he asked. "Twenty," I responded. After a while more, he said, "You can take your clothes off if you want." "Right here?" I asked. "Of course here!" he barked. "What is wrong with you?"

Although that was a good question coming from most people, on this particular day, I was sure I had met my superior with regard to mental defects. I complied.

As I undressed, I felt frail and cold in the bare room. Completely terrified, I began to coach myself. *Just take your clothes off. Don't look down. Pretend like you're still dressed. Act normal. Keep your clothes close in case he tries anything. You can grab them and run.* Once I was completely undressed, I just stood there; my thin lanky body trembling, arms strapped at my side as if I had forgotten where to put them. Looking beyond him, I was trying desperately not to feel his eyes on me. Praying he wouldn't touch me. *Focus on the money. In a few minutes you will be out of here and you will have money. You and Alyssa can get high. Project yourself outside of here. Think of being in the car with Alyssa. Please don't leave Alyssa. How long had it been? My God, what if she left?* As I calculated what had happened thus far, I deduced that I had only been in for around forty minutes. *She wouldn't leave, would she?*

I was sure he could sense my nervousness. I was anything but sexy. I looked like a prisoner getting ready for an anal cavity search; a bit stiff, head straight up, looking off into the distance, expressionless, a sexy vision indeed. "Ok! You can get dressed!" He barked. *Thank God.*

In the blink of an eye, I was fully clothed again, sitting back in my seat on the couch, attempting to recover from that very uncomfortable task by appearing to take a small, relaxing sip off of my wine. A few moments later he said, "You can go now." Although every part of me wanted to run out of the door like I had a firecracker up my butt, I got up slowly, snatched my purse from off of the couch, did my best to smile at him, said "thank you" and casually walked out of the door.

As I walked out I recall feeling three things. Guilt. I had just taken his money and not given him anything. Sadness. He had no one. And curiosity. What had happened to this man that left him so alone? No family. No friends. No tree.

The only person he could get to come over on Christmas Eve was someone he had to pay. Something was seriously wrong. I found myself absorbed by his level of anger and separation from society. In a strange way I felt connected to him. Although his isolation was more apparent, we were both alone.

I could not remember a time in my life that I was happier to see Alyssa's face. I practically ran down the front path and jumped into the car. As we tore out of the neighborhood, I recounted the insanity of the past hour to her.

We had to deliver the money back to the call service lady, but getting high was a priority. I had to mentally purge the last hour with drugs. Since Alyssa wanted coke and I wanted heroin, we went to Buena Clinton. We bought a piece of tar heroin and some coke. Thankfully, I had a needle back at my motel. We ran out of heroin too quickly, and as usual, I was left in a state of paranoid insanity yearning for more coke.

By the time we called the lady at Star call service, I could barely speak and I was having a hard time not taking the remaining money to get more drugs. The only reason I did call was the intense belief that something horrible would happen if I didn't. She had my driver's license and my address. I knew someone would come for me. My jaw was locked and I was unable to speak much more than a whisper when she answered. Fortunately, she did most of the talking after hello.

"I can meet you in the gas station on Fairview Road in an hour, but if you want you can go on another date first, we have a man waiting. He is close by. You can see him and bring me all of the money after, in just one trip." I knew I wanted more coke, which meant I needed more money, so I agreed.

Never really thinking about the inherent sex act I would eventually have to perform, in my mind, I went straight from her question to the money, then the drugs and agreed. This was an internal communication problem that I would continue to experience over and over again. I would completely miss the bad part. From the question to the money without any thought of what was in the inevitable middle.

We should have been back at my mom's hours ago. It was now after midnight. The guilt of knowing they were sitting there all night was heart-wrenching and only made me want to get high even more. I could not think about it. It was now too late. Leaving my dad to wait after he had flown out here. Never returning to Madie. My child. My angel. Who was I? Who had I become? It was unbearable. It was too late. It was done. It hurt too much to face myself. My self-hatred increased and as it did, so did my need to feel numb.

The guilt I endured day after day, time after time continued to worsen and with it my sense of self worth diminished. My need to medicate would choose itself over the people in my life and drive me deeper and deeper down in an effort to shut off my feelings. I was the kind of person that even I would hate. Leaving my own child waiting on Christmas? I needed to forget. I needed to get high.

Having agreed to do it again, we left the motel. By the time we got down to the next house, the heroin had taken off a good deal of the coke edge. This was good. Although still inflicted with cravings, I was no longer hearing voices and my hand and jaw had settled down. I was left with the occasional paranoid thought and I was very pale and jittery. This I could deal with.

We drove up to a large house in a beautiful neighborhood. This time it was much different. The man who answered the door looked like a businessman. Upon entering I could see that the house was richly furnished, with expensive pictures and accessories. The man was about fifty years old. He looked like someone my mom would date. As I scanned the room I quickly deduced that he was married. There were pictures in the entry-way of him with a lady around his age and kids. I couldn't figure out why a nice man with a wife and family called a service, but I thought of my family and realized that maybe they weren't normal either. That being said, the normalcy of the home made me feel safe. He had kids. And I figured that I didn't have to worry about AIDS because he was married. This was much better.

Much to my surprise, this one really knew the drill. As he walked me through the foyer into the family room, he pointed to the kitchen counter. There were a few hundred dollar bills and his license. He said, "Go ahead make the call." And he pointed to a phone. After the call, he simply told me to follow him.

He took me into the master bedroom with lush furnishings. There was a huge bed that was way too high to mount without a jump and again more pictures on the dresser. As I glanced toward the pictures he said, "Oh. My wife is on a trip." I just nodded. He said, "You can take your clothes off and get on the bed." I followed procedure. All I could think about was getting this done and the money. As I stripped my clothes off, I felt uncomfortable and anxious. What would he want me to do next? Would I know what to do? At this point I started to get really scared. This would be the first time I would actually have to do something. I was a wreck. I needed to calm down and I knew it. For the sake of making it through this, I tried to talk myself into a better state. *Ok, Lauri, he is a normal guy, a safe guy, a husband, a dad. It will only take a few minutes and then you will have a bunch of money. The sooner you start, the sooner you will be out of here with money in your hand. Just get it over with…*

He stared at me while I undressed, smiling. *Yuck!* I was completed grossed out. At the point I was fully undressed, he climbed on top of me missionary style. When he pushed inside of me, I clenched my eyes and looked the other way and began to chant in my mind, *Just a few minutes…just a few minutes…just a few minutes…Focus on the money, just a few minutes and the money is yours…Think of something else…The car… Alyssa…the money…more drugs. Just a few minutes and it will be over, focus on the money, focus on the money…*Finally he let out a noise and it was over. Disgusting and wet. I was horrified and at the same time thankful. It was over.

That wasn't too bad. It was less than five minutes. He pointed me to the bathroom. I cleaned up. The moment I was dry again, I could make like it never happened. *It is over and I had a lot of money again. No harm done. Safe.*

Alyssa was amazed when I was back in the car within minutes and found that he had even paid me extra. It wasn't as bad as I thought; just a few minutes. I realized that night that I had the ability to get as much money as we needed and now having gone through the "real deal," I knew I could do it. There would no longer be a struggle for money in my life. I was clearly able to handle it and the money was inexhaustible.

The focus on money hid the desecration of my body and my soul from my view. By the time I was conscious of what I was doing to myself, it would be too late. I would be so far into the depths of hell that I could no longer climb out.

We decided it was best to drop the money off to the lady now, before we got high and accidentally spent it. We called the lady and, as planned before, met her at a gas station. Alyssa stayed a minute away in the car where she could see me, but not be seen by others. Much to my surprise, the call service lady appeared normal. She pulled up in a white Mercedes coupe, freshly detailed with shiny rims. She was about thirty two years old with lush black hair that was just past her shoulders, which appeared to have been set with curlers, shiny and cute. Her glasses made her look smart and stylish, like a well-to-do librarian type. She had on nice black slacks and a grey sweater set. Her matching jewelry looked like real gold, and had petite diamonds. She was not an addict type by any means, but she was certainly up late at night. By this time it was almost two in the morning. She said thank you and explained that she was having wine with some friends and needed to return to her condo. She asked me to call her again the next night and told me I did well for my first night.

Before she walked away she said, "When you are new we usually start you off slowly, one date every few days. Thanks for being so available. Call me tomorrow; I will let you know what I have." As I walked away I actually felt like I had accomplished something. Not only had I made a ton of money, she said I did a good job. I felt good.

Alyssa and I darted off to Buena Clinton and then back to the motel. For the next few hours, I was incapacitated as I shook from fear in the bathroom tub with the door locked. Even Alyssa was surprised to see the progression of the addiction and the level of psychotic behavior I was exhibiting. A few hours into the paranoia, I slowly opened the bathroom door to look in the room. I had to know if "they" were out there. When I peered out to see only Alyssa, I knew from the look on her face that she was scared of what was happening to me. But she said nothing. By the time I had completely calmed down, the sun was coming in and I could hear birds outside of the room. I crept out of the bathroom and said, "Let's go." Alyssa did not say a word about my prior state. We pushed it under the carpet and just went on, as we did with everything else in our lives.

As we reentered my mom's house, it was dead silent. My mother and Madie were fast asleep in my mom's room and the house had been shut down for the night. My father's return flight was just hours away, so he was long gone. The embarrassment that my mom must have experienced was unthinkable. Waiting for us, telling my dad we would be there soon, telling Madie mommy would come home soon. Devastated. I hated myself.

When I returned to the bed I lay in earlier, my eyes were pegged open. I could not sleep and I was certainly in no shape to interact with humans. Hopefully they would sleep for a few hours more. Anyone seeing me would know I was on death's door. Madie was the only person who couldn't see it. Being so young, unless I was very high or she could feel my heartbeat, she was oblivious. The safety of my mom's house with the smells that lingered from the food and Madie's baby powder brought about an intense awareness of the evil within me. I had to stop hurting her. Even if she didn't know, I knew.

As I lay in bed that early morning, I recalled something Beatrice had said. "If you ever want us to watch Madie, we will. We love her like our own." They wanted to adopt her. I would never let that happen, she was all I had, but right now I thought maybe they could watch her and I could get help. That would be good.

Beatrice lived just a few houses down from my mom. Once the drugs wore off, I grabbed the stroller from the garage and Madie and I walked over. They were happy to see us. All of the kids came out of their rooms to see Madie. They loved her. Although it was difficult to ask or even think about, I knew if she watched Madie I could get help. I knew I needed help. It would only be temporary and Madie loved playing with the kids. Although I needed help, I truly had no idea what "help" meant. I had no knowledge of a place to go for help; I just knew I needed something. It was more of an idea than a formal plan. Although it sounded like a rational idea, I could never leave Madie. I never got up the nerve to ask, I left that day without saying a word.

Lack of understanding of what "help" meant was an understatement. I specifically recall one day when I was hitchhiking after a long coke binge. I was desperate for help and I felt dead inside. A man picked me up to give me a ride to where ever I was going. Although he was quiet for most of the ride, at the end he said, "It is obvious that you are in need. Jesus can help you. If you call him out, he will be there." For lack of a good response, I did not respond at all. Then he said, "This looks like where you want to be dropped. If you want help, just ask him. Jesus help me, Jesus help me. Say it over and over again and he will come."

Well, as silly and ridiculous as that sounded, I was out of ideas. There I was after he dropped me, alone on the street, chanting, "Jesus help me, Jesus help me." Being a good addict and quite compulsive, I probably said it thirty times; nothing happened. Being a Jew I had no idea who Jesus was or what I was asking for, but bottom line was I was out of options.

When Madie and I returned to my mom's she said nothing of the night before and avoided eye contact, as usual. Again, the Burns Conflict Resolution Plan: Bury it. The lack of communication only piled on the unresolved conflict within me. I was being buried alive. Layer after layer, the shame and humiliation just piled on. Having no other access for "how to be" or "how to change," I was destined to repeat the same mistakes over and over again.

I kept on reliving the hardship and pain I caused. The experience she must have had with my dad and Madie that night. All of them waiting patiently for our arrival, hour after hour, losing hope and worrying about what could have happened. No call, no return. My poor baby, I wanted to be so much more for her. She was so perfect. Why couldn't I just be good? I knew more than ever that God would take her from me. I never deserved her. I was incapable of taking care of the most perfect gift. He was coming to take her and I knew it.

Interestingly enough, although I didn't like my dad, I also felt shameful for leaving him sitting there. I had no reason, excuse or explanation for who I was or why I did the things I did. How do you explain that? It didn't even make sense to me. It was as if I was possessed. I was a thousand times more disappointed in myself than they were in me. I knew every time I opened my mouth to say I didn't know why I did what I did, although completely true, it sounded like a copout. It only served to escalate things. This is something I believe every addict feels at some point of their addiction. No escape out, trapped in a vicious cycle of disappointment.

That night, when I returned to the hotel, Brandt was watching TV. This was one night that I would not use no matter what. Still experiencing the after effect of the night before and the remorse for the monster I had become, I just couldn't do it. But by morning, things were different. I was very sick. I needed at least one shot.

Brandt didn't have any money and I knew the Call Service lady had specifically said, "Call at night." As I sat on the bed, I began brainstorming. I needed to get well. I had to figure out a plan. One bad idea after another raced through my mind, until I suddenly came up with something.

I recalled an experience a few months back when I was driving with one of the guys from Shady Acres to pick up. As we drove up the boulevard headed for the dealer's house I saw a girl hitchhiking. On our way back with the drugs, I saw her again. Only this time she was hitchhiking in the opposite direction. I said, "Wowcc, she is really confused. The poor girl has no idea where she is going."

It was at that point that I learned the facts of life—street life that is. He quickly brought me up to speed. "Lauri, are you serious? She is not looking for a ride. She is working. These girls work the streets all day; they hitchhike up and down doing tricks to get money for drugs." Ok, now I felt stupid, but also intrigued. I knew nothing about this life. I assumed these girls were "real" junkies. But not wanting to appear even dumber, I did not ask any more questions.

Now sitting in my motel room, reflecting back on that day, I thought, *I have been hitchhiking for years. Hitchhiking was never a problem for me. At this point, I have had sex with men for money and nothing happened to me. I haven't changed, still the same old Lauri. If I had changed, Brandt would have noticed, but nope, still the same old Lauri.* I pretty much forgot about the sex thing right after it happened. As soon as I picked up, it was gone, blocked out as if it never happened. I could just continue to will myself to forget about it. It's not like anything bad happened. Anyway, worst case scenario, I can just hitchhike towards the dealer's and maybe someone will offer me some money. I can make the final determination right at that time. If I am freaked out, or the guy is creepy, I could just say no. Worst case scenario, I hitchhike, turn around and come back. No harm, no foul. But if the guy is cute and has money, I could get well and that would be great. Within a few minutes I began preparation for my mission. I retrieved my military style Sketcher boots from under the bed and started to tie them on. Better safe than sorry. Always good to have sturdy boots.

As I started to prepare, Brandt started asking questions. This was something I hadn't thought about, but I was always quick on my feet when it came to making stuff up. I told him that I had an idea, a scam, an idea to make money. He always trusted that since I was older and I knew a lot of prison guys, I could pull something off. I explained that I knew some guy; a friend of Gabriel's that I could probably get a front from. He didn't need to know the specifics. He was just happy that I might be able to score. All was well. I can assure you that if he knew what I was about to do, he would have tried to stop me. Brandt was young, and although using drugs, he was completely monogamous in his thinking. He was barely out of high school and not near the level of desperation that I had achieved. Bottom line, he wouldn't have to know. I would get money and return with drugs. Once I gave him his shot, there would be no further discussion.

32

M Y EXTERIOR WAS SO HARDENED BY THIS POINT THAT YOU COULD never see the pain beyond my eyes. People often told me that I was mysterious. "Hard to read," they would say. They said I had a distant look in my eyes. They could never tell where I was or what I was thinking. The truth of the matter was since I could never see myself from an outsider's view I had no idea what they were talking about. I know now that any part of me that was real was so deeply injured, it was miles away. Like a tortoise, you could look at me all you wanted, but you would never see me. Under the protective armor, there was only more armor. I had disappeared years ago.

Although I never really thought about it at the time, the sensation of others touching my body had ceased to mean anything long before that first night as a call girl. The separation began with the requirement to hug my dad after being beaten, continued with that summer night many years ago in the dirty sleeping bag of the man that stole my innocence and stored his baby in my body, and became permanent the night my body reacted without my permission in that small Catalina bed. I would never again connect with my body in any way that would leave me vulnerable. My body was no longer a part of me. Being fully disconnected from it and having no other use for it, I would sell it to others in return for money to numb the ongoing torment of the memories from my childhood and the horror of my existence.

I surrounded myself with people who saw something in me to counter the worthlessness I felt from within. Although it wasn't a conscious thought, it was clear on many occasions that I derived a sense of self worth from some of the lowest life forms. Not caring how corrupt they were, whether drug addicts, men cheating on their wives, or pure perverts, as long as someone still valued me, I was okay.

And my friends, especially Gabriel, always made me feel valued. Honor among thieves is a much different kind of honor than that of most normal people. In our world I knew that regardless of what happened, Gabriel and his friends would always be there for me. They never changed. They were consistent.

Coming from the insanity that I grew up in, where you couldn't trust anyone and you never knew what was going to happen next, I needed this stability. I needed to know who I was dealing with. And I did.

We were in this through thick and thin. If someone hurt me, Gabriel would be there. And although we loved each other, it was unspoken but clear that if you died in the course of using, like Alvin that day, you would be sacrificed for the safety of the remaining pack. As cold as it was, it never changed. We all knew the risks we were taking and these were the values we lived by. We were all in this together. A family that lived and died for each other. We were strong and consistent in our beliefs.

One of the core beliefs that I carried with me that day when I walked out onto the streets came from a roommate in Anaheim a few years back. It served me well, so I kept it.

It was the day after my roommate was hit in the face by his girlfriend and they ended up breaking Madie's leg. I remember asking him, "Joe, if your girlfriend is as crazy as you say, why don't you break up with her?" I will never forget his answer. It resonated with me for many years after and still unconsciously on the day I walked out on the street. "It's the sex," he said. If I had no other value, I knew sex would secure me. Even when his girlfriend disrespected him on every level, the sex would make all of her defects acceptable.

Just as my father's eyes created a mirror of self-hatred for me, the men that liked me created a mirror of acceptance that made me feel powerful. Throughout my life, from the time I was small, my perception of "me" was determined by the eyes of the men that surrounded me. It started with my dad and continued throughout my life. As the quality of the men I associated with became more and more corrupt, so did the activities I would engage in for acceptance. As long as my audience was happy, I was ok.

The day I walked out on the streets, I was primed for it. I was going to prove it to all of them. Everyone who ever told me I couldn't. I was in charge now. And if I die, I will go down with a fight. When they strip my body of clothes, they will reveal the flaming skull head tattooed on my back and see that they didn't kill me, because I was already dead. I feared nothing and thought of nothing. Nothing was taken from me that I hadn't already given. No one could truly hurt me, because I couldn't feel.

I walked out of our hotel, crossed the street and stuck my thumb out. Although the girls I had seen were further north, I figured, if I get one good ride, I will be there.

It was then that I realized, as I had with the call service, I had no idea how to do this. Was I supposed to say something when I got in? Proposition the person? I had no clue. I decided I would just hitchhike and see what happened. With no solid plan in mind, I just went with it. If nothing happened, maybe by the time I got back to the hotel, it would be late enough for me to call STAR. The bottom line was, I was heroin sick and had nothing else on my calendar.

The first guy picked me up just minutes after I stuck my thumb out. "Where you goin'?" *Hmmm…didn't think about this…*"First Street!" jumped out of my mouth. I don't know why I chose First Street, other than that it was the beginning of what I knew to be "the area." Since I had been hitchhiking for years, this part of the process was very normal to me. It was the transition to money and sex that I still had to master and I had no idea how to do that, yet.

He was a regular guy, about thirty-five and not bad looking. He asked me about my day, where I lived, and what kind of music I liked. Although I struggled to transition to asking for money, it just didn't fit. There was no way to go from "What band do you like" to "Hey do you want to pay me for sex?" He dropped me off promptly on First Street and said, "Have a *great* day!" I waved goodbye as he drove away.

When I slammed the door shut I thought, *OK, that was a no go. Now I am on First Street, still no money and no plan. What a loser. How the heck was I going to do this?* Maybe the girls I see on the streets know the guys that pick them up? Maybe I need to dress differently? The girls I had seen on the streets were not dressed up like prostitutes. Not like on TV. As a matter of fact, they were quite the opposite. They were hopeless looking. Torn jeans, hardened leather skin, missing teeth and a void empty look in their eyes. Over the past few months, I had seen the same girls over and over again, standing on the street with their thumbs all day long, every day. They never left the area.

I am still good looking enough that this gig should be easy for me. I mean if these guys are picking up homeless-looking girls, I should be a huge step up. After all, I am an escort girl. As a matter of fact, anyone that gets me on the street today should pay extra premium because unlike the others, I was freshly showered and I had a full set of teeth. Furthermore, this may be the only chance they will have at a "normal girl" because I am sure I will never do this again. I have a high paying job at STAR Services. This was a one day gig, just to get over the hump.

As I stood on the corner where the first man dropped me, a white Plymouth pulled up. There was a chubby white man in his early fifties driving. "Need a ride?" "Yes," I said. As I got in, I noticed the car was a mess. Old paper coffee cups on the floor, remains of fast food containers and the ashtray was overflowing with butts.

As we pulled away from the curb, he said, "So do you really need a ride?" "Actually I need money," I replied. He said, "Well are you willing to do something for the money?"

I said, "Well what do you want me to do?" He said, "Well I'm not going to say it first, you could be a cop." I looked at him like he was crazy. I mean clearly I was a kid for cripes sakes. I wasn't old enough to have gone to school to be a cop, but I humored him.

"Do I look like a cop?" "Ok," he said. "I will give you $80 if we get a room." *$80 dollars? He must be kidding. But from the looks of his car, I could tell he wasn't living the high life.*

I quickly responded, "Are you kidding? $80? I usually get $150." "Are you crazy?" he said. "You are lucky I am offering $80!" He went on to say, "Look kid, maybe you don't know the drill around here, but I can get a head job for $20 and sex for $40 from any one of the girls out here. Take it or leave it. I can easily get someone else."

That sounded extremely cheap to me and the guy was a total slob, but he was probably right. The rates out here were probably a lot lower. I mean, for cripes sakes, look at my competition. These girls would probably take anything you offered them. The truth was the guy knew the drill and I didn't. Not only did he know the prices, he also knew the girls. I was lucky to land a regular.

Then I started thinking. *I promised Brandt I would return with money. I have to return with money and drugs or he'll think I'm a loser. I didn't come all the way out here to fail. I had to save face with Brandt. I can get it over with quickly. Brandt will be so surprised when I return with drugs. My second ride and I had this thing figured out. In less than two hours I can return with drugs and money. I knew I could do this thing. As disgusting as this man is, I have to start somewhere. Then at least I will know the drill.* I took the deal.

At the motel we got out of the Plymouth and walked up to the small office window. Before we got there, the man turned to me and said, "If they ask, you are my daughter." As I stood there, I realized this guy had no idea if I was eighteen. He was probably trying to avoid any suspicion of child molestation by the hotel manager. That made sense. Lord knows we didn't want any heat, so I agreed.

The old Asian man at the office window seemed to know the man. As he grabbed the money from his hand he barked, "One hour; then you pay again!" I couldn't believe it.

The man behind the window knew what we were doing? He clearly knew the man. What kind of person needs a room for an hour? And more importantly, why would you want a room with your daughter for an hour? I assumed this was just something you had to agree to if they asked. The man at the motel knew what we are doing, and surprisingly enough, not only did he not care, he offered special rates. Well, I guess it can't be that bad if everyone knows.

I was sure everything was kosher and this man would not hurt me because he knew the hotel manager was in the loop. While that made me feel safer, it also made me feel extremely embarrassed. The Asian man thinks I am a freakin prostitute! Like one of the toothless girls from the street? I was a regular girl with a boyfriend and a daughter. I was sure he could tell. Maybe he did think I was his daughter. Who knew?

As we opened the door, the smell of old ashtrays and spilt beer wafted through the air. The brown-stained carpet was crushed down and rippled much like the one at Shady Acres and the worn bedspread was covered in dark flowers to hide the stains. This was definitely not a room you would want to spend the entire night in. It was disgusting. As he walked over to the side of the bed, he began to unzip his pants and remove them. Completely repulsed, but knowing I had made the commitment, I followed suit. *Just get it over with Lauri, and you will be out of here in no time.* Then he sat down on the bed. I did too. It was hard like a box, no sign of springs. He immediately instructed me as to what I was to do. "Come here." I was completely disgusted, but as always, I started to coach myself. *Just a few more minutes Lauri and you will be on your way home.* Just as I endured hugging my father after he beat me, I knew I could endure this repulsive man. If I just went with it, it would be over soon.

The stench of the room, the disgust of the dirty old fat man and the awkward silence that amplified the disgusting sounds of his body were horrifying. The second it was over, I jumped up, grabbed my clothes, ran into the bathroom to wash the disgust from my body and pulled on my clothes. The smell hung in the air. I needed to get out. I grabbed the money from the dresser and headed for the door. As the sunlight hit my eyes and the cool breeze hit my face, I took my first breath in what seemed like an hour. I pushed the disgust out of my mind. It was over and I had money. As I quickly crossed the parking lot to leave, the man exited the room and yelled, "Hey, the key! You have time on the room, take the key!"

Since it had only been about fifteen minutes since we entered and he had rented it for an hour, I guess he was telling me to return the key later. I realized this was probably what the other girls did when they had a room. Use it until the time was up. Although I only planned on only doing this one time, I now realized if I hooked another guy in quickly, I could make twice the money. Maybe I wouldn't even have to call Star that night. As disgusted and dirty as I felt, I could do it just one more time.

I walked south on the street, heading towards where the man had picked me up. Within five minutes, a dark car pulled up to the curb. It was a man about thirty years of age, not bad looking and the car was clean. Without much hesitation he propositioned me, told me he was on his lunch break and just needed a quickie and asked me how much. Following the lead from the other man, I said $80. Although he looked surprised and mumbled something about being broke, he then said, "You look like you're worth it."

In less than ten minutes I was back in the room. This time was easier. The guy was in good shape, not bad looking, and most importantly, he wasn't my dad's age. Within a few minutes it was over. I returned the key and crossed the parking lot with $160 in my pocket. As I walked to Buena Clinton to score some drugs, I felt powerful. I had left the motel room this morning with nothing. I was rich. I had almost as much as I got from my welfare check for two weeks and it had been less than two hours. Since a balloon of heroin was only $10 at the time, I returned with two balloons, $20 worth of coke and a wad of cash. Brandt was both happy and surprised. He didn't ask any questions.

Although you would think I must have undergone a horrible psychic change that day or had a good deal of mixed feelings or fear about what I did, I didn't. I immediately felt better when the drugs were injected into my body. At the end of the day, back at the hotel, I felt powerful. That was how it started.

Even though I vowed it would only be that one time, for the next few months, I would wake up with the same conversation. *You've done it before. You know how to hitchhike. If it doesn't work out, you can call the service.*

Each morning I found someone to watch Madie and I walked out onto the boulevard and stuck my thumb out. I got into strange men's cars, rented rooms and did whatever they told me to. Although I continually found it disgusting, I became a master at focusing on the afterthought, the money. After a short time, I became so delusional I started to believe I had hit the jackpot.

I learned the ropes very rapidly. The guys would never say what they wanted for fear of being arrested or setup, and I couldn't proposition them for the same reason. But if the guy said it first, then I knew he wasn't a cop or it would be entrapment. Within a few weeks, I spent my first full day on the streets. From morning 'til night. It was also the first time I would buy a used needle. It was customary for junkies who hung out in Buena Clinton, who didn't deal and had no game (method of making money) to search the trashcans and bushes for used rigs and sell them for a premium. Not knowing where it came from, the floor of a carport, trash, or even rented to several people throughout the day, at the point when I became really sick, it didn't matter. *The way it is going, I won't be alive for long anyway.*

I bought a used syringe for five dollars. The needle was bent and the numbers that measured the amount in the cylinder were worn off from use. As I walked away, the man warned me, "Be careful not to push too hard Mija. With the bend in the needle, it could break off in your arm." I understood the risk and accepted it. I needed to get well. It was early yet and if I could get well, I could make more money.

This was the day I learned about "the twist." The first time I heard it, it sounded unreal. With no comprehension of how it could occur or if it even existed, I thought the girl who told me was just trying to scare me, make me turn away from the streets. Not really grasping the full weight of what she was saying, I just listened. I could never have imagined the magnitude of what she was trying to tell me. There was no way I could have prepared myself. By the time I realized it was "real," it was too late.

I was on the streets just over a month when I met Tammy and her girlfriend Criminal. Tammy had AIDS. Everyone knew it, not only because her girlfriend would warn you when you wanted to share their needle, but also because anyone could plainly see it. The disease was eating her alive. Scabs consumed her face and body. Any normal person having taken a gander at Tammy and Criminal coming down the street would have gladly given them room to pass.

Criminal walked and held herself like a man, but her breasts gave her up as a woman. Hardened by her life and years on the streets, with a leathery, scarred grimace, she was unapproachable. You could tell from looking at her that she had spent a good deal of time in prison and was more comfortable inside than she was on the outs. You could also tell from her armor that she was not interested in chatting. Dressed in men's Dickies, a shirt buttoned to the top like a gang member and the word *CRIMINAL* tattooed in old English writing on the side of her neck, she was angry. For the most part, people avoided any eye contact with the pair out of sympathy for Tammy's apparent illness and fear of an altercation with Criminal.

I was surprised the day Criminal approached me. I was standing at the bus stop on Fifth Street awaiting the next car, when I turned to see her behind me. "Got a light?" she said with a cigarette dangling from her mouth. I immediately noticed that although Criminal looked extremely dangerous from a distance, her insecure, meek voice gave her up as a scared little girl.

Talk on the streets from the other girls was that unless locked up, Tammy and Criminal were inseparable. They were in love. After speaking with her for just a few minutes, it was clear that being inseparable from Tammy had less to do with being in love and more to do with not wanting to be alone. I provided her with a matchbook. She lit her cigarette, threw her match to the ground and avoided eye contact. Eyes fixed to the ground, she began to kick the match and talk. Under that tough exterior, she was too shy to even look at me. I assumed she found me attractive. Not looking up from her shoes, her face was flushed with embarrassment as she spoke.

"So how come we neva seen you around here? You don't look familiar to me. You do any time?" "Not really," I replied. "Just juvie when I was a kid and a few little things as of late." Like Gabriel had taught me, *keep it quiet, don't brag.* She ran through a list of people she knew, comparing names from juvenile hall, jail and the streets to see if we had any common friends. When she came up dry, she just continued to talk.

"Have they questioned you about what happened a few weeks back?" she asked. Having no idea who "they" were and not wanting to appear stupid, I just replied, "No." She continued, "It was at the Firelodge Motel, guy pulled a twist on some chick, cut her all up. They found one of her eyeballs cut out on the bathroom counter." Criminal knew the girl! She was a regular on the street. "They're looking for the guy; still haven't found him. Police are asking questions. They're cool; they won't arrest you, just tell them what you know."

She went on to tell me, "The twist happens a lot out on the streets and when it does, you need to get yourself out quick. Use everything and anything you can think of. Think your way out. They get crazy. You don't want to end up like that. The twist is when a guy looks normal when he picks you up and somewhere in your time with him, he changes. He goes psychopath. It is as if he turns around and then he's someone else. He looks at you one way and then he looks back around and it's completely different. It is dangerous. You must get out or he will kill you."

I will never forget the first time it hit home what she meant. Although she was very blunt the day she told me, I couldn't have imagined the seriousness of what she was trying to transmit. In a world with no rules, void of sanity, moments away from your own death and knowing it, the desperation and pleading that will buy you one more second of life is timeless. *You must get out or he will kill you...*Although it didn't happen immediately, once it did, I would never be the same again.

Returning home that night, after hours on the street, I had a wad of cash, drugs and ongoing thoughts of that poor girl in the Firelodge Motel. I needed to relax. For the life of me, I couldn't figure out why someone would do that. I was sure I hadn't met any of those crazy guys and from now on, I would be on guard for anyone who looked weird.

When I walked in the room Brandt was asleep. I woke him up, walked out to the payphone and called over to Gabriel's. Now that I was home, I needed a new needle before this one broke in my arm. Gabriel was not there, but Lexie was. Knowing I had drugs, she came over. Not able to wait, I was in the bathroom struggling with that broken thing when she arrived.

For the next several hours we spiraled down into the pits of hell. When the cop car pulled up in front of the motel room, we had no idea. I was sweating profusely, my mouth was caked with white chalk in the corners and I was on the bed rocking in my own private hell, trying to calm down. After several hours of hiding behind the bed, I had started to return to a more normal state. It had been about an hour since Brandt took Madie in her stroller to get some snacks from the store. We both agreed that anytime I was using drugs, she needed to be away. Lexie was standing in front of the open bathroom door, having just exited when we heard the knock...

Before I could think, Lexie went straight to the door and opened it. When I saw the police officer there, it validated every ounce of paranoia I ever felt. My heart jumped out of my chest! Lexie completely opened the door exposing not only the contents of the room, but also the spoon and needle sitting on the toilet tank! It was a straight shot from the door; he couldn't miss it! What was she doing?!

As the policeman man spoke, he surveyed the room with his eyes. I couldn't hear what he was saying because I was terrified of what he would see. When he looked over Lexie's shoulder to the bathroom beyond, his eyes widened and he said, "Well, well. What is this?!" Before anyone could respond, Lexie said, "Can I talk to you alone?" She walked out of the front door of the room and shut the door behind her. They walked just far enough to be out of my sight. I couldn't believe it! What was she telling him? I could only imagine. *"See the crazy girl in the room, they are her drugs, I am just trying to help her.*" Or maybe she was telling him that I had a child and she was just down the way! My heart and mind raced. I had to escape! The only way out was the front door. There was no window out! I was going to jail! What about Madie?

A few minutes later, I heard the loud clicking of the officer's large shoes as he approached our door again. About to jump out of my skin, I was dumbstruck when the handle turned and Lexie entered alone. The police car's engine roared and he drove away.

I will never know what she said to that man, but it was enough for him to forget what he saw. Clearly Lexie was a rat. I needed to stay far away from her. Unlike the others, she could not be trusted.

When Brandt returned, I told him what had happened. We agreed it was too hot and we needed to get away for a few days. Although we had paid for a week, it didn't matter. For all we knew Lexie could have told that cop to come back later. We couldn't stay.

When we arrived at Lucy's parent's house in Irvine, a nice family community, she said, "You can only stay here for a few days. Lay low and stay quiet. Brandt has to sleep somewhere else. My parents would never let a guy spend the night. You and Madie are okay if you are quiet." Lucy's parents had rules, but as long as we followed them they were pretty cool. Although Lucy knew we shot up a lot, neither of her parents had any idea about our lifestyle.

I was able to make it through the night, but I woke up the next morning very sick. When Brandt returned in the morning, after crashing at a friend's house, we immediately jumped in the car and headed towards Santa Ana. With the remaining money, he would take me to pick up while Lucy watched the kids. We would give her some in exchange for her services, so all was well.

On our way back from Buena Clinton, I glanced in the mirror and saw the lights. The police! "They are pulling us over!" I had never seen Brandt so petrified. Not knowing if he was going to hit the gas or the brake, I was surprised when he pulled to the side of the road. My head raced. *Why are they pulling us over? Were we speeding?* I quickly took in the enormity of the situation. We had picked up and had heroin on us. All five balloons were in my mouth. This was the very reason they packaged the stuff like this. Safe transport and immediate disposal, if necessary. If I needed to, I would swallow it. This amount of heroin would kill me if it released into my system, but the theory was that if it was tied tightly in a rubber balloon, it would exit at the other end the same way it got in. I was counting on it.

As Brandt pulled the car slowly to the curb, I said, "Stay calm. Please just stay calm or he will know. Crap, I wonder how long he has been following us? Since Buena Clinton? Just stay calm."

The officer walked up to Brandt's windows and said "Please step out of the car." I was still terrified, even though I knew I could swallow at any time. Just the presence of the police frightened me. I moved the balloons between my back teeth and my cheek. I tried to appear calm. *Just stay calm Lauri.*

After performing a thorough search of the car, questioning us on our origination and destination sites, and coming up with nothing, he said, "You realize you didn't make a full stop at the stop sign back there. I am not going to give you a ticket, but full stop next time or I will surely write you up." I knew it was Brandt's innocent nature that got us off the hook. Whew!

Just as he was about to walk away, the cop turned toward the top of the car and said, "Well, well. What is this?" My eyes followed his as he peered into to the rubbery inner lining of the open sunroof on Brandt's black Jetta. I couldn't believe it! A Rig! He had a Rig hidden in the rubber lining of the sunroof and it was open! You could clearly see it resting there in open view!

"Well, well, looks like someone is going away." He told us to get out of the car, put our hands on our heads and turn around. My knees trembled as I got out of the car. What were they going to do to us? Then he said, "Is this car registered in your name?" Brandt responded, "Yes." He completed the conversation, "You have the right to remain silent..." Brandt's head hung down and I avoided looking at him. The car was impounded, Brandt was taken to jail and I watched as they drove away. No car, and no money, but I still had drugs in my mouth.

I hitchhiked back to Lucy's, I got well and she got high. The difference was that I was addicted and she wasn't. When you aren't addicted, the drugs actually made you feel lightheaded. For me, they just made the pain in my body subside and returned me to a "normal state." Basically, at this point, I needed the drugs. I stayed at Lucy's for the next two days, complying with her parent's house rules. I was too afraid to return to the motel and still in shock about Brandt.

We got into a routine in no time. Lucy would watch Madie and I would go out and make money. I never told her where I was getting it. I just told her I had a connection to get free drugs and that if she watched Madie, I would come back with it. As long as I turned up with drugs, she was okay.

It was about this time that I first felt humiliation about my actions. I believe it was the lack of sleep, level of sickness and the time of day that got to me. I had left Lucy's the night before, and although I said I would return in a few hours, I was still out, and the night had come and gone. For the first time, I was standing on the boulevard with my thumb out during morning rush hour. The people in the cars were going to work. I had been up all night. Then my head kicked in with thoughts I had not heard before. *What if one of my mom's friends sees me? Or better yet, my mom? On her way to an insurance appointment. Look at me, I am a mess. Pale, skinny and desperate, just standing here with my thumb out. What would I say? What would they think? Well I am just hitchhiking, right? Yes, they will just think I am hitchhiking. Stop tripping Lauri.* And I did. The feeling of humiliation and shame left as quickly as it arrived.

I never realized that this thing that what was supposed to be a one-time gig had become a lifestyle. By this time, my arms had fresh needle marks all the way up and down on both sides, both old and new, fresh scabs and blue and green bruises and lumps. I kept my arms covered at all times. If anyone saw them they would be horrified by the self-inflicted abuse and seriousness of the situation. As long as I didn't look at my arms much, and no one brought it to my attention, I was fine.

As the car pulled over, I got in and forgot all about my mom and people possibly seeing me. I was safe inside of the car, no longer on display on the street corner. I felt better. The good-looking man in his late forties asked, "Where are you going?" I said, "Just up the road." He said, "Up the road where?" I said, "By Westminster." He simply said, "Ok."

A few moments later he said, "Are you looking for money?" I said, "Maybe, do you have money?" He said, "Maybe. What will you do for it?" I said, "What do you want me to do?" I had this thing down—never be the first to offer.

At that point he made a U-turn; I assumed he had a spot in mind. He pulled into a gas station parking lot that was no longer in service and stopped. He looked at me and smiled. I smiled back.

The words that fell out his mouth were like a knife through my soul. *"You have the right to remain silent…"* Before I could take in what just happened, several white cars came rushing in around us. *"NO! NO! NO! You don't understand. I am not a prostitute. I was just doing this temporarily, just some money for me and my kid. Hell I didn't even proposition you. You brought it up first! You have the wrong girl! I am not a prostitute. I have a boyfriend! I have never even been slutty. Ok, so I messed up for the past few weeks, but a prostitute? NO!! I am a mother. I have a kid.*

I am a kid…

This was the moment I realized what I had become. As they put the handcuffs on me, passing cars slowed and I could feel the gaze of curious eyes judging me. My head hung down in fear of someone driving down the street and recognizing me. There I was. Standing in shame, facing the trunk of the white car with my head down surrounded by vice cops. The men arresting me did not make eye contact. Afraid that they would see the child that I was through the broken facade, I was glad. Although fully clothed, I stood naked.

The men arresting me knew that I did not deserve the tears. No one had done this to me. I had chosen this. Like it or not, this was who I had become. The curtain of ego that protected me had fallen. I could feel the thick film of disgust that hung around my presence and I knew that others could see it. They too were disgusted.

My head pounded as the muscles tightly contracted and my stomach churned in revulsion and pushed to release any food that might have served to comfort me. On an unconscious level, even my body knew how worthless I was. The churning of my stomach within its empty lining, was also a reminder of what I had become. I had chosen drugs over food for several days. Nauseated as I was, there was nothing to release.

I stood silently as the police spoke to each other about paperwork and schedules. Where older people had once approached me with compassion and advice about what a great kid I was and how I could turn it all around, I had now fallen below what is considered worthy of human contact. I was the dirt of the street they had to sweep to keep their town clean. I could feel their disgust.

As we drove away, handcuffed in the backseat of the car, I avoided looking out the window. Although I knew it was there, I did not want to see the disgust in the eyes of people in other cars. I hung my head down and my long hair draped over my swollen face where mascara marked the path of my dried tears. All of the pain I had caused my daughter, whether she knew it or not, clearly defined what type of a mom I was. I had abandoned my daughter to perform disgusting sexual acts on dirty old men. I didn't deserve her. I deserved nothing better than death.

And then it hit me. My baby. I want my baby. I want to hold her and smell the innocence of her hair, her skin and her love. My eyes welled up again, but I would not allow it. As instantly as I missed her, I turned it off. I was ashamed to even think of her. She was pure innocence and I was pure evil. I didn't deserve to think of her. The revulsion hung in the silence of the car as the police car entered the large gates of the Orange County Jail. Devastation, humiliation, fear, sadness, self-hatred, loathing and disgust enveloped me. I lifted my head to be escorted out of the car.

The next few hours were spent in a shared cell, barefoot, sitting on a cold metal bench with other girls picked up for drugs or prostitution, and a few drunks. The crying stopped the moment I entered the jail and saw other girls also being arrested, hearing the familiar sounds of the bars, yelling girls and jangling keys. I knew that crying would only serve to alienate me.

The only part of the twelve-hour booking process that I can recall was the phone call. I had one phone call and I was not looking forward to it. I had to call Lucy. By this time, I had spent hours talking to the other girls. They told me that I got a bum rap, my arrest was entrapment, what to say to the judge and not to worry, there was a mandatory ten-day sentence for first time prostitution arrests. They told me to plead no contest and it would be fine. Although I had no idea what that meant, I planned on doing it. They also told me that the judge would probably release me on my own recognizance, pending sentencing, due to the overcrowding of the jail and being that this was my first offense. I was in a very different frame of mind by the time I had to make the call.

What should I say? I am a Prostitute? I know I had been doing it, but I wasn't really a prostitute. Not like one of those toothless girls. Man, this thing was a mess. If I say I was arrested for prostitution, Lucy will think I am a prostitute—I mean a real one, like on Baretta or something, a streetwalker, high heels, dresses and pimps. Do prostitutes have pimps? I didn't even know. *You need to be clear, don't confuse this Lauri*. This is just something I was doing to get back on my feet... think...Ring...Ring..."Hello, Lucy?"

"Yeah, it's Lauri. Uhmmm I have a problem. I was arrested. Yeah, arrested. I guess I had a warrant. They saw me hitchhiking. Mixing a bit of truth in there always helped me to feel *more honest*. I don't know how long. Well, the girls here told me it takes a few days to find out. Can you call Beatrice's? She lives by my mom's. I don't want my mom to know I am in jail. If you call Beatrice's and your mom can drive Madie there, she will probably watch her. Tell Beatrice not to tell my mom." She agreed. Not having another call coming, I hung up only hoping everything would go well, but knowing I would have no way to confirm. I returned to the cold metal cell bench, and fell forward with my head on my knees. As I rocked, I tried to squeeze the pain and devastation out. I was worthless. *I can't even protect my beautiful baby.*

What would happen to her? At least she is at Lucy's. Lucy won't let anything bad happen to her. I don't deserve her.

The only time I ever thought about my failure as a mom was when I wasn't focused on getting money or getting high. Which was almost never. My whole life was consumed with getting more. I spent the few hours in that cold cell contemplating where I went wrong with my life; how the hell I had screwed everything up so badly. I thought about what a loser I was and how I did not deserve to even breathe fresh air. Death was too good for me. I hated myself. Aware of the gift that Madie was, I was determined that I would do everything I could to never be separated from her again. I was committed to the idea that this would not happen again. I would return to school. Get a job, rent an apartment. Not see any of my old friends. I was the scum of the earth and I knew it. Deep in my core, I knew death would be too easy for me. I should be punished severely and the fact that I wasn't only made it worse. At least if I was beaten for what I had done to my child, I would have paid for it. I should have been beaten or had limbs cut from my body. I needed to be punished and I knew God knew that. Afraid that something would happen to my daughter to pay the price for my sins, I swore this would never happen again. I needed to know she would be safe. I had to make it right.

Jail was the first time I would go through the sickness completely without getting well. The first twenty-four hours I slept. After that, I woke up drenched in a sweet smelling sweat, choking as the trap door in my throat slammed shut. Over the next few days a dull severe pain radiated from every bone in my body and I shook. The pain increased as the hours went by. Rocking back and forth, rubbing my legs, it was almost unbearable. After the first twenty-four hours sleep would not return. The pain kept me sharply awake. The knowledge that I could not get drugs under any circumstances was the only thing that helped me to make it through psychologically.

Some of the other girls that had spent time in jail knew what I was going though. They said, "She is melia," which was street slang for being heroin sick. "Don't worry, mija, you will be okay. Hang in there." There were a few girls who were talking to me, but I avoided the majority.

I stayed in jail over the weekend and pleaded no contest in court. To this day I have no idea what that means. The judge released me and told me to report back in the next month to serve the remaining days. Since I didn't get well the day I was arrested, I was on my third day of sickness and had seen the worst of it by the time I was released. The girls in jail told me it takes three days to kill a small habit, then you start feeling better. Although my bones still ached, I had a stuffy nose and I still reeked of syrup, I was doing much better.

It was about four in the morning when the bars finally slammed open and my name was called for release. I was sitting on the bench waiting to get my few belongings and get out. I felt the sense of relief already. I was going home. I could see Madie. I was so happy, I could barely think. It was very early in the morning, so I would have to hitchhike. I couldn't go to anyone's house this early. I had to come up with a plan. As I walked out into the cold morning air, it was still dark. The sun had not risen and the streets were empty with the exception of street cleaners and a few cars. I walked out to the main boulevard hoping to hitch a ride with someone going to work.

The first car that picked me up was a man. When I got in he said, "Do you want to make some money?" *I thought, no! Are you kidding! Not this again!* I was sure he was a cop trying to see if I would do it again. I said, "Look, I just got out of jail because a cop thought I was a prostitute; for all I know you are a cop." At that point, he opened his glove compartment and exposed some weed and a pipe and said, "Does that look like I am a cop? Look, we'll get a room, smoke some weed and mess around a bit and I'll give you some money. I'm sure you could use money. No big deal." Knowing I had no money and nowhere to go, I thought if he rented a room I could rest. Yes, I needed rest. This would be the last time. I will get some rest and some money and be on my way to my new life.

The man rented a room in the most God-awful motel back on the boulevard close to where I picked up. He had his way with me and left. I had no interest in the weed. It only intensified the sickness. Now alone, I was not only sick, but I also had the stench of the old man on me. The disgust surrounded me. I needed to get rid of it. Although I could get rid of his smell with a shower, I knew the only way I could extinguish the sick feeling in my gut was with heroin. Heroin always made it all go away. I needed to forget.

One little shot, dull the pain, get rid of the flu and I could rest until daylight. Within a few minutes I had left the room, and began walking to Buena Clinton. Luckily, I was only a few blocks away. It wasn't until I rounded the corner into the neighborhood on foot that I realized; these guys may not be up at five a.m. I arrived there to find that much as I suspected, the place was quiet. The usual activity of the neighborhood did not exist at this hour. He must have heard my boots thumping on the pavement, because appearing from behind a car in the carport of the old apartments, I saw a man's head pop up. "Hey mija, you need something?"

I loved the way the Spanish people called me mija. It is my understanding that mija means daughter, or young girl. It was very endearing and made me feel cared for. "Yes." I replied. "No problem baby, I will take care of you," he said.

"I have some of the best chiva around. My name is Serjio." Chiva is heroin, and I was in need. Sergio was nice enough, not only to sell me some, but also to let me use his needle. Hidden behind the tire of the car, he had everything we needed. A needle, a used coke can and a cigarette filter. He set the small piece of tar heroin in a dent on the can. He did not have water to melt it in, so he asked me if I would mind spitting in the can to create water. He said he did it all the time. He explained that he would heat the mixture with his lighter to burn off my impurities and it would be better than water because it came from my body and was going back in. Sounded logical to me. Within minutes I was well. Sergio was very nice. In just the few minutes I spent with him, he really seemed like a good-hearted man. He really seemed to care. As I walked away he said, "Be safe, mija."

When I got back to the motel, I fell fast asleep. By the time I woke up it was three p.m. Too scared to go back out on the streets again after the arrest, I decided to get some change and phone the call service. I needed to know if they were mad at me for not calling. I figured as an excuse for calling, I could just tell them that I moved and wanted to give them the new address. Although I was scared to work the streets, I could use the service to get some money and rent an apartment for Madie and me. Then we could have a whole new life.

I was surprised to learn that not only were they not mad at me, the man in the wheelchair, who I learned was named "Bob" had called several times to request my service again. They told him they would call him if they heard from me again. The lady in charge said she would try to get a hold of him and instructed me to call back in one hour. I felt better. I had a plan. I still had my job and I actually had a customer that wanted me. Things were looking up. Now having been exposed to the streets, I felt a much greater sense of safety with the service, and unlike the last time I dealt with them, I was now relaxed. Almost as if the lady and I were now friends.

I couldn't figure out why that man was calling for me. But at this point I realized he probably wasn't thinking of killing me, because asking for me would blow his cover. I figured he had other motives, but I had no idea what they were. And frankly, I needed to find out what happened to this guy, why was he so alone. This would be my chance. Since he had asked for me, he might actually be open to talking. I needed to know.

When I phoned the lady back, she told me she had located him at home. She gave me his number and said that he wanted me to call him for arrangements. I dialed his number. Consistent with his nature the last time I saw him, he was very short in his communication. "Hey, I want to go to a movie." I guess when you're paying you don't really have to ask, you just state the facts. Then he said, "I will pay you like I did last time."

He took down my hotel address and said he would be by in two hours. For the life of me, I couldn't figure out how he was going to get there. Being in a wheelchair, I had no idea how you drive without feet, but I didn't ask. Lord knows I didn't want to upset the crazy man. If he said he would be there, I assumed he would be. Intrigued and scared I waited. I was glad I hadn't called Beatrice yet. Given the fact that no one knew I was out, I could delay picking up Madie for one more day. Then I would have money.

When I returned to my motel room from the payphone, I sat on the bed and switched on the TV. It was New Years Eve. Not only was this guy alone on Christmas, but he was also alone on New Year's Eve, and for some reason, his best idea was to spend it with me. I was intrigued. This guy really had no one. *It never crossed my mind that I had no one either.*

When I heard the engine I peeked out of the window to see him sitting in front of my room in a silver Mercedes. *Hell, this guy does drive. How, I didn't know.* I threw my shoes on, locked the door and got in his car. Just like last time, he was bitter and direct. When I got in the car there were no hellos or pleasantries, he simply barked, "Put your seat belt on!" I did. He was good at giving orders and although I didn't put it together at the time, I was used to this kind of treatment from my dad.

Although, I normally didn't take well to being ordered to do things, with him I didn't seem to care. He was clearly not capable of much more. Remembering his bitter nature, I now knew I wouldn't get any information out of him. He hadn't softened up at all. I didn't know what movie we were going to, but I hoped it was a short one.

As we pulled out, without trying to appear nosy, I glanced over at the driver's side. His feet were by the front of his chair, nowhere near the pedals and he had extra buttons and sticks by the driver's wheel. He operated the entire car with his hands. I still had no idea how it worked, but given that his car was in good shape, I figured he was used to it and wouldn't crash. We drove for over an hour and ended up in Los Angeles, a whole different county. I could not figure out why he would want to go so far for a movie. When we stopped he said, "Get out." Sure that this was all a trick and he was going to leave me in LA, and not wanting to piss him off, I figured I could always hitchhike back and did as he asked.

Feeling like an idiot, I saw immediately why I had to get out. His wheelchair was in the backseat. He had to move my seat up to get to it. That was when I noticed his arms again. With his strong muscles, he grabbed the chair with one hand, pulled it over him and laid it on the pavement outside of his door. Then he retrieved the wheels, one at a time, pulled them over his head and reattached them to the chair. With the chair completely assembled, he hoisted his body out of the car and onto it. After readjusting himself, he pulled his blue bandana out of his back pocket and tied his feet to the chair. He grabbed his backpack from the car, threw it onto the back of his chair and swished around like a stuntman, catching a bit of air with the right tire, in a flawless 180. "Let's go!"

I was surprised to learn that not only did we go to the furthest movie theatre in the world, all of the actors were unknowns and there was no talking! We had to read the damn thing! What a gyp! Clearly this guy had no idea where to go to see a good movie. Having not read anything in quite a while, I dreaded the thought of having to read this entire movie. I was bored already and it hadn't started. The movie was called "The Vagabond."

After about twenty minutes of watching and thinking about getting out of there, I was reading the words almost involuntarily and stopped thinking about the money. Much to my surprise, I liked it. The friggin' thing had no words and I liked it. I didn't think about the money again until the movie ended.

He drove me home right after the film. As I opened the door to get out at the motel he handed me the money and said, "I am going to give you my number. I want you to call me direct. I want to go to another movie again. I will pay you." Aware now that neither of us required pleasantries, I took the number, closed the door and walked away.

Although Bob and I didn't talk much on the entire drive home, which was over an hour, having spent Christmas and now New Years with him, I felt slightly connected to him. This guy made my isolation look like child's play. I needed to know what happened to him.

I didn't return to Beatrice's until two days later. I arrived at her door broken and desperate to get my Madie. When I walked in the house Madie was in front of the TV snacking with the other kids. When she heard my voice, she turned and yelled "mommy!" and ran up to hug me. After she wrapped her little arms around my leg, all of the self-loathing went away. She was safe and she loved me. It was going to be okay.

After a few minutes of small chat, I told Beatrice that I was in "transition," looking for a new place to live and all. She told me that she thought it would be a great idea if she watched Madie for a few days while I found a room to rent. She pointed over to the living-room and said, "She is doing fine, playing with the other kids, eating good and watching TV. I would be more than happy to watch her until you are ready."

She also said, "Look, I know you have a lot going on. If you need to go somewhere, to get some help or something, it is perfectly okay. I will watch Madie. You can go get help and tell me when you are ready. I can watch her for a month or so. It will be fine." Knowing that all I ever had in life was that little girl and wanting her desperately to be with me, I knew Beatrice was right. I had nowhere for us to go. I needed to get back on track.

I had every intention at that moment of getting help. I made a call to the old motel and they had returned my welfare check. I called the Social Services Department and they told me to come in for an appointment and provide them with my new address and they would give it to me. This is how it always started. It was a catch twenty-two. I needed money to get a room so that I had an address. I knew the only way to get an address was to have money, but I also knew I would not go back to the streets. So I told the lady I would call her as soon as I cashed the check and rented a place. She was okay with that.

Even though it had been a good deal of time since that day my sister first took me to the old wood shack with the hippie people, scared to go back to the streets and in hopes that they could save me, I hitched there from the welfare office.

33

THE HIPPIE SHACK WAS RIGHT NEXT DOOR TO THE SILVER NICKEL where I used to hang out with the bikers, but by this time I was much too broken to ever show my face at the bar again. In fear of seeing Toby, or someone who knew me before, I avoided the place. Weighing less than ninety pounds with bruises all over me, I would rather die than have someone see me like this.

When I arrived at the wooden shack, there was no meeting going on, but there was a small group of people sitting around a coffee bar. Attempting to fit in, I went up to the bar and ordered a coffee with the remaining change from the bottom of my purse.

Although I never really understood what the people did at this place, I knew they were all trying to stay sober. I figured if I just sat there, maybe something would rub off on me. I had no other plans, and it certainly couldn't hurt. The crowd had changed, the hippies seemed to have relocated and there was now a mixture of really old people playing cards and teens in leather jackets without motorcycles. I always thought leathers were for protection in the event that you fell off your bike, so I didn't understand leathers in hot weather without a bike, but to each his own. I didn't make eye contact for fear of being talked to. I was sure they would see my scabbed hands and determine that I was not one of them. I felt like death warmed over. Avoiding direct contact, I just sat there staring at my coffee.

I was surprised when the man behind the bar said, "Hey aren't you Nadine's little sister?" From the pin on his shirt I could tell he was the manager of the place. He must have recognized me from the one time I came with her. He was about seventy years old, with red leathery, sun-damaged skin and was wearing a golf shirt and tan pants. He said he had been sober for over ten years. And then he just talked and talked and talked some more. Clearly, he wasn't someone I would normally engage in small talk with, especially with all the young people around, but he just wouldn't let me be. Asking me questions about my sister, my baby, my mom. I had no idea who this guy was. Even though I gave short answers to his questions, he continued.

He began by explaining how he knew my sister. He said, "Nadine used to come over to my house and I would 'help her out' financially." Nadine always had a knack for hanging around with old men with money, but surely she wasn't dating him? This guy was an antique, for cripes sakes.

I always despised Nadine's flaunting her men with money. Every time I saw her, she would start in. "Hey Lauri, I met this guy with a lot of money. Look at the necklace he bought me. It's real gold with a real diamond. He is rich. He gives me money whenever I want it. He takes care of me. Whatever I want, he buys it for me." The whole thing made me sick.

The way I saw it, we were complete opposites. She would play up to rich men pretending she cared about them so that they would be her sugar daddy. I couldn't stand it. I could never pretend to like anyone. Clearly the men I got money from had no illusions. I wasn't interested in them, just the money. This wasn't an act pretending to be in love with them. This was a business deal.

I had something you wanted and you had something I wanted. No emotions involved. I provide, you pay. It was a job. I recall thinking of the Navy commercial on many occasions: *it's not a job, it's an adventure* As far as I was concerned *this was a job, not an adventure* and that was it. I made my mind up very early on that I would never depend on anyone. I would work for my money. I would never be dependent on a man. It was fine if you took my body; it was never mine anyway, but my heart, never. I would never pretend. The men I was with knew I despised them. They got what they wanted and so did I. The money was mine because I earned it. I was hard and direct. Make the deal, do the deed and walk. None of this pretend, prissy stuff. I hated the men, and taking the money was one way I could get back at them for everything they ever did to me. Even sitting with grandpa talking about my sister was making me sick to my stomach.

He went on talking about Nadine and what a great girl she was and how long they'd known each other. I assumed, since he was sober and manager of this facility, maybe he just liked helping young girls. When he mentioned that they had dated a few times, I was horrified. Feeling totally embarrassed to be talking to this old perv, I told him I had to go. I went to the check-cashing store, cashed my check and rented a motel room. I called my case worker and gave her the address. I was on my way to my new life.

For the next five days or so, I showed up at the wood shack and for the first time in years, I did not use drugs. Every time I would show up, the old man would attempt to talk to me. Whenever there were meetings going on, I slipped in and sat right by the door and left before it ended. One day, on my way out, he approached me. He said, "You know, if you need money, I could help you like I did Nadine. We could go to my house." Being almost out of money due to paying the motel rent, I thought, *Well, if Nadine knew him he can't be all bad. I know he's not a cop because he is the manager of the club.* Thinking that it couldn't hurt, but still unsure of exactly what he wanted, I said, "Ok, I guess so."

When we arrived at his house, he made his intention clear. He wanted to tongue kiss me for money. I found the whole idea completely repulsive. Girls on the street never kissed. I learned almost immediately from the girls on the street that kissing was taboo. They could do whatever they wanted below the neck, but never, never let them put their tongue in your mouth. It was far too intimate. We could shut down our minds and let the men do whatever they wanted to our bodies, but kissing was an act of love and caring that had no place in prostitution.

I was completely disgusted by this old man, but needing money I let him kiss me for about ten seconds, gagged, thought, *I cannot do this* and headed for the door. I guess he was used to this response because he cordially handed me the money without complaint and drove me back to the wooden shack.

The next few times he asked me, I told him I was busy. The last time I saw him, he was more insistent that ever that I come to his house. Using every resource he had, he said, "Hey if you want to come over, I have an old car sitting in front of my house. You can use it as long as you want to in order to get to meetings. I don't need it." I was clear that his motive was more about inserting his tongue in my mouth again, rather than my health, but the car was something I couldn't pass up. I knew if I had a car I could visit Brandt, who was still in jail. I had not spoken to him or visited him since he was arrested. Knowing a car would serve me well, I complied.

It was a beautiful aqua blue 1960 Chevrolet with a white leather interior and wood dash. I was amazed that he would let me use it. Sure enough, after a ten second slimy, disgusting kiss, he let me get in, handed me the keys and I drove away. Over the next few weeks, I would go over to the old man's house whenever necessary to extend my use of the car and get more money. It was gross, but I was out of options. I was showing up to the shack intermittently in hopes that I would catch this sobriety thing, but knowing no one, I would end up with the old geezer and leave in the car with some money as a bonus. Unfortunately, I started shooting up again to get the disgust out. I realized that I couldn't be with a man for money without using something to extinguish the disgust. It went hand in hand.

When I first went to the old shack, I had no idea what the people were doing there. All I knew was that there was hope there. With the old man working the place, I was trapped. The only place that had hope was also the place I was trying to escape. It was all so confusing. But, I continued to show up. Amazingly enough, over the next few weeks, I was able to put a couple of days together at a time without shooting up, but each time I ran out of money, I would see the old man and shoot up.

One day I was leaving the old shack after sitting in the very back of a meeting. I was more desperate than ever. I had two days without shooting up, and I needed to stick to it this time. But, I knew I needed something more or I was going fail again. Not understanding anything about the strange people at the shack, I remained adamant that I would continue to show up until I found "the answer." Something, just anything. I needed help.

I had sat in the corner right next to the door and heard nothing, but as the meeting ended I heard two guys talking. One of them, named Jesse, said to the other, "Sometimes I go to a detox and talk to people who are fresh off the streets. It gives me hope and keeps me sober." He mentioned a place called Sober Street. As I walked back to the old blue car in the parking lot, the thought rattled around in my mind: *Helping street people helps them.*

I jumped in surprise when Jesse yelled from behind me, "Hey, where are you going?" "Nowhere," I said. "You want to hang out?" he asked. I thought, *Hang out?* He has obviously confused me with a normal girl. I don't hang out. Life was a lot more serious for me. I certainly have not *hung out* in a long time. Frankly, I wasn't even sure what he meant.

Before I could even think of what to say, I blurted out, "What about Sober Street?" I had no idea what Sober Street was, where it was, or what we would do once we got there, but I had heard there was hope there, so it was on my mind. When I opened my mouth, it just seemed to fall out. "Okay," he said. "I know where it is. Let's go."

For the first time in a long time, I started to feel good. We were going to help people. I felt a sense of peace that I hadn't felt in a long time. The dust flew as we departed the old shack parking lot on a mission.

Jesse was a cross between Howdy Doody and Fonzie. He tried to pull off a tough guy look with his leather jacket and goop in his hair, but his spiked, dyed black hair and freckles gave him up as a momma's boy. He was a cute kid about nineteen years old. Seeing that I had no regular friends and with Brandt still in jail, I figured a friend might be good.

We were less than three blocks away from the wooden shack when Jesse said below his breath, "I really feel like getting high." That was all it took. The junkie bond took over. Although just seconds ago, I was feeling good and proud to be on a mission, now in the car with my new friend, getting just a little bit of heroin didn't sound like it would hurt. But the problem was, neither of us had any money.

I explained to Jesse that I had worked the streets a bit to make some money and I had gotten arrested and didn't want to do it anymore. I told him I was committed to my new life. After a brief discussion about what it was like and how much money I made, we agreed that I could do it one more time, but only once and we would have to go to a different place, not on the boulevard where I got arrested. I told him it usually took about fifteen minutes, then we would get drugs, but I would never do it again. I was committed to staying sober now. We agreed that I would work one last trick, we would get high once and that would be it.

Even though I had always worked the main boulevard, I suggested an alternative street for working girls. It was one of the other streets the girls talked about when I was in jail. Now having a few days of sobriety, and having been arrested, I was much more aware of everything. I was completely grossed out about having to go on the streets again and scared of being arrested again.

I parked the car by an all-night donut shop. As I exited the car, Jesse remained in the passenger side. I said, "Don't worry, I'll be quick!" Although I left him the keys, he agreed he would stay put, drink coffee, smoke cigarettes and wait. So off I went. It was 2:00 p.m.

A few blocks later a silver Cadillac with dark tinted windows rounded the corner in front of me and pulled to the side. This was standard signal from a trick. As I approached the window on the passenger side, it rolled down and I saw a black man driving. One of the other rules we had on the street was *never get in the car with a black man.* Criminal had made this very clear in one of our early morning smoking discussions and I heard it again in the booking cell in jail. Although I wasn't totally clear on it, I remembered they had told me that black guys are dangerous. White girls should never go with black men. Stick to WHITE MEN ONLY.

As I bent over to look in the window he said, "Hey you looking for a date?" I said, "No." He said, "Aw come on, lets go. It will be quick." I said, "No, that's okay." He pulled his wallet out of his pocket and exposed eight $100 bills. He held them like a hand of playing cards. It was certainly more money that I was used to seeing from tricks on the street. He separated them like a fan and flashed them in my direction. "I will give you a C-Note every thirty minutes, I promise." Keeping in mind what Criminal had told me, I stuck to my guns. I replied, "I don't think so."

"Come on girl, I don't want sex or anything, I have these friends in a band. I just want to swing by there and I don't want to go alone. I just want someone to go with me, like a date. It's embarrassing to show up alone. Just pretend to be my date. I will pay you good." *Hmmmm... he didn't want sex and he has money, so I am not really breaking the rule. But go somewhere? What about Jesse?* After thinking for a minute I said "Well, I would love to help you, but my friend is waiting for me at the donut shop and he is expecting me to get back really soon, so I can't leave the area."

He replied, "No problem, get in and we will drive by there. You can tell him exactly where we will be and how long we will take." Sounded good to me. When I got in the car, the safety locks engaged and the window went up. He said, "You know what? We are going to be back so fast, your friend won't notice."

Even though I was a bit concerned about the automatic doors, my fear eased up when he started to talk about family and the recent holidays. He seemed very normal and dressed like a businessman. I was sure he was right; we would be back so soon it wouldn't matter. As we entered the 5 freeway northbound, I assumed the place was a few exits up. After about fifteen minutes, I expressed concern. He said, "Don't worry, it is a short drive. We will go in, you will meet my friends and then we can go. They will probably have some cocaine if you'd like." I told him that was okay, I was looking to stay sober. I told him about my daughter and that I wanted to straighten out my life.

The longer we were on the freeway, the most apprehensive I became. But each time I expressed concern, he would alleviate it by reiterating,

"Your friend will wait, and you will come back with tons of money." Then he tossed a hundred dollar bill on my lap. "See. The longer we're out the more you make. Don't worry so much. You will have fun and you will like my friends." He was probably right. The fact that I was completely sober was making me so hyper-sensitive that I was getting paranoid. He talked more about his family and his friends. I was going to be fine. He was very nice.

By the time we pulled off of the freeway, we were in Los Angeles somewhere. I have no idea where we were, but it was instantly clear that there were no white people here. He pulled into a parking lot and stopped the car. As he began to open the door, he said, "Come on." I tentatively asked, "Where are we? I thought we were going to a club?" He said, "Well this is the band's motel. We will meet them, do some coke in their room and then head out."

We were on the second floor of the motel, when he unlocked the door and said, "After you." I took only a few steps in to the room when he slammed the door with a loud bang. The fear shot through me as I looked into the crazy eyes of this suddenly enraged man. As he lifted his arm to smack me he yelled, "YOU EVER BEEN FUCKED BY A PIMP BEFORE?!!" He grabbed my hair and lifted me off of my feet and threw me against the sharp corner of the dresser. I began to scream, but he held my neck and slammed my head repeatedly against the headboard until I was starting to lose consciousness. "YOU SCREAM AGAIN AND I WILL KILL YOU, DIRTY BITCH!" He tore the clothes from my body while yelling, "WHO DO YOU THINK YOU ARE WORKING MY STREETS?"

He sodomized me until the blood running over the wounds became one large screaming wound. I had no strength left to stop the slamming of my head against the headboard and the beating of my limp body beneath him. By the time he began to drag me into the bathroom, I was unable to stand. He threw me on the floor and said, "KNEEL IN THE BATHTUB BITCH!" I crawled in over the metal rim and knelt as the blood poured out of me onto my knees and covered the shower floor. When I saw the gun rising toward my head, I knew this was it. I would never see my daughter again. It was over. Then as I faded in and out of clear consciousness, I heard Criminal's sweet voice. *Use whatever you can, you need to get out or you will die.*

With the cold gun pressed against my head, I muttered, "Please, Please, Sir. I really just started doing it... I didn't know, I swear I didn't know it was your streets." He continued to scream, "*FUCK YOU, YOU DIRTY WHORE!*" *I had mentioned my daughter in the car. He knew I had a kid!* "For my daughter, please let me go home! Please I will never come back."

"Fuck you bitch. You're no mom, you're a fucking whore!" he screamed. With the gun pointed at my head, he was not up for talking anymore, he took one more step towards me. I knew I was gone. I knew the last second of my life would be alone in a hotel room with a pimp. *No goodbyes. Alone. Knowing this was the end, with no chance of living, I decided I would say one last word to God before I go. Not feeling deserving of anything for myself, knowing God hated me and the piece of shit I was, I prayed out loud, for him. The pimp.*

In a quiet voice, just above a whisper, I muttered "God please forgive him for what he is doing. Forgive him God."

Expecting those would be my last words, it was all I had left. It was at that moment that his arm dropped and he left the room. He came back with the clothes he had torn off my body and threw them at me. He said, "Clean your dirty self up, bitch."

He followed me, with the gun in his jacket pocket, as I slowly navigated my steps back to the car, trying my best not to fall because of my wounded body. The blood had already drenched through my clothes and my face was badly beaten. The few black people around the hotel avoided eye contact with me and seemed to give this man his space. They looked away as we passed.

He ordered me into the back seat. We pulled out of the lot and into a 7-11 just blocks away. He pointed the gun into the back seat. He said, "You will walk in there and get me a 7-Up to drink. If you say anything to anyone I will kill both of your asses." As I approached the counter, the cashier looked at my bruised face and then looked away. He took my dollar and returned the change. Every part of me screamed, call 911! The words never exited my lips, for I knew he was watching me from outside.

Ten minutes later we were driving down a busy boulevard and he began to talk. "You are mine now. You will work in Vegas. We are leaving tonight. You belong to me. You will talk to no one without…" Suddenly his voice stopped and he jerked the car to the curb and disengaged the lock. A tall pretty blond girl rushed to the car and jumped in the front seat. She was crying and breathing hard as the words poured quickly out of her mouth. "He took my money and he hit me, and then…" I couldn't believe it; she was talking to this monster as if he would protect her. What kind of fucked up chick is this? It was at that moment that through the corner of my eye I noticed the amount of traffic on the street and the fact that the door was still disengaged from letting her in. The pimp was so involved with the girl in the front seat that this was my only chance. I had to take it.

I flew out of the door and ran as fast as I could in the opposite direction of traffic, down a side alley and onto the intersecting street. I never looked back. The pain shot from my broken body and my whole body tensed as it prepared itself for a shot in the back. I threw my thumb out and the very first car pulled to the side. I jumped in and slammed the door. In a state of panic, I looked out of my window and yelped, "I am going to Orange County!" The man replied, "I will take you as far as the freeway."

As I glanced forward I could see the pain in his eyes as he peered through the rear view mirror and got a better look at my beaten face, swollen eyes and torn blood stained clothes. Seeing his expression, tears involuntarily filled my eyes. I had to blink them away. I didn't want to upset him further by crying in his car. Humiliated, I turned my head as far as I could away from his view and stared out of the window. As much as I tried to push it down, and breathe normally, my chest continued to convulse in silent, systematic crying below my torn blouse. He never stopped driving. He drove me all the way back to the Donut Shop in Orange County. I got out and turned to say thank you. He looked very concerned but said nothing. I was thankful for the rescue he provided, but felt bad that I had affected him. I didn't mean to do that. Not knowing what else to say either, I closed the door.

Five hours had passed and I was stunned to see the aqua Chevy still at the donut shop. When I saw Jesse's silhouette in the car, my breathing accelerated but I held the tears back. I would not cry again. I was not a wimp. In a firm voice I spoke to myself. *Straighten up Lauri.*

Then it hit me. *He waited for me. This guy that I barely knew waited. He didn't steal my car or leave. He waited.*

As I opened the car door, Jesse's eyes were already streaming with tears and he let out a gasp of labored breathing. I sucked back the tears and no longer looked at him directly. I blinked my eyes to refrain from crying and, out of respect for him, I would not watch him cry either. I started the car. For the remainder of the ride, we did not make eye contact or speak.

When we arrived at my motel, I got out of the car and walked to the room. The dried blood rubbed against the wounds, intensifying the pain with each step. Even though the pain was almost unbearable, I would not let Jesse see my suffering. Attempting to walk at a normal pace, I would not baby myself. The man was right. I was a whore and a horrible mom. I deserved this. Each sharp pain reminded me of what a worthless whore I was. I deserved it. I had left my child. No matter how hard I tried to push it away, the images kept on jumping back in. *The gun...the potential end of my life in that room with that monster. The cold silent nothingness that would have been the end of my life...It kept on coming back...I couldn't shake it. It was still there with me, reminding me. The end... Just hours ago, I saw the end.*

Jesse followed me to my room. I unlocked the door and sat on the corner of the bed, my eyes immediately transfixed on the curly piece of green yarn where the carpet had been torn.

*Although it was completely quiet, it was still alive, screaming... slamming...pain...the end...my end...*I could not look away from the yarn. My eyes felt huge and I could not will myself to move. I just drifted. I wanted to be alone. Just leave me alone. I felt uncomfortable not talking, but had lost the will to speak. I could feel Jesse's stare. In my peripheral vision, I could see him pacing back and forth. While there was something deep inside that wanted to respond to him...say something...anything...anything...anything...no words came...green yarn....

Finally Jesse spoke. "I am going to get some money for dope, I will be back."

When Jesse returned an hour later, I hadn't moved. Eyes transfixed. Pain, silent, no thinking...*blank...carpet...numb...bladder full...pain... no move...bladder full...carpet...carpet.*

When Jesse realized I was just as unresponsive as I had been when he left, he injected me. When the drugs hit my belly, I retreaded further inward. I was so far within myself, I was gone. No more thoughts sending messages to my mouth that would invoke speech, no more words worthy of moving my mouth to speak. Jesse sat in silence for a while and then left. "I will be back tomorrow."

Jesse showed up the next day, but again, there were no words. I had to believe he too could not think of anything to say. Even though he had no idea what happened that day, he knew. Words seemed insignificant. Sometimes tears would stream down my face involuntary and I would wipe them, void of empathy. I had done this to myself and I knew it. Thoughts of the man out there kept me in the room, but not wanting to comfort myself with food, I was a prisoner to the noise in my head. That afternoon, after receiving a large shot of heroin Jesse had brought, I spoke.

"Who did that?" I am sure he did not know what I was saying, but in my mind it was clear. "The plug from the air conditioner. Who unplugged it?" *Or had someone come in and unplugged it. Was he here?* I was sure Jesse knew I was crazy. I did not repeat it.

For the next few days I was unable to respond normally. Jesse came by and brought me drugs. I have no idea where he got the money. I assumed from his parents. He probably lied to borrow money. Even though I had only known Jesse for a few days at this point, he took total responsibility for me without so much as a request. He was all I had that day. Given my lack of social skills and inability to discuss feelings on any level, I never thanked him. At some level thanking him would also mean that I had to admit I needed him. I was too strong for that. I didn't need anyone. But deep down inside, I was sure he knew.

By the next day, I threw the entire event away. Blocked it out of my mind completely…as if it never happened. I walked out of my motel door, strong, confident and more hardened than ever. I returned to the streets.

The event was gone, but my armor was thicker than ever. There was an evil animal dwelling inside of me. I could feel it. I had a newborn state of recklessness that far exceeded anything I had ever felt. I failed to care if people saw me on the street, arrest didn't scare me and I certainly didn't care who knew that I was a prostitute, or a heroin addict for that matter. There was a coldness about me; others could see it and I could feel it. The anger and hardness comforted me. *F with me and I will kill you.* It was forever present thereafter.

Three days later Jesse and I returned to the motel to see three police cars out front. Then I remembered the prostitution charge. They had my welfare address. As I slumped down in the seat, I knew they were there for me. Although three cars seemed excessive, I had a feeling. Jesse said it was probably coincidence. He insisted they would never have three cars for a chick. We decided to play it safe anyway.

The plan was that I would hide underneath a low riding station wagon that was parked in the hotel parking lot and Jesse was given the task of walking through the motel entryway to identify where the police were going. If they were coming for me, he would come back and give me a signal or tell me.

After about twenty minutes of lying under the car with my head pushed to the left by the dirty low hanging car parts, I heard shoes to my right. I scraped my face against the car frame to turn my head. It was the police, standing inches away. They stood and talked for a few minutes, but never looked under the car. Thank God. Since I couldn't see beyond the next car, even after they walked away, I stayed put for the next thirty minutes. I had no idea if they were still in the area or not. When enough time passed that I felt safe, I crawled out from under the car, black grease all over my face and found Jesse. "Yes," he said. "They were at your door. I couldn't come back to tell you because they saw me."

I had to go to jail and I knew it. It was only a matter of time before they would come for me again. Determined to turn myself in, I thought, *I can get sober in there like last time. It is my only chance to get Madie back.* I had a plan. I would work a few more tricks and turn myself in. I figured it was a good plan to clean up. I might spend four days in there with good time and time served, but that would help me to kick my habit. A few more tricks and I would go in.

That night I was working the streets when an old man pulled over in a nice car. He said, "Hey there lady, would you like to go grab some dinner with me?" I told him, "Thanks, but no. I am not hungry and I am trying to get some money." He said, "Well, I'll tell you what, you don't have to eat, just go with me and I will pay you. We can go right here to this nice Steakhouse." He pointed into the parking lot beyond at "The Barn Steakhouse." I thought, *Geez; I can have sex with someone in ten minutes and be on my way. If I go with this guy to eat, it could be over an hour!* I replied, "Look old man, I am not interested in eating. I am only interested in getting more heroin. Your little meal is going to keep me busy for over an hour. I am not interested in going with you. Please go so that other cars will stop."

"I will pay you $200 if you go with me." *Hmmm that didn't sound bad, but I needed to get well.* "For how long?" I replied. He responded, "One hour, tops." So, I thought, *What the hell, just watch him eat. I can rush him along.* I jumped in and off we went. He looked around seventy years old, a short wrinkly guy with thick white hair. Total square, but I could tell he had money.

Not hungry for food, I had him buy me a Bloody Mary. I thought the V8 would give me some of the vitamins I was lacking from not eating. I sat; he talked. I have no idea what he talked about, other than when he asked me about my background. I explained that I was

Jewish, which seemed to really impress him at some level, which I didn't understand at all.

About forty five minutes into watching him eat, he pulled out a wad of pictures from his jacket. They were all girls from about fifteen to eighteen years old. Said they were "his friends." *Interesting*, I thought. They probably don't think so, but whatever, grandpa. He told me several times how pretty I was and talked about my being Jewish and how wonderful that was. He also spoke a lot about what a great surgeon he was, and bragged about his career as a professional boxer. After listening to him stroke himself for almost forty-five unbearable minutes, he paid me. As I was leaving he asked if he could see me the next night. I explained to him that I was going to jail the next day and would not be around. Interesting old man, a bit perverted with the pictures of the young girls, but easy money.

The next day, I drove to the jail to turn myself in. When I was about two blocks from the jail I had a thought. Knowing I was going in, I thought I should take advantage of it. Bring something in. Since I wanted to clean up, I thought pot would be good. I didn't like pot, but I thought it would help to secure a peaceful stay if I brought it for the other girls. There was a young street gang that controlled the streets close by and sold wack, I thought they might have pot in that neighborhood. Within minutes I found a kid with some pot and was on my way. I pulled over near the jailhouse and hid it, *in my 'backyard.'*

I made it through the search okay, and even though my initial plan was just to give the pot to someone when I got there, I couldn't. My system was so backed up from the heroin addiction, that it got sucked somewhere inside of me and let's just say it was *unobtainable*.

I made the mistake of telling one of the older ladies near me that night that I had it and would give her some *"when I could."* Within a few minutes I was quietly instructed by one of the biggest dikes in the cell that she would like to talk to me in the bathroom. In the small bathroom, I was shoved up against a toilet and surrounded by five massive and angry looking girls. The biggest spoke first. "I hear you have something. I also hear that it is *stuck*. We are going to help you get it *unstuck*."

Let's just say within a few seconds the bag became A LOT easier for me to obtain. Having known what happened with the pregnant girl last time, I had my hand up and out within mere seconds. They ripped the filthy bag from my hand and scurried away like hungry rats. *Whew, not such a good idea after all.* But no one bugged me for the remaining days, which was good.

On day three, when starting to feel better, I called my mom collect from the payphone in jail. Much to my surprise, she accepted the call. I figured I could check in with her and see how Beatrice was doing with Madie. Since I was now late to pick Madie up, I was embarrassed to phone Beatrice directly. Almost immediately after accepting the call, my mom informed me that she knew I was in jail. She said 'a man' had been calling her house. A doctor something or other. She said he had met me and taken me to dinner and wanted to bail me out of jail. My mom asked who he was and if she should give him my jail information. I explained that I was in jail to detox and didn't want to be bailed out. I told her I was trying to straighten out my life. Tell him to stop calling. When I was at dinner with him, he asked me my last name. He must have hunted down my mom through the phonebook. Very strange.

When I left jail a few days later, I went to my mom's house for food. I figured since she knew I was trying to get clean, she might be open to letting me in. She did, and told me to eat quickly. She was going out and didn't want me there alone. She asked again about the man and I explained to her very casually that sometimes I see men who have money. I figured, what do I have to lose? She already knows I am a mess, maybe she would offer me some suggestions. Our relationship couldn't get any worse.

Much to my surprise not only did she not freak out, she gave me a furry jacket that she thought would be nice for me to wear. As confusing as that was, I took it. She also gave me the man's number. "Here is the man who has been calling for you." Although I was surprised again, I also realized I had nowhere to go and he had told my mom he would help me. She probably thought he would take care of me. Lord knows, no one else could.

When I called him, he said, "Well, well! Lauri, how nice it is to hear from you! I spoke to your mom. She seems like a very nice woman. She said you have nowhere to live. Maybe you and your daughter would like to stay at my apartment." He said he had an apartment in the Lillywoods in Garden Grove and I could stay there for as long as I needed. Since he hadn't made an advance at me, I thought this might work. But I wouldn't bring Madie to his house. I needed to somehow save money to get our own house. Maybe he would help me get an apartment. For now, Madie was safe at Beatrice's.

He picked me up from my mom's house and drove me to his apartment. When I arrived, he said, "I have a gift for you." He gave me two gold Krugerrands and explained that I should save them and he also gave me money. Totally uncomfortable, but with no better plan, I slept on the small couch in his living room. The next morning he made his real intentions known. He told me that he liked that I was Jewish and beautiful and he would like to marry me! *What is he talking about? He was like seventy-five years old or something? Jeezzz!* I explained to him that I was not in love with him, but he didn't seem to care. He kept on saying, "I will take care of you financially. I am a retired doctor. I will buy you anything you want. I will take care of you and your daughter. You can have anything you want for the rest of your life!"

This was just not my thing. I couldn't live with some guy and sleep with him day after day for money. This was more Nadine's style. I get in and out with the money and forget about it. I would never sleep in the same bed with an old man. Gross. Absolutely not. For the next few days I went out during the day, picked up, came back and slept on his couch. Every time I came back, the pleading for me to marry him intensified. *There was no way.*

After the third day of hanging around the place and picking up money and gold coins, he said, "Please marry me, I will give you whatever you want." Then I started to think, *If I say I will marry him, he will have to get me a ring. If he gets me a ring, I can sell it and get more heroin.* Within a few hours we were at the ring shop. I bought an $800 wedding ring. To me that seemed like a lot of money. By the end of the next day it hit me, I am going to have to marry this guy! Bring the ring back! I knew I couldn't get near what the ring was worth, I didn't want to give up my spot on the couch and I couldn't marry him because I thought it was bad karma. Go figure. After all I had been through, this was truly my first thought of bad karma. Something to do with marriage, God and vows. Although I had nothing to do with God anyway, somehow this thing just seemed very wrong.

I returned to his place to tell him that I would not marry him under any circumstances and that was that. I even left the ring out on the counter. As I was heading for the door, he said, "Take a walk with me." I said, "No, I have to go." He reiterated, "Please if you take a walk with me, I will not bother you anymore about the marriage thing after today, I promise." So I agreed.

About a block away he approached the driveway of a little cottage house. He said, "Come on." He walked up to the front door and knocked. When the lady answered, he said, "I see you have a car for sale, can my friend drive it?" I had failed to notice the 633 CSI BMW parked in the driveway with the sign on it stating $49,999 firm. I looked at it and said, "I don't want to drive it." He asked for a moment and stepped away from the lady. He explained to me, "If you agree to marry me, I will go to the bank right now and buy you this car for cash." I knew he was trying to trick me and I wasn't about to fall for it. So I said, "Prove it." He said, "Ok." He told the lady, "We will be back." About an hour later he was handing the lady $50,000 in cash. I couldn't believe it. I had a $50,000 car! And it was all mine! Woweee, this was a great scam! My friends would not believe it! I could sell this thing for $50,000! The part I failed to remember was the karma, God and all that. The only thing going through my head was a $50,000 trick! Ha ha! They are never going to believe this. *I also forgot the part about having to marry him.*

The next day I was standing in the Little White Chapel in Vegas being married to grandpa. When he later attempted to get me in the sack, I did everything I could do avoid it. Although I messed around for money, it was a wham, bam thank you ma'am. Not only did he want to sleep in a bed with me, he wanted to kiss me! Ughhhh!!! Nooo! I had to get out! What a mess!

The next day we arrived back at grandpa's apartment. Up until this point, I had avoided sleeping with him by saying I was sick, tired, or had a headache, but it was becoming clear that he was not having that anymore. Just moments after our arrival, he erupted from the room with boxing gloves on and pinned me up against the wall with his arm against my throat. He was stronger than I thought he would be for his age, and all I could think was *professional boxer and he still had the gloves.* I was not going to allow it. I fought back with everything I had and screamed, "Get the fuck off me, I will kill you!"

Like an angel from heaven, the apartment door crashed open and in rushed a biker from a few doors down. Not any biker, but a biker I knew! From years ago at Savannah's! He was one of the guys who used to hang out with the Vagos. He was Savannah's brother's friend. Not knowing it was me, he had rushed in to help whoever was yelling.

Within moments he had the old man against the wall and told me to get out. Before I could leave, the police were at the door. A neighbor must have called. When they inquired what was going on. I told them and they saw the boxing gloves on the counter. They asked, "Do you want to press charges?" I thought GREAT! He will be gone and I will get the apartment to myself for a few days and then I can escape! "Yes! I want to press charges!" As they took him out in handcuffs he turned and said, "I need the pink slip to my car!" The officer replied, "You don't need anything where you are going."

The pink slip? After he left I saw it. The pink slip was on the counter and had yet to be signed. My friend explained to me that whoever signs it, owns the car. All we had to do was register it and it would be mine.

I left with the pink slip and his credit cards, never to return. As an alternative to working the streets, two weeks later I was at the gas station putting gas in people's cars with his credit card and collecting their cash when the detectives pulled in. They impounded the car and told me if they found me doing this again, they would take me to jail. I was glad they didn't take me to jail this time. I was certainly not ready to stop using again. One of the detectives gave me his card and told me that he just had to verify that this was, in fact, my car. I guess it just didn't make sense to be driving a new BMW and hocking money for gas. He told me to call him about the car the next day. I was pissed off that they took it, but they didn't arrest me, so I stayed quiet.

The following day, I called the detective. I wasn't really sure what I was going to say at first, but when he greeted me in a friendly manner, I thought, heck he's already seen my record. No harm in telling the truth. I told him that I was working the streets, and how the guy tried to get me out of jail, called my mom, gave me the car as a wedding gift and was going to beat me to sleep with him. Much to my surprise, the detective said, "Well, it sounds like this is your car then. When do you want to pick it up?"

I have to assume he was horrified that this old man was looking for kids on the street and thought maybe this would teach him a lesson. He allowed me to pick up my car that afternoon. For the next few weeks, I drove the uninsured 633 CSI. I was proud to tell people that I had a $50,000 trick that I didn't even sleep with. I left the old Chevy at the apartments and never saw it again.

Believe it or not, this all happened in less than 90 days from the time Brandt was arrested. I realized that it was only a matter of time before he would get out, so it would be best to go see him and let him know what had happened. Now that I had no warrants, I could go visit him at the Muick Farm, where he was doing time. I thought, *he is going to be so happy when he finds out that I pulled off a scam this big. When he gets out we can sell the car, get an apartment and get Madie back and celebrate!*

But, when I visited Brandt he was so focused on the fact that I got married while he was in jail, that he couldn't hear the rest. It was as if he thought I was cheating on him. He just couldn't get past it. He kept saying,*"You married someone?"* Needless to say, that was the end of our relationship. At the time, I thought he just hadn't been on the streets long enough; he didn't understand that you do whatever it takes to make money. Gabriel, Jesse and all of the guys in the neighborhood completely understood, but Brandt, on the other hand, seemed stuck on the marriage while dating me part. Go figure.

In the next few weeks, I decided the BMW was going to bring me bad karma and I knew I had to get rid of it. My mom saw it and said it was ridiculous to be driving such a nice car with no insurance. After a series of conversations, I decided I would trade the BMW for a 280Z and $2000 cash to rid myself of the karma. I realized later that the Z was worth a lot less than the BMW, but I had no practical knowledge of such matters. Either way, I figured the car was free and now the bad karma was gone.

I paid for two months at the motel with the money and still had some left over. It was about this time that Gabriel hooked me up with his friend Frank. The last time I had seen Frank was the night of the coin robbery when Alvin almost died. He had been in the car with a sawed off shotgun that day so we really didn't talk, but I remembered him.

Gabriel told me that Frank and Sadie, his wife, had a call service. They had been running all kinds of girls through it until the cops kicked in their door and arrested everyone. They did some time and had to shut the service down. Now, back out, they still had all of their customers' contact info and Sadie has resumed activities. She did all of the tricks herself. With no other girls working there, they kept things very clean. Gabriel suggested that maybe I could help Sadie. This way I could continue to make money and it would be with known people. I wouldn't get arrested and I could secure an income. It sounded great.

The first day I showed up at their hotel, it was clear that Frank and Sadie were serious users. Neither one of them were in good shape. Frank's legs were swollen to about twice their size due to abscesses and some sort of strange fluid retention, and Sadie was just plain tired.

Frank had lots of guns and was adamant about not going back to prison. They were dangerous. For the next few weeks, Sadie and I answered the calls and we also took calls from another service. Much to my surprise, a few of their customers were women. At first it was interesting, not knowing what to do and all, but after just a short while,

I came to prefer the calls from women. When I was on the calls with women, I didn't need to shut my mind out. I was all there and I felt connected. I would like to think that was because I had never been violated by a woman, but I knew that I had. As much as I tried to understand it, the only thing I could come up with is that I hadn't been violated by women *as much* as from men.

Sadie and I were a two woman show. We did all of the tricks. Going to men's homes and meeting them in hotels while they were on business trips, I was safe from arrest and danger. One thing that became more and more apparent as time went on was the type of men who engaged in this activity. Regardless of whether it was the street, or a call service, a lot of the men were normal. Family men, business men, religious men, teachers, doctors. More times than I could remember, especially on the streets, the guys had the same speech, "Do you have any diseases because I am married. If I bring home a disease to my wife, I will come back and find you. You better be clean!"

They would give me some long lectures on what would happen if I gave them "something" and they gave it to their wife. I could never understand it. I didn't have anything, but if I did, they would trust me to tell them? And why are you sleeping with me if you have a wife? It was none of my business, but I knew beyond a shadow of a doubt that you couldn't trust men. It was all around me. Frank was letting his wife go out and screw all day long, Most of the guys I knew still had crushes on me, even knowing how I made money. Even my mom didn't seem too appalled.

For the crew I hung with, selling yourself was as ordinary as being a cigarette smoker. The guys did robberies and the chicks did tricks. That was just the way it was. Gabriel specialized in banks. But as he explained to me as we got older, he didn't actually rob the bank. It is too risky. He would just rob the teller. It was simple enough that it could be done with a note and a plastic gun. You get in and out with no hassle. Of course, you make much less money; rather than hundreds of thousands, it is only about $2,000 to $3,000 a pop, but because of the reduced risk, it was the preferred method.

Due to the high volume of calls, Sadie and I were running ourselves into the ground. The money was constant, but there was never enough drugs or soap to wipe the disgust from our dirty bodies. It was only a few weeks before the police became aware of our activity and I had to return to the streets. I drove my Z to a local motel parking lot and walked out onto the boulevard.

The day I returned to the streets, it took hold of me. Drug sick, desperate and without a better solution, it consumed me. Like one long day, light and dark, light and dark, the days merged together. Now almost twenty-two years old, needing to fix more and more to function normally, my body began to shut down on me without my permission. My heroin use had reached a level that was unmanageable and my mind was deteriorating.

The amount of time that I would be able to numb the pain erupting from my aching bones became less and less and there wasn't enough heroin to make it subside. The syrup sweat that seeped out of my skin when I was sick became a permanent state, and even when I was well, there was a coating of stickiness on me. My body began to react without warning and I lost control over it. Until the moment I was able to acquire heroin, I lost control of my bowels.

The period of time between picking up and shooting it into my body became shorter and shorter in an attempt to keep from messing myself. My bowels would give out the moment I saw, smelled, held or sometimes even thought about heroin. I had to rush from the dealer's to a safe place to inject before I crapped in my pants. The best solution became to hit the closest bathroom, dealer, gas station or fast food, sit on the toilet and let go of my bowls while shooting up. On more than one occasion, I did not make it to a bathroom. Rather than go in my pants, I would run into neighborhood bushes and let go. My body was done and I knew it. Unable to stop, over the next few weeks, it got worse.

I met a young hippie couple in Buena Clinton. They were from a different county and not familiar with our area. She was a cute girl named Amy with long curly brown hair and her boyfriend was named

Jack. Jack looked like he came from money, but had been down on his luck for quite a while. Amy was in complete awe of him. In their mid twenties, they were completely in love with each other and heroin. Although they seemed to know the drill pretty well, they were happy and healthy. They smiled a lot and still had color in their skin. They had no idea what they were headed for, although they should have gotten a clue by looking at me and the others. But remembering my first look at the girls on streets, I had no clue either.

In need of a needle, they picked me up and took me with them to a parking lot to slam. I let them use my needle in exchange for drugs. The deal was they would use the needle first and I would go last. Sitting in the back seat of their car, I wrapped my legs around one another and squeezed as tight as I could to keep from messing myself until the needle came my way. As was customary, the moment I injected myself and the warmth hit my stomach, I would regain control of my bowels. I just had to be calm. *Breath in and out Lauri, relax. It's almost here, you are almost better . Just make it better.*

Just moments after I injected myself, the two of them started hitting me! Stretched over their seat, reaching into the back seat, they were hitting me and saying, "Count! Count! Mother F'er! Count!" They were smacking me across the face and screaming at me. I threw my arms out to protect myself, but with four arms hitting me simultaneously it was nearly impossible to avoid being hit. Simply blocking every few punches was about all I could do. I was sure I had gotten into the car with the friggin' Manson family. Happy hippies when I met them, now deranged and out of control lunatics! Finally I screamed, "STOP! GET OFF OF ME!"

Much to my surprise, as soon as I yelled, they stopped! They turned around and the guy said, "Let's get out of here." He started up the car and we left. The fact that they stopped so abruptly and returned to almost a normal serene state again was just as scary as the outburst. I knew I had to get away from them, but they did not stop. As if running from some unknown force, they just drove and drove and did not speak much.

Several hours later, they finally stopped when Amy had to go to a restroom. Wanting to escape the weirdos, I said that I too had to go. When I walked into the small bathroom, Amy went immediately into the stall and I walked up to the small sink to wash my face. The moment I looked in the gas station mirror, I knew something was very wrong. Although they had managed to hit me a few times, this didn't make sense. My arms and chest were covered in blue and red marks, more like large bruises. As if reacting to some kind of spirit take over, my body was turning colors. I was petrified.

When Amy came out the stall, she looked at me and saw the shock in my eyes. With almost no reaction she said, "You are lucky we didn't leave you. You were dead for almost two minutes." We were about to give up when you came to again.

Although surreal, now stringing the pieces together, the hitting, the return to normalcy and the bruises, I knew it was true. I had died. It hit me like a wall. No memory, no white light, just black. I was dead. Every time I saw my body in the mirror, I was reminded. Death was close.

Now intensely aware of the quietness in the car and the aimless driving, it was clear that they were affected just as much, if not more, than I was. Several hours later, still driving aimlessly, Jack spoke. "Tomorrow we will go to the methadone clinic. We will go back to Long Beach (they were renting a loft there) and tomorrow we will go to the clinic for help." I had no idea why they cared enough to try and help me, but in fear for my life more than ever, I just nodded, emotionless. The only thing I knew about the methadone clinic was from the lady in the battered women's shelter. I had no idea what to expect.

We spent the whole next day there. They said they had to test our blood to make sure we were addicted prior to prescribing it. They said if we weren't addicted, it would kill us. By the end of the day, we were all approved and given a small cup of liquid to drink. We were told to come back every day for the next week and that they would wean us off the heroin. The fact was that kicking a methadone habit was worse than heroin. The drink they prescribed produced the same warm affect as the heroin did, but it took longer to hit. I realized immediately that I was not only addicted to the "well" feeling of the heroin, but also the ritual with the needle. Without the ritual, it just wasn't the same. I was addicted to the entire process. I needed it. Over the next few days, as they dropped the dose, the pain in my bones increased and I began to experience nightmares like never before. After six days with the dose dropping, I returned to heroin.

As my body was weakened, I became more desperate. Selling myself for less and less money, I had no limits to the levels I would sink. One day at the park with five young men, I gave them a discount, one at a time in the back seat of the car. When two wanted to come together, although scared, I agreed. Completely aware of the revolting creature I had become, the monster inside of me left me no choice. It made the choices now. First I had a disease, then the disease had me. There was nothing I wouldn't have done to get more heroin. Nothing.

Knowing I was at my end, without any thought in mind of what I was going to do once I got there, I drove my Z to my mom's house. It was about seven o'clock on a Friday night. She was home alone. When she opened the door and saw me, she looked disgusted. She let me in, sat on the couch and put her head in her hands.

My emaciated body was covered with bruises from missing when I shot up. I stank from the sickness and my clothes were dirty. Going to the laundry was just not in my schedule anymore. Then there was my hand. A few days earlier I had shot up into my hand. I would not normally do this, since I always missed due to the small rolling veins, but I was out of options. My arms were calloused with scar tissue and I was covered in bumps and bruises. Even if I did get a needle in my arm, it was unlikely to hit blood through the coarse scar tissue. To make matters worse, I had scabs lining up and down my arms, making it impossible to see the actual vein beneath. My hand was the only option left. The end result was that I missed and over the next few days my hand had blown up like a large golf ball was inside it. By the time I arrived at my mom's, my hand had grown to the size of a small balloon. It looked like the golf ball was imbedded beneath the skin and my entire hand had hardened like a claw. Although I could move it if I really wanted to, the pain kept me from doing so. When my mom finally looked up she said, "So what is going on with you?" I said, "I need help with my hand." She took one look at it and started shooting off questions. "How did you get this? Did you go to a doctor? What did you do to yourself?"

After we were both satisfied that I had done this to myself by shooting up in my hand, I said, "I need help." "What kind of help?" she asked. I said, "I don't know." "What can I do for you?" she asked. "If you could just let me sleep here for a few days, I may be able to stop." Unable to commit to anything, she said, "Why don't you go lie down and we can discuss your options later." Already feeling sick and needing to sleep, I walked like a zombie into my old bedroom and fell asleep instantly.

Less about twelve hours later, I woke up in excruciating pain. My throat closed sooner than expected and I rolled out of the bed in a panic, landed on the floor on all fours and gasped for air! My mother must have heard and came running into the room. This was the first time she would actually see what occurred when I would stop. She panicked to help me, but it was no use. The trap door in my throat would be closed until it decided to open again. Unable to talk, I held her at bay with my arm, while continuing to gasp and attempting to calm myself. I needed air! Just a pea sized bit of air! I was going out and I could feel it! Much to my surprise, by the time a small bead of air got in, instead of returning to a state of exhaustion, my body responded violently. My spine locked back and knotted up in a spasm as if being pulled backward in a vise. I twisted around on the floor and kicked my legs violently, attempting to break the lock, but it was no use. I screamed and scrambled about reacting to the pain, but it only worsened. Within a few minutes my mom had managed to manipulate my thrashing body down to the garage. Before I knew it, we arrived at the hospital emergency room.

I lay in the emergency room bed moaning as quietly as I could. Trying not to appear baby-like, but desperately needing to stop the pain. By the time the doctor pulled the sheets back to see me, he had a plan. Now having spoken to my mom, seen my arms, and realizing I had done this to myself, he thought he would teach me a lesson. Not providing me anything for my back yet, he took a hold of my hand and said, "I hear you have an abscess. We will need to treat this first."

He called the nurse over and removed a scalpel from the table. Even though he explained to me that this must be handled first due the seriousness of the infection, when he stuck the knife in my hand I was acutely aware are of two things. Number one, you would normally give someone some kind of numbing injection before sticking a knife in them and number two, he was going to teach me not to do this again by showing me how much it hurts. Little did he know, it was the *how much it hurts* that kept me "doing" these kinds of things. Pain was not new to me. He cut my hand open, drained the fluid and sent me upstairs. He told my mom that the muscle spasms were a result of severe withdrawals from heroin. When I arrived upstairs they medicated me. I can't tell you what it was that they gave me, only that I did not remember anything else, except one blurry memory. A tall thin black man came to my room to see me. I have no idea who he was, or why he was there, only that he didn't work at the hospital. He came to tell me something that would give me hope. For the life of me, I couldn't remember what. Only that he was there and then gone.

Released to my mom's care, I spent the next week sick and unable to sleep. On the second day she took me to her holistic healer. The woman had me drink ginger soup with herbs and massaged my temples. Knowing my problem was much more than a few herbs and a massage could resolve, I reluctantly went along with it. Much to my surprise, while she was massaging my head I was able to sleep for ten minutes. In the midst of the sickness, ten minutes seemed like forever. If I hadn't looked at the clock on the wall, I would have sworn I was out for several hours. One week later, where in the past I would have been better, I still hadn't slept. I was hallucinating and the pain blaring out of my bones was unbearable. When my mom left for work one morning I returned to the street to get better.

Having lost track of where I was going or what I was doing from day to day, I spent the new few months plunging to new depths of despair. The day I regained active consciousness, I was sitting in a dark room on a couch in a house in Long Beach. It was Christmas again. Exactly One Year since I left my Angel behind in a plan to get help.

The house was dark because the heavy curtains were all drawn. The Christmas bulbs were flashing on the tree, and the only other source of light was the ray shining from beneath the bedroom door at the end of the hallway to my right. I had been there for several days, without sleep. I was unable to differentiate between the voices in my head and the voices coming from beneath the door, down the hall.

I had no recollection of how I got there, but I was acutely aware of the situation I was in. I was not alone. There were three other people in the house. They were in that other room. A man in his forties, who had been dolling out the cocaine for the past few days, his twenty-one year old wife, and the man's father who was in his mid sixties. Up until now, I had been comfortable with the situation. A bunch of drug addicts just doing what we had to do to get by. The girl and I had been turning tricks with men that had visited for cocaine, but now things had changed. The girl had explained to me prior to retreating to the bedroom that it was customary for her to have sex with her husband and his dad together for cocaine. This information brought about a mental sobering that I hadn't experienced since arriving at my mom's. I did everything to get her not to do it. I pleaded with her to get out, that it wasn't okay. That it wasn't the same as being with strangers, that she needed to stay with me in the living room, to refuse to do it, but she wouldn't listen. Now in the bedroom, all three of them were together. As the disgusting noises erupted from the room, the revulsion and panic consumed me. No!

I could feel another presence here. The devil was undeniably present. The stench filled the small house and made the air so thick it was suffocating. I struggled to get a breath of fresh air. My heart pounded and my mind raced. I needed to escape. My pale face and stringy long hair dripped of sweat, my jaw was permanent locked to the left and my sleeves were covered in dried blood. The terror of opening the front door to the bright sunlight, the sound of the cars on the street and people stirring about, sent shivers up my spine. I needed to get out. I was frozen in fear by the life beyond the door leading out and the death consuming the house from within. My head darted back and forth from the room to the door, the room, the door, the room, the door. Crouched over and rocking, I glanced at the tree. Like an angel's wings being tragically torn from its small body, it wept. As my eyes clouded with tears, the flashing of the tree brought back a memory of my baby…The tree…life…death…my baby…life…streets… death… Madie…life…

It was at that moment, as if catapulted from an outside force, that my body bolted up and I ran out of the door! As if the devil himself was on my tail, I dared not look back. My Z was parked out front. Having no clear recollection of how I ended up at this house in Long Beach, or where I was going, with my stiffened body and hands clutching the wheel so hard that it hurt, I drove…and drove…I needed to straighten this whole thing out; I was desperate. It had been a year.

A year since I left my angel. I stopped at a gas station and called the old shack. By this time, I knew the number because I had called the old man there so many times. Thirty minutes later, I pulled up in front of a treatment program called the Redwood Revival Center.

In an act of desperation, and without an appointment, I ran in as if being chased by an army and demanded to see the person in charge immediately. A tall man pointed down the hall and said, "Go to the office."

As I turned the corner to the office, a frail white-haired old man sat in a large leather chair. Although everything about me said this was an emergency, he did not acknowledge my presence. He calmly went about shuffling papers and flipping files. I was sure hadn't seen me, or heard my labored breathing, until he spoke. Without lifting his head or making eye contact, he calmly said, "Sit."

For the next few minutes, he continued shuffling papers. Tending to whatever business he had on his desk, he did not look up. Giving the last pile of files a swift tap on the table to straighten it up, he set it aside and lifted his head. Leaning back in his chair, he took a deep breath and looked at me. "What can I do for you young lady?" I immediately responded, "I need help!" I think it was the first time I had ever said it out loud. I was immediately aware of how weak it made me sound. I was barely twenty-two, five-foot-five and eighty-nine pounds. This kind old man looked at me as if I was a child, and at that moment for the first time in a very long time, I felt like one.

He said, "Well, I believe you do need help. But this is a treatment center for alcoholism. Clearly you are suffering from something other than alcoholism." I was immediately aware of the black tracks and green bumps and bruises that marked my tiny hands, and although the long flannel shirt hid my arms, the dried blood stains halfway down on both sides and my tracked hands told all. "I am an alcoholic! I might do drugs, but I drink too!" He grinned. His caring eyes smiled. I felt guilty for even saying it.

Although I used to drink Jack Daniels and Seagram's, it had been a long time since I had picked up a drink. With a compassionate look in his eyes, and a quiet voice he said, "I cannot help you here, you are not an alcoholic." He looked down at his papers and resumed shuffling them.

Although I cannot explain how I knew, two things were crystal clear. This was a man with a huge heart and immense integrity. No matter how much he knew I needed help or how much he wanted to give it to me, he would not break the rules. Even though he had said no, everything about him said he cared. He cared deeply. I don't know how I knew, but as I left the room, I felt it. As he dropped his head to reshuffle the papers, he put in a word for me, with someone, somewhere else.

I walked into the parking lot, got in my car, hung my head and wept. I needed to get help. I needed to be with Madie. My baby. In respect for the man, I pulled slowly out of the lot, rather than tearing out, like I normally would have done.

I drove slowly and aimlessly down the street. Before I hit the traffic light, I saw the answer! A liquor store! Knowing this man could help me with an alcohol problem, I would make it happen! I can live in my car in front of the building and drink until I became an alcoholic! I removed my boot and shook it and the last of my money fell out, $17.26. I would drink for days, weeks, even months if I had to, but sooner or later, I would be an alcoholic and they would have to let me in! I returned to the car with a large bottle of Seagram's Seven and I pulled in front of the building. Even though I was quite a distance from the old man's office, the large bay window behind his chair was a direct shot across the field from where my car sat.

I figured at some point someone would notice that I was there and by the time they did, I would look like, smell like and be an alcoholic!

It was less than a half hour later when the tall man that initially pointed me to the office came out and knocked on my window. When I rolled it down, he said, "What are you doing?" I replied, "Drinking. Because I am an alcoholic." He looked puzzled and said, "You can't stay here." I defiantly replied, "I am going to stay here until you people help me! I will stay as long as I have to in order to prove to you that I *am* an alcoholic!" He looked both bothered and confused and walked away.

Not ten minutes later he returned to the car and knocked on the window again. When I rolled it down he said, "Floyd wants to see you," and walked away. Not knowing the name of the old man in the office, I assumed he was Floyd. Suspecting I was in trouble, but having no other plans, I got out and walked back into the facility and returned to the old man's office. This time when I entered his office, the old man was looking up, as if he was waiting for me. He did not say a word. I walked in and like a child about to be scolded, I returned to the chair I had sat in just moments prior. With seriousness in his eyes, he just stared at me. Then he spoke.

"This is a 30 day treatment program. You will apply for SSI. The counselors will help you fill out the forms. If you follow the rules of the program you can stay for up to 90 days..." I couldn't believe it! I was in! Much like when Charlie returned the Gobstopper to Willy Wonka, he was just waiting me out! Although I guess it was a bit different, as Charlie had to display honesty and I did quite the opposite, but I truly believe the old man wanted to help me and now I had made it possible for him to follow the rules *and* help me.

I spent the next five and a half months in the Redwood Revival Center. We had classes all day for the first thirty days, and meetings, much like the ones in the shack, almost every night. We also had a family night. After thirty days, I was able to leave the center on passes for up to eight hours at a time. I would always pick up Madie and spend the day with her on my weekend passes. Beatrice was nice enough to continue to watch her until I got better. All I wanted was to get better and get her back. Now that my mind had cleared from the drugs, I couldn't understand how I ever could have wanted anything else. I really started to feel like everything was going to turn out okay after all.

It was also during my time at the Redwood Revival Center that I met "Tommie." While hanging out with one of the other residents on a day pass, we stopped at her boyfriend's parents' house. With nothing else going on that particular day, we planted ourselves in front of the TV and watched sports with a bunch of his guy friends. Bored out of my mind, and knowing nothing about sports, I shoved chips and dip in my mouth while they watched. We were about an hour into our very uneventful visit when she busted in the door. She flew through the door in a dark blue sweat suit, huffing and puffing, chucked her large baseball bat to the floor and in a deep masculine voice said, "Hey!" She was 17-years-old and absolutely stunning. Short black hair, standing straight up from hair jell and the largest chocolate brown eyes I had ever seen. She was the female version of Ralph Macchio, the karate kid. Having known gay women my whole life, I had never felt drawn to a woman, up until this very moment. It was love at first sight.

Knowing I was too messed up for her and also too old, I did not act on my feelings other than to mention it to my friend after we had left there. The very next day my friend revealed that she had told Tommie, and Tommie felt the same. For the next few weeks, I made it a point to go anywhere where there was a possibility of seeing Tommie. Every time I saw her, I flirted with her, but clear on the fact that she was too young, too normal, school sports and all, and I was a mess, I did not pursue it further...at that time. But I thought about her all of the time.

In the Redwood Revival Center, they talked a lot about God. They repeatedly talked about the need to pray. I had an issue with this. Pray to the same God who stuck me with a bad family and had me thrown away, tied to a bed? He hated me. I knew him, but I couldn't look to him for help. He was out to hurt me. I knew they wouldn't understand at the center. They really seemed to like the God thing. Not knowing what else to do, I prayed, with a lot of skepticism, but I prayed. One night they held an meeting at the center and a man with a cane came in. He said, "Be careful what you pray for. I prayed to slow down and I got hit by a bus. Now I pray with very clear instruction."

Now this was something I could relate to. The God I knew did stuff like that. It seemed like this guy was the only one I had met so far that had the same God I did. I said nothing to the man, but from that point forward I prayed reluctantly to a God I didn't know or trust with very specific and direct instruction. *Please watch over my baby and make me better.*

I also had a strange experience with Lucy. Having reconnected with her when I got to the center, she announced that she had gone "Christian" and invited me to her church. On one of my passes during the week, I decided to visit. To say it was weird is really an understatement. There were people yelling and throwing their hands in the air, and believe it or not, a bunch of them were on the floor, flopped over and weeping. Frankly, I was embarrassed for them. Feeling completely out of place, I just sat down in a chair and observed. It was crazy. The part I found even crazier was that to anyone just walking in, I was the one that was out of place! I was the only one sitting down like a normal person. The rest of them were convulsing all over the floor. Unfortunately, my refusal to conform gave me away. A young man and two women spotted me. They approached me and said, "Would you like to talk?" Talk seemed a couple of notches up from watching the circus freaks. Not knowing what we would talk about, I said, "Sure." They led me beyond the stage to a private room and we sat down. Or more accurately, I sat down. Two of the three remained standing. One of the ladies sat across from me, looked me straight in the eyes and asked, "Do you know God?' "Yes," I replied. She went on. "Do you know Jesus Christ as your God?" I said, "No, I am Jewish." "Do you realize you are not praying to God if it is not through Jesus?" she said. I just stared at her. Then she said, "There is only one way to God and that is through Jesus. If you are not praying through Jesus, you are not praying to God." This came as a huge surprise to me! In complete confusion I said, "Then who am I praying to?" She replied, "You are praying to an evil spirit pretending to be God." I thought about that for a minute, or two. Very disturbing to my twenty-two year old mind.

I replied, "So an evil spirit has been keeping me sober?" "Yes," she replied. "Because I am not calling God Jesus, he is not listening?" "Yes," she replied. "Why would an evil spirit keep me sober?" "To trick you into making you think he is God," she replied. Now really considering this, I said, "I love my daughter more than anything in the world and I can tell you one thing for sure, I don't care what she calls me, I will feed her. They say God is ALL love. This really doesn't sound very loving to me." Not knowing how to respond, both she and her associates just stared at me. Now completely confused and not really wanting to hear anymore of this insanity, I got up, walked out and left the church.

The whole thing sounded crazy to me and even though on a logical level I knew it made no sense, it still affected me greatly. The small amount of faith I had before was now in even worse shape. Not knowing who the heck I was talking to anymore, in order to cover all bases, I started my prayers with 'God, Jesus or whoever is there.' Let's just say this was not good for me.

I stayed at the center for the next five months. It was the longest time since I was in New York that I was able to go without drugs. And this time, I was completely sober. I learned a lot about alcoholism, the symptoms and the signs of relapse, and for once I enjoyed being around the people. On an average day there were at least thirty recovering drug addicts and alcoholics living there. I was so grateful to wake up feeling normal and not in pain anymore; whatever it was that was keeping me there was working.

The next Saturday, my roommate Gia and I drove to Beatrice's to get Madie to take her to the movies. We were going to see "An American Tail." It had our song, "Somewhere out there."

> *The words to the song seemed to help her.*
> *They talked about being far away, but still together.*
>
> *They talked about love being able to get people through.*
> *A world where love fixed everything.*
>
> *With no real understanding of how I was going to fix this,*
> *the song gave her the hope that I couldn't give her.*
> *It said all of the things I couldn't say.*

Having sung it to Madie each time I visited, it reinforced the idea that I would come back for her, and frankly, the song killed me every time. I couldn't believe I had ever left my angel for drugs. The only thing that kept me from falling apart when I heard the song was that I knew Beatrice was taking good care of her and that I would get better and get her back.

When we arrived at the movies that day something was bothering Madie. She seemed grouchy. This wasn't normally the case when I got her and even at the age of three she was pretty good at communicating when something was wrong. Being raised around mostly adults, she communicated much more directly than most three-year-olds. But on this day, she was just disturbed and not really talking. Much to my surprise, she started crying on the way into the theatre and refused to go in. I couldn't understand it. We had talked about it on the phone and she seemed very excited to see the movie. I knew she wasn't tired. It was eleven in the morning. She had just barely woken up.

I pulled her aside, away from Gia, to talk to her. I sat on a bench in the movie theatre with her on my lap and we rocked. I sang her baby song. *Mommies little princess, mommies little pumpkin, mommies little baby girl...*She pulled away from me and got down on the floor. She stood and looked at me and started crying. She pointed at her bottom and said, "Todd." Todd was Beatrice's oldest son. He was fourteen at the time. Not knowing what she was saying, but immediately assuming the worst, I grabbed Gia and we headed out. Petrified that something might have happened to her, we sped out to the local hospital emergency room.

Four hours later, the detectives departed the hospital with the small dolls that they used to interview my baby. Small cotton rag dolls with realistic private parts. Confirming that something had indeed occurred, they left to obtain a warrant for Todd's arrest. In a state of shock and completely broken, I returned to the center, with my baby. I had left her there. I left her in a place where they hurt her. I hated myself. The more I thought about it, the angrier I became. These were the best, most normal people I knew. How could this have happened? What about my prayers to God? I could never accept what the lady at the church told me about the evil spirits pretending to be God, but now I surely accepted that he was not listening. Or more directly, he was still out to get me. And this time, it was unforgivable.

By the time the police phoned me at the center to tell me that the arrest was made, I had been crying for so long, my eyes were swollen. At the same time, I was trying to be strong for Madie because she needed to see that I was okay. That was the only way I could assure her that she was now safe. I was glad he had been arrested. It couldn't have happened quickly enough and as far as I was concerned, arrest was too little and much too late. He needed a worse punishment. I wanted him to go to hell. I wanted him to die! How dare he hurt my baby? Other thoughts raced through my mind though...

I thought about my class, and the fact that most kids that are abusers were abused themselves. Then I thought about his sisters acting so sexual that day when I was babysitting them. Back then, I thought I was overreacting due to the information from my class, but something had happened! Then I thought about the dad, and that strange doll he showed me! I was such a fool! How did I not see this?! I hated myself!

Something else still bothered me. Beatrice. What if her husband is molesting her kids and she didn't know? She was always so sweet to us. She must not have known. She must be in shock. I was feeling guilty for arresting her son after she was so nice to us, and although I wanted to kill him, I was feeling bad for her, so I phoned her from the payphone at the center.

She answered, "Hello." I responded, "Hi Beatrice, it is Lauri. I guess you know what happened." She said. "How dare you do this to us after all we've done for you? Todd was already in counseling for this. He was getting better, and now this." As if the phone were covered in poison, I held it from my face and screamed, "YOU KNEW HE DID THESE THINGS AND YOU HAD ME LEAVE MY BABY THERE?!" I banged the phone at the receiver several times and threw it against the wall. It dangled at the end of the long wire cord twisting and hitting the wall. I crouched down with my head in my hands attempting to process what I had just heard.

I couldn't believe it! Not only had God been out to hurt me, but Beatrice knew as well! I am so F'ing stupid, I left my kid there! I shouldn't have left her! My already swollen face was heating up with rage and my baby, my poor baby. I wanted to kill someone. In a state of shock, I knew I could not leave Madie again. Floyd said Madie could stay with the girls in the independent housing for two days while I figured something out. Two days later, I left with a boy I liked from the center and Madie to rent an apartment.

I signed up for victim witness, per the detectives' instructions and I got counseling immediately for Madie. I knew from my class that we would need to talk about it and process the feelings or she would bury it and it would make her very sick. I had to do everything I could to help her heal from this.

I had prayed for only two things while I was at the center; to stay sober and to keep my baby safe. This prayer crap wasn't working and I knew it. With growing rage, no job, no one I trusted and anger at God, I was in bad shape. More than ever I had a complete distrust for everyone and everything.

In the beginning of my stay at the Redwood Revival Center, I really thought I had felt something, a presence, like someone was listening when I prayed. Trust it or not, I felt "something." But for the past few months, since the church thing, the feeling of a presence dissipated. It was just a useless routine, brush your teeth, wash your face and mutter a few prayers into nowhere. Now I was sure I had always been alone.

Within two weeks of leaving, I stuck a needle in my arm again. The moment I put the needle in, I felt it. I realized that even though I had felt alone, something was there. The only explanation I could come up with was that I had grown so used to it. It must have become a part of me, and therefore unable to be felt as something separate.

The moment the drugs hit my blood, I felt the presence leave. I knew beyond a shadow of a doubt, that I had made a serious mistake, but it was too late. The old thing returned, filling every inch of my being. Having no understanding of what it really meant, I knew only one thing for sure. I was not alone before. Even when I felt like I was talking to the air, I was not alone. In the matter of just a few seconds, something good left and something very bad returned. The transition was undeniable.

Back on the streets again, leaving Madie with the other junkies while I went to make money, within a few weeks my mom found out and came and got Madie. I knew this was best and frankly, I was relieved. I hated myself for not being able to protect her. I didn't deserve her. This was the end for me. Over the next six months, any part of Lauri that remained died.

I became one of them. The streets became my refuge, the only answer left. Sedated from morning until night, I needed to stay numb. I needed to forget. Every time I injected myself, I went further and further away. I wanted to go away permanently. The men on the streets couldn't hurt me any longer. I was already dead. I had been beaten and raped so many times, I now failed to care on any level. One day I stopped caring altogether.

I was now working the streets throughout the night with a total disregard for my own safety. On many nights, I was out there when only one or two cars remained on the road. My boots were the only sound, until the hum of an engine and ongoing headlights appeared.

Having been alone with so many lunatics, I was now acutely aware that the next car could be the last car.

I remember many nights when I saw the twist coming. I became an expert at seeing the change. Raped and beaten by so many men, I lost count. I sensed when the end was near. There was a point where something in me still cared. In desperation, I would plead my way out. I would comply with any and all requests to save myself. There was no limit to what I would or wouldn't do. *Just let me live, so that I can go turn another trick and make myself feel numb again.* Rape after rape, beating after beating, I shot the pain away. Numb again. One day I stopped fighting.

A man picked me up in a large truck. Just moments after entering the car, he sped out of control. He pulled into an alley and exposed a large knife, which he pressed against my throat. "I have no money. You will do whatever I want." Where I usually would have fought, my body fell limp, my eyes vacant. "Do it. Take what you want. You don't need the knife. I don't care. Take it."

It wasn't my words that alerted me that I had given up, but rather the man's response. Just seconds ago he had been filled with rage and anger, prepared to do whatever he had to do in order to violate me. Now, looking into my eyes, he became instantly solemn. His hand fell open and he dropped the knife on the seat. He turned his eyes away from mine and stared out his window. I gently opened the handle and got out. There was nothing left to take.

Each day new memories piled on the old, making it more and more difficult to be sober for even a short while; the rapes, beatings, my mangled arms, my baby. There were some days that stuck out more vividly than others. These were the days that no amount of drugs would erase.

Unfortunately, this was about the time Tommie found me. Having thought about me since I left the Redwood Revival Center, she sought me out. The day she showed up couldn't have been any worse. Already on my way to the dealer to score, she intercepted me at the door of the place I was staying. Visibly sick with addiction, she instantly knew something was wrong. Wanting to shield her from my life, I just looked at her and said, "I have to go," and started to walk. Emotionally charged by my state and our connection, she said, "I am going with you!" I turned and said, "No, you have no idea Tommie. It is not good, just go home." After a few minutes of useless bantering, I gave in. When we arrived at the dealer's, I was so sick I needed to fix there. I turned to look at Tommie, her head was down and she continued following me. Trailing right behind me, she followed me into the restroom. I begged her not to witness this, but she insisted. Unable to choose anything over the drug, I fixed in front of her. Leaving there a few hours later, she had tears in her eyes and said, "I will be back." She was driven to save me, but unfortunately she had no idea what she was up against. Before she could find me again, I was gone. I loved her too much to subject her to any prolonged exposure to me or my dirty life.

A few days later, sick out of my mind and attempting to hide from anyone who knew me, I showed up to a known dealer's house for heroin. The drugs here were not the best, but it was one of those days I just didn't want to see any other humans. Sickened by my own disgust, I just wanted to be alone. The routine at this dealer's house was to go around to the side yard and knock on the window. The window was covered with a heavy curtain, but there was always someone on the other side. Seconds after I knocked, the window would slide slightly open and a man's voice would erupt from beyond. "What do you need?" I would verbalize my order and hold out my money. A man's hand would come through the ripped screen and make the exchange. I never saw a face.

I intentionally went there to avoid humans, but on this day it was different. When I went to the window and knocked, a woman's voice responded. When I made my request clear, she muttered, "Come to the door." My need for drugs far exceeded my need to be alone, so I complied. When I arrived, she told me she was on her way out and her husband had been arrested. She had a bit of stash, and said I could use the bathroom to get well, although she added that her nephew was home, but wouldn't be bothered by me. She closed by saying her husband would not return and that was the end of their sales. She handed me what she had and left. I have to believe the only reason she let me in was because I was a young girl. This certainly wasn't standard procedure. I went into the bathroom and within a few minutes of frantically trying to fix myself, I clogged and broke my needle. The plunger disconnected from the stick. I was completely deranged when her nephew knocked on the bathroom door. "What are you doing in there?" he said. "Nothing," I replied in a frustrated small voice.

"Come on, open up. I am cool," he said. Realizing I had no reason to be in there without a needle, I had no reason not to. I opened the door a crack and looked at him. He couldn't have been older than eleven. A cute skinny kid dressed like a mini gangster with his long shorts, white tee shirt and socks up to his knees. He had large brown innocent eyes and the voice of a child. "Do you have drugs?" he said. "What is it to you if I do kid?" I replied. "I just thought maybe you would share," he said. In a frustrated voice I said, "Look kid, I am not sharing heroin with a kid. You are way too young to do anything like this." As he peered through the crack of the door, he noticed the mess on the sink… the blood, the spoon with liquid in it and the broken needle. Finally he said, "Look, open up. I have a brand new needle and if you share, I will let you use it." I was horrified. Let a child shoot up? Are you kidding? There is no way. Then he said, "Look girl, it's not like I don't shoot up already, I do it all the time. If you do, I will let you go first."

My bowels began to give way and I knew I had to have it. Against everything I ever believed in or wanted for a child, I agreed. I was conflicted, but unable to choose this child's life over my addiction. I turned my head as he injected the remainder of my drugs and no amount of sedation would ever let me forget that day.

Then there was the "rainy day." Unlike most days in California, on this day the rain came down in buckets. Having no money for a hotel room, and knowing that the guy that I left the Redwood Revival Center with was recently evicted, I broke into his old apartment for shelter. I drove there in the 280Z, entered through an open window and returned a few hours later with drugs. That was the day I met Brandy. Brandy was a younger girl who had just started to work the streets. She had no shelter. When I told her about my circumstances, she asked if she could join me. Seeing that she was soaking wet, and in a state where my heart was completely hardened, I thought, *What can she give me for it.* After a few seconds I had it. "If you give me half of everything you make, I will bring you back to the apartment with me." She agreed.

We decided we would work the streets together and only take tricks that were willing to pay for two. Shortly after we walked out to the road a car with two men pulled over. One Hispanic man who claimed to have lots of heroin on him and a white man whose face had been burned in a house fire. His face was melted away and his ears and nose were burned beyond recognition. When Brandy saw him, she looked at me with tears in her eyes and nodded no. Completely void of all compassion or sympathy I replied, "Then you will sleep out in the rain."

I failed to recognize myself. The evil had consumed me. I took the drugs, and they took me.

The men returned with us to the apartment. I slept with the man with the heroin and the other man just hung around. After a few hours of deliberating and unable to bring herself to be with him, Brandy opted to return to the rain. Two days later I awoke from a heroin induced slumber to find the men gone. They had taken something extra, my 280Z.

It was in the cards. Karma that is. I heard it was totaled a few days later. There was nothing left now. I spiraled down into the depths of a hell I would not wish on anyone. I saw and experienced awful things that only a person delivering their own death sentence would allow themselves to be subjected to.

Depleted of everything, I was now one of them. As the young drug addicts drove up the road, they might look out of the car window at me and say, "Why is that girl going south when she was just going north a few minutes ago?" And someone would enlighten her on the facts of life. "This is what she does, she is a prostitute. She is out here every day making money to feed her addiction. She probably works for less than $40, but will take anything you have. She needs it to live. There is nothing else now."

The streets owned me.

Late afternoon, the street full of cars and the sun setting, I stood in front of the donut shop, walked over and bent down and picked up a cigarette butt off of the street. There was still some white left on it; it wasn't finished yet. I straightened it out, knowing I could get at least a few good hits off of it.

I walked into the shop, nodded at the man behind the counter, picked up a matchbook from the little cardboard box and walked back out into the warm sun. Sitting down at the bus stop, I carefully cupped my hands around my little prize. I had to make sure the flame lit the end all at once. When they were real stale, they would burn too fast sometimes. Engulfed in the process, I barely noticed as the car pulled up alongside the curb, until they beeped lightly. My attention shifted. From the bench it looked like two men were in the car.

I walked over, took the last big pull off the old cigarette butt and returned it to the street. Before I could speak, the young man on the passenger side nodded as if to say, get in. I entered in the rear door and shut it. I assumed they were used to the drill when they didn't speak.

The driver glanced at me in the rearview mirror and then immediately returned his eyes to the road and pulled away from the curb. When we got on the freeway onramp, I knew. Something was wrong, very wrong...

By this point, I clearly knew the signs. Getting on the freeway was bad. Even though I had been raped and beaten in alleys, behind motels, or trapped in a room, only the most ferocious of the lunatics took me out of the area first. When we entered the freeway, I always knew. Today could be the day I die.

Before I could fully take in what was occurring, the driver had accelerated and was frantically weaving through traffic and the man in the passenger seat was growing visibly apprehensive, as if he wanted to take over the wheel to make him drive faster, he became increasingly frustrated. His facial expression was what you might expect of someone in a getaway car with a trunk filled with money. It was as if the man driving could not go fast enough for him. It was apparent there was a destination in mind and wherever it was, he needed to be there now. As the passenger's panic increased, my heart banged inside my rib cage. Something was very wrong!

I quickly took in my surroundings. The car was barren of any trash, belongings or paraphernalia which might provide insight into who or what I was dealing with. As I glanced out of the window, I realized the freeway was packed, although we were moving quite rapidly. There were cars everywhere. Traffic hour. I guessed it was around 7 p.m. but couldn't be sure. I had long since lost track of time and days. I only knew I had to get out. The fact that neither of the men had spoken yet only increased my inner panic. Something was very wrong! As I continued to scan the car, I was surprised to see that the door handles were still intact. As I pulled on the handle gently, the resistance told me that it was still operational; this is good.

Noting the speed at which we were traveling, and the distance between the cars, jumping was out of the question. I would surely be run over almost immediately. Now, making eye contact with a man in a neighboring car, I knew what I had to do. It would be my only chance. I had to let the other drivers know I was in trouble.

I jumped out of my seat and threw my torso over the front seat and lunged for the wheel. If I jerked it hard enough, they would hit someone. Even if they didn't pull over, someone would get our license! The passenger's fist bashed my temple so hard that it caused me to retract before I was even able to get a grasp the wheel. Bang! Sharp white lights of pain shot out in my head. "Try that again and you die!" the driver said. Sensing the enormity of the situation and in a state of severe malnutrition and stress, my mind just checked out. I lost all memory of what happened next. By the time my mind checked back in, it was almost too late.

34

I AM STILL IN THE BACK SEAT, ONLY NOW THE MEN ARE THERE WITH me. The driver is on my left side; his accomplice is on my right. My neck hurts. I drop my head and see my bloodied, torn shirt hanging from my pale body. It is at that point that I notice my exposed breast and the driver's gun. Holding it firmly between his legs with his hands wrapped tightly around it, he is breathing rapidly. There is pressure on my left leg; the driver's foot is on top of mine. The only portion of my pants that remain on are tightly wrapped around my boot with my underwear. My other foot is bare. The car windows are completely fogged up, but I can still make out the forest outside. We are in the woods. Everywhere I look there is nothing but dense forest. My head is on fire, pulsing. I feel bumps of pain. My bottom burns.

The men are yelling, at each other. The accomplice seems to have changed his mind. The more he tries to convince the gunman to stop, the angrier the gunman becomes. He lifts the gun to my head and presses the cold barrel against my temple. His hand forcefully shakes with the intensity of their argument. As their anger escalates toward each other, the gunman's anger escalates toward me. Spitting in my ear in Spanish, I no longer understood the words, but I feel the intensity. His accomplice is calmer. He appears to be reasoning with him. He is speaking in English. Someone had died. A prostitute killed him. My death would even the score. "The puta dies today!" the gunman screams. The voice in my head shrieks, *No!* I squeeze my eyes shut, willing them to go away. *Just make it all stop!*

As the gunman shifts in his seat, I instinctively turn his way. His blood-red eyes pierce through my soul with an intense rage that my frail mind is unable to sustain. I drop my focus to the floor. My pale thin legs vibrate with the trembling of my body, my eyes widen and my stare takes me away for a moment.

Jolted back to the scene, the gunman grabs my head and forces me into an upright position. Pain shoots through my face as his left arm hits my lip and he reaches across my head. Clumps of my hair are balled up in his right fist with the gun; he is using my head for leverage as he lunges on top of me. I retract in pain. He forces himself inside of me, his hand clamping on my ribs like a vice. It burns. He has been here before. As he violates me, his gaze returns to my eyes. The accomplice looks away and his head drops. I am gone again, somewhere else; not somewhere safe, just somewhere else. Away.

His heavy, limp body drops on top of me. I feel his hot breath sting the side of my neck. Everything is quiet now with the exception of his labored breathing. My body is stiff. I dare not move. I don't want to remind him that I am here. He climbs off of me. There is no sound. Without so much as a word, he silently returns the gun to my head. It's cold.

That's when I heard it—the voice in my head—distinctly. Everything stood still for just one second. *"You know what Lauri? They don't know who they have here…you want to die…they want to kill you…you all want the same thing…Why don't you let them know? If you scream loud enough, they will get scared. Scared someone will hear…they will pull the trigger…It will all be over. Your whole life, you always wanted it to be over. Your dad, the gun, the institution, the streets, your baby…you have nothing to live for anymore…. Make it end now.*

This is it, the end. I am ready.

Without so much as another thought, I erupted in a hair-curling pitch, "KILL ME! KILL ME! KILL ME NOW!" I screamed so loud my body shook, my face burned with heat and the raw skin in my throat stung in pain. "KILL ME!" And then it went black.

35

I WAKE TO A COLD CHILL AND THE STING OF SHARP TINY PEBBLES penetrating my cheek. Exhaust fumes fill the air. The sound of large boots crushing small pieces of gravel beneath them is like thunder against my throbbing head. There is a white van. As the memories of the woods come rushing back, my heart begins to race. *Where am I?* I quickly scan my surroundings. We are on a road now; it is dark. The van's headlights are the only source of light. There is a tall black man standing above me. He is alone. The hum of the van's engine echoes through the canyon. There is no other sound.

As my vision clears, he kneels down beside me. Gently wrapping his arms around me, he begins to lift me up. The cold asphalt burns as it separates from my sticky skin. For a moment, his face appears directly in front of mine. It is different. Not like the gunman. His eyes fill with tears and he whispers, "You are going to be okay."

My legs dangle beneath me and I struggle to regain my footing. I drop my head to look at my limp feet and I see my shirt. Ripped and bloody, it is the only clothing that remains on my small frame. My foggy state of mind is the only reprieve from the embarrassment of my exposed bottom. He carries me toward the passenger seat of his van. Tan cloth seats come into view. *Wet…Blood…Cloth seats…* "Please, No!" I struggle against him and twist fiercely using my foot to push away from the van. *My blood will stain the seat! When he sees the seat, he will be mad! No more pain, please, no more…*I fall unconscious again.

With just a brief memory of the man delivering me to a hospital, I do not remember anything else until I exited the taxi at the donut station. The man or one of the hospital staff must have paid for the taxi to take me home. Having no home to speak of, I was on autopilot.

For months now, when being asked "Where do you want to go now," after a trick, I would return to the donut shop and walk back up the boulevard in pursuit of more. By the time the taxicab stopped at the small donut shop it was morning again. I exited the cab with just the hospital gown on, slit up the back. Torn shirt underneath, I walked slowly out to the bus stop barefoot and half naked in excruciating pain and stuck my thumb out. I needed to get numb to make the pain subside and to forget. I needed to do it one more time to make it go away...

The next day, I phoned my mom, "Mom, I need help." She hung up on me, which was well-deserved. Having broken her heart over and over again, she couldn't endure another time.

Then I called Bob. The man in the wheelchair from the call service. Bob had returned to the streets several times over the past years to find me. Not to take me to the movies anymore and not to spend time, but to plead with me to get help. Somehow in saving me, Bob would save himself.

Now, having gotten to know him in the depths of my addiction, he laid it all out on the table in an effort to save me. Bob was brutally abused as a child. He has a mother, father and a sister. At the age of fourteen he left home and never returned. His parents never sought him out. When he was injured in Vietnam by the piece shrapnel that permanently severed his spine at the age of nineteen, they phoned his family. His mother came alone to the hospital and left the same day. Having no way to resolve what happened in his mind, Bob became an existentialist. As he explained it to me, there is no God, no power, no angels, nothing. We are alone.

Bob's friends in Vietnam were the only family he had. Remembering the friends that were addicted to heroin and died out on the field, he made it his responsibility to save me. He hunted me down on the streets, had long talks with me and gave me money for rehab with broken promises from me that I would go. I never had any intention of going, just getting the money.

"Hello?"

"Bob I need help." Silence…Having used him for so long without any sense of remorse, he was completely done with me. In a frustrated emotionless voice he responded. "Lauri, I will take you wherever you want to go. But I will not give you a dime."

36

As I waited for Bob, I only knew one thing for sure. I needed to go far away, to a place too far to hitchhike back from. I could not trust myself. I would be getting sicker soon. When the sickness hit, I would start to deal with the monster within. If the drive was within a reasonable distance I would be able to make it before the pain started and the haunting memories set in. I could not make any promises to myself or anyone else. All that I knew was that I had to be far enough that the monster wouldn't make me return.

I don't remember much about how we found the place or the drive, but I do remember the arrival and my state of being. The long driveway led up to a small light blue cottage that sat on top of a hill. There was an old rusty swing set just to the left of the two cement steps leading into the small office situated in the kitchen.

I lugged the large black garbage bag I had with me out of the back seat of Bob's old Mercedes and up the small cement steps. It was all I had left to show for my life. All that remained.

An average looking man in his early fifties opened the old screen door and said, "Are you Lauri?" When I replied, "Yes" he said come in." Bob remained at the foot of the steps due to his wheelchair and the absence of a ramp. From the bottom of the steps Bob yelled, "I'm just dropping her off. Do I need to wait or can I go?" The man answered, "She should be fine," and directed me to sit down at a small kitchenette table. After a few minutes, I heard the car door slam and the engine roar, Bob was gone. Not having spoken yet, I sat at the small table with my large black trash bag at my feet. The man said nothing. Other than the sound of the papers he was rummaging through on the kitchen counter, the house remained quiet. The contrast of the beautiful warm sun pouring in through the window against my pale weak body was difficult to resolve. I was a human virus.

My pores were drenched with sweet sweat and the familiar dull pain erupting from my bones was unbearable. As broken as I felt, I kept my head up and vibrated my legs ever so slightly to deflect the pain. I avoided any additional movement as I didn't want to bring attention to myself. I was dirty inside and out and I was sure this man knew it. He was probably avoiding eye contact so that I wouldn't see the judgment in his eyes. The silence fueled the voices within my head. *Your car has been stolen by the filthy man you let inside of your body. Your welfare is gone. You have no money. How many warrants do I have? You married a 70 year old man who preys on children for sex. You abandoned your angel, the gift from God you never deserved. What are you here to save? You have nothing...Quiet.*

After a series of questions about my last drug, drink, living situation and income, the man requested to look through my bag. More embarrassed than offended, I set it in front of him. As the man in the office picked through the dirty pieces of clothing, I was humiliated and felt sorry for him for having to touch my disgusting stuff. My bag smelled from the same putrid sweet stench that emitted from my body. As he pulled the few small orange needle caps, he avoided eye contact and did not show a response. Thank God for small favors.

He was certainly not a talker. After a few more minutes of shuffling through my belongings, the man handed me my bag and said, "Good. I will show you where your room is. You can rest if you want." We walked through the empty living room into a bedroom. He explained that I was the only girl there and I would have the room to myself until a new girl arrived.

In the room there were two twin beds. He stopped at the door and said, "Make yourself at home." Then he gently shut the door behind me. I stood unable to move for what seemed like several minutes, but was probably mere seconds. It was broad daylight, the sun blazed through the windows and the birds sang. The beautiful, flowered bedspread and dainty white furniture gave off an air of purity and innocence. I began to cry. I was not worthy of this room and certainly not this beautiful bed. I refused to sit on the bed for fear of dirtying it. My dirty skin stunk and my clothes had not been washed in months. I was dirty through and through. The man did not know who I was, or where I had been. If he had known, he wouldn't have been so kind. People like me, who do bad things, do not deserve rest.

As I approached the bed, I dropped my bag to the floor. My aching legs, too tired to hold my emaciated body, gave in and my knees folded in unison. Sitting on my folded legs on the floor with my head resting on the edge of the bed, every bit of pain I had endured since I was a child flooded over me like a blanket, making it difficult to breathe.

Up until now, I had assumed that each time I was raped, beaten or brutalized in any way, once I put in a needle in my arm, it was gone. The medicine would hit my stomach, soothe my mind and make it go away. Now on the floor of this small house, it was all with me. The badness enveloped me. The large dry pulsating knot in my throat grew. I began to sob and within moments I had reached hyperventilation. I heard myself mutter, *God help me.* My breathing slowed and my mind kicked back in.

God? Help you Lauri? Really? God? How many times had you asked God for help before? The room with the pimp? The woods? How many times have you made deals with God? You have treated God like you've treated all of the men you have used. You made promises to God. Please save me and I will...And he always came through for you. The moment you were okay, you turned your back...And then the next time...God Please help me. God has gone away, Lauri. He is not listening to you. Quiet. Alone.

I wept and begged for his help...

As if it was the only voice, and no other sound existed, my resounding prayer pounded through the gates of heaven with an undeserving request for permission out of hell. Although I heard no response that day and felt no resolve, he whispered quietly to his angels...*One more child home...*

OVER THE NEXT SEVERAL YEARS, THIRTEEN PEOPLE WERE PLACED IN my path to guide me. Eight of them were teachers; they provided me instructions I would need for the task that was before me. The other five were angels, people who were put in my life at crucial times specifically to get me over a hurdle. I call them angels because they were not someone I knew or paid to help me. I could never figure out where they came from or why they did what they did. They were just placed in my path for a specific purpose and then disappeared. Today I believe everyone has teachers and angels; unfortunately in most cases, they fail to notice them. The man in the white van was Angel number one.

37

I REMAINED AT THAT LITTLE HOUSE FOR THE NEXT WEEK. THERE were other people there, all men. I don't remember them. I avoided all human contact with the exception of one mandatory meeting. During the meeting, I sat silent, avoiding eye contact and returned to my room upon dismissal. Although I didn't speak with the men, I will always remember their breathing.

As the sun went down each night and darkness closed in, I could hear the long labored breath of the male residents from down the hall. Unable to sleep, I spent the next seven nights awake. During the nighttime I would make my way to the living room and with no other occupants around, I felt safe.

Perched like a small bird on the couch, rocking to the beat of the sleep breathing, I rubbed my aching legs. The book was there, on the old wooden coffee table alongside the couch. It was the same blue book that they read at the hippie shack. On the second night, I picked it up hoping I would find the answer. I read the first paragraph and could not remember what I read, so I read it again. I could not remember what I read, so I read it again, and again. Having no other answer, I read the same paragraph, over and over even though I was completely resigned to the fact that I had lost the ability to interpret the words.

In a state of insomnia and with the pain growing daily, I will always be thankful for the bathroom. Since there were no other women I had the bathroom to myself, complete with bathtub. I crept out of my room several times a day to run a hot bath. The heat was a welcome reprieve for the pain emitting from my bones. The bathtub was my sanctuary.

The week at the little house went by quickly. The day before I left,

I walked outside for the first time. There was a small swing set on the grassy area on the side yard. I sat on the swing and leaned back. With my head tilted up, I soaked in the soothing heat of the sun. The wind blew softly through my hair and the smell of the nearby ocean floated like a sweet perfume through the wind. I opened my eyes and took in the brilliance of the vast blue sky. Tears quickly filled my eyes. I remembered the last time I felt the wind, the sun, the smell of the grass. Suddenly, I was back on my little swing set in New York. I was ten. That was when it began...

For the thirteen years that followed, I had begged that the gates of Hell would open and let me in. I knew that was all I had coming, so I thought let's just get it over with. I begged to die right up until that moment in the woods.

That day, on the small swing set, the whole world spun on its edge when it hit me. The gates of Hell had opened, but I was not going in, I was walking out.

With nowhere to go, I called Bob. He agreed to let me stay with him until I figured something out. It was, without a doubt, a very temporary agreement. He was not comfortable having a long-term visitor and I was not comfortable being one. But knowing this might be the only chance I had, he agreed. I stayed in the pretty guest room at his house. Arriving at his home and entering the room, I instantly flashed back to the last time I saw it. The night of my first trick. At this point, I was clear on two things. One, he probably didn't lure young girls in here to kill them. Secondly, there probably wasn't a body in trunk in the next room. But there may still be guns.

I never would have imagined that it would end right where it started. The scary man in the wheelchair saved my life. I have since come to realize that anyone can save a life. With a home and a car, he gave me a bed and a ride. Having no God, no friends, no family and no love, he had the one thing I needed: Hope. He had hope that I could make it out. Although he never said it, I knew. The spark of hope from a completely broken man was enough to carry me back through the threshold of life.

It would be twenty years before I would possess the insight and courage to look him in the eyes and crying say, "You saved my life."

I stayed at Bob's house for one month. During that time he never made a pass at me. I am not sure if it was due to my condition or out of respect for my new life. Either way, it may have been my saving grace.

Even though I felt done, it seemed like the drugs had a hold on me and wouldn't let go. I was three weeks into my stay before I regained the ability to sleep. Still wrestling with the pain of the remaining drugs in my bones, I developed a habit of rubbing my thighs to deflect the ongoing ache. I had no idea where I was going from Bob's, but I had to think of something, some way to get some money to start my life over again. With no one else to call, I phoned my mom. When I called her, she told me about a place called New Life for Women. She was referred there by a friend. Having told them about my situation and my inability to pay, they said they would accept me in their 30-day program with an agreement to pay later.

This really wasn't the kind of "plan" I was looking for. Thirty days in a program with women? It sounded like another group home. Lord knows I didn't need any more of that! How could this possibly be good for me? Hadn't I had enough of this?

With no other plan to fall back on, on February 13, 1987 at the age of twenty three, I was admitted to New Life for Women. Strangely enough, this place was less than a mile away from my mom's house and we never knew it existed.

New Life consisted of five houses in the same neighborhood. The home for the new girls was the largest. It was a long, ranch-style home, with five rooms and two beds in each room. Like many of the homes I had lived in, the focus was on accommodating a lot of people rather than being fashionable. There was a long wooden table for meals and an even larger kitchen. In the pantry, there were five loaves of bread and in the fridge there were five quarts of milk. They were ready to meet the needs of several women who hadn't eaten regularly for months. The smaller houses were for women who decided to stay on board after the initial 30-day program. At those houses, the girls went to work during the day and paid rent. I was just looking to do my time and get out.

The only thing I remember about my arrival was the YMCA. After I interviewed with a woman who told me about the program, of which I remember nothing, I was dropped off to join the house residents down the street at the YMCA. I arrived to find eight young women jogging up and down bleachers and then around a small track. As the woman dropped me off, she pointed over their way and said, "Go on and join the girls!" I thought, *You have got to be kidding, right? What is this? A military operation? I haven't slept in almost three weeks! I can barely stand; I am certainly not ready to run a marathon!*

Not wanting to cause a problem my first minute there and fighting against every fiber in my being, I slowly joined in. Lord knows I didn't want the girls to think I was a wimp. Luckily, about two minutes later, when I was already about to pass out, the leader of the group announced, "Okay girls, TIME!"

I quickly learned the most important rules of the program. No visitors except family members on "family group" night, no phone calls and no leaving. The only person I longed to call was Madie. I had to talk to my baby. Madie was four years old at the time and the memories of all my failures as a mom were crashing down on me more with each day that passed. My inability to reconcile how I could have hurt my innocent baby and then abandoned her was causing me to spiral down emotionally. The day my mom showed for family group, I would be faced with one of the hardest choices in my life. Sobriety or Madie.

It was my third day at the program when my mom showed up. She started by saying unfortunately she would not be able to watch Madie any longer. Rambling on with something about work and rest and needing her "own life" at this stage of the game, I couldn't believe it. My head was spinning. I finally have a plan and I am actually committed to it and she is giving up now? I knew it! I shouldn't have been stupid enough to think I could do this. Every time I try to put my life back together something goes wrong.

38

I SAT QUIETLY AND MY BODY STIRRED WITH A MIXTURE OF FEELINGS self pity, anger and doom. *I freaking knew it! They say they want to help, but they never do…it's a lie…I am nothing…no one cares…why even try?* While my head was busy spinning with this new information, my mom was still talking , but I could no longer hear. I shut down right after, "I can't take care of Madie."

Then a strange thing happened. I don't know if it was the absence of drugs or what, but for the first time in my life I tuned back in and heard what my mom was saying. "Look Lauri, Madie has been through so much already. You have let her down too many times." Normally this kind of talk would immediately shut me down with anger, but for some reason I kept on listening "I think for once in her life, you should work on not disappointing her. Do it right this time. Take the time you need and come back when you are ready to be a real mom for the rest of her life." The words *for the rest of her life* echoed in my head. I couldn't have wanted anything more. She continued, "I spoke to a lady about voluntarily putting Madie in a foster home." That was my breaking point.

I erupted. "NO! I will not put my kid in the system. No way, out of the question, absolutely not. Not an option!" After everything my little princess had been through, you think I am going to put her in the system? Me? Put MY kid in a foster home? Are you crazy? My poor Madie had been through so much already.

At the age of four my poor little angel had more life experience that most eighteen year olds. She knew what drugs looked like, knew to be quiet around police and had more than her share of disappointment and trauma from me. Enough was enough. We were supposed to be making things better, not worse!

My mom continued in the background. "There are a couple of families that already say they will watch her for a while if you stay here and get better." My head was spinning. What was I going to do? I really wanted to do it right this time, for me and Madie, but now I was trapped. I knew if I left I would return to the needle and the streets. This was the only chance I had. My new plan was falling apart and I didn't see a way out.

Then I came up with an idea. "I will only agree if Madie wants to go there. If she likes it at the foster home and agrees to it, then so would I. But if she doesn't, there is no way I will ever leave her there." Having spent her first years of life exclusively with adults, Madie communicated well and was not afraid to tell us what she felt. I thought this would be the true test. I ended with, "And it must be temporary and voluntary. I will not do it unless everyone agrees that I can get her back at ANY time." This was non-negotiable.

The next day the counselors allowed me to leave temporarily to visit some foster homes with my Madie and my mom. From the moment I saw her, I was conflicted. I missed her so much, I didn't want to let go. The smell of her hair, her skin; my angel, I needed her and she needed me. The closer we got to our destination, the more apprehensive I became. How could I leave my daughter with complete strangers? I stared out of the window and tried to shut out my head. I had no options. Do this, or return to the streets. I wanted to stay with her more than ever, but I had nothing to offer.

The first foster home was in an apartment complex. The residences were all two-story townhouses. When we knocked on the door, I heard the voices of small children rushing towards us. A soft tap on the glass window to my left drew my attention. As I glanced that way, the curtains swung open and two small faces appeared and disappeared just as quickly. Then the front door opened. A woman around thirty with long blonde hair and green eyes stood before us. A young boy stood by her side with his arms wrapped around her leg like the branch of a tree. She smiled, looked down and said, "You must be Madie!" Then she introduced herself as "Ms. Lynne." Entering the living room, she directed us towards a large couch. Madie sat on my lap and I wrapped my arms around her in a protective mode. Ms. Lynne quickly explained that she was a single mom with one adopted son, and three other foster kids; two little girls and a boy, all under the age of five. The house was littered with toys, stuffed animals, and games. The smaller children left the room, but occasionally peeked their heads around the corner to get another look. "Ms. Lynne" explained that she was a daycare counselor and that all of the kids stayed with her all day at work. She said that I could visit every week without a problem as long as we scheduled the visits. She ended with, "It's my understanding that Madie will be staying while you're in the program and she would be moving back in with you after." I nodded. *This was good; at least we were all clear, this was only temporary…*

Then she asked if I had any questions. I told her that the final decision would be up to Madie. I would not leave her anywhere she didn't feel safe. She agreed that was important. Even though we were only there for a few minutes at this point, I was almost certain Madie liked the place. I could see she was drawn in by the toys, and had been exchanging eye contact with the little ones around the corner since we entered, but I needed to be sure. Looking into her eyes, I said, "Sweetie, if mommy goes bye-bye, would you like to stay here and play?" Looking up at me she said," Yes, I want to play" and pointed at the toys. I am sure at this point Madie had enough with hanging around with adults. Being with other children would be good for her. Even as I made the decision, I was brutally aware that Madie had no idea how long we were leaving for. It just killed me. It took everything I had to leave her there. That day, with my head screaming, *you are a terrible mom and a failure,* I left my baby at the home of a stranger. It was the hardest thing I had ever done in my life. Stone cold sober, I left my angel at a foster home.

Aware of my anguish, my mom did not speak on the drive back. I stared out of the car window in silence. I felt horrible. I just kept thinking, at least there are no boys or men there. She should be safe. I had no idea if I was doing the right thing. I just didn't know anything for sure anymore.

For the next week or so, the program kept my mind busy enough during the day to stop thinking about Madie. At night, alone in my room, it was different. When the lights were out and the room was quiet, I would cry silently into my pillow. I had to make it better. I just had to get her back.

As much as I thought New Life was like every place I had ever been, there was one thing that was very different. That one thing would be the very thing that saved my life. They liked to talk. I had survived my entire life without anyone ever asking me about my childhood. Tucked away deep in the archives of my mind, it was gone. Festering like an infected wound hidden under layers of bandage, it seeped out in every part of me, but I had never noticed.

39

I N New Life, they wanted to know everything about our lives. They had us write and write and then when we were done, they told us to write some more. In the groups, we read what we had written and talked and talked and talked. The other girls cried a lot as well. I found this disturbing. I couldn't understand what the heck they were all crying about. Sure bad stuff happened, but it was in the past. I thought they were all weak little babies. There was no way I would ever sit there and cry and let people feel sorry for me. How humiliating. I was embarrassed just watching them. When I talked it was about drugs, and the streets. I had dealt with my past and it was over. I was not going to play the victim.

There were a few different therapy groups at the house to accommodate the number of girls. My group was led by a licensed family counselor in a little office in the back of the independent living house. The room had three small couches around the perimeter and the therapist's desk at the far end. During the group, all of the girls sat on the couches and the therapist pulled her rolling chair into the open space. At the end of the first group, we were all given writing assignments. Depending on where you were in your stay at the place, the assignments varied. They ranged from your history of drug use, to beliefs in God, to family history. Now that I had completed drug use, she gave me the assignment of writing about God. She probably thought since I was new she would save family history for last and give me the easy stuff first. Boy was she wrong. Family history would have been a welcome reprieve, but God? I had no problem telling the other girls that my family history was just that, 'history.' Lord knows I wasn't going to cry about it. My dad is an asshole and everyone knew it, end of story. But God? Now that was opening up a can of worms. Not feeling confident enough to voice my opinion yet, I accepted my assignment silently. We were instructed to bring back our writings the next day for group.

For the remainder of the day, my mind just whirled around and around. The last time I was sober I had prayed to God and asked him to watch over Madie. That was it, just one thing. And she got molested! I couldn't believe I was back here again. This time, I was not going to enter his trap. I trusted him last time and he made it clear, just as he had when I was a kid that I had nothing coming: Nothing but punishment. Opening the door to God again was something I could not do. With Madie so far away now, I had to be sure that she was safe. I had to keep him from her.

Later that night, I tossed and turned in bed trying to figure out a solution. If I wanted to stay sober and complete the program, I knew I had to do my assignments. I knew I couldn't read any lies I had written about believing in a God. That would only worsen the situation. He and I would both know I was lying. This would only bring on more curses. We both needed to leave this one alone. Unable to think of anything honest to write, I wrote nothing.

The next day I returned to group defeated. When it came around to my reading, I explained my issue. I told them about what had happened last time and not wanting it to happen again. The counselor was much nicer than I thought she would be and gave me another night to complete the assignment. She explained that not only could I find a different God than the one I had last time, I could even make up my own God. She said it is very important that I believe in "something." It is a big part of making this thing work. One girl in the group said, "You can use anything—a frog, a tree or even a door knob, as long as it isn't yourself." I thought this sounded crazy, but the rest of the group, including the counselor, seemed convinced. I said I would think about it and get back to them the next day.

That night was horrible. The only thing that kept going through my head was what had happened to Madie at Beatrice's and how I was responsible for leaving her. I hated myself. I had to find something I could believe in, but I was coming up dry. I tossed and turned for several hours knowing I couldn't return to group empty-handed. Remembering what the girls said about "your own God," I thought about the type of man I would want God to be. As the ideas poured in, they molded him. He would be like my grandfather. He would speak the truth. He would be like Floyd at the Redwood Revival Center, quiet natured and filled with wisdom. Of course, he would have to be old, having created the world; it was just came with the part. I would like it if he was cool, kind of like that guy Carlton back at the group home in Stonybrook NY, someone I could talk to. I would need to really trust him. Above all, I would have to be sure he liked kids, someone who would watch over Madie. I drilled my brain trying to think of someone who met the specs. It was around three in the morning when it hit me. Tired, but content, I showed up to group the next morning with my new God, ready to go. We were almost done with group when the counselor finally asked, "Lauri, what did you come up with? "

"George Burns," I replied with confidence. I had seen the movie "Oh God, Book II" several years ago and I was certain this God met all the specs. He was cool, holy and would never allow a kid to be molested. For cripes sakes, his best friend was a kid. I knew without a doubt, I could trust George. Although I expected some pushback or laughter, the group was completely silent and a few seconds later accepted it as a valid choice. From that day forward I prayed to a guy that looked like, and for all intents and purposes, *was* George Burns.

The last assignment was family history, which wasn't nearly as tough as you would have thought. After hearing about all the other girls, I thought my story was just more of the same, a bit boring at that. Crap happened to everyone, same story, different day. For the life of me I couldn't understand all of the crying. I absolutely hated when people over-dramatized in an effort to get people to feel sorry for them. That was not my style.

I returned the next day with one small paragraph. It went something like this. My dad was abusive. I went to juvenile hall, became a ward of the court, went to group homes, started shooting up coke, became a heroin addict and a prostitute and ended up here—in about that many words. The whole group seemed affected. The counselor questioned my "matter of fact" style in communicating the details and my lack of emotion. I just stared at her blankly. I had no idea what she wanted from me. I did the assignment. Regurgitating the details like a movie about someone else's life was normal for me. Maybe they didn't get it, but I was not one of those mushy girls. It was just my personality. After few more questions about my lack of emotions, I ended by saying, "You guys don't really know me. I'm from New York, it's just how we talk, direct and all."

My emotionless state only drove the counselor to push me harder. Determined that she would break through to me, each day she pursued me more, asking for additional details and information about my childhood. Every day I showed up with the expectation that she would shift off of me and on to someone else, but she didn't. As far as I was concerned, these other girls weren't getting their money's worth. They had paid good money for this program and each day they spent on me, they were getting gypped. I answered whatever she asked. Even though I had never spoken about this stuff before, it was extremely easy to answer the questions. I had to believe I would have talked about it all along, but no one ever asked. Having spent the past week listening to the girls in group spilling their family secrets every day, I was not only ready to talk, I needed to talk. With the kind of stuff they were talking about and all the crying, I needed to set an example. I had been through a lot of worse stuff, and hell, you didn't see me crying. I was going to set the get-over-it example. When the final push came, I thought, "Okay, give em' the mother lode. The night with Aunt Nora and the gun and ending in Central Islip. When they see you are over it, maybe they will get over their stuff too."

That day the counselor requested to speak with me alone. When the other girls left, she directed me to move from the couch to sit in the small chair directly in front of her desk. Then she spoke. "Lauri, you know if you don't get rid of the secrets about your dad, you will never get well. I want you to think about meeting with your dad and talking to him about what happened." I thought, "Lady you are out of your mind; I don't even talk to my dad." She continued, "I know it sounds big, but just promise me you will think about it." Knowing it wasn't an option for me, but wanting to sound compliant, I said, "Okay, I'll think about it." She handed me the card of a friend of hers, an outside therapist. She said, "I want you to call Sandy when you leave here. It is very important that you continue therapy." For the life of me, I couldn't figure out why I was so important that I needed to continue therapy. What about the other girls? Seemed to me they *really* needed therapy. I had nothing more to talk about. I was fine.

The next day in group, she started with me again. "Well Lauri, what do you think about talking to your dad?" *Oh hell! Just when I thought it was over!* I quickly explained that while I was interested in completing all of my assignments, this one was not possible. "My dad and I haven't spoken in years. He doesn't even live in California. He lives in New York." Ten minutes later the whole group had me mentally cornered. Having told them he worked at the airline, the counselor asked if he ever flew to California. Knowing that secrets would get me high, I had to tell the truth. In a defeated tone I said, "His regular flight is from LaGuardia in New York to LAX." That was the final nail in the coffin.

The next thing I knew they were all chattering about how great it would be if I could confront my dad in person. My counselor suggested I call him to tell him I have the disease of addiction, that I am in treatment and that I need to see him. She closed with, "He will come." The fact that I already knew he wouldn't was the best thing I had going for me at this point. It was my way out of this. Having to do all assignments only meant that I would try. If he refused, that was out of my control. Not wanting to go back to the streets, I had to do my part and make the call. She closed by saying "We can make the call tomorrow." For now, I was off the hook.

That night, my roommate and I sneaked into the kitchen. It was well after bedtime, but we knew there was left over apple pie from dinner on the counter. We were having trouble sleeping and she said, "Heck, who's gonna' care anyway. It'll be stale tomorrow." Acting as if we were twelve years old, we tiptoed silently from our room into the kitchen on a mission. Standing in the dark kitchen, shoving apple pie into our mouths as quickly and quietly as we could, my roommate started to laugh. Her laughter was contagious. Within a few seconds I was grabbing my gut to stop the pain. We laughed so hard that we cried. By the time we caught our breath we were doubled over on the floor with pie on our hands and mouths, our faces wet with tears. I looked into her watery eyes, and my brain kicked in. *When was the last time you laughed Lauri? When was the last time you laughed so hard you cried? It was Passover, 1973. My cousin David was leaning back in his tin chair when it suddenly folded up. Launching forward, he landed with his chin on his plate of food. Laughing until we cried, we were hysterical. I was ten. The sadness returned.*

I remembered laughter. I had completely slipped away from life and I hadn't even noticed. I had been numb for so long, I forgot who I was. Where had I gone? It was at that moment, I knew I had to find myself again. I would do whatever they told me to.

The next day came much too soon. I sat with my counselor while she dialed my mom's number and handed me the phone to ask for my dad's number. My mom was intrigued and asked why I wanted it. Luckily my counselor had coached me prior to the call. She told me to say it was requested by staff in the office. The last thing I needed was to discuss this plan with my mom. She would freak. As I suspected, my mom assumed it was to collect money and released the number. When I dialed my dad's number, I remembered his busy schedule and found relief in assuming he would be gone on a trip. I would just leave a message with the number on the small business card in front of me, and he would never call back. That would be the end of it.

After the second ring, a man picked up. "Hello...Hello...who is this?" *Oh crap! It was him! Now what?* Although we had rehearsed my response, I really didn't think he'd answer. I wasn't ready for this! I blurted out the specific parts I could remember. It went something like this: "It's Lauri. I'm dying. I mean I have a disease. They want you to come here!" Frustrated and embarrassed I handed the phone to my counselor. Jeesh! I screwed that up!

I cannot tell you anything that the counselor said after that, as I was spiraling down into my own personal hell. The only thing I remember was when she hung up the phone and looked at me with serious eyes and said, "He will be here day after tomorrow." I knew he would be pissed when he found out I wasn't sick, but for now that was the least of my problems. My father was coming.

40

I SAT ON ONE COUCH, MY FATHER SAT DIRECTLY ACROSS FROM ME. THE counselor was seated in her office chair to my left. I was cold. Completely shut down. In an effort to avoid looking at him, I stared at the counselor as if waiting for instructions. Her voice was a muted annoyance in my mind, as if in another language. I heard nothing, until she looked directly in my eyes and said, "Ok Lauri, tell your dad what we talked about. Tell him why he is here."

I stared over my dad's shoulder out to the small backyard of the house. I reeled back in my mind to when I was twelve. *The principal was talking and he was angry. Once again, I had failed to follow the rules. Only this time was going to be the last. My lack of response and eye contact only angered him further. As his voice rose, I receded deeper and deeper into myself. He would not break me. I would not even shudder an eye lash. I watched as the boys played football out on the field. I was there with them now, no longer in the room. I was gone. I was a wall that he could not penetrate.*

With my dad sitting across from me now, I mentally exited the room. I stared out to the small yard beyond the counseling room. I needed to go away.

I was jolted back into the room, by the counselor's voice. "Okay Lauri, tell your dad what we talked about." Unable to make eye contact with my father and now having somehow lost the ability to block this out, I looked the counselor directly in the eyes and said, "I have nothing to talk about."

Clearly this whole idea sounded cool with a bunch of chicks sitting in group, but now sitting directly across from my father, I knew this was a big mistake. As if the universes had collided, he should never have entered back into my world and certainly not in this place of safety. Although I was 23, I felt 6, small and afraid.

My eyes involuntarily clouded with tears. Blinking repeatedly, I fought to make them go away. *Just put yourself outside Lauri; go away in your mind.* The counselor's voice continued, "Lauri, your dad flew 3000 miles to hear what you have to say. You are safe here Lauri, just talk." As I looked up, I noticed that my dad looked impatient, as if this whole thing was just one more mess that I had created. The counselor's annoying voice echoed in my head, the room was spinning. All of a sudden, the flood gates burst open. I started spewing words out and crying uncontrollably. Like pellets shooting from a machine gun, they shot out in all *directions at once.*

"WHY DID YOU HIT ME?! WHY DID YOU HATE ME?! WHAT DID I DO TO MAKE YOU HATE ME SO MUCH?! WHY DID YOU PUT ME IN THAT PLACE?!

Shaking uncontrollably, I angrily wiped the tears from my eyes. I was conflicted with feeling like a stupid, weak child and needing to be strong. My vision cleared and I could see his head was dropped down. Appearing completely humiliated, I could tell from his body language that he was beyond embarrassment. Having me talk about this crazy stuff in front of this stranger was definitely not okay. My labored breathing was the only sound in the room. With deep breaths, I attempted to regain control of myself. I would not be weak around him, not again, not now.

Knowing the counselor was waiting for him, he finally lifted his head and looked directly at me. In a firm voice with taut lips, he stated, "If you had only fed the dog, it would have been different."

Before the counselor could react to the insanity of his response, I was up and running. *I had to get out! I had to hit something! Break something! I had to hurt something! I had to hurt myself! I couldn't believe this was it! I had gone through all this to have him say, "Feed the fucking DOG!" I fucking hate myself!*

I was just about to grab the door knob to exit the small house when God clearly spoke to me for the first time. "It's not about what *he* said

Lauri. It's about what *you* said." At that moment the world stopped and a different kind of self-talk kicked in. For the first time in a long time, I had a truly positive thought. *"Do you realize what you just did Lauri? You took your life back."*

I had just released the secret, the thing that had been killing me ever since the day they threw me away. *No one wants you...your own family dumped you...you are worthless...you are stupid...you are ugly... everyone will always leave you...*

As I looked back, he remained in the room, demoralized and alone. *Feed the dog...*If nothing else, I felt sorry for him. Alone with the counselor, he would face the coward that he was. From that day forward, I would speak the truth about abuse and nothing would stop me. His lies almost killed me. I let him keep his dog food story and I walked away in truth having taken my life back. As I grabbed the knob to exit the house, I returned the secrets to the man that rightfully owned them and I walked away completely free.

> *I FEEL IT IMPERATIVE TO MENTION THAT HAD I NOT confronted my dad and released those secrets, you could just close the book now and return me to the streets. There is no going forward without that day. You must leave everything on the old path to move forward to the new one. Leave no stone unturned, and you too will be free.*

After releasing my burdens with my dad, I opened up everywhere. I started talking at the house meetings and at the outside meetings they took us to. My counselor told me, "You're only as sick as your secrets, Lauri." Since I wanted to stay off the streets and get my baby back, I talked as much as I could. Unfortunately, one of the outside meetings they took us to was at the old wooden shack. When we pulled into the parking lot for the first time, I knew I was in trouble. Hoping the old man no longer worked there, I said nothing to the staff. Following my housemates through the parking lot toward the structure, I spotted him. Even worse, he spotted me. "Lauri, how are you?" he yelled from where he was sitting with a bunch of old geezers. "Fine," I responded. "In New Life Recovery Center now." Thinking that would get him to back up, I walked close to my housemates and proceeded into the building. It appeared to work, but this would prove to be a temporary situation. He left me alone for the first 30 days I was in the program.

My time in New Life flew by. Before I knew it, I was called to the office to talk about my exit plans. When the lady in the office handed me the exit form, I knew I was in trouble. Having built my whole life around drugs and crime, I had nothing to fall back on. I had no income, no job experience, nowhere to live and no plan. How the heck was I going to get Madie back? I didn't even have a place for us to live, let alone food. Sitting there with the form and pen, unable to touch it to the paper, I froze. Noticing my level of anxiety, she said, "Have you considered our sober living houses?" She explained, "It's a lot like the New Life program, but you go to work."

Even though one month ago, being in this home for girls sounded like a sentence from hell, at this point I would commit to whatever I had to in order to stay. Within a few minutes we came to agreement that I could move to the Sober Living House #1 and find a job. I was ecstatic! In the midst of completing all of the necessary forms for admission to that program, the lady discussed the rules: curfews, chores, weekly meetings, going to outside support groups and then the explicit get-a-job instruction.

It wasn't until a few days prior to my move into House #1 that I actually started to process the get-a-job instruction. It went something like this. Sign up with all of the temporary agencies on the list and be completely honest on your job applications. Always smile and always shake the hand of the person you are interviewing with. Eye contact is important, it shows self-assurance. It is also important to tell them you are a hard worker. Tell them you will do a great job! Don't assume they know. They don't. But most important, be honest.

I don't know why I didn't hear this when she said it in the office, but now just 48 hours later, it hit me. BE HONEST on your application. Are you kidding? How is that going to happen? Under prior job experience, what am I going to put? I was in sales? I sold my body? Under pay rate? I started off at $75/hr and worked myself down to $10. How the heck would this land me a job? I knew it was the rules, and I did everything I could to follow them, but this was my limit. Regardless of what she said, I had to lie and I knew it.

My first job application had a section for name and address. For once in my life I had a real address that wasn't a motel. It also had a section for prior job experience. I wrote the name of my mom's business. If she wanted me to do well, she would have to vouch for me. The last section of the application was for office skills. It listed things like shorthand, typing, computers, 10-key and switchboards. As I reflected back I realized I had typing classes in both 7th grade and the few months I spent at the business college. I also studied shorthand when I was there. Although I couldn't remember much, I was sure it counted for something. Not wanting to be stuck in a job I couldn't handle, I checked Shorthand—Beginner. And then the clincher; at the bottom, it said "Computers"—Beginning, Intermediate or Advanced. I had never even seen a computer, only a word processor, but I loved the idea. With a great amount of confidence and nothing to back it up, I checked Computers—Intermediate. The lady taking my application really seemed to like that. She said, "We have a great deal of jobs for folks with computer skills!"

Two days later the phone rang at House #1. They had a job for me at FedEx, working on computers. I couldn't believe it. I had a job. I was so happy I could have screamed, but at the same time I was scared to death. I knew nothing about computers. I rolled around in my bed all night unable to sleep. In the morning I borrowed a business suit from my roommate and headed out. By 6 a.m. I was at the bus stop preparing for my journey to my new job. Sitting on that cold bus bench, in that stupid looking suit, every impulse in me cried out *You look like an idiot sitting on this bench, stick your thumb out and get a f***g ride.* I could feel the eyes of the people who passed by staring. *Look at the loser who doesn't have a car.* Then I started thinking about money. *$7 per hour? I made almost a hundred dollars an hour doing nothing. This* *is crazy. They actually want me to do work like a slave for $7 per hour? I could make more in an hour doing nothing than I could in an entire day of actual hard work.*

Feeling like the biggest loser ever, I fought the urge to make money the old way or hitchhike. I arrived on the job safely, but I was a wreck. I had no idea how to talk to people or how to act for that matter. I had forgotten what to do with my stupid arms. Feeling totally uncomfortable, they hung by my sides like wet noodles. I was a complete social misfit.

To top off the awkwardness, my weak computer skills were identified very quickly when I couldn't figure out how to turn the damn thing on. Long story short, I lasted only three days. I was completely devastated when the lady handed me a check and said, "We will be hiring the other temp. You are no longer needed here, but best of luck to you. You can leave now; you don't have to finish out the day." I was even more embarrassed to tell the girls at home, so I didn't. I just said it was a short assignment.

For the next few months, I went through jobs like crazy. Needing to pay rent and get food, I failed to notice the obvious reason I got fired from the first job. I continued to sign up at all of the temp agencies as a computer person. Reflecting on what the lady in the office said, I took her words to heart—well some of them. I learned to give strong handshakes, look people in the eye and tell them, "I am your woman!" Much to my surprise, she was right. I got hired a lot! The bad thing was I also got fired a lot. I didn't know a thing about computers.

This was also about the time that the old man at the wooden shack started in on me again. In the habit of attending the shack with the girls, I instinctively walked to the big house and jumped into the van on weekends. The day he approached me, I was in between jobs and broke. As I stood at the coffee bar, he came up from behind me, put a hand on my shoulder and whispered, "Lauri, how are you *really* doing?" I knew what he meant immediately. He was asking how I was doing with money. Thinking that he may just give me some, but without expecting anything now that I'm sober, I said, "Not so good." He responded by saying, "I have no problem lending you a few hundred bucks. Why don't we go for a ride to my house to get the money? I will have you back before the meeting ends." Unfortunately, with my focus on the mention of $200 I blocked out the rest.

The moment his hand reached into my pants, anger and repulsion consumed me. I wanted to kill him. The fury rose so quickly it was all I could do to keep my teeth clenched. I needed to make him to stop. There was nothing to shield me. I felt like a child being abused and the worst part was that I had invited it! Even though I said nothing, with my head turned away, he realized quickly that I had changed. He stopped immediately, retrieved the money from the kitchen counter and directed me toward the car. Neither of us uttered another word on the way back to the hippie shack. The deed was done and I felt dirty and worthless. To make matters worse, I couldn't use drugs to make it go away. It sat with me for days. I felt like a whore. And now I had a secret. The very thing they told me not to do.

That was the last trick I ever turned. Embarrassed by my actions, I told no one immediately, but as the days went on it stewed within me. I felt that I was no longer being honest and it affected all of my relationships because I knew. It was clear from that day forward: I could not abuse myself and stay sober. I also learned that bad money doesn't go to good places. There was no way I could pay bills with that money; it went specifically to fix my insides with the only vices that remained: Shopping and smoking.

It was several job assignments later that I was able to walk into a new job and instinctively know how to turn the computer on. The job I kept the longest was in a factory that made dental materials. My job was producing mainframe reports. Since they were running custom software, they had to train anyone new coming aboard. I was trained on their programs and took to it like a duck to water. The lady who ran the computer department, Tootsie, really liked me. And for once I didn't feel like a misfit. Tootsie was one of our people. She was about forty, hair permanently disheveled. She smoked, cursed and complained a lot and always looked tired. She was dating a man twenty years younger and they shared an immense love. Unfortunately their love was not for each other, it was for skunk weed. She was the supplier and he was her best customer. She was his "sugar momma." Not knowing much else about her, I knew one thing for sure. She was one of us. She never smoked at work, but she would allude to their wild nights at home. I had no interest in hearing about it, but I humored her. Even though it was only weed, I could see from her appearance that it was affecting her. Prior to my stay at New Life, I never would have noticed, but something had changed. I knew it was none of my business, so I never said anything. As long as I never socialized with her outside of work, I was safe. As time went on, it was not irregular for Tootsie to come into the computer room and say, "Hey kiddo, you have worked enough today. Take the rest of the day off with pay. Go home and have fun."

I never told her where I lived or anything about my life. But one thing was clear, even though I was sober, I was still magically drawn toward my people—addicts. Like distant family members, we had an unexplainable magnetic bond. I had to be sure that the only ones I let in were the sober ones.

Now that I was in House #1, I was able to visit Madie. For the first few months, the girls from the house helped me with rides. The way she looked when I would pick her up was like a knife in my side. She looked beautiful. Ms. Lynne always took the time to put her in a pretty dress with matching tights. It killed me. Every time I was reminded of how she never looked like this when she was with me. In an old hotel room, eating cereal in front of the TV, on most days we didn't even get dressed. I was a horrible mom.

Madie was always excited when I showed up. She would run up screaming, "Mommy! Mommy!" When I would leave she would scream and cry, "Please don't leave me mommy!" This killed me. Ms. Lynne assured me that she was always fine as soon as she knew I was really gone, and that it only lasted a few minutes. That knowledge helped a little, but I would still cry myself to sleep on those nights. No matter how much it hurt, I remembered what my mom said: "Make it count this time. Be her mom for life."

Up until this point, I hadn't thought much about a car because it seemed way out of my reach. The only thing that entered my mind in regards to transportation was a motorcycle. I had seen a beautiful motorcycle in a magazine, cut out the picture and hung it on my wall next to my bed. Falling asleep, gazing up at it, I thought maybe if I looked at it every day, someday I would have it.

Over the next few weeks, I began to feel guilty when asking the girls for rides. I knew it was a hassle for them. Lacking a good plan, I went to my mom's office for help. By this time she was working for herself in a small executive suite just north of our sober living. I explained my issue and asked if I could just borrow her car for the sole purpose of picking up Madie more regularly. Much to my surprise, she informed me that she had bought liability insurance on the 280Z without my knowledge a few months back. When it was stolen, she filed a claim and received a check for $10k. She was holding it for me until she felt I was responsible enough to have it. I was ecstatic. I could get a car and a motorcycle for ten thousand dollars!

When she heard my plan about the motorcycle, she was pissed and refused to give me the money. She immediately launched into a pitch about how stupid I was and my lack of responsibility. She ended with "You are a complete moron, Lauri Burns." That was about the time I lost it. Even sober, when my mother started in on me, I instinctively hit red. I cut her off with a hair curling scream. "That is *MY FUCKING MONEY. YOU GIVE IT TO ME NOW OR I WILL PUT MY FOOT THROUGH YOUR COMPUTER! I FUCKED SOMEONE FOR THAT MONEY! MAKE A DECISION NOW LADY!*"

With tears in her eyes and shaking, she got up, went to her file cabinet and threw the check at me. "TAKE YOUR FUCKING MONEY!" I walked out. I felt like crap. The 'old me' had returned and I didn't like it. I learned very quickly that my mother was one person who could take me back regardless of how much work I did when I was away from her.

Being impulsive and needing to fix the guilt I was experiencing, I went straight to the motorcycle store. I immediately located "my bike" on the floor and told the salesman that I wanted to test drive it. He said, "No problem, I just need to see your license." As you can imagine, it had long since expired. I explained to the man that I had it in New York, but that was a while ago. He grinned and said, "No license, no ride." He went on to explain the liability for the shop. As usual, I was working plan B.

"What if I buy it right here and now?" "If you buy it, you can do whatever you want with it," he replied. In less than an hour, I bought my dream motorcycle and headed out. I purchased a car a few days later. Over the next few months, my bike would cause me additional trouble at my sober living. The old ladies on the board thought it was inappropriate to have it on the front walk up to the house. I, on the other hand, did not. I needed it safe. The closer it was the better. I was a constant thorn in their side.

After a few months of non-compliance, the lady who ran the board held a meeting at our house. One of the primary topics to be discussed was "my motorcycle." I cannot tell you exactly how the meeting escalated, but it did. Long story short, when I became heated I did what I knew best, attacked back. Although I am certain the conversation never warranted it, I went above and beyond when I called her the "C" word.

To increase the drama, after I dropped the C-bomb, I got up and left the meeting without permission and went to my room. The moment I got to my room I realized my mistake. I was trapped. I should have left the house! Unfortunately my room had only one tiny window up by the ceiling and no other access out. Left with no other choice, I grabbed my motorcycle keys, threw on my leather jacket and headed past the girls in the house meeting and out the front door. They all sat in silence as I stormed past them like a two year old. Knowing I was only compounding the problems, I couldn't stop myself.

I jumped on my bike, revved it up enough to be annoying and pealed out. Screaming down the twisted road, I took my anger out on the throttle. When I finally wore myself out, I stopped at the small bay that backed up to our neighborhood. Parking my motorcycle, I stomped with my large boots though the dead weeds that littered the bay and sat down by the water. Now what? I can't go back! Realizing the only money I had was the dollar in my pocket, and I wasn't going to return to the streets, I thought, "Fuck it! I will just sleep here at the bay. Then they will see what I am *really* made of!"

When the wind started to kick up a less than an hour later, I began to shiver. Just imagining spending the night out here was dreadful. In just a few months at New Life, I had become a complete wimp. I spent the next few minutes thinking about my actions and everything they taught me. Three things were clear. Number one: I had to make amends to the old crow for dropping the C bomb. Number two: I also had to apologize to the girls for leaving during group. And number three: The most painful of all, after my heroic "bad ass run out, motorcycle stunt" this would be the first time in my life that I would go back and apologize for anything. It marked the last time in my life I ever ran away from my own home. On this day I realized, even though I had been running away for years, it was never the house, it was always me. This was the day it finally dawned on me that wherever I went, I was there. I needed to fix myself, not my residence.

After apologizing to everyone and accepting my consequences, I agreed to start therapy. I picked up the card that my counselor had given me and called the lady for my first appointment.

Two days later I was in her office. Much to my surprise, she was Jewish and even though you'd think I would be repelled by that fact, since everything about my childhood was intertwined with my Judaism, it was quite the opposite. For some reason, I felt safer. I spent the next few weeks getting to know her. I had visits twice a week to start. She said I could pay later. I still don't know if my payment arrangement was simply because she was friends with my counselor at New Life or the information she conveyed to her—*this one REALLY needs help.* Either way, I went.

She was a loud woman about forty, with shoulder length brown hair and a huge smile. She was so happy at times that it was scary. She would almost scream when she'd come to get me in the waiting room. "Oh come in, Lauri, come in!" Then she'd close in on me for a huge hug. Equal to her free style of loud and unlimited happiness was her ability to pour out tears. If tears were any sign of healing, she should have been paying me for therapy; because I did all of the talking and she did all of the crying.

41

ANDY WAS VERY DIRECT. SHE LEFT NO STONE UNTURNED. ON MY first meeting, she said, "Honey, tell me, has anyone touched you sexually in a bad way?" She had no idea what she was in for. She asked all the questions, and without any emotion, I answered them. She had a habit of saying, "And how do you feel about that?" And I had a habit of answering, "I don't feel anything, it happened ten years ago, I am fine today." The bottom line is that by the time anyone did question me about my childhood abuse, it was buried so deeply, even I could no longer access it. We went on for months like this. She tried and tried to get me to feel something, but it was fruitless. I was a wall. The truth of the matter was that I felt nothing and I was convinced there was nothing there to feel.

In addition to therapy, I continued to pray to George. I put my prayers in an old shoe box. This came as a suggestion from an old man I met one day at the wooden shack. He seemed to have more wisdom in his small toe than I had in my entire being, so I listened. He said, "Once in the box, you leave it alone kid, that's it. The big guy has it. You leave it for him to handle." From that day forward, I wrote my prayers on little pieces of paper and dropped them in them box. Having total faith that George had my back, once in box, I trusted it was covered. This worked so well that other girls in the house followed suit. All of their boxes were for the BIG God, but the concept still worked.

I continued to get better in some areas, but the family dysfunction continued. Whenever I was around them, the violence and insanity returned. They knew all my buttons and pushed them frequently. Although I never lifted a finger to hurt anyone again, the threats, cursing and throwing things continued. Everyone in the Burns family participated. It was a family tradition. I hated myself when I acted like this. I tried and tried not to react to their fighting, but I couldn't stop. I just couldn't change when I was around them. Sandy, my therapist, explained the reason for this.

She said, "You have been making progress, but it is important to surround yourself with healthy people to continue on this path. Imagine you are ten years old and you want to play with a two year old. The two year old doesn't have the ability to come to your level. The two year old cannot ride bikes, or even talk like you do. Your only choice is to go to their level. You are going to have to revert back to baby talk and baby things in order to communicate with those who haven't grown up emotionally yet." This is one of those concepts I would remember for years to come. I had to pick healthy relationships in all areas of my life to keep from going backwards.

To add to the confusion, in the first few months of my sobriety my mother drove me to visit Madie. On the ride home she said, "It's funny; I recently remembered that when Nadine was little, she told me that your father was trying to kiss her, like a 'girlfriend.' Completely confused by the fact that she told my mom, I said, "Well, what did you do?" She responded, "Nothing, I wasn't sure what it meant."

This information was disturbing. It added to the ongoing insanity that I was trying to work out in therapy. Lord knows I didn't need more material to work on. I had my hands full as it was. The fact that it was still unresolved brought back the insanity and fueled a huge argument. I couldn't understand why she brought it up if she wasn't going to admit it was true. I started to spiral downward as the memories came rushing back. After about four months in my sober living home, I had to take a break from my mother. Stuck in our old patterns, she continued to verbally abuse me and my efforts to change my reactions to her were fruitless. I was accustomed to calling my mom for help and she was accustomed to telling me what a worthless mess I was. The bottom line was, I was trying to get better, but with no help, she was staying the same. Each time we fought, I would revert to violence and suicidal thoughts. In an effort to change, I needed some distance. Upon Sandy's advice, I told my mom it was more about me than her, but I needed to take some time away. She didn't understand, but I did it anyway. My mom was clearly sick from prolonged exposure to me and my dad. But knowing that didn't help her to get better. She needed to seek her own help.

This was when I really started to change. A friend had told me about a jail for juveniles that needed help. They needed volunteers to come in and talk to the kids about not doing drugs. I couldn't have been more excited. I signed up immediately and went in whenever they asked me. I loved those kids. Before I knew it, I had one year sober and they put me in charge of the outreach. When I went to the Department of Probation for my badge, I was sure they would say, "You have got to be kidding!" Instead, they looked at what I had written, including my prior arrests, and assured me that I would be great! I left that day with a badge that said Orange County Department of Probation—Lauri Burns. Who the hell would have imagined that? I was on cloud nine.

Most of the volunteers would come in, talk and leave. I couldn't get enough of these kids. The counselor in charge ended up giving me special permission to stay late to chat with the girls. As time went on, he also allowed me to bring in food and candy on holidays. Normally, this was out of the question in jail, but he made an exception.

I was quickly approaching my one-year commitment at the sober home and had yet to formalize a move out plan. In addition to my one-year plan at the home, there was my plan to take Madie back in a year. I was lucky to discover two other girls who wanted to move out as well. All equally scared, we decided to rent an apartment together and maintain all of the house rules we were accustomed to, chores, curfews, etc. Since they had no credit and I had horrific credit, we were fortunate that one of the girl's parents cosigned for us. With little money and no furniture, we begged and borrowed and stole to furnish the place. Yes, I stole.

I stole my sheets from New Life. Having slept on them for over a year, I thought who would want them? So I took them. By the time we moved, we had everything we needed. The plan was to spend a few months living independently before attempting to take Madie back. This way I would be comfortable in my new life by the time she returned.

Just a few days into our new life at the apartment, the Director from New Life called our place. Not knowing why she would be calling me, I just listened. "Lauri, in our staff meeting this week, one of the counselors suggested that *you* would be the perfect person to run our Aftercare Group. I am hoping you would be interested. We have also agreed that instead of paying you, we will credit each hour back to the outstanding balance for your stay in our program." I couldn't believe it! They wanted me to be the counselor for the alumni! Happier than you can imagine, I exclaimed, "Yes! I would love to do it!" Then she said, "Oh yeah, there is one more thing. You will need to return the sheets you stole before you start."

Embarrassed and honored, I showed up week one with the folded sheets under my arm. I continued as After Care Counselor for the next two years. The Director taught me a valuable lesson about parenting that day. Sometimes the best way to address a mistake is to mix it right in with some successes. I clearly understood that they believed in me, regardless of my shortcomings and her open-hearted forgiveness would empower me with the humility to never steal again.

My life was moving forward quickly and my little shoebox filled as it did. Still unsure of myself, I knew George would not fail me. The apartment with the girls came to a sudden halt when one of them started turning tricks and the other tried to kill herself and was admitted to a mental institution. Who would have thought that I would be the last man standing?

Desperate to get Madie back, I was determined that I would not fail. I called each apartment ad in the Sunday classified section and was able to secure my own place. It was in a less-than-desirable neighborhood, but with a very small down payment split up over a few months, it was mine. I was one of the few white neighbors in a largely Spanish area, but I didn't care. The neighbors welcomed me and I felt at home there.

Now on my own, I knew I had to do more. I needed to stay clean and knew I couldn't count on my own thinking. I still had the juvenile jail commitment, but it wasn't enough. By this time I had a good deal of sober friends, and I didn't want to fall off like the other girls. My friends were all sober and crazy, much like me. I found that I was still attracted to the same type of people. I rode motorcycles with a bunch of sober guys and I also hung with a good group of girls. We attended sober events throughout the area and hung on tight to each other for fear of being picked off from the group.

In an effort to increase my odds, I signed up to run a group at a local park for drug addicts. I volunteered for the board meetings, brought services to the jail and I started a meeting at my apartment for women needing help from alcohol and drug addiction. At the time there was a men's group that was really big in the area. It was called "Canines on the Curb." My girlfriends and I were familiar with "the Canines" and although they were all fairly cute, their group was also very "military like." We didn't like that. In an attempt to let them know what we thought of them, and to start a strong women's group of our own, "Pussy on the Porch" was born.

"Pussy on the Porch" met at my house weekly and was strictly for women and their children. It was a small meeting. We drank coffee, smoked cigarettes, gossiped and laughed. Our only rule was "stay sober." Afraid to be alone, I rented the room that would be Madie's to another girl in the program. Her name was Tessie. Tessie was newly sober and attended the Pussy's.

I was about three months into my new apartment when Ms. Lynne called to tell me it was time to pick up Madie. I was home alone that day. Agreeing to set up a plan, I told her I would call her back. When I hung up the phone, the magnitude of the situation set in and I froze. Having picked her up so many times looking pretty as a button, I instantly remembered what kind of mother I was. The voices inside said, *"You will fail her again. You're a bad mom."* I remembered all of the reasons I used drugs. Just the littlest thing, and I would use. My head started to spin as I imagined the nice life she had become accustomed to at Ms.

Lynne's and the little apartment in the crappy neighborhood that I had to offer. *I probably can't even get her to school on time. How about meals? I didn't cook. For months I had been eating out. How could I do this? I will fail her. I spiraled down so quickly I didn't see it coming.* By the time the phone rang again a few minutes later, I had already broken the large mirror in the bedroom and was holding a shard of glass above my wrist. Jolted out of my mental plummet by the ringing of the phone, I instinctively picked up the receiver. "Is Tessie there?" "No," I responded. "She's out." Wanting to get back to my suicide attempt, I quietly waited for the person on the other end to say "*Ok*" and hang up. When nothing came, I said, "Do you want to leave a message?" She said, "Tell her Misha called." Again, I waited, but she was still there. "Are you okay?" she asked. Knowing that I was talking in a totally normal tone, I had no idea what she meant by that. I replied, "Yes, I'm fine."

For the next hour I could not get her off the phone. Before I knew it she had the story and would not let go of me until I agreed to two things. Number one, I would not kill myself and number two, I would make arrangements to go pick up Madie. Misha was my second angel. A stranger calling from who knows where, at just the right time, with an intuition that something was wrong. She intercepted my path and redirected me. I can't tell you how many times since that day I have looked over at someone; someone I didn't know, but for reasons I can't explain, I knew they needed help. Thanks to Misha, I no longer walk away. Today I respond to the higher calling and say something. Today I listen to the voices that whisper so quietly they can barely be heard, the chatter of the angels.

A few days later, I did as I promised and picked up my little princess. I could not have been happier. I had missed her so much, I couldn't get enough of her. Afraid to be away from her again, a strange thing happened. Overwhelmed by the intense guilt from my past, the feelings turned outward and I became one the most overprotective mothers you'd would ever want to meet. In addition to my over protectiveness, the fear returned. Even though I was sober, in therapy and doing well, I was still convinced I didn't deserve her and she would be taken from me. Much like my fear of her dying of SIDS as a baby, now I thought she would be kidnapped. When Polly Klaas was kidnapped, my paranoia intensified. Polly, who was taken from her room while her parents were just a few doors down, affected me greatly. Paranoid that someone would come steal her in the middle of the night, I couldn't sleep. It became a compulsive habit to wake her up in the middle of the night and tell her to move into my bed. Locking my bedroom door from the inside, I returned to sleep knowing I could protect her. This fear never went away completely, but since then I learned to live with it.

It was shortly after Madie moved home that I met him. I saw him at the podium of a meeting. With tears in his eyes, he spoke about the experience of putting together a bicycle for his nephew who was five. With the combination of his love for his nephew and his sensitivity, I fell for him. Within two weeks we were dating. Along with the onset of our closeness came a storm of panic and fear. I knew I was in trouble when I went to tell one of my friends that he was moving in and within seconds I began to shake and tears poured from my eyes. I was petrified. Luckily she was older than me, and had years of healthy life experience. She replied, "Lauri, a relationship will take you through your issues quicker than any therapy you could ever pay for. If you are ready for the ride, just hang on to your seat and you will come out better at the other end." Lastly she said, "Just remember one thing: Never cancel a sober commitment for a man or it will be your first of many bad choices. If you keep sobriety number one, you will come out fine."

I don't think even she knew how right she was. Concurrent with my work with Sandy, and my growing relationship, came the flashbacks. The closer he and I became, the worse it got. Before I knew it, any touch in a sexual way produced a large surge of terror. Fighting the impulse to push him off and scream at the top of my lungs, I did nothing. Conflicted with the knowledge that he was not the bad guy and not wanting to expose my brokenness, I would remain still and let him continue as the tears saturated my pillow in the dark room. Having processed no actual thoughts, my body remembered.

Over the next several months, the body memories grew, my

relationship diminished and I fought with Sandy's help to make it all go away. Still unable to produce emotions in therapy, we were getting nowhere fast. I was having a hard time keeping up with my new life, while my old life came crashing back.

Unable to extract an emotional response out of me after several weeks of treatment, she suggested we try an "exercise." "I want you to ask little Lauri how she feels about what we've been discussing and I want little Lauri to respond. We have done this before and it seems to work quite well. I am going to give you a pen. Since you normally write with your right hand, I want little Lauri to respond with her left hand. We use this method to access our inner child. I'll leave the room so you don't feel any pressure from me. Any questions before I go?"

What did she think I was, like Sybil or something? Although I thought she was out of her mind, I did as she instructed. Shortly thereafter, she came back into the room excited to hear what "Little Lauri" had written. I looked her in the eyes and said, "Sorry, I'm not Sybil. No little Lauris came out while you were gone. It's just me in here." And I slid the paper toward her.

It had been a long time since I had felt any emotion about my past. I was cold. Like watching a movie about another person, I was completely disconnected from anything that had happened in my life. She looked at my sloppy response and somewhat dejected, read it aloud.

Having exhausted all of her resources and coming up dry, Sandy suggested a group. She had four other women clients who had all suffered sexual abuse. In an effort to create healing by sharing our experiences and work, she decided to formulate a weekly group in addition to individual therapy.

Karen had been molested by her father, Sheena was touched by a man on a bus, Meg by her brother and Melinda by her uncle. Each time we did an assignment, Sandy would reference the abuser. She would say things like, "Picture him in front of you now." Three of the other girls wept continuously throughout the session. Meg and I would just smirk and pass looks. Meg, who was molested for years by her brother, didn't get it either. We both thought, *What the f* are you crying about now...my*

God, get over it! We thought they were sappy babies wanting attention. Unable to produce a single tear, we joked about making a sign on a stick that had sad on one side and happy on the other and holding it up when appropriate. The truth of the matter for me was that each time Sandy referred to the abuser; I didn't know which one to pick. My dad? The man in the alley? The man in the Pinto? The pimp? The men in the woods? Having too many people to choose from, I failed to process anything.

I was about six weeks into group when I finally broke. Meg was a no-show on this particular day, so it was just me, Sandy and the weepers. Sandy was working on stems. A stem is when someone begins the first part of a sentence and the rest of us complete the second part. For instance, Sandy would say, "When his hand touched me, I felt _____." And we would have to complete it. With growing intensity the girls screamed out answers and wept, "Scared! Dirty! Petrified! Terrified!"

As their alarming voices rose, I felt a surge of panic. In a flash of light, all of the faces of the men who had ever hurt me came barreling in on me, one after another; their hands, their eyes, their bodies, their breath. Until in sheer desperation, the tears burst from my eyes and I completely lost control.

I began screaming. *"STOP! I CAN'T TAKE IT ANYMORE! THERE ARE TOO MANY! "YOU HAVE ONE FUCKING PERSON TO DEAL WITH!!! ONE FUCKING PERSON!!!!! DON'T YOU FUCKING UNDERSTAND?!!! ONE FUCKING PERSON! FUCKING STOP!! STOP!!!!!! STOP!!!!!!!!!!!!!!!!!!!!!!!!!!!"* The room fell silent.

Snot dripping from my nose, tears soaking my face and shirt, I shook violently. Grabbing the large pillow that lay beside me, I lifted it in front of my face blocking their view. Sandy instinctively got up, sat next to me and reached for my arm, but I immediate pulled away and backed further away from her. Rejected, she refrained from touching me again. Backing into the corner of the couch, I found a safe shelter and continued to use the pillow as a barrier from everyone's view. Over the next few minutes, my anger shifted to embarrassment. I took a deep breath and pushed it all away. One thing was clear. I may have cried, but I was not one of them. I was stronger than that. This would not happen again!

And I was right. It was several years before I was able to process feelings related to my abuse again, but as time went on, I learned to tell Sandy, "I'm sad." Or "I'm angry." The ability to talk about the past and genuinely feel it took almost a decade. The years spent in my childhood, learning not to feel were necessary for my survival. I would not have made it through otherwise. In order to heal effectively now, it had to be undone. Equal to the amount of work ahead was my feeling that my safe shelter was all that I had.

The walls were the only things that ever protected me. I was, and still am, petrified to take them down completely. With intense trepidation, I have taken baby steps. I know I will never be fully unprotected, but unlike the steel walls I had before, I can now confidently say I now have a garage door, only down sometimes.

As I pulled away from the group and went back to individual therapy, I told Sandy that I was worried about bringing up the past while trying to move forward with my new life. I also told her I was worried that I was not benefiting from therapy because I couldn't cry. What she said next has stayed with me always. She said, "Anything you feel—body memory, sadness or anger, is inside being let out." She explained that all of the stuff I went through and didn't feel is still in there, waiting to come out. Once out, it is out for good. Although some feelings may be similar, they are never the same one twice. Each time I felt or talked about something, regardless of whether I cried or not, I let one more memory out. She assured me that bit by bit, someday it will all be out. And that day, I would be completely free.

One of the additional benefits from learning to express my feelings was that I was no longer explosive. I learned to tell people when I was upset in "real time." Sandy also taught me to do it in a healthy way, like I am angry about what you said to me, or you hurt my feelings when…I learned not to attack, use name calling or accuse. I learned to take responsibility for my feelings, and believe it or not, I changed. The explosions I had when I was a kid were simply due to the buildup. One by one the hurts would pile up inside and then one day, almost without warning; I would hit red and explode.

Even though my anger was dissipating, I knew for sure by this point that I had no business being in a relationship. As the days went on, we grew more distant. I became fearful of intimacy due to the ongoing flashbacks, and he became angrier. Not understanding it had nothing to do with him, he took it personally. He put more and more pressure on me and I pulled further and further away.

As part of my therapy Sandy told me it was imperative that I listen to my body. When I felt unsafe, I must abstain, even if it didn't make logical sense. Feeling scared and going forward anyway would only stunt my healing. In an effort to teach me to love my body, she was persistent. Knowing I had to give everything up to heal, I told her about the hippie shack. I finally cleared the last secret. I told her how it felt afterwards and that I regretted it. This was hard for me, but I knew she wouldn't judge me, and she didn't. She responded by saying, "I am proud of you for telling me." I had no idea how much that secret was weighing me down until I finally let it out. Like a small splinter that you couldn't pull out, I knew it was there. Even though it was just one secret, it kept me from feeling 'okay.'

Now I had a bigger task: Respecting my body. For years I had been ignoring my body. I didn't feed it when it was hungry, I had gotten in the habit of delaying my need to go to the bathroom, and I had always given in to sex to avoid an argument. Having grown numb to my body on the streets, it didn't really seem to matter. But now as I continued that behavior, the flashbacks increased. She taught me that no one should place demands on another. Right or wrong, I needed to listen to my body now. I could no longer be a victim to others. This was just as confusing for me as it was for him. We both knew he wasn't hurting me, but the combination of intense therapy and being intimate was putting him in the position of bringing on flashbacks just by touching me. All intention aside, like a time machine, just by putting his hands on me, the rapist would return. Although I knew we should break up, I couldn't.

In addition to my issues, Madie was also having issues. She had gone to therapy for a few years after the molestation, but shortly before she went to Ms. Lynne's it stopped. The day I discovered her standing at the second story window threatening suicide because I told her to put her Barbie's away, I immediately put her in therapy again. Afraid that she would turn out like me if she buried the abuse, I knew it was imperative that she learned to talk about it now.

Maddie's case worker at Victim Witness set her up with Dorothy. Dorothy was an older professional-looking woman in her fifties. I had nothing in common with Dorothy, but Madie loved her. Madie continued to see Dorothy for the next five years, and today attests that it was Dorothy who inspired her to pursue her dreams as an adult. Through our individual work with our therapists, Madie and I were able to talk about issues as they arose and formed the most healthy parent/child relationship I could have ever imagined. I learned what not to do from my parents and both of us learned what *to do* from Dorothy and Sandy.

I was about two years sober when my job at the dental factory ended. Toward the end of my employment there, Tootsie started to get strange. Paranoid is the best way to describe it. A few months later, she died of a brain tumor. Tootsie showed me unconditional love for absolutely no reason. She would never know how she carried me. Unable to relate to 'normal people' since I was fresh off the streets, Tootsie was my assigned guide. Just crazy enough to make me feel normal. She also taught me how to use my first computer.

Due to my actual experience on computers at this point, it was much easier going forward to obtain a job. I spent a year working at a real estate firm. The most lasting thing I took from this job was my best friend, Linda. I was only there a few days when I met her. Linda was a black girl about my age, thin and pretty. She worked the front counter and seemed to run the place. If you needed anything, Linda was the 'go to' person. I was sitting at a small round table with my head down, eating chips, trying to mind my own business, when she and another girl stopped right next to me. Not really taking notice of me, Linda continued talking loudly to the other woman. "And you know my mom, she said girl those 'hos work the streets and they don't care who it is." She continued with her colorful depiction of a street prostitute. Grabbing an invisible rope of some sort, she swung it in circles, swirled her hips around, rolled her head with attitude and gave her best impression of a black prostitute. "Nigga, my b'ness is on ho stro…" It was without a doubt the worst depiction of a prostitute I had ever seen. I couldn't hold back. Giggling beneath my breath, I instantly fell in love with this girl. We didn't actually talk until later that day, but after that, we were inseparable. Linda was crazy and crazy funny. As far as I was concerned, she was just what the doctor ordered. She told stories, jokes and was always good for workplace pranks. When Linda told a story, she held nothing back. Linda was irreplaceably my best friend sent straight from heaven. Like salt and pepper shakers, different in appearance, we were the same inside. Even though Linda had never been on drugs, her family was a mess and she had been equally damaged by the time she was a teen. Both in desperate need of a friend and anchor to hold onto, someone you can tell anything to, we are still best friends today.

42

I LEFT THE REAL ESTATE FIRM WHEN MY MOM'S INSISTENCE THAT I focus on a 'real career' started to make sense. Noticing that I was staying sober and showing up to work, she wanted me to learn her business, insurance. Aware that we probably had too many issues to work closely together, she suggested that I work at a major company and train in anticipation to take over her business later in life. Not really knowing if insurance was what I wanted, I liked the idea of a 'real career.' Even more attractive was the fact that my mother told me the money was unlimited. Now that, I liked. The final clincher was that I didn't need any college and I could take the test as soon as I wanted. Much to my surprise, I studied and passed the test very quickly and was hired by a large agency. It was also about this time that my boyfriend insisted that we move out of the bad neighborhood. We agreed to move into a nicer neighborhood since we now had two incomes. We found an adorable little house in between my mom's house and New Life. It couldn't have been better.

My boss at the insurance agency, Cindy was about a year older than me and quite my polar opposite. Cindy had light brown hair that was cut short and neatly laid against her head. The tips were frosted and stood perfectly in line behind one another. Her makeup was light, but attractive. She wore business suits with short skirts that showed off her perfect legs. Her nails were always freshly manicured, even though she seemed to work day and night. For lunch, she ate a burger, fries and a cookie, but it was not a problem, because she sped up her metabolism by running three miles every morning before work. Her car was equally impeccable, a white BMW with cream colored seats that smelled like new leather, fresh off the lot. Cindy was married to her high school sweetheart, still friends with her best friend from childhood and had a great family upbringing. To top it all off, she was always happy.

As I walked past her office in the morning, she would lift her head and with the biggest smile yell, "Hey Lauri! We are going to close the big one today! I know you can do it!" With a huge smile and dimples, she was absolutely flawless. She would still be yelling about how we are going to bring the big daddy home as I rounded the corner. In order to fit in, I would produce the most energetic voice I could and respond, "Yes! We are! You got that right Cin'!"

All the while thinking, jeesh, what have I gotten myself into? I barely knew what insurance was, how the heck was I going to sell it? My saving grace was that they had classes a few days a week for the newbie's. The more classes I attended, the more confident I felt, but I was acutely aware that although I wanted to earn money, I wanted to close the big one more for Cindy's approval than anything else.

About my third week in, Cindy began to mentor me personally. With all the positive energy you could possibly imagine, she would race up to my small cubical, lean in towards me so the other agents wouldn't hear her whisper, "Lauri, I have a great meeting today! I want you to go with me. You do the paperwork and I will give you a percentage!" Honored to watch her in action, I was game.

Watching Cindy work was nothing short of amazing. Exiting her car with her black briefcase in hand, she strutted through the door with confidence and announced her presence to the receptionist. Regardless of the size of the office or the status of the man behind the desk, it was the same every time we entered. A huge smile, a firm handshake and a self-assurance that was undeniable. After asking a few questions about his financial position, (salary, investments and insurance) she had no qualms about going into for the close. Pulling a small calculator with jewels for buttons from her black briefcase, she began rambling numbers off and pushing buttons at speeds so fast it was hard to believe. Based on an investment of 20% which you will need if you plan to retire at the standard of living you are used to, it would be x dollars per month, approximately $ per year, at the rate you've been saving in your present annuity of x%, and an investment of x%, which is reflected in the worst case scenario of our money manager's ten year history.

By the time she was done, the man on the other side of the table had his pen in hand and his checkbook out, ready to sign. "Make the check out to…in the amount of $xx, xxx.00—and I will walk this right into underwriting myself." She was definitely a class act.

As much as I wanted to be just like her, I knew we couldn't have been more different. After all, she finished high school about the time I finished probation. She came from a normal family and mine was straight out of an Alfred Hitchcock movie. Her clothes were pressed and ironed; and mine were thrown in the dryer to get the wrinkles out. She knew about investments, politics and life. I had no idea who the President was and I couldn't keep my bank account in a positive state to save my life.

Cindy gave me all of her best tips. "It takes money to make money Lauri. Always invest in your business, buy leads; you will make the money back if you sell just one or two. Get a nice briefcase, a good calculator and a great closing pen. Gotta have a good closing pen! Always be prepared, have everything with you. Now is the best time to make the close. Firm handshake and consistent eye contact is important. Never say, 'I don't know.' Only say that is a great question, I will find out and get back to you! Sell something. If you can't close him on the most expensive deal, close him on the least expensive deal, but close something. Don't leave without a check and don't be afraid to ask for it. It is all relative; what seems like a lot of money to you is nothing to him. One thousand dollars to a man who makes six figures is like ten bucks to you. Treat it like ten bucks. Don't ask him, tell him. You can make the check out to xxx for $ xx.00 and I will get this started right away!"

Knowing I couldn't go from my current state of insecurity and uncertainty to being anything like Cindy, I did the next best thing: I became Cindy. Yes, that's right, I became her. I would sit in my car alone before the appointment and I would close my eyes and think, *OK, you are Cindy*. I would picture myself looking like Cindy, acting like Cindy, and when I felt like Cindy, I would finally get out. I walked like Cindy, talked like Cindy and closed like Cindy. For all intents and purpose, I was Cindy. When it worked, I was amazed!

Cindy was my first teacher. Cindy taught me that I could recreate myself any time. My clothes, my words, my body language and my accessories would define me to the world. Unable to see under the covers, they saw what I gave them. I always thought people could see through me, to the inside. For some reason, I felt like 'they knew.' Through Cindy I realized I was the one providing them with that information. Although I continued to dress comfortably at home, torn jeans, motorcycle boots and wife beaters, at work I was the 'new improved Lauri.' In the beginning, I felt like an imposter, kind of like Superman, changing identities. But as time went on the separation between my home and work got smaller.

I quickly found my niche with attorneys. I needed to get in and out quickly due to my lack of experience in just about everything. I never wanted to be caught in a conversation above my head and look like an idiot. Fortunately, attorneys are way too protective of their expensive time to visit with me. Making more than God for a few minutes of work, they didn't want to spend a lot of time with the 'insurance lady.' They wanted the terms and the price right up front, and unlike the other agents who insisted on giving a sales pitch about the history of the company, I had no problem getting right to the numbers. I got very good at walking in, going right into reading off the terms and the price and asking for the check and much to my surprise, they liked it. My blunt no-nonsense approach was a winner.

It was ten years later before it hit me why this was so natural for me. I had been giving men terms and numbers for quite some time! Even though I only worked at the agency for about a year, I continued to "be Cindy" for the next several years.

In addition to Cindy, a man named Nathaniel who worked at the agency changed my life dramatically. Nathaniel was a black man and the area we worked was upper class and predominantly white. Nathaniel was one of the most successful agents in the place. Earning well over six figures, he wore the finest suits and sat in one of the largest offices with a beautiful view. For the life of me, I could never figure out how this guy had made out so well, given the nature of the snobby white people in the area we worked. One afternoon, Nathaniel came into the telemarketing room where us "newbies" worked and said, "Hey guys, I am going to create a motivational success tape at a recording studio tomorrow. I think I would do much better if I had an audience, and I was wondering if you would like to join me." I couldn't believe it; I would have done anything to learn his secrets, and I now I had the chance.

Nathaniel spoke for more than an hour and I was captivated by his integrity and tunnel vision to success. When we first got there, Nathaniel told us about his first job. At the age of 17, he landed a job at the local mall in a shoe store. His first day there he was trained by the manager about where to find the proper types and sizes, how to treat the customer and how to sell the right shoe. Let loose as a rookie, day two he was on his own. A few minutes after the mall opened an average looking man walked into the shoe store with his son and daughter in tow. His daughter was looking for running shoes. Nathaniel measured her foot, showed her the running shoes they had in stock and proceeded to help her try them on. As the young girl stared at her feet in the mirror, Nathaniel could not shake the feeling that he was not being completely honest. Nathaniel had passed a sports shoe store earlier that morning as he entered on the other end of the mall. He knew that store had just what she wanted. Unable to quiet his mind, he told the man, "I know what your daughter needs and unfortunately, we don't have it here, but there's a store down at the other end of the mall that has what she wants in stock." Thanking him for his honesty, the man and his children walked out and headed for the other store. Nathaniel's manager was not impressed. Overhearing the conversation from the cash register, he held his tongue until the customer was gone. But the minute they were out of sight, Nathaniel was given a firm warning. "You are here to sell our shoes, not refer people to our competitors."

Both Nathaniel and his manager were surprised the next day

when the man returned with all three of his children. Impressed by Nathaniel's honesty, he returned to purchase all of their shoes for the new school year. That man was Nathaniel's best customer for the entire two years he worked at the mall.

I found this story extremely interesting. It was a level of honesty I had never accessed. I had learned in New Life that it was bad to keep secrets, but not what it meant to "really" tell the truth. I later learned this was called "integrity."

Nathaniel told us that he knew he would be rich. He had actually told himself he would make a million his first year in the business. In order to achieve his goal, he set up his whole life to support it. He said, "Let me start by saying you need no experience whatsoever to achieve your goals. You hold the keys to your dreams, and you always have. As a matter of fact, you are the only one that can unleash them; no one else has the power. The process is simple, but requires consistency. Over the course of the next few minutes, he gave us the formula to materialize our goals and dreams. He told us six things that needed to be done. In order to remember it, I created a single powerful word that represented everything he told us. This way, I would not forget anything and I could pass it on. I chose the word MASTER because it fit the words and the action necessary. In order to pull this off, I knew I would have to master his techniques.

M – Maintain the belief that you can do this. Do not let the smallest amount of doubt slip into your mind. You must not only believe you can do it, you must plan on it.

A – Add to your goal every day. If it is a monetary goal, set money aside a little bit every day. However small, you must keep the forward momentum. If it is a goal to start a new business, design your logo, begin a client database, create a mission statement, research similar businesses, interview people who started a business like yours. You must add something every day.

S – See your goal. You must have a picture that represents your goal in a location you are sure to view every day. If it is money, you can have a picture of money or what you will buy with it—a house, a car. If it is a business, make a business card with your name and title on it. Put it in the bathroom where you get ready. See it every day.

T – Talk about your goal. Talk about your goal as it exists now. Talk about it repeatedly and to everyone you know. Describe it. Breathe it into life. "To speak is to create."

God said, "Let there be light, and there was light." Words create. With every person whom you bring in to supporting your goal, your goal is that much closer within reach.

E – Eliminate negative people. Only talk about your goal with people that support it. If there is someone who puts it down or doesn't believe you can do it, don't share it with them, and if at all possible, separate from them. They are the number-one enemy of your goal.

R – Relationships with others. Whether you like it or not, you become like people you surround yourself with. You pick up mannerisms, phrases and beliefs from the people closest to you. Choose a few people that have been successful in life and have what you want. Spend time with them, whether in the office or leisure time. It makes no difference where. It is only important that you watch them. You will pick up their successful energy.

He then said everyone and everything around you should support the attainment of your goal. You will speak your goal into existence. Nathaniel mastered his goals and upped them every year. Now one of the top guns at the agency, he was inspired to share it with others. He closed by saying that all of the world's heroes had one thing in common; they knew the end before they started. They saw the finish line clearly. Some of the most successful people had nothing more to start with other than knowing the destination. I floated out of there that day with an excitement that was barely containable!

When I was driving home, I started to think about it. "Words create." It was intensely powerful when he said it and I knew he was right. Talk does create. For me it had created more negative than positive, but I could see it. When one of the girls at my meeting said something about Terry, a girl we all knew and the fact that she was known for using people for money, I began to relate to her like that.

Even though I hadn't verified the information, she just became that person. It was hard to go back from there. Now when I saw her, instead of seeing Terry, I saw "User." In the same way, I imagined, if someone were to say, "Everything she touches turns to gold," I was sure I would be drawn to her. I knew he was right. Words create. Good or bad, they can change everything.

It was because of Nathaniel's talk that day that I began to surround myself with successful people. In both my work life and my sober life, I looked for people who were admired and successful. Not quite ready to socialize with anyone, and scared to death I simply attended events where I knew they would be and I watched.

I didn't have any concrete goals in my head, so I didn't try to MASTER anything immediately but by the time I did, I was ready. Nathaniel was my second teacher.

The last person I met while at that agency was Ron Johnston, a pastor. Cindy was an avid church go'er. The closer we became, the more she insisted that I should attend church with her. Not wanting a repeat of what happened at the last church, I did everything I could to back out. When the "I'm Jewish" thing wasn't flying, I knew I was doomed. I had to go at least *one* time and then I could tell her I didn't like it. It was Christmas time when she finally got her hooks in me. Entering the massive building with hundreds of nicely dressed, happy people was just nerve wracking. I surely didn't fit in. Given where I had been, I felt that they might as well just grab the pitch fork and throw me in the fire right now.

When Ron Johnston walked up and opened with a joke, I was able to breathe again. Then he spoke about big churches with bells and stained glass and the stiff 'perfect people' who attended these places. He ended with, 'we are broken people.' At that point, I was able to take a deep breath and relax. Then he told a story, a personal story about his family and how he didn't meet his mom until he was an adult. I felt like he was talking right to me that day. He spoke of the brokenness of his life and how he struggled to put the pieces back together. Over the next hour and a half, I laughed, I cried and I got goose bumps as the man on the stage connected to me at the most intimate level you could imagine. The one thing that Ron said that day that I would never forget was in regards to Martin Luther King Jr. He said this man trusted God so much, that he said something like *"Even if he had a dagger pointed straight at my chest, I would rush into his arms…I trust him so…"* Ron was my third teacher. He seemed to have a strong anchor and I desperately needed one. I knew I had to learn from him. For the next year, Madie and I went to the church every weekend in anticipation of hearing Ron speak. I never really changed religions, I just loved hearing Ron. I was able to put my crazy head to rest when it would say, *what are you doing in a church? You're a Jew!* I decided to treat it like a buffet; I would take what I wanted and leave the rest. I took the inspiration and hope and left behind the hell, sin and fire. Knowing judgment was not something I could believe in, I took the jewels and left the coal.

About this time, I really started to settle in to our new home. Since our address had changed, I updated our sober meeting location in the directory. Two weeks later the new address appeared, and the minute it did, we knew. That was when the lady came. She introduced herself as a member of "the committee" for sober meetings. She said "they" sent her to find out what was going on at this "Pussy on the Porch" place. She reiterated that there was some "concern" about the name. She wanted to know what *occurs* at "these types" of places. Surprised by her insinuation that anything was going on, we were baffled. The girls and I explained that it was a joke of sorts on "Canines on the Curb" and the history behind it, but frankly she didn't get it. She insisted that it was inappropriate and she was pulling it from the directory. Basically what that meant was that no new women would ever find us. With no ability to reach new people, we had no choice but to just go forward with the same small group every week. In no time it became like a soap opera: Coffee, smoking and gossip on our own personal true life sagas. What a bore. We were all surprised the night a new girl walked in.

43

IT HAD BEEN ABOUT THREE MONTHS WITH JUST THE USUAL DRAMA queens at that point. Sitting down on the living room floor across from me, the new girl just listened. She had long black hair, piercing green eyes and seemed very relaxed even though she didn't know any of us. I guess we kind of had a way of making other girls feel at home with our overfilled ashtrays, feet on the table and unfiltered sharing about our true life tragedies. We had created a natural atmosphere for dumping. With only two minutes to the close of the meeting, none of us expected her to say anything. She said, "Hi, my name is Denise and I am an addict. I think your meeting here is really great and you guys seem to have great lives, but I can't do this thing. I have an eleven year-old daughter and we live in a crack house. As a matter of fact, she is there right now so that I could come here. I can't go to one of those recovery places like you guys did, 'cause I can't leave my daughter alone at the crack house." Then she stopped.

Feeling sad and conflicted by what she just said, I left the living room and went back into my bedroom and closed the door. I sat on my bed and put my head in my lap. By this time, I had begun taking Ron Johnston's words to heart. He often said, "Listen. Just stop and listen and you will know the answer." That night, in the silence of my room, my thoughts were clear and consistent. *Lauri you could take her...watch her for a month. She could go to school with Madie and sleep in Madie's bunk bed...Madie would like a friend. One more mouth to feed, what could it hurt? Her mom could go and get help. If it weren't for the people who helped you...*Just considering it brought about a warm flow of love. Everything felt right again.

I returned to the living room and interrupted the girls chattering in the kitchen. "The girls and I will find a place for you to get help, and I will watch your daughter until you get out." She immediately agreed. That night a man named Ed had driven Denise to the meeting. Knowing that he was still waiting outside, she rushed out and promised to return the next day to drop her child off and go into a sober home.

Ed was overweight, sloppy and unattractive, but Ed had two things that Denise wanted: Money and marriage. Money so that he could support her, and marriage so that she could continue to get money by holding the fact that he was cheating on his wife over his head. Basically he was her sugar daddy. A sugar daddy is similar to a trick. The difference is that with a sugar daddy the girl is committed to "only" him. I never could have done the sugar daddy thing. I had to get in and out. The thought of having to get mushy with some old man, ugh! But when you are using, you do what you have to. The very next day Ed pulled up to the house with Denise and her daughter Jodi. When Jodi entered, I was pleasantly surprised. She seemed self-assured, headstrong and very outspoken. She was tall for her age, a bit overweight, with medium length, brown hair and the same piercing eyes that her mom possessed. Not wanting to extend her painful departure more than necessary, Jodi's mom stayed for a few minutes, said she would visit soon and left. Denise called me from the recovery home about twenty minutes later to confirm that she was admitted.

The next day, I signed Jodi up for school and although they were four years apart, she and Madie got along just fine. They walked to school together, did their homework together and for a short period of time, couldn't get enough of each other. We only had Jodi for about two weeks when she started feeling comfortable enough to let her true colors show. Before I knew it, she was stealing, lying and sneaking boys into the house. Jodi was my karma. She was everything I was as a child and more. Unfortunately for her, she didn't realize at first that she was messing with the master. I knew all of the tricks and then some. She couldn't get away with anything. One day I came home from work early. When I walked in, she appeared from the back hall.

Walking towards me, she said, "Hey, how was work?" That's when I knew something was definitely wrong. She was way too friendly and interested in me. Scanning the room and the outside window, I took a deep breath and sat down on the couch. Plopping on the couch next to me, she attempted to draw my attention away from the back yard. I looked at her, smiled and asked, "Who is the boy behind the tree in the yard?" She, of course, replied, "What boy?" I immediately knew what I was dealing with. Jodi was the "I have no idea" type of kid.

Now this was a tactic I would have never employed. Not only was it doomed to failure, it was just plain silly. But Jodi was committed to it. Time after time, whether it was something broken or stolen, even if caught red-handed, I would get the same, *I have no idea what you're talking about,* response. I understood. When nothing in your life seems to be going right, the ability to pull a fast one from time to time may be the only thing you have left.

Unfortunately, my boyfriend didn't understand. As her behavior escalated, so did his insistence that she needed to go. Explaining that she was ruining our lives, and that she was a bad influence on Madie, he gave me the ultimatum. Jodi goes, or he goes.

By this point, our relationship was at an all time low anyway. We had no intimacy due to my ongoing therapy, flashbacks and continual pressure from him. I was becoming more interested in church and he was becoming more and more interested in his punk rock band. And lastly, but most importantly, I could not give up on the kid or her mom. I was clear on the fact that for some reason beyond my level of understanding, I had been plucked out of hell. Now I had a home. Not a motel, but a home. I had never had it so good. Still unable to explain how I was lucky enough to have made it out of the darkness of my past; I refused to leave anyone behind. Insistent that he provided me no other choice, I told him the child was staying. Within a few days, he was gone.

Even though it wasn't working between us, I became seriously depressed. Over the past almost two years Madie had grown very attached to him and I felt responsible for her loss. I was angry with myself for hurting Madie, confused and sad. Knowing that I could not give up now, I needed to counteract the depression. I did not come this far to fall now. My head was filled with negative thoughts and I desperately needed to get something good in there. I knew the only way to do it was to shove it in!

In an act of desperation, I went to the church office and bought a crap load of tapes from Ron Johnston's past sermons. I listened to them day and night. When Madie was around, she listened with me. The tapes helped us both transition through this time successfully.

As much as I was doing my best to make this transition a smooth one, my "ex" was having other thoughts. Just about the time I thought I would make it through this, Cindy called me into her office. When I walked in, she said "shut the door." A bit concerned, I closed the door and sat down. She said, your "ex-boyfriend" called here today. He started telling me all kinds of things, the most shocking of which was that that you were a prostitute." My entire body stiffened up immediately with shock and despair, and then she said the words that I thought I would never hear. "My God! Couldn't he have come up with something more believable! A prostitute! Ha! He is absolutely crazy! Like I was going to believe that!" *Whew…breathe Lauri…breathe…*I have since learned that it is in the darkest times that God's light shines brighter than ever.

Through the breakup, I learned that I needed positive and consistent "input" to keep me strong. Regardless of how much therapy I had, when things went bad, the old tapes played. *You are a loser, you will be alone. No one wants you.* Some friends suggested giving positive affirmations, saying things to myself like, *I am good. I am smart.* Frankly, it took years before I could actually believe any of that. In a bad mode, I would just start stirring around the same old crap. The only way to get better thoughts was by implanting them. Good input produced good output, and the more positive stuff I listened to, the more positive my thoughts were. Even today, if I hear my old tapes play in my head, I immediately seek input. I have tons of CDs in my car, just in case, from inspirational speakers like Pastor Ron. When I need to replace my thoughts with better ones, I just pop something new in.

Another valuable lesson I learned during that time came from Pastor Ron. One day in church he told us to take out a piece of paper and a pen. He then said, "Don't you wish you could find the perfect mate? I have the answer! But first, let's find out what you need. Put your pen to the paper and write it all down. Don't hold anything back. Funny, handsome, sexy…Put it all down, I want a *big* list." So, I did— *dark hair, funny, no cursing, no anger, generous, talks about feelings, sober, doesn't play head games, no silent treatments.* I just went on and on and on. After a few minutes he said, "Okay, pens down. Now look at your list."

Then with an evident seriousness he said, "If you want to find the person on the list, *YOU MUST BECOME THE LIST.*" Oh, no! Had I known I would have held back a little! I looked at my list to see how deficient I was. Well clearly I had the basics; funny, sober, but emotionally healthy? God, no. The silent treatment was one of my all time favorites. I learned it from my mom. Truthfully, it never really worked anyway. The longer I went without talking, the worse the anger grew. In an effort to clear the path to my soul mate, that day I embarked on a journey to become "my list." I didn't date anyone for just over a year, and after that, although I dated, I referred back to my list often to gauge my progress. Let's just say it took a while.

I also bought a bible during that time. I know, I am Jewish, but I thought I would just peruse through and see what you guys had on the other side. To tell you the truth, I didn't understand most of what I read. But I did see one thing that stuck with me. I am paraphrasing because I can't remember the exact words, but it said something like, "God can turn all bad to good." I remember reading it and just pondering the thought. I thought about my childhood and the flashbacks I was having and I promptly said, "Nope, sorry, I don't think so." And I closed the book.

44

IT WAS ABOUT THREE WEEKS AFTER THE WORST OF THE BREAKUP passed that I realized Jodi's mom hadn't called or visited. She had visited a few times in the first two weeks, but had not been by since. Not knowing how much longer I could support all of us, I called the sober home to talk to her. I knew it would relieve some pressure if I knew when she was getting out. When the man answered the phone, I said, "Is Denise there?" He said, "No." "When will she be home?" I asked. He replied, "She's doesn't live here anymore. She left about three weeks ago."

I had a hard time processing what he just said. After a few awkward moments, I said, "Well, I've got her kid." He responded, "We don't do kids, we do recovery. Call Social Services." I heard a click and just stared blankly at the receiver. Left? Three weeks ago? Left? I drifted away from the phone and sat on the couch. *Well surely she's coming back. I mean she isn't going to leave her here. But she left three weeks ago, and we haven't heard from her…three weeks…*The poor kid, what am I going to tell her? Her mom is gone? Is it not bad enough that she left her at a stranger's house, but now her mom is gone? Not wanting to upset Jodi, I waited a few more days just to see if Denise would call. A week later, when nothing came, I knew we were facing the inevitable. I sat down in the bedroom and explained that her mom may be away a bit longer than we expected. Still hoping she would return, I just explained that she was unable to visit right now. Then I started some general conversation about family. Within a few minutes I determined that Jodi had a grandma and an aunt, but she couldn't stay with either of them. She also had a dad, but she had never met him. As the weeks went on, I knew I would have to break the news to her. Not understanding why her mom hadn't called, she began to internalize it and started thinking her mom didn't love her anymore. Finally I told her in the best way I could about the power of drugs and what it does to loved ones. Unfortunately, she already knew all about it.

She was fairly quiet for the next few days, but when she finally started talking again, much to my surprise, she said nothing about her mom. She was upset about her hamster. Her hamster, Sammy, was still back at the crack house. She was sure he wasn't being fed and would be dead if we didn't get him. When I suggested we drive over there, she became extremely nervous and said, "What are you, crazy? They are scary men. They have guns. You can't just go there; they are not going to let you in. A white girl? You've got to be kidding. They don't even know you." And maybe she was right, but knowing there was an animal in the house that may die, I was determined. I knew how it felt when I lost Pepper. I just couldn't let him die. The only hope for this little girl's sanity was to rescue the only thing she had left, her hamster. If it was the last thing I did, I was going to rescue that little guy.

It was two days later, when I was getting changed from my work clothes to prepare to go to juvenile hall for my meeting, that it hit me. Pulling out my laminated badge, I stared at it. There it was in bold letters, PROBATION DEPARTMENT, my picture in the middle and my name at the bottom. This was it! Just the break I needed. I stood in front of the mirror, pulled my hair back and with a real serious look said, "Probation, Officer Burns." Heck, wearing the right business suit, I may be able to pull this off.

Today I realize that this was one of the craziest stunts I ever pulled. If it hadn't been for my childhood mischief, I never even would have tried. As we pulled up to the front of the house in the small gang neighborhood, Jodi looked like she was going to have a nervous breakdown. Her eyes welled up with tears and she was saying, "I don't know. I just don't know. I want him back, but I'm scared." I, on the other hand, was scared, but determined.

Knowing that if I thought about it any longer, I might change my mind, I said, "Look, you stay in the car. I am going to go up to the door. If they don't let me in, I will just leave. I will not let them hurt me." Pulling together everything I had learned in life thus far, by the time I got out, I was Cindy Cop. I had the confidence of Cindy with the cop attitude and walk. Thank God for small favors; I had the cop walk down. Lord knows I had encountered enough of them at this point to do it well. In my dark suit, with my probation badge pinned to my upper lapel, I strutted up to the front of the house and gave a sturdy knock and waited. A large Samoan man opened the door and a frail nervous woman stood behind him.

Surprised to see a white woman in a suit at their door, I was sure they thought they were in trouble. With a harsh stare and a firm lip, I looked directly into the eyes of the large man, pulled my badge from my jacket, held it up to the screen door for inspection, and before he could say anything, I blurted out in a firm almost masculine voice, "Officer Burns, Probation Department. I have the minor Jodi Goodman in custody. I am here to retrieve her pet and belongings." Like a Marine standing at attention, I continued to hold my badge firmly against the screen and stared straight into the eyes of the huge beast as he looked over my shoulder and saw Jodi sitting in the car.

He swung the door open and said, "Come in, officer." At this point, I didn't know whether to panic or celebrate. It wasn't over yet. He looked at the frail woman and said, "Hurry up, grab a bag! Get the kid's stuff." We walked through the living room where several large, dirty men were sitting around. The room was quiet. I could feel their eyes on me. I kept my posture stiff, avoided all eye contact and marched behind the woman, focused on the goal: Sammy. Having spent a lot of time in drug houses, this was familiar territory for me. I acted "as if." *We're coming to get you Sammy…Hang on…*

I just prayed he was still alive. When I entered the dirty room, the lady pointed at Jodi's pile of clothes on the floor. Next to the pile was the small wire cage with her hamster, alive and well. Attempting to conceal my emotion, I helped her shove the clothes into the bag. And then with little more than a glance, I grabbed the cage and the clothes and marched out the door. As I reentered the car with the hamster and clothes in tow, Jodi laughed and cried at the same time. When we hit the first light, we high fived and giggled. We couldn't believe it worked. This was the stupidest stunt I had ever pulled, but for once it was for a good reason.

It was a few days later that I was chatting with someone about being twenty six years old and having a twelve-year-old left at my house, and the funny insight of trying to parent a child who is just like me. Overhearing my conversation, a man whom I didn't really know approached me, concerned. He said, "I can appreciate your good heart in wanting to take this kid on, but do you realize if she hurts herself or gets sick, with her mom now gone and no note, you can't even get medical care for her?" He continued, "If she breaks a leg, or worse, gets critically ill, you will not be able to get her help." Not knowing what to say, I said nothing. He closed by saying, "You should call Social Services and see what they can do to help you."

Now after hearing from two people, I thought maybe they were right, I should at least call. The next day, on my lunch break, I came home and made the call. I explained the situation to the social worker that answered the phone. She responded by saying,"You need to drop the child off here at the children's home."

I said, "What? Drop her? No, I don't want to get rid of her. I want to help her. I just want to know if you can help us." Lord knows, I would never drop a kid off at an institution, not after what I had been through. The lady said, "Your only other option is to apply to be a foster mom." Now that was something I could do. She explained the process, told me about the services they offered and told me what I needed to do to get started. Over the next week, I frantically filled out paperwork, got a TB test and scheduled myself for foster parenting classes.

To add to the insanity, this was about the time my dad called. Having gotten the number from my mom, he phoned my house. Direct as always, he said, "Lauri, this is dad. I am going to be in town on Tuesday and I want to see Madie. I will take you to dinner. Please call your sisters and tell them to be there." Immediately reverting back to the way I was with dad's orders and my expected compliance, I said okay and hung up. Knowing how much I had changed, I was sure he wouldn't have the same power over me. I was healing.

I don't remember where Alyssa was the day he showed up, but Nadine came. At this point, Nadine had gotten sober and had a son. She had gotten pregnant from a relationship that was short-lived. She and her son Andy lived close by. I never asked my sisters to get sober. I didn't want to push it on anyone. But I guess after seeing me go from the streets to a being a normal person with a job and a house, she was inspired and followed suit. Alyssa also tried to get sober too. She went back and forth from drugs to sobriety, but with Nadine it stuck. Knowing that we were both sober now, I felt confident that together we could handle a visit from dad. Even though were still distant from each other, I thought our common "sobriety" bond would keep us strong. Boy, was I wrong.

Unfortunately, he was coming on a Tuesday—Pussy on the Porch night. When I told the girls what was going on, they agreed to run it for me in my absence. Up until this point in my life, other than with Sandy, I really hadn't talked much about my dad. Talk about my past was more focused on the streets and drugs. Feeling that my family was crazy, I still carried the stigma that if anyone knew, they would think I was crazy. So even though these were my closest friends, they knew little to nothing about my family. Not wanting to expose Jodi to the insanity of my family, I suggested she stay home with the meeting as well.

Going out to dinner with my dad was strained to say the least. He took us to a local Italian restaurant. After a few casual questions about life in general, we were stopped. Struggling to find anything to say to each other, the noise was mostly limited to the sucking of spaghetti. The only thing that saved us from long gaps of silence was the fact that Madie was a chatterbox. Talking about the funny kids in her class, and her many short-lived adventures, we survived, almost.

Everything seemed to be going the best I could expect, when my father pulled up to my house to drop us off. I was surprised when he said, "Well, I will come in for a few minutes before I go." It was at that point that I looked at my watch and realized the meeting was still in session. It ended at 9 p.m. and it was 8:52. I suggested that I go inside, see if they were almost done and come back out to get them when it was over. As I entered the house, the girls were standing up for the closing prayer. We did this at the end of every meeting. A sort of level setting to take the world on again for a few more days, nothing fancy, just a generic, please watch over us. I ran over, joined hands with the women, prayed our silly little prayer and returned to the front door to tell them the coast was clear.

When I opened the door, my whole world collapsed. The next few seconds seemed like a lifetime. The brown Lincoln rental car my dad was driving remained parked in front of the house. But Madie was in the back seat alone. My gaze quickly shifted to see my father and sister standing behind the car. At first glance, I thought they were getting something out of the trunk, but as my eyes registered what was happening, the insanity of my childhood came rushing back.

My father was standing in the street facing the car and my sister was standing with her back to the trunk, facing my father. As I opened the door, they immediately jerked away from one another. Not being able to react quickly enough, I saw their lips separate. And like a sledgehammer as they pulled away from one another, I saw my father pull his hands from beneath my sister's shirt. Nausea instantly consumed me and my entire being shut down. All systems failed simultaneously. I was gone.

Shutting the front door, I moved in a trance-like state past the living room table where the girls stood chattering excitedly and continued past the living room and into the back hallway. Turning into my bedroom, I walked through the door and stopped. My head dropped and my eyes transfixed on the small pieces of carpet protruding from beneath the wood on the legs of my dresser. My eyes grew as they studied the small fibers of the carpet and the fibers grew. They were everywhere. I was gone. *The girls I knew and trusted most in the world standing just a few feet away and my childhood was back...my past and my present...and I was stuck somewhere in the middle...the carpet...I was gone.*

In a catatonic like state, I couldn't move. Several minutes later, I heard the final slam of the front door closing and the resonating silence that remained. Finally it was over. They were all gone...*quiet...silent... alone.* I was catapulted out of my safety zone without warning when my sister burst through my bedroom door. "So hey!" The shift was familiar and disturbing. *I remembered it instantly...this part of the game I knew clearly...pretend it didn't happen...shove it down. It will all slip away...*

Like a roulette wheel I spun, unable to choose a stopping point, caught between the old games, my newfound therapy and my safe haven, my mind whirled...Denial...Isolation...Truth...denial...isolation...truth... denial...isolation...truth...

On this day I would be forever thankful for Sandy's voice as it pushed through the barriers of my mind. *"They cannot hurt you anymore Lauri, you are on the other side."*

As her voice resounded in my head, I reengaged with my sister. For the first time in my life, the brave Lauri I had found in therapy would shield me from the abuse and deception that nearly killed me. An air of confidence infused my being. I held my head up high, took a deep breath and with everything Sandy had taught me, I looked my sister in the eyes and said, "You are smiling? I don't understand, after what I just saw with dad? You are smiling?" Grinning at me, in a condescending voice, she said, "Lauri. It's dad. You know it's not me. It's dad. You know how weird he is."

"Nadine, now I know. This is not the first time this happened; this has been going on for a long time." Embarrassed, she said, "There is nothing I can do. It is him, Lauri!" Not able to deny it, now I knew for sure. I looked at her and said, "It is you, too. You came here tonight knowing what he has done to you and you continue to talk to him. You have not even tried to stop it. You're allowing the abuse to continue and you're sober now. Nadine, until you sever your relationship with him and get some help, our relationship is over. I will not communicate with you until you end this." And I left the room. Unable to address her issues, it was years before she showed up at my home again. And by the time she did, she was completely broken.

When I reentered the living room, my father was standing by the coffee table and Madie was sitting on the couch. A few seconds later, Nadine erupted from my bedroom, gave my dad a hug and promptly left. I assumed he had given her a check, hence the reason for the hug. She had to secure her next payment. It was all much too clear now. When she shut the front door, I was alone, with him. I stood in the kitchen and he stood in the living room. It was completely silent. Emotions fired through me like water rushing from a garden hose. I was completely stopped.

My father looked beyond the room into the hall. My thoughts raced...*get out...get out...get out of our home...Get away from me...get away from my daughter! Get out..!* But I remained frozen. After what seemed like an eternity he announced, "I'd better get going." As uncomfortable as it was, with my old self wanting to fix it with a hug, I remained in my transfixed state, silent and still. He exited and quietly shut the door. Left in a whirlwind of complicated feelings, and needing to isolate Madie from my emotions, I said, "Mommy is going to bed now sweetie. Why don't you go in the room with Jodi and get ready for bed as well." I rarely cried or broke down in front of Madie, believing I was her bedrock, I remembered the shelter for abused women and that desolate motel we stayed in and promised to myself, I would never expose my weakness to her again. I needed her to know she was safe. In an effort to eliminate fear or worry from her small world, I projected a positive, "everything will be okay" façade. Today I realize that wasn't the best method of preparing a kid for an emotionally healthy life, but being "mom and dad" I thought I had to be strong. Madie was much more aware than I ever could have imagined. I learned years later that she had seen everything that happened with my father and sister. Luckily, she already knew that I was trying to protect her from the experience by not talking about it. I say luckily, because the flip side would be to think that I had no reaction to it.

Wanting nothing more than to close the world out, the anger was insurmountable. My mind reeled as I reflected on my childhood, the institution; Nadine's secluded room, "the gun"... Just when I finally thought it was all over, it all came rushing back and crashed into my new life like a locomotive through a sanctuary.

In the middle of the night after hours of tossing and turning, unable to break the spell of emotions, I jumped out of bed and I withdrew a pencil from the drawer. I scratched the following note in large bold letters:

DAD—IT DISGUSTS ME EVEN TO CALL YOU THAT. YOU NEVER DESERVED THAT TITLE... THE ONLY REASON I EVEN HAVE ANYTHING TO DO WITH YOU IS BECAUSE YOU ARE MY DAD! IF YOU WERE A STRANGER I WOULD BE SICKENED BY YOU! WHAT KIND OF MAN TOUCHES HIS DAUGHTER?!!! WHAT KIND OF MAN BEATS HIS KIDS!!! YOU ARE A SAD EXCUSE FOR A MAN!!!! FATHER'S ARE SUPPOSED TO PROTECT THEIR CHILDREN!!!! I ALWAYS BELIEVED THAT SINCE YOU WERE MY DAD, I HAD TO KNOW YOU! BUT IF THE ONLY CHOICE I HAVE IS A DAD LIKE YOU, I CHOOSE NO DAD! GOD IS MY FATHER NOW. STAY THE FUCK AWAY FROM ME AND MY KID!!!

And I sent it.

Even though it was Nadine and my dad who were involved, the dirt stuck to me like a film of disgust the next day. As if I was weighed down with mud, the happy skip in my walk had vanished. As I walked by Cindy's office and she yelled her usual greetings to me, I sped past to hide the building tears. Approaching my desk that morning, I straightened up and strained to smile. When Cindy approached my desk, she looked frightened. She said, "Lauri, what is wrong?" The moment I looked her way, my eyes involuntarily filled with tears. "Come to my office...come on...let's go." *What the hell was I going to say?* She pulled me in, shut the door behind me and asked again, "Lauri, what is it?" I struggled to get control of myself. By the time she shut the door to her office, the flood gates flew open. All I could tell her was that it was a "family thing." She seemed to understand and didn't pressure me further. She offered to give me the day off, but I refused. If I returned home, I would be alone with *it*. I couldn't have that.

Wanting more than anything to help me, Cindy was more vulnerable that day than I had ever seen her. In an effort to make me feel better, she started talking about her own struggles. Coming to California from her hometown in Michigan with nothing, she had worked as a waitress in a Mexican restaurant. Struggling to make a dime, she was broke and hopeless on the day someone from the agency came in to the restaurant. Impressed with her service and friendly nature, he asked her to come to his office at the agency the next day where he hired her on the spot. Indebted to him for his kindness, she had worked relentlessly since being given that opportunity. This new information only increased my respect for her. She and Nathaniel taught me some very important things. The overriding theme: It's not where you come from that is important, it's where you are going.

It took weeks for the filth to subside. I couldn't scrub it off. During that time, Sandy and I met twice a week. We did stems on my father and she fed me enough positive affirmations to get to the other side of it. If it weren't for Sandy, I never would have made it.

From that time forward, I became the loud and persistent voice that would fight abuse at all levels. Whether protecting myself, a family member or a total stranger, I would never sit silently again. It was two days later that I received a call from the social worker who had received my foster care application. She asked if I could come to the agency the following day.

When I entered the place the next afternoon, I was immediately reminded of the many institutions from my past. After sitting in the lobby for several minutes, a man with a badge on his jacket unlocked a large door and called my name. He escorted me into a small room with a metal table, a few chairs and a large window that appeared to be a two way mirror. Sitting down across from me, he opened my file and smiled. He said, "First of all, I want to congratulate you on your newfound sobriety; that is great. I know how hard it can be."

I thought really, you do? Because if you did, you wouldn't have said, "newfound" for cripes sakes! I have been sober for more than three years...what sounds newfound about that?! "And I can tell you really like children, but the issue is this." And then he looked down at my file, and read it off from the sheet in front of him. "Prostitution. Receiving stolen goods. Warrants.

As much as I'd like to approve you, you really aren't foster mom material. But I don't want you to give up. We have a rule at the agency. After seven years of sobriety, we will consider someone in recovery. Since your charges are misdemeanors, if you come back with seven years of sobriety, we will see if we can waive them. But for now, you need to go home, get the little girl who is staying with you and drop her back off at the county children's home. We will find her a suitable home for placement."

I walked out of there heartbroken. The drive home was twenty minutes, but it seemed like twenty years. I just kept on hearing "drop the kid off..." *Drop the kid off? She was abandoned by her mother, and now the only person who is really helping her is going to drop her off at a building? An institution?* They clearly had the wrong girl. After everything I had been through, I was the last person who would drop an innocent child off at an institution. Knowing I couldn't break the law, I was traumatized. I knew I had to do it. Ed was there when I got home. By this time he knew Denise was gone and was concerned about the child he had brought to my home. I explained what had happened and that I would need to take her to the "children's agency." He too was conflicted. He certainly couldn't bring her home to his wife and kids, but he felt responsible. He said, "I'll tell you what. I will pay for an attorney so that you can get guardianship. I know a guy close to here. I'll pay the bill, if you'll keep the child." I agreed. This was Ed's solution to leaving without visiting again and feeling ok about it.

The very next day, I went to the attorney's office. The attorney explained that we needed to send a letter to every living relative of Jodi's telling them that I was filing for guardianship. If none of the relatives disputed it, I would be awarded guardianship. The attorney located the addresses of the relatives and sent the letters out. A few weeks later, after receiving no responses, we went to court. Jodi went with me. We were sitting in the back of the courtroom waiting and our attorney was talking to the judge when she walked in. She walked right past us. If it hadn't been for her long black hair, I wouldn't have even recognized her. *I knew she would come back!* I was sure she was pissed that I was trying to get guardianship of her kid. I never could have predicted what happened next.

She walked straight up to the bench and in a loud firm voice said, "I want Lauri to keep Jodi. I am a bad mom, I can't take of Jodi. I am a drug addict." My mind spun. *A drug addict? For cripes sakes she took prescription pills and maintained a full time job as a waitress at Coco's. I think we are unclear on who the "real" drug addict was in this equation.* "She is going to be better with Lauri." Then she turned and quickly stormed out of the courtroom. As she passed us, Jodi jumped up and ran for her calling, "Mom! Mom!" But Denise brushed her off and kept on going. Just as I got up to follow her, the judge hit his gavel and said, "Guardianship granted." Then there was silence. We won. Or had we?

I was only getting guardianship so that I could take care of her until her mom returned. I wasn't planning on keeping her forever. I was only twenty-six and now with two kids, and one of them was half my age! I loved Jodi; she was so much like me as a child, but I was way in over my head and I knew it.

Completely confused, the more I thought about it, the more pissed off I became at God. When I was in the room praying about keeping the kid, a few months back, everything felt right. I thought he was in on the deal with me. Her mom could get sober and I could help her out, but now this? Now the kid is hurt even more! What is the point of this? I had a bone to pick with God for sure. Somehow, he agreed with my taking the kid initially, but must have gone on vacation and forgot us after that. Ron Johnston always talks about an "aha" moment. When something happens, like you get fired or you break up with someone and you wonder why. He said that later, when something better comes along, you say, "Aha! That is why that happened!" I was sure there would be no "aha" for this day. This was just bad. Jodi was a crying mess. I have since learned that sometimes the distance between the event and the "aha" is longer than you could ever imagine, but it always comes.

In an effort to put my life with my ex behind me and lower the rent for Madie, Jodi and myself, I rented a less expensive house on the same block. The insurance thing was okay, but as time went on they reduced my base salary and I was on straight commission. I could never tell when the commission checks were coming. Sometimes they would accidentally skip a month. Having no insight into the fact that people were dependent on the money, they would chock it up as an administrative error and promise to pay the next month. We were so strapped for cash that on a few occasions it was necessary to pick up food from a church that served needy families in order to eat and on more than one occasion our electricity was shut off. I felt like I was failing Madie again. I wanted her to feel like a regular kid. I was tired of being the mom who couldn't pull it together. Even though I was sober for years at this point, I still felt different. Different from the other parents and different from the "normal" people, but I didn't want Madie to feel it. I had to make it better for her.

A few months later, Bob, the man who picked me up off the streets, delivered a computer to our apartment as a housewarming gift. Being in a wheelchair and not realizing that our new home was two stories up, he handed it off to me with explicit instructions on how to hook it up. I fell in love with that computer. At night, after the kids went to bed, I was fixated on it.

A few months later, when my video card died, Bob bought me a new card and some memory. Still unable to get upstairs, he walked me through replacing the parts over the phone. Shortly after that, curious about the electronic flow through the computer chassis, I signed up for a Saturday class at a local college. It was in that class that I learned how to put a whole computer together from scratch. I absolutely loved it!

Our first test was on binary, hex and decimal conversions. When the teacher told us the test was in one week, I studied like crazy. I bought several books and learned the basics. It was quite a feat because I knew nothing about Hex or Binary. I walked into the class the next Saturday with my brain saturated with numbers only to find that everyone else had calculators!

We weren't expected to master the numbering systems in a week, and frankly the teacher was surprised I had. When he offered me a calculator, I declined. I had to know if I could do it. When I passed the test with 100% I knew I had to return to computers. That weekend, while sitting in the living room watching TV, I spotted an ad in the Pennysaver that read, "Job Training Partnership Act (JTPA)—tuition paid in full in for people who qualify." One of the possible training opportunities listed was Computer Networking. The small print referred to the inability to earn an income due to absence of education. I just knew I had to try. A week later, I received the application in the mail, filled it out and returned it. For the first time in my life, I was happy I was broke. With my base salary now gone and working on straight commission, I qualified! A few weeks later, I was called in for a formal appointment. The lady I met with told me that although I was approved, there was a long waiting list, anywhere from one to six months. She closed the interview by saying, "But you never know." I left elated! I couldn't believe I might be able to get an education in the one thing I loved most in the world! I was so excited, I couldn't sleep that night! About four in the morning, after rolling around for hours, I jumped up, grabbed a piece of paper and scribbled *"computer school"* on it and dropped it in my GOD box. For the next few hours I slept, knowing George had my back.

It was three weeks later that the lady phoned me at work. She said, "Lauri, did you see the news this morning?" "No," I replied. She said, "Well, I wanted to call you before you found out and got upset." My heart sank as I listened. She said "The funding for JTPA has been cut. My boss came into my office this morning and told me. He said that's it, we are closing out, the government has cut all of our funding, so finish whatever you have in your approved pile and send a letter to the remaining applicants, telling them we are sorry.

"As soon as he left my office, I looked at the approval pile sitting on the right hand side of my desk. Your file was on the left because I was just working on it. When he was out of my sight, I picked it up your folder and dropped it into the approved pile. No one will ever know the difference. Lauri, you will receive the funding even though the program closed." I couldn't believe it! I could not understand why she did this for me, but I felt like I was the most fortunate person alive! This lady, whose name I didn't know, was angel number three. Little did she know, she would dramatically alter the course of my entire life.

Within two weeks I was enrolled in school full time to be a Certified Network Engineer. With my incoming commissions being just enough to pay our rent and necessities, we scraped by, but we survived. I loved my classes and studied harder than I ever had in my life. Following Cindy's words, "it takes money to make money," I bought practice tests online and studied all of the time. There were five tests ranging from basic computer hardware to advanced computer communication protocols. Much to my surprise, one of the main ingredients for being successful in this field was knowledge of binary numbers. Since I accidentally learned them in my old class, I was the binary queen. I made over 1000 flashcards for each test, and knew all of the answers. I was so determined it was scary! When I aced one test after another, the teacher put me in charge of mentoring the other students. For once in my life, I was happy to be in school. They told us when we were nearing graduation that we could easily ask for $30,000 at our first job! I was so excited that the moment I graduated, I rushed out to interview.

I already knew I was good at interviewing, but now I really had something to back it up with: Skills!! One of the first interviews I had was with a software company as a Call Center Manager. When they told me I would be working exclusively on their software, I knew it wasn't what I wanted. I wanted to build networks, but I went on the interview anyway. I figured it was a good practice.

I walked in as Cindy, and rolled in two things that Nathaniel had taught me. Talk and Maintain. I *maintained* the belief that could I do it and I *talked* who I was into existence when I boldly looked the man in the eyes and said, "I always succeed, it's just my nature!" The clincher came when the man asked me how much salary I wanted. Since I didn't really want the job, I put myself way out of their limit. Their ad said $32,000 so I asked for $45,000. I figured this way I was sure not to land the job, but I had the chance to practice interviewing.

I thought I would just die the next day when he called me and said, "Lauri, I am calling to congratulate you. We believe you have what it takes to make this place run and the CEO approved your requested salary. We will pay you $45,000 to start."

Hell! Now what was I going to do? I didn't want the job! But $45,000!!!!! This was crazy! I had to take it! Ecstatic and confused, I enthusiastically accepted the job I didn't really want.

45

MY FIRST DAY THERE, THE MAN THAT INTERVIEWED ME SAT ME down at a computer and said, "Take a few days and learn our software." He launched the program for me and walked away. Then he turned and said, "Oh yeah, try to break it. It has not released yet. You will be our QA tester. If you can break it, then we need to fix it before it goes out."

I had so much fun my first day, by the time five p.m. rolled around I didn't want to leave. I loved computers so much that as far as I was concerned, I was being paid to play! I did so well that they got rid of the other folks and made me the sole support for the United States and Canada when the software rolled out.

As well as things at work were going, things at home were escalating, especially with Jodi. She was hanging out with bad kids, stealing and refused to take any instruction from me. She was now fourteen years-old and we hadn't heard from her mom at all. I would come home from work to find her and her friends lying on the roof of our two-story condo, smoking cigarettes and laughing. If I gave her any instruction, she would just smirk and walk away. If I grounded her, she would say *F* You!* and walk right out of the house slamming the door behind her. Madie was learning what not to do from watching her. Even though they shared a room, they could barely stand each other now. In an effort to keep her side of the room clean, Madie put a large strip of masking tape on the carpet to separate their sides. Madie was upset that Jodi wasn't respecting me, but I explained over and over that she was just hurt and reacting the only way she knew how. I did everything I could think of to help Jodi. I talked to her, brought her to Sandy, and tried to make her listen at our meetings, but she didn't care. I didn't know what to do. I only knew I couldn't let her go. Not after her mom had left her.

The day I came home and found that our home had been burglarized, all of that changed. Entering the house, it was immediately apparent that something was wrong. Furniture was tossed about, things were strewn about on the floor and when I entered my room, my computer, which was normally on the desk, was lying on the floor, tipped on its side. When I realized what had happened, I lifted my mattress to check on the rent money I had been saving. It was all gone.

In a state of shock, I sat down and tried to absorb what had happened. I began to take inventory in my mind of everything I had of value so that I could determine if it had been taken. As I glanced up on my dresser, I noticed my jewelry box. It was still partially open, the way I had left it that morning. When I jumped up from the bed to check, I was surprised to find that all of the jewelry remained. I began to survey the house. Much to my surprise, although things were tossed about, nothing else was missing, just the money. Well, let's just say, not such a good idea to burglarize a burglar's home. I didn't know much about life, but one thing I did know was burglaries. All of the doors and windows were locked. Surely the window in the back yard would have been optimal for a burglary. Hidden by the large fence, none of the neighbors would have seen. When I checked the upstairs roof window, it had been broken. Who would break in on the second floor where God and everyone could see them going in? Only a kid who has been hopping the fence and entering that way for months. This was my moment of clarity. I thought I had been helping Jodi, but I had only been hurting her by not giving her consequences for her actions. I knew I had to make a change immediately. I called the police and when they arrived, I took them aside and explained the situation. I told them I didn't want her arrested, but I wanted to scare her. We agreed that if she denied it, they would say they found her fingerprints. She was so young she would never realize that fingerprints are not on file until you are arrested. The police waited while I drove down the street to pick the kids up from the Boys and Girls club. I said nothing on the drive. When we returned to the home and she saw the police car, she looked out of the car window to avoid eye contact. Entering our home, she denied the whole thing. When they sat her down and said, "Honey, the game is up. We have your fingerprints," she fell apart. She started crying and immediately offered to return the money, which was still in her room. The police and I agreed that they would put handcuffs on her, read her rights and take her to the local police station. After they determined that she had learned her lesson, I would pick her up.

When I came to get her two hours later, the officer at the desk said "good luck!" with a sarcastic tone. "She has been joking with the officers all night and frankly, I don't think she cares about you." I was baffled. I got home and phoned my friend from Pussy on the Porch, Colleen. Colleen was a school teacher and she had a lot of experience with kids. By the end of our conversation, I knew what I had to do. It would be one of the hardest days of my life. I sat Jodi on the couch and told her I didn't feel I was helping her. I told her I really wanted to make it work, but we both knew she didn't respect me. I told her that every time she broke a rule, I moved the line because I didn't want to abandon her. I had moved so many lines that it was doing both of us more harm than good. I humbly admitted that I felt like a failure as a parent. I had run out of ideas. Then she responded by saying something that explained everything and would help me immensely. "You don't understand. You're trying to be a mom, like Denise. I hate the mom person. I don't want a mom."

I realized at that moment that she had so much anger at her own mom, that by stepping into that spot, I took on everything that was due to Denise. That day we both acknowledged and accepted that fact. Over the next few minutes, we talked more like friends than parent/child. I accepted that she didn't want a mom and she accepted that I couldn't live without rules. In genuinely hearing her and respecting that decision, we began to grow closer. While listening openly to her we came up with a plan together. I told her I wanted to be there for her emotionally, but the only way to fix this was to take me out of the mom role. Confused as hell, but also needing to regain my sanity and stability in my life with Madie, we agreed she could not stay without following my "mom" like rules. Accepting that she wasn't interested in following rules, and putting my ego aside; we looked for another place for her to stay and agreed to move forward like friends. By the next day, she had found the perfect place. It was a church that took kids. This church was different in that it was run by bikers. Even the pastor was a biker. They took in both drug addicts and wayward kids. We called and arranged for her to move that weekend. Even though I felt conflicted, I knew it was the right thing to do. The only time I ever thought about my actions as a kid was when I got consequences. I needed to love her enough to let her go. She was a lot like me as a child. She just wanted to be free, to have a voice in her own mixed-up life. In giving her that, I showed that I respected her. Finally, someone was listening. She remained at that church for the next few years, bonded with the other kids there and grew to know a loving God through them. By simply stepping out of the mom role, our relationship shifted to one of friendship, love and respect.

Madie on the other hand was a whole different thing. She went from having a mom who was using drugs and irresponsible, to growing accustomed to my paranoid quirks. In addition to sneaking her into my room at night to avoid a kidnapping, we had our own personal "code word." In the event that anyone ever came to pick her up from school saying her mom sent them, they would need "the word" or she wouldn't go.

My paranoia grew when at the age of ten she asked if she could ride her bike to school. Convinced that someone would steal her from me, I outright refused. I couldn't let her just head down the street alone. Madie became more and more frustrated by my over protective nature and it became a frequent topic of conversation. Finally, in an effort to try to allow her live a normal life, I came up with a plan that made me feel safe, while still letting her ride her bike. I agreed to allow the bike riding, but only if I could follow her in my car. From that day forward, she rode her bike and I drove behind her at a rate of about five mph. It was the craziest thing you ever saw. The day we realized the true insanity of it, a lady pulled up alongside her bike. I was sure she was trying to get my baby. Instead, she rolled down the window and said, "Honey are you okay? Seems like that car is following you." Embarrassed, Madie smiled and said, "Yeah, that's just my mom. She follows me to school." In an effort to save her any more embarrassment, the next day I dropped a simple note "keep Madie safe" inside of my GOD Box and let her ride alone like the other children.

Still working at the software company, I was learning a lot about "normal life" stuff from the guys I worked with. During lunch they talked a lot about news, sports and technology. Since I knew nothing about any of these matters, I just chewed my food and listened. One day I overheard my boss talking about home loan rates. Excited about the fact that the rates had dropped lower than ever, he spent the whole day looking up information and announcing what he had found. I really didn't understand what he was talking about, but somehow his information planted a seed in my mind about the possibility of buying a home. This is certainly something I had never thought about before, but now that I had a good paying job, I thought maybe I could actually do it. Then I could really give Madie a normal life. Unfortunately at this point, even though I was making more money, I was spending it all. We were eating out, had a cleaning lady and had all of the cable channels. I had nothing in savings and still bounced checks like crazy.

I started to think about what Nathaniel said. Add to it every day, maintain the belief, and talk about it. Using just pieces of his "MASTER" concept, I came up with a plan. For the life of me, I knew I couldn't save money, but I had an idea. I could trick myself. When I signed up for work they asked me if I wanted my check auto-deposited to my bank. Knowing that if I had a negative balance it would suck my money up, I said no at the time. But now I was on to something. I wrote down my idea and threw it in my bedroom drawer for safe keeping.

A few nights later while tucking Madie in to bed, I brought up "the plan." I knew if she agreed, I would put everything I had into it, but I had to know how she felt. I told her I knew it had been rough, everything she had been through with my drug use, the molestation, the foster home and our struggles to stabilize and although we were doing okay now, I wanted more for her. Since we were both in therapy, it was normal for us to have open and intimate discussions like this. Madie and I talked about everything. Everything that was healthy to talk about that is. I was very careful about the level of information. There is a fine line between what should be talked about and what shouldn't. Clearly she never knew about my life as a prostitute. I found this kind of information totally inappropriate and disturbing for a child's mind. But we often talked about the impact that the molestation had on her and how she was doing in therapy.

On this night, I explained to her that since it was hard for me to get close to anyone other than her and my best friend Linda, I didn't know if I would ever get married. I assured her that I liked being a single mom, and I had everything I needed. Then I closed with, "But I want to be able to give you everything 'normal' families have." Although she insisted she was happy and everything was fine, I continued, "I was wondering what you'd think about buying a house in a real family neighborhood."

She was immediately excited about the idea and started shooting out questions faster than I could answer them. I answered as much as I could with my limited information and then rolled out "the plan." I reminded her about when we were on welfare and barely had any money. I explained that I was making a lot more now, but that we were using it all. I told her we needed to change our habits. I found a bank that was really, really far away with a strange name I never heard of. It was closed on the weekends and had no ATMs, so even if we were desperate we couldn't get money out. I knew exactly what my shortcomings were and as crazy as it was, I armed myself against myself. I had already confirmed that they could take direct deposits from my paycheck. I also confirmed that the payroll company could split my check. Half to me in the form of a check, and the remaining half to the bank in BFE via auto deposit. Then the more difficult part of the plan.

We would pretend that I was only making half as much money and we would live like that was true. We would have to cut our cable, take lunches to school and work, and now the clincher, we would have to share my bedroom and get a roommate. Much to my surprise, she was all in. Starting the very next payday, I deposited my first $1000 into the remote bank and within a week, we had rented the room. For the next several months, Madie and I talked excitedly about "the plan." Each week when the Pennysaver came we would sit on the couch and look at the houses, imagining what we could buy someday.

I couldn't believe it when ten months later we had $10,000 in that bank! Even though we had a few more months to go, we couldn't wait. That next weekend, Madie and I embarked on the journey of finding our new home. On our third weekend, we saw an ad for "new" homes and we were very surprised to find that, unlike cars, they didn't cost more than the used ones. Curious to see what they looked like, we drove twenty miles south on the freeway.

When we pulled up there were big flags outside and a sign the read "Kaufman & Broad Homes." As we entered the office, there were two sales women. One was sitting with a couple chatting and the other lady said, "Welcome! Please take a brochure and walk on in!" And she pointed to the path out to the homes. There were three homes on the path: Models A, B and C. Madie and I walked into model A.

It was like no other home I had ever seen. It was a three story with the entryway providing a clear view all the way from the top floor to the bottom. Madie and I held hands and walked through, silently taking in every detail. It had cathedral ceilings, kitchen, formal living room and master bedroom upstairs and a view from the kitchen window that left us spellbound. Looking out onto the vast mountains in the canyon, it was absolutely magnificent.

Still not speaking, I clenched her hand as we continued downstairs to the large TV room and just beyond that, two children's rooms. It was absolutely amazing. Afraid to say anything that might get Madie's hopes up, I continued on as if "just looking." Although we looked at Model B and C, my mind was still back on A. I pulled the insert out of the brochure and it read Model A—$174,000. I was sure we didn't have enough. Readjusting my expectations, we walked back through the new homes to the office. When the woman behind the desk asked, "Any questions ladies?" I replied, "No thanks." Although she probably assumed we weren't interested, she would soon learn differently when we returned for a "walk-through of Model A not only the next day, but every weekend for the next six weeks.

The ladies in the office became accustomed to our visits. Seeing Madie and me coming through the door again, they would yell, "Hey girls! Coming to look at your house?" We would smile, say yes, and walk through to Model A. We would sit on the couch and talk about how nice it would be to relax here after work, go into the children's room and talk about the different ways to decorate it, walk into the kitchen and look at the appliances again, and then we would leave. Not only was I under the impression that we would have to save a lot more money to get this place, I was scared to death to commit to anything this big. It was way out of my league.

One Saturday morning we drove up and there were balloons out in front of the office next to a large sign. It read *$10,000 off move in costs this weekend only*. When we entered the big French doors of the office, the lady at the desk said, "Hey there, girls. If you make a decision this weekend, we can not only give you $10,000 off, but we can also throw in some goodies: Upgrades, a washer & dryer...Before I knew it the lady had convinced us to just sit down with her. She began printing off sheets of papers with numbers on them while chattering about the great bonus this weekend. The most memorable part of our discussion was the payment, $1800.00 per month. It was almost double what I was paying at the apartment. There was no way.

Noting my apprehension, the lady said, "Look, Lauri. Go home, grab your taxes from last year and come back. Today I am going to teach you how buying a home really doesn't cost any more than renting an apartment when you do your taxes right." Madie and I rushed home and returned with my tax file. In less than an hour the lady showed me how I could claim more on my taxes, get more back at the end of the year and subtract the property taxes from the payment and pay it in lump sums. Bottom line, by the end of that day, Madie and I were signing paperwork for a brand new home! I couldn't believe it! I was scared to death! And Madie was in heaven. Since the home wasn't built yet, along with the paperwork, the lady gave us a sign that said LOT 78. It was a cardstock that was pulled off the front of the house, which she replaced with a SOLD sign. We carried that LOT 78 sign around with us in the car everywhere we went. Now, instead of looking at the model homes every weekend; we drove to the dirt lot where our house would be with our LOT 78 sign in tow. We watched the wood going up, picked the carpet and the tile and stood at the frame that would someday be our kitchen window. I couldn't believe it. From where I had come on the streets, this kind of stuff just didn't happen. Just Madie and me?! Alone, with no help?! It was like a dream!

The day we moved in was one of the best days of our lives. We went to Target and decorated Madie's room with all of her favorite things, all Winnie the Pooh. We even decorated the guest room in case she had a friend spend the night. Our home was on a cul-de-sac surrounded by mountains. Since they were all new homes, all of our neighbors were moving into their homes at exactly the same time, so we met everyone very quickly. It was straight out of a movie. We were in heaven.

Due to our limited resources, and unlike our neighbors, our home was surrounded by dirt for more than three months. But we didn't care, we had our own home. I quickly learned it would be over $10,000 to put in landscaping! After a few days of watching the neighborhood fathers digging and plowing for sprinklers, I was determined. If they could do it, so could I. One of my girlfriends and I hired a day laborer for the digging and over the next weekend, we learned how to glue pvc pipes, drain pipes and worst of all, we learned that sod is very heavy! By 6 p.m. on Sunday we were suffering from severe heat exhaustion, but we had done it! Two chicks with absolutely no experience installed the entire lawn, drainage and sprinkler system. Not a day went by that I didn't drive into that neighborhood, see my lumpy, self-installed lawn and thank God for my life. It was beyond my wildest dreams.

About a month after we moved in to our home, I was on a tech support call at work helping a customer and before I could thank him and hang up, he said, "Where are you guys located?" When I told him, he said, "How would you like to come and work for me?" Not knowing who he was, I just listened. It turned out he worked as a manager for one of the largest computer networking firms in the United States. Within a few minutes I had set a meeting with him. And a month later, I was working for him as a Systems Engineer. He started me off at the same salary I was making, but now I had the chance to do exactly what I wanted, build networks! I was the only female engineer at that location. I worked with a group with five male network engineers and a male manager. The guys on my team made it very clear from the start that this was a man's job, not for chicks. That only made me more determined to succeed. Each time I solved an issue, the guys on my team would chock it up to "luck." Luckily I had enough therapy at this time to realize they were just insecure. So I would just smile and nod.

I was there just under a year when my boss told our group that he was going to enroll us all in classes to receive an additional engineering certification. The certification was on the most popular networking software. It was called Microsoft. It would be six months of night classes and we would have to pass five classes and extensive tests, but upon completion, he would give each one of us a raise of $15,000! He enrolled us in classes immediately. We had only attended one class when he informed us that the training budget had been cut and we would have to hold off on classes until further notice. I was completely bummed. I really saw myself making the $60,000!

Remembering what it took to pass that first six months of school with the classes, flashcards and practice tests, I was sure that I could do it. But without the classes? Remembering that everything we learned in class was also in the book, I thought about what Cindy said: *It takes money to make money* and what Nathaniel said: *Maintain the belief you can do it.* That weekend, I went out and bought a whole set of books called Microsoft Systems Engineer—Self Study. For the next six months, every weekend, Madie went over her friend's house and I came into work and studied. I brought my practice tests, books and flashcards and studied quietly in the computer room for at least eight hours, Saturday and Sunday. After months of studying, I scheduled my first test and I failed. I was completely bummed. Before leaving the testing area, I asked the teacher, "How long do I have to wait before taking the test again?" He said, "You can come back tomorrow if you want." Unwilling to fail, I said "Great, I'll be here!" I studied the entire night, cramming the stuff I missed into my brain. I sat out in the car looking at the flash cards right up until test time. That day I passed my first test!

With four more tests to go, I started the process again. The next test, passed! The third test failed…Studied more…failed…I refused to give up. I had come too far! I studied more…and passed! Before I knew it I had my MSCE Certificate in hand! I had done it! With no classes! When I showed to work proud to show my boss, he was stunned. I was given a raise to $60,000.

As time went on and our lives improved, I continued to put everything I had into my work. Forever grateful for everything I had been given in life, I was happier than ever. The dark track lines that scarred my hands and thin arms from my drug abuse were a constant reminder of the darkness I had walked out of. Luckily, no one else ever knew what they were, but every time I glanced down, I was reminded of how my life had been saved. I can honestly say that I was not the best engineer. There were a lot of guys that were better than me, but I was grateful for my life and it was evident to everyone around me. Knowing I had walked out of the darkness into a miracle life, I was always uncontrollably happy. I had somehow transitioned from being "the awkward girl" who didn't know how to interact with humans, to being "Ms. Sunshine." Over the next few years, I was recommended for one job right after another and was thrust up the ranks of the company. I quickly advanced from being a Network Engineer, to being a Sr. Systems Engineer and leading large teams. Before I knew it, I was promoted again to System's Consultant. Now I was going out with the sales team, selling the deals, writing up the contracts, and managing the budgets.

One day the Vice President of the company called for me while I was out at a customer's site. The site was at least an hour from the main office and I was sure there was trouble, a system down or something. He often recommended me to work on outages, and although I was honored by his confidence in my skills, it also made me very nervous.

I was in the break room when I was told there was an urgent call from the VP at the home office. When I picked up the receiver, he said, "Lauri, this is Dave." I was a nervous wreck! Trying to be Cindy in this very nerve racking moment, I confidently replied, "Yes, Dave, how can I help you?" Then I just listened. Although you would think what he said next would make me happy, it only made me more nervous!

"Well Lauri the reason I am calling you is that I don't know if you are aware, but over the past three months we had a contest at the company. The contest was to identify the best System's Engineer in the company. The way the contest worked was that managers and directors would send in recommendations as to who they thought was best. And as you know Lauri, we have over 8,000 engineers at our company. I am calling to tell you that you were one of three engineers selected. You and a guest will be going to Paradise Island in the Bahamas for an all-inclusive one week stay. Congratulations!"

I was such a wreck I had no idea what to say next! Nothing like this had ever happened in my life! I still didn't know how to handle direct "praise." It was very foreign to me and made me uncomfortable. If you can believe it, I felt guilty! I was an absolute mental case. The confidence that these people placed in me was so alien to me, I wanted to just lie down and die. I was afraid to see the VP after this conversation and the worst of it was that I was planning a hard drive upgrade for him the next day! I was sure I would fry all of his data. I was on the verge of a breakdown.

The hard drive upgrade went fine and a few weeks later, Madie and I flew off to the Bahamas for the vacation of a lifetime! When we returned from the trip, the Vice President saw me and asked how the trip had gone. I thanked him profusely. When I turned to walk away, he said, "You know Lauri, most people go to these things for a romantic vacation, with a significant other. I was surprised to hear you took your daughter." Even though I was dating at the time, taking someone else had never crossed my mind. Knowing he would never understand that my daughter was my most "significant other," I just smiled.

46

IT WAS JUST A FEW WEEKS AFTER OUR VACATION THAT I RECEIVED A call from my older sister, Nadine. Besides holidays at my mom's house, I hadn't spoken with her since the incident with my dad, but I could tell from her voice that something was seriously wrong. Weeping into the phone uncontrollably, she said, "Lauri, I need your help. It's Andy!" Andy was about seven years old at this point. In her muffled, disconnected voice I heard, "I beat him so bad, I am afraid I will kill him. I hit him in the head a lot. I need to bring him to you now! Please Lauri, I need your help! I need to have him taken away from me. Please help me to get help!" I told her to get in the car and come over immediately.

The moment we hung up I called 911. The social worker was the first to arrive. When my sister pulled up, I instantly honed in on Andy. He was a horrible mess. His eyes were red from crying and he appeared to be in a catatonic state. Speaking so quietly I could barely hear him, he softly tiptoed towards Madie's room. It was all I could do not to break right there. But the social worker was upstairs waiting for us. Madie knew what had happened and had been crying just thinking about it. By the time Andy entered her room; she was under control and smiled in an effort to cheer him up. "Hi Andy," she said in a voice scratchy from crying. With his head down, he let out the smallest "hi" and continued to stare at the ground. I closed the bedroom door. For now he was safe.

When I entered the kitchen Nadine was already sitting with the social worker. He had a folder and began to ask her questions. I just sat quietly listening. He asked questions like, "What brought the fight on?

Where did you hit him? How many times? Why is he taking medicine? Is this the first time this occurred?" She started off by talking about how hyper he is and that she can't handle him and *that's when she broke.*

As if she were trying to hold back water behind a dam, her words poured out so quickly, it was difficult to understand her. In a high pitched, broken voice she said, "I hate Andy because he is a boy and I hate boys because my dad used to put his tongue in my mouth." She continued to talk, but I had completely tuned out, trapped in a world of my own. I could no longer hear their voices. My head screamed inside. I was completely paralyzed as the whole thing flashed in front of my eyes. I don't know why it didn't hit me this way when I caught her with my dad a few years back, but now the whole thing came twirling around. *You mean you hid a gun and had me tied to a bed in a fucking straight jacket and this shit really did happen!!!! I was right all along! And I was never crazy?!!! You mean I was never fucking crazy?!!!*

Here I was, twenty years later, sitting at a table with the very girl who conspired with my dad to put me away after witnessing his beatings on me for years. And now she was hitting her own son and thought I was going to *help to put him away?* My whole world had spun around so quickly I didn't know what hit me. The hypocrisy of the whole thing was nauseating. I had to do something. *This would not happen again!* I had heard about the cycle of abuse in my classes, but this was mind-boggling. A whole lifetime later and the insanity was repeating itself! Nadine finished by saying, "I need him to go away. I just can't handle him." Before I knew it, the social worker closed the folder and looked at me and said, "I will be taking Andy to the Peppertree Children's home. We will give him a full checkup and a psychological evaluation and then we will find him a safe place to live." *No! No! This can't happen again! I refused to watch another child be institutionalized because the parent can't stop hitting them! They were taking the wrong person away!* Before he left, I asked if I could speak with him alone. My sister was so out of it, she didn't notice. The social worker and I walked downstairs into the TV room. I only had one thing to say. *"I want him."*

The man explained that even if I wanted him, he would have to take him to the children's home today, take pictures and do an assessment, but a social worker would call me in the morning to see if they could approve me for custody. It was absolutely heartbreaking to watch him drive away. He was just a tiny little peanut, incapable of understanding what was happening to him. He was so small I could barely see him in the car window as the man pulled away with him in the back seat of the car. He was scared and alone. I needed to get him back. Nadine left in a state of despair and Madie was equally traumatized. "You are going to do something mom, right?" "Of course I am sweetie." Madie loved children and of all the values I instilled in her, she was clear on one thing: It was never okay to hit a child. A child herself, she was just as protective of kids as I had ever been.

The next day a social worker called and arranged for me to come in after work. She gave me a packet to fill out and some instructions. She also said I would have to get a TB test and fingerprints. This was my second time applying to be a foster mom. Between the trauma of the recent event and the knack that I have for blocking bad stuff out, I totally forgot about the fact that I was denied with Jodi so many years ago.

I completed the packet, TB test and fingerprints in record time and got it back to their office. It was one week later that the lady phoned and asked me to come in. It was in the meeting in the little room with the two-way mirror that I remembered being denied years ago. As she opened the file, I stiffened up. *Oh, God, not again. Not with Andy!*

When she opened up my file, she looked me in the eyes and smiled. I instantly felt judged. I knew what was coming. *So what, I was a prostitute. Get over it! Can't you see I have changed?*

But when she spoke I was completely taken back. She said, "Lauri, when we tell people to come back when they have seven years of sobriety, no one ever returns. But here you are. I read your file and your reasons for wanting to be a foster mom. Based on what you wrote, a few days ago, I put together a recommendation to waive all of your crimes and approve your application to be a foster mom. I am happy to say that the agency has accepted my recommendation. It was all I could do not to cry. I couldn't believe it. Angel number four. This lady didn't know me from anyone. She looked at my record from the past and for reasons I will never understand, she took a chance on me. I floated out of there with her recommendation in my hand with a plan to pick up Andy in a few days.

Nadine called me that same night. Having been informed that I was getting custody of Andy, she was very upset. She said she didn't want to see him again, and that if he was with me, she would have to see him at my mom's at holidays. She wanted him to go somewhere else, so that she didn't have to think about it anymore. She closed by informing me that I couldn't have him because she would be getting him back. Now that she was engaged in a battle with me, she immediately enrolled in an anger management class and started working with the social worker on the steps to get him back. I was very upset at first, but saw later that, although it wasn't her intention, she got the help she needed and she never hit him again. It also took me a while to realize that she was a victim too. She suffered from untreated sexual abuse. Unfortunately, since she was one of the people who had put me away, it took a bit for me to get over that enough to see it clearly.

The reason I tell this story is because of the things that came as a result of these events. Number one, I learned that "hurt people, hurt people." Although Ron Johnston had said it many times, I never really "got" it until this experience. Having never dealt with what happened to us as kids, the wounds festered inside of Nadine. Even thought it didn't bother her on the surface, and she may not have thought about it much, it came out on others. After that time, I began telling women I worked with in recovery that it's better to find someone you trust and tell them your secrets than to have it come out on the people you love most. You can ignore it, but it won't ignore you. It still has a hold on you.

Ironically, it was at this time that I really started to consider what had happened to my dad. Because of the event with Nadine, it hit me that it was possible that he was abused and that his abuse on us was a result of that abuse. It was the only logical explanation. I told Sandy and she agreed that something definitely had happened to him. This whole cycle thing hit me in a way that empowered me. I saw how the horrific events in my life could repeat over and over again through the lives of others in our family chain if nothing was done. I decided I would be the one to break the chains of abuse in our family. Two things affected me that week. One was something I heard on a noon-time radio show, and the other one was out of the writings of Gandhi.

I was listening to a talk show one day at lunchtime. There was a caller who had an issue with her sister. Although it had absolutely nothing to do with me, somehow it morphed into my new mission. The caller was complaining that Christmas was coming and that she always bought stuff for her sister's kids, but her sister never bought her kids anything. Her question was, "Should I continue to buy them stuff when my kids get nothing?" The psychologist hosting the said, "Oh, I get it. Your sister is such a selfish nasty person that your solution is to be just like her?"

Through that radio show, I saw that everyone in my family was the same. We had all modeled my father's behavior with our inability to love one another. Later that day, I was eating Chinese food and happened on a quote from Gandhi in a fortune cookie. Not knowing about who he was, I unrolled the small piece of paper. It simply stated, "Be the change you want to see in the world." Those words resonated through me in a powerful way. Be the change...

On that day, I decided I would be the change in my family that would stand for love. Wanting nothing in return, I decided I would model love to the one person that needed it most and was the least deserving, my father.

I would set the example. I would not continue the pattern of hatred and anger any longer. I would stand for love and I would be love. As uncomfortable and awkward as it was, I would force love into his life against his will. I would expect no reciprocation. If nothing else, I would clearly yell out to the world, "The abuse stops here." My first letter to my father went something like this.

> Dad, I realize we haven't talked in a long time and I
> told you I hate you. The truth of the matter is, I was

very angry at you, and yes, there were many times that I hated you. I have been in therapy for a while now and I am starting to heal. I have learned through my work in therapy that "hurt people, hurt people" and it is very possible that someone hurt you as a child. I am sorry if they did. It makes me sad. I also learned that it is possible no one ever showed you love as a child. I am sorry for that too. I have decided that I am going to continue to love you dad, no matter what. There is nothing you can do to make me stop loving you. I am going to continue to send you cards to remind you that I love you unconditionally.

Love Lauri

47

I CONTINUED TO SEND LETTERS AND CARDS TO MY FATHER ON A regular basis for the next five years. I did not receive a response for the first two years, but I never expected one anyway. It just felt good knowing I had broken the chain.

In addition to my letters to dad, more than anyone, I knew I owed my mom a huge amends. Even though she wasn't the healthiest of people I knew, she stuck by me through all of my insanity. I think the fact that I was a mom now made the whole thing even clearer. I couldn't imagine how many sleepless nights she must have spent worrying when her crazy daughter did things like hitchhike to the river. Or how many times she thought she was going to get the call from the police telling her that I was finally dead. Understanding the love for a child through my relationship with Madie, I knew that I had hurt her immensely. In an effort to repay my mom for the pain I had caused her, I made an effort to spend time with her on a regular basis. Starting off with a letter to her making a formal amends for how much I had hurt her, I made a commitment to take her to dinner one night a week.

Two days before Christmas the phone rang and a lady on the other end said "Is Lauri there?" "Yes, I said, this is Lauri." She said, "We have you on our list of foster moms, and we have a fifteen year old here who ran away from Vegas. Her dad was sexually abusing her and her mom left at birth. She jumped on a Greyhound bus and headed out to California alone. She is in custody now. I am wondering if you have space for her."

I was still on her first sentence in my mind—*you have me on A LIST?! I am a foster mom? I can pick up ANY kid! I am a FOSTER MOM!!!* I had gone though the classes for Andy, but when my sister took him back, I never gave it another thought. In the next few seconds it actually hit me, I AM A FOSTER MOM!!!!

It is Christmas time... we have an extra room...we decorated it for a girl...I could give a kid a life for Christmas! She needed a mom... She was alone... I was a foster mom! We had a brand new house and her room was just waiting for her...I couldn't believe it...It couldn't have been more perfect. "Yes!" I shrieked. "We have plenty of room! When can I get her?" I would have jumped in my car that second! But since it was too late in the day, the lady scheduled the pickup for the following day after work. At this point, I was thirty three years-old and Madie was fifteen. Madie and the new girl were the same age. It was absolutely perfect. The entire next day, I was so anxious I could barely think.

When I walked into the Children's Home, I still felt like a juvenile delinquent. Vividly aware that they had seen my file with the prostitution and stuff, I felt like all of the workers were thinking...*Okay here comes our "test" case.* I stopped in at the front window and told the worker that I was here to pick up a child. He asked me for my driver's license and insurance card and looked my name up on the system. Within a few minutes, he said, "Ok, proceed back." When he popped the lock to release the large steel door, I was transported back in my mind to Juvenile Hall. My anxiety escalated.

When I entered the waiting room, there was a "control desk" exactly like the ones we had in juvie, but now the people behind it were my age. They took my paperwork and asked me to be seated. There were large plastic couches everywhere and colorful animals painted on the walls, kind of like a big kid's room. I was excited, happy and petrified all at the same time. For me, it felt like a "break out." Remembering how much I hated these places when I was a kid, I felt like today would be the day it would all turn around. Instead of going in, I was going to help to break a kid out! I knew we were just walking out normally and legally, but something about it felt too good to be true! The door to the right of the control desk was the one the kids would enter though. Every time the door swung open my heart pounded. For the next thirty minutes, I was a mess. Each time the door opened, I reacted. First a large fat boy, then a tiny kid you could barely see behind the desk, a few counselors assisting toddlers...By the time she came out I was pacing the floor, unable to sit still.

When she walked through the door, all time stopped. Out walked a beautiful child, shoulder length, silky black hair, normal height, but thin as could be. She looked like she hadn't eaten in weeks. Her big brown eyes told so much. One glance at her and I could see that she was scared to death. She scanned the visitor's room with discernible dread in her eyes, unsure of which one they had picked to be her new mom. I would later find out that her step mom had abused her as well. I can't imagine the terror of being assigned a family you've never met. She stood perfectly still as her eyes made their way from one side of the room to the other. There were several older women and a tiny ancient Japanese lady who looked to be pushing eighty sitting on the couch to my right. Panicked that this might be her new mom, her eyes stopped at the old woman and she swallowed hard. She was jolted back to awareness when the lady at the control desk, barked, "Papers please!"

Returning her attention to the desk, she handed the small stack of release papers over and stood, frozen. The worker took the papers and with her head still down, pointed over in my direction and said, "Your new foster mom is waiting." Julie spun around quickly. Our eyes met and I waved and smiled. I could see the relief in her eyes. *Thank God they aren't sending me with granny...*

In the next few moments, while they worked on the release papers, God surrounded me. My recent life on the streets flashed before my eyes. Empty and lifeless, nothing left to believe in, left for dead on that canyon road. And now here...How did this happen? I am a heroin addict...a prostitute...And now I am here to pick up a kid? I realized that things had changed and all...I was sober, working, doing well... but still. How does child welfare services choose an ex-heroin addict, ex-prostitute to be the perfect mom? Although I felt like I would be the best mom she ever had, I still couldn't understand it. Something had occurred here...something I would never be able to explain. A judge from a much higher place had slammed his gavel down on my life and demanded grace. The tears welled up in my eyes as the realization hit me. It was a miracle. Just as a group of passersby see a statue, shed a tear and claim a miracle, I made my claim that day. It is a miracle when the life of a prostitute was saved so that she could return to the trenches and reclaim the wounded children left behind. I couldn't have planned this. By some sort of strange magical power and without any planning on my part, I was somehow guided back to the very place I started. On this day, I would have the power to intercept someone else's path. But more than that, I would get to be her mom.

I was so excited to have Julie, I chattered all the way home. By the time we got to the house, she was completely aware of where we were going, and who would be there. She knew all about Madie and all of the animal's names and where we found them. Each one had a story. Knowing how scary it is to go to a strange place as a kid, I tried to build her comfort level as much as I could. She knew that she would have her own room and that we had bought new sheets that were still in the package, so she wouldn't feel like she was sleeping in someone else's bed. This had always been important to me. I remember the smells of the different homes and the creepiness of sleeping in a stranger's bedding. She needed her own things with familiar smells on them so that she felt safe.

Desperate for the mom that she had never experienced, by day two, she was calling me mom. So excited that she finally had a mom, she used the word every chance she could. Sometimes she would shove the word mom in to the same sentence three times. "Mom I am going to do my laundry mom, okay mom?" This did not fare well with Madie. Although they hit it off immediately, and she was excited to have a sister, she had no idea that this meant she would have to share her mom. Equally proportionate to Julie's need to say the word mom was her need to be nurtured. Even though she was my same size and weight, around 110 pounds at the time, spotting me sitting on the couch in the TV room, she would plop right down on my lap! Sensing her desperate need to be loved, I worked with her to set appropriate boundaries and taught her to sit next to me and we would hold hands. Again Madie was not happy.

On our first night out to dinner, Julie, Madie and I went for Italian food on the lake, one of our favorite spots. Half way home Julie announced, "Oh mom, you left money on the table, I grabbed it for you!" She had taken the tip.

Up until this point, at the age of fifteen, she had never been to a restaurant. We had no insight into what her life was like before, but the damage was evident as the days went on. Her emotions were all backwards and sideways; she would be sad when we were happy and laugh when something went wrong. It was never as apparent as the day her social worker visited. Her social worker was about thirty-five-years-old and very friendly. We loved having her visit. It was mid-February and the wood steps leading up to our porch were covered with a thin coat of ice. She had made it up to the door safely, spent about an hour at the house talking to us and then headed out. As I opened the door, I warned her, "Please be careful, it's very slippery." Holding her folder in one hand and a large coffee from Starbucks in the other, she turned to say one last goodbye as she proceeded down the steps. Suddenly, her foot hit the ice and flew up, throwing her whole body down on the steps. She banged down the steps with a force that was excruciating to watch. By the time she hit the bottom step, there was coffee all over her and Julie was laughing hysterically! Struggling between helping her and closing the door so that the social worker didn't hear Julie's out of control cackling, I shut the door and reopened it several times before instructing Julie to go downstairs so I could go outside to help the worker.

Over the next several months, we all worked together, Madie, Julie and I to learn appropriate boundaries, and establish everyone's role in the family. Struggling with their jealousy for the first few months, I couldn't do anything right. They fought about everything. If I brought home Del Taco, with a seven up and a coke, they fought over who would get what. One day in the midst of a heated fight, I broke. Entering Madie's room, I sat on the bed and started to cry. This was very out of character for me, as I am not the emotional type, but it had built up so long I couldn't take it. I walked in and yelled, "Stop! I love you both! I can't take it anymore! It isn't going to be perfect! I will not always have two cokes! It doesn't mean I love you any less! It only means I bought two different drinks!" Whatever I said must have penetrated because they never argued over my love for them again. Over the next year, Julie's need for attention normalized and the girls grew closer to one another.

48

SEVERAL MONTHS LATER, WHILE SITTING IN THE TV ROOM ALONE, the phone rang. I will never know who the man was on the other end, but on this day Jodi's life would be forever changed. When I picked up the phone, the man said, "Hey, is this Lauri?" "Yes," I replied. In a soft, almost secretive tone he said, "Word on the streets is Denise is dead." I recognized his heavy Hispanic accent and cholo lingo instantly. He was from the other side, the "old world." "Word on the streets?" I replied. "What does that mean?" Although I knew what he was saying, I wasn't going to accept it. Denise, of course, was Jodi's mom. How would this gangster have gotten my number? It had been years since she left. I was immediately defensive and began shooting questions at him. "Word on the streets? What kind of thing is that? How valid is word on the streets? How did you get my number? Who are you?" He ended by saying, "Word on the streets lady. It's real. You figure it out." Then he hung up.

Sitting silently with the dead phone in my hand, I just stared at it. *Are you kidding? Word on the streets?* By this time, Jodi was doing better. And now this! Calling to tell her a stranger had just called and told me *word on the streets is that your mom's dead* just wasn't reasonable! I was considering my options when I remembered the tour of the coroner's office in my child development class. This was where they took people who had died. I knew if this information was accurate, they could tell me. I immediately dialed information and got the local coroner's number. The man that answered connected me right to the coroner. In a rattled state of mind, I rambled off the details of the past few minutes. Then he said, "What is the full name of the person you are looking for?"

I spelled it out for him. He said, "Let me put you on hold one minute." The next minute seemed like a lifetime. I heard a click as he reentered the line. The words stung as he bluntly said, "Yes, we have a body here with that name on it."

I hung up the phone and tears poured out as the magnitude of the situation hit me. *No...she's not gone...Dead...? It couldn't be...Oh, Denise...why didn't you come to us for help...? What happened to you...?* I wept as I pictured the body of the broken girl who came to my meeting so long ago, now lifeless in the cold freezer. I was devastated. Preparing myself for one of the most difficult things I would ever have to tell someone, I prayed and dialed Jodi's number. She answered on the second ring.

"Jodi?" "Yeah, it's me, what's up?" she replied. Still the same outspoken little girl I met years ago, she was tough as nails. "Something happened to your mom." I knew the minute it came out, it was not the way to begin. Her response only confirmed that. "What happened to my mom? Is she hurt?" Now she thought she was just hurt. I knew I should have just come out with it. Not wanting to delay the inevitable any longer, I said, "No Jodi, your mom is dead."

"What?" she said in a trembling voice. Having no other way to explain it, I recounted the events of the past few minutes. Jodi quickly transitioned from her present state of shock to anger. "Where is she?" she demanded. "At the coroner's office," I responded. "I will pick you up now, we will go down together." "No," she commanded. "I will go alone! I will go down there and see if it's my mom!" I wanted to comfort her, but I was all too familiar with her ongoing anger and stubbornness. Even though it had been years since she first stepped into our home, she had yet to deal with the abandonment and unfortunately it came out in the forms of anger and control in all areas of her life. Much like I was as a child, she wanted to be alone, trusted no one and needed no one. Wanting to do the right thing, I thought, *Lauri, this is no time to make a squabble.* That day Jodi went down the coroner's office and identified her mother's body alone.

Somehow, the death of her mother brought about forgiveness for the lady who left her behind that I never would have thought possible. Learning that her mother drowned in a bathtub after overdosing on cocaine, something became clear to Jodi. Her mother wasn't capable of being a mother because she never loved herself. She died as she lived, alone. For the next few weeks, I struggled with God. Having her walk out of court years ago was nothing compared to this betrayal. I was really angry. Why would a loving God put a child through all this? I simply didn't get it. Even though I was sure I would never understand his reasoning, the truth is my "aha moment" still hadn't arrived quite yet.

Over the next few years, Jodi and I got closer. Understanding that she would always be guarded, I took whatever she gave of herself. She was nineteen years-old when I had landed her a job as a receptionist at the large computer company where I worked. By that time she had also given birth to my first grandson. He was beautiful. Sitting alone with him one morning when he was almost two years old, he played with checkers on my bed. In a language that only he could understand, he chattered away while making little piles with the chips. Taking in the innocence and beauty of who he was and everything that Denise missed, I mourned her loss. Tears falling from my eyes, I spoke to her. *"Do you see your grandson Denise? Isn't he beautiful?" Someday I may understand why I was spared and she wasn't but on that day, I mourned her loss deeply.* Over the next few years, Jodi drifted closer and apart several times. Never able to reach her, I loved her when she allowed me to, and accepted each time she pulled away. Knowing what she had been through, I understood.

It was about nine months after Jodi came to work with me that one of the top salesmen at my firm was offered a job elsewhere. He was hired as the CEO of a local consulting firm. Wanting to take me with him as the Director of Information Technology, he offered me $90,000, a car allowance and an office. He basically said if I need anything else to make the decision, I would get it. I couldn't believe the offer, but I was conflicted. Having been at my company for almost five years, I had a sense of loyalty toward them. After talking to my senior management and considering the endeavor, I decided to take the offer. I was only into the new job a few weeks when I realized I had made a mistake. It was a new office, so there were no engineers, the salesmen were not seasoned and they had no customers. In an effort to make it work, I sold all of the new deals, wrote the contracts, hired the best engineers I knew from school and started the ball rolling.

When the man who ran my office started making advances on me, I reported him to the owner of the company and asked that I be reassigned. When the owner told me I had to "deal with it" or resign, I gave my notice. I was not upset with them. I knew that I was the new "guy" on the block and they had no history with me. For all they knew, I was one of those crazy people who cries lawsuit at every corner. I understood the complexity of the situation, but I also understood I could not stay and work for this man. I had lost all respect for him. Standing outside of the small office that day, panicked by being jobless, I was devastated. Not being a smoker at the time, I had bummed a smoke off the receptionist and squatted outside as they cut my final paycheck.

I had come too far at this point. I could not let it all go downhill now. The new Lauri, a morphed version of Cindy, rose up that day and spoke to me. *You know Lauri, you've been running this place. Think about it. You brought in the customers, you wrote the contracts, you hired the engineers and you lead the team. What did they give you that you didn't already have? A fax? A printer? You can get that at Staples. With a few simple things and a cell phone, you can do this yourself!*

That day I made a deal with myself. I would give it thirty days. If I didn't have income coming in within thirty days, I would go out and get a regular job. Lord knows I didn't want to be one of those stubborn people who would watch their world come crashing down while they held onto unrealistic dreams that never came to fruition. I was a parent. I had to be logical. I had enough money in the bank to carry me sixty days, so with the amount of time it would take to get payroll setup on a new job, I knew thirty days was my limit.

This would be the first time I would truly MASTER something, using every part of the tools I had learned and Cindy's advice, "it takes money to make money." The next day I went out, and with the money from my check, I bought a printer/fax and I called a customer whom I had worked for years ago and liked my work. I said, "Peter, I was wondering. If I decided to start my own company, would you have any work I could do for you?" "Well, certainly Lauri!" he replied. "I have some work right now that you could do. Why don't you come by next week and see me."

I made a few more calls and they all went just as well. Then I called the five best engineers I knew. I told them I had a great idea and I setup a coffee meeting with them. We all sat down in a coffee shop and I laid out the master plan. "Look, you guys know how it is. We work for a company and they charge $125 an hour for us and they pay us $45. I have a plan that will make us all rich. I will sell the deals. I will charge the customer $125 an hour and pay each of you $100 per hour. I will do the sales, the contracts, and all of the accounting." They loved the plan! With the utmost confidence in my ability to close a deal, we came up with a name that night and I filed the fictitious business name the next day and we all got business cards. I started making calls like crazy. I **maintained** the belief we could do it, I **added** stuff every day as I got our office together, I **saw** it on the business cards and the letterhead, and I **talked** about it constantly. There was no one to **eliminate** because everyone I talked to knew we could pull it off and as for **relationships**, the guys on the team were some of the most brilliant people I knew. By this point I had been Cindy for so long, people had the same confidence in me that I had in her. Like Nathaniel had taught us about talking about it as if it existed, when I spoke to the customers I never said, *"We are thinking about starting a business, or we are considering,"* I would say I just started a great new company. Much like I learned while selling insurance, I gave them the bonus right up front. I would say, "I have the best engineers I know and to top it off, no salesmen! We have found the biggest problem with computer consulting these days is the communication barrier between the sales team and the engineering team. Now you can talk to the engineers directly; no more shmoozy sales guys or over-priced deals. Knowing exactly what it takes to get the job done, we will get it right the first time." The customers loved it!

I called people all day every day. I was committed to being successful, and everyone knew it. I met with the engineers daily to talk about our plans for success. I closed two of our biggest deals right off the bat. With all five guys working, I was making $125 an hour for myself and $25 off each of them, so I started my new job at $250 an hour. The first year, I brought in over $300,000 with plenty of time off to relax with the kids.

The part that always inspired me most was that when I lost my job, I was at a crossroads. The choice was to plunge into a deep depression of sorrow or to create something. We had nothing when I first picked up the phone, just a small printer, some cards and an idea. I had just lost my job. But I refused to let my circumstances weigh me down. Inspired by the successful people before me, I changed my perception from that of being at the bottom, to the vision of being at the top. In a space where anything was possible, the whole world was open to me. I had no limitations. I clearly saw where I was going and I spoke it into existence! I picked up the phone and I painted my vision into the minds of others with an excitement that was undeniable. For the first time in my life, I mastered a dream! Over the next few weeks I was in heaven. I thought this was "it." The grand finale, everything I had ever wanted and dreamed of. Little did I know, it was only a test bed for what lay ahead.

Two years after I started writing letters to my father, he started writing back. At first it was just a card with two words on it, Love Dad. I understood that he was doing the best he could. Realizing how broken he was, I also began calling him. Committed to being the person who would stand for love in our family, I would simply call to ask how he was doing and tell him that I loved him. Our conversations were short and limited, but I didn't care. I was going to spoon feed him love whether he liked it or not.

A few years later we started to meet for dinner when he was in California or I was in New York. We never spoke again about what happened. After all we had been through, now we just focused on the new stuff. As our relationship slowly grew, I focused on his good qualities and our commonality. He is very good with money. I enjoyed hearing what he knew about investing and he enjoyed telling me. We both love motorcycles, so that was a good area for discussion, and after he retired, I was able to share my love for remote control planes and computers with him. Our conversations were very robotic since I was not used to having a dad and he was not used to having a daughter. I learned a lot about my dad over the next few years, but the thing I learned that was most important, I found out through a casual discussion with my foster daughter Julie.

Madie, Julie and I went to New York City for the Fourth of July. On our second night in town, my father met us for dinner. This would be his first meeting with Julie. Both of my girls knew about my childhood and that I was with "being the change for my dad." They knew me well enough to thoroughly understand why it was so important. While waiting for our food my father was making casual conversation with Julie. "So you are a foster child?" he asked. "Yes," she responded. Then he said something I could have never imagined. "Did you know I was a foster child?" he asked.

"No" she replied. My ears suddenly perked up, but I dared not speak for fear of missing the rest of this. "Yes," he responded. "I lived in an orphanage until I was three. Then a very nice lady took me home. Her name was Ana."

I couldn't believe it. That nice lady who used to bury me in her long hugs and shower love and food on us was a foster mom! Recognizing that since he never mentioned this before, he must have had some hardship, I dropped it for the time being. I understood he was just trying to make a connection with Julie.

I reflected back on being a child and wondering how such a loving woman could have raised such an angry man. Now I knew. My only regret was that by the time he told us, my Grandma Ana had passed on. We would not discuss my father's childhood again until ten years later, when he finally broke.

49

IT WAS ALMOST A YEAR AND A HALF LATER WHEN I WALKED OUT OF my house one day and noticed that there were "FOR SALE" signs everywhere in our neighborhood! I had been so busy working, I had hardly noticed. Not understanding where everyone was going, I asked my next-door neighbor. He was just pulling the trash bin up his driveway when I approached him. "Hey Brian, I was wondering. Don't you think it's weird that everyone is moving out?" He looked at me quite seriously and said, "Oh no Lauri, it is time. You see, our homes have appreciated to a point where they may not go up anymore. This is how it works…" Having known me for the past four years, he and his wife were accustomed to bringing me up to speed on the "facts of life." They were aware that I had missed out on a few years and were totally accepting of my shortcomings. "Now is the time to sell your home. Take the money you make on it and put it down on a larger home. You keep doing this, and before you know it, you own a wonderfully large home! You work your way up!" At this time, both Julie and Madie were eighteen. This was our home, the home we always wanted. We were supposed to move? I was so confused.

It was two weeks later when I decided to have a realtor visit. Having now completed the initial paperwork, she left the *for sale* sign leaning on my front porch with instructions to place it on the lawn that afternoon, I knelt on my front lawn and had a conversation with God. It went something like this: *God this is our dream house. You brought us here and gave us this home as a gift. I don't know if it's right to sell it. It is everything I ever wanted. They tell me to do "your will," but frankly I don't know what your will is. I am going to make a deal with you. If it sells in under 30 days, that means you wanted me to sell it; if it doesn't that means you don't want me to sell it and I will remove the sign.* I pushed the stick into the hole in the ground, covered it up and walked back into the house.

Three weeks later, our house sold for more than any other house in neighborhood. Sure it was immaculate inside, but with the lumpy lawn and sparse gardening, I thought, *How the heck?* Since I hadn't *really* thought about moving, I hadn't been looking for new house. But now that my home was sold, I thought I'd better find a place or we would end up homeless. On that beautiful summer morning, even though I didn't understand his decision, I thanked God for his direction, pulled my motorcycle out of the garage and jumped on it to ride through the canyon looking for homes for sale.

About five miles from my house, I saw the first sign of the day. On a large hill, four colorful flags waved in the wind next to a big sign that read "New Homes." As I climbed the tree-lined hill with my motorcycle the gargantuous homes came into view. This neighborhood was way above my pay grade, but since I was there, I figured I would walk through anyway. It would give me a chance to see more recent trends in décor. I was acutely aware they weren't going to welcome me in the new homes office anyway, given the fact that I was wearing my favorite torn jeans, biker boots and riding a motorcycle. I was sure I didn't fit the part of a potential buyer.

When I walked through the door, the lady at the desk closest to me looked up from her paperwork and blurted out, "Lauri! I am going to sell you your second home!" *It gives me chills just to write it today, because God surely couldn't have been more in the mix on this one.* Turns out the lady from Kaufman & Broad that sold me my first home had been offered a better job as a Sr. Account Executive with Centex Homes just a few months prior. When I walked through the door, she recognized me immediately. It had been four years since she sold me my first home. Amused by her remark about me purchasing a home in this expensive neighborhood, I smiled and replied, "Yeah right. Not in this neighborhood! I am just coming through to look at the paint!" She smiled back at me and in a reassuring tone stated, "Look Lauri, we did this once, we can do it again. Just go home, get your taxes, bring them back and let's just look at it. I am sure you are making more money now; let's just see what we can do!" There we were again looking at the numbers. When she said "You can do this Lauri," there were two things going on in my head. Number one, *well she was right last time. I bought that house and four years later, I had 100,000 in equity.* Number two, *I should call someone for advice.* Knowing my dad had a wealth of knowledge when it came to investments and realizing how valued he would feel if I picked him to help mentor me in this decision, I called him.

I quickly brought him up to speed on what had happened and the fact that I needed to buy a new home. I told him that I knew from our conversations that he was savvy with money. I told him how much I had in cash and the purchase price. I also told him I was scared. I could tell by his voice that he was moved by the fact I was calling him. There was a nervous excitement detectible. It was at that point that I realized, he never had to the opportunity to mentor any of us kids. After the abuse it was over and done; he lost his role completely as a parent. This was his first chance to "really" be a dad again. He started by asking me questions about terms and rates. I communicated the information back and forth between him and the sales lady. Then he said "Lauri, I am going to tell you something very important. The difference between people who make it and people who don't is their ability to take risks. If you react to situations in fear, you will never get anywhere. Successful people take risks." I closed by saying "Ok dad, I trust your experience and I will do it." That simple call healed mountains. From that day forward he had an excitement in his voice that I had never heard before. He was part of something in our lives, something good.

An hour later, I was signing the last of the paperwork for a four-bedroom house with a loft. When I walked out of the office that day, I was on top of the world. I looked back to wave goodbye to that lady who had helped me for the second time and it seemed almost surreal. My little sister Alyssa always says "Is it ODD or is it GOD?" Clearly that lady was Angel number 5. Placed in my path at just the right moment, two times! She unknowingly prepared me each time for what was coming next.

Within two years I was acutely aware of why I had been led to purchase that home. When the children's agency found out that I had moved into a larger home, the phone rang off the hook! I became recognized as the woman who would take the most difficult kids to place and they couldn't give 'em to me fast enough! God led me to a larger house because he had more children for me! Over the next few years, we became accustomed to a full house. There were times when I had four to five teen girls all at the same time! Passing around the story at the agency of the girl that grew up in the system and became a foster mom, they just kept on calling. Just like I was drawn to the kids in the group home, the kids I took were drawn to me. Knowing I had walked their path, they requested time after time to be placed with me. Each time they called me from the agency; it was like that first Christmas. I couldn't wait to pick up the next one!

By the time I finish this book, I will have had twenty-four children in my home. My daughter Julie, who was my first foster child, is now twenty-seven. She is married and lives down the street from me. Still closer than ever, Madie was the bridesmaid at her wedding.

During the time Julie lived with me, she denied all contact with her father. Unable to deal with the toxic relationship, she shut the door on her old life when I became her mom. The workers pushed for just one visit or even a letter, knowing that her healing depended on the healing of her past, but she was adamant; no visits.

On her eighteenth birthday, I asked Julie if I could meet her dad. "I won't tell him where you are, just that you are okay." Her answer was, "You can do whatever you want, but I don't want anything to do with him." *Remembering what it was like when I was the bad parent, remembering the nights I cried myself to sleep, knowing now that most of the parents were abused children themselves, and all along hating what he did to her, for some reason that I still can't explain, I had to see him.*

When I arrived at the restaurant, he was already there. Although he avoided eye contact as much as possible, his blaring-red, bloodshot eyes told all. Still smelling of stale booze from the night before, I was surprised he had driven so far without crashing. Knowing what it was like to be trapped in a world so painful you needed to anesthetize yourself to deal with it, I felt his pain. Even though most people stopped at the fact that he had made inappropriate advances to his daughter, for some reason, I saw beyond it that day. I saw a man condemned to hell. Sitting at the table with me, he was so far down he couldn't even look at me. Like I had learned to do with my dad, that day I showed love to a man that was not only not deserving, but was unable to accept it.

I looked at him and said, "I want you to know that although I have had your daughter for the past three years, I will always know that you are her dad. I have a daughter of my own. I know what it is like to be separated from her. Like you, I did some very bad things. I will never forget what it was like when she was taken from me. I felt like the devil. I knew I had failed. I hated myself for who I had become. Unable to explain it, I couldn't resolve how I hurt someone I loved so much. The more I thought about it, the more I plummeted. It got to a point that I couldn't even get up anymore. A few years back, I met some people. These people were just like my friends, except they didn't use drugs or drink. I started to hang out them. In fact, I surrounded myself with them. Soon after that, I got my life back and was able to be a mom again." Not saying much more we continued eating and made small talk. My intention was not to fix him, only to let him know I wasn't judging him. When we left I gave him a friendly hug and told him to call me anytime to find out how she was doing. When I walked away, I felt good. Like God was smiling on me.

He called me the very next day. He said, "Lauri, guess what I did today? I went to one of those meetings you told me about with the nice people. Today is my first day of sobriety."

It was seven years later that Julie married her soul mate. The little girl that I had met so many years ago, had become one of the most beautiful, confident women I knew, and she was my daughter. I had the honor of walking her up the aisle on the happiest day of her life. As I looked over to the other side of her, there stood her father with seven years of sobriety. Tears pouring from his eyes, he looked at me and mouthed, *it's because of you that I am here.* The tears ran down his cheeks and his chest convulsed with emotion. Tears immediately filling my eyes, I felt the intensity of his emotion. I took my finger and pointed up towards the clouds and mouthed back, *it is because of him that we are here.* After the ceremony, crying simultaneously, I took him aside and said, "It is because of him. I was dead. He picked me up and plucked me out of hell. I would not be here otherwise. I only gave you what I was given: Forgiveness." With tears in his eyes, he smiled, gave me a big hug and walked off.* Since that day, I would learn over and over again that the most powerful kind of love is that which is undeserved. Julie and her father remain close today. He started his own business, married a sober woman and remains gratefully sober.

50

RITA CAME TO LIVE WITH ME WHEN SHE WAS SIXTEEN, AFTER failing several placements. Most of the failures were due to her non-compliant behavior, but unfortunately some were also due to abuse at the hands of a foster parent. Rita was different than the others in that she didn't choose me, I chose her. Her sister Susan was living with me at the time and Rita was in a different foster home. It was common knowledge that they hadn't communicated with each other since Susan escaped from the home in which they were being sexually abused. To date, there was no single time when both girls were stabilized in one place long enough to see each other. The day Rita's foster mom called me and asked if she could arrange a visit so that the girls could see each other, Susan and I were ecstatic. She was finally going to reunite with her long lost sister. When the morning came Susan sat nervously in the living room and I responded to the knock at the door. The foster mom was young, like me, and Rita was about fifteen, very pale, a bit homely looking and thin. She, like Susan, looked nervous.

We all sat down in the living room, but neither Susan nor I was prepared for what happened next. Without warning, Rita launched into a hair-curling pitch, *"HOW COULD YOU LEAVE ME THERE? YOU LEFT ME WITH HIM! YOU FUCKING LEFT ME WITH HIM AND HE RAPED ME! YOU KNEW HE WOULD RAPE ME! YOU LEFT ME FOR HIM! I HATE YOU!!! I FUCKING HATE YOU!!! YOU LEFT ME BEHIND! HOW COULD YOU DO THAT TO ME? I FUCKING HATE YOU! WHY DIDN'T YOU TAKE ME WITH YOU?!!! I HATE YOU!!*

By the time she finished she was standing over Susan, face beet red with a fiery anger, shaking with rage. Susan was huddled into the smallest space on the couch, shaking behind a large pillow that she used to protect herself from what might be coming. Afraid that Rita would launch on top of her and start beating her, I had moved in closer. When she was finally out of breath, the room fell silent. Unable to come up with any words suitable at this point, I took a deep breath and released. Completely wiped out emotionally, I muttered the only thing that crossed my mind. "I could use a cigarette." I didn't smoke, but not able to have a drink, I needed something. Then the foster mom said, "Come on, it's done, let's go." At that moment it became crystal clear to me that this crazy lady had planned this. She actually thought it would be healthy to have Rita come over to release her anger on Susan. Two days later Susan was gone. Unable to deal with what had happened, she returned to drugs and the bad people who had been molesting her.

A week later a call came in from Susan's social worker, Greg. "Lauri, I know this is going to be a weird call, but I had to make it anyway. I know Susan is gone, but Rita's foster mom dropped her off this morning. She needs a placement. I know she was a mess when you saw her, but she really needs a home. I thought I would call you on the far out chance that maybe now that Susan left, since you have an opening, you would take her."

I couldn't have been happier. Even though she was hysterical the day I saw her, I knew the anger only too well. When I arrived to get her at the children's home, she was quiet. As we exited the facility, she walked beside me lugging the big sack that was slung over her shoulder containing all of her life's belongings. Embarrassed, she looked up at me and said, "I have one question. Why do you want me?" She was completely baffled as to why after the horrendous behavior she displayed in my home, I would have any interest taking her. I looked down at her and said, "Well I am assuming it was just one *very* bad day. I am sure you are not like that all of the time. I have had some bad days myself."

51

I T WAS 2:00 A.M. ABOUT A MONTH LATER WHEN I WAS AWOKEN IN THE middle of the night. At this point, I had three girls in the home. I was startled and confused. Did I hear a noise? I usually sleep with earplugs to avoid being woken by my kids, who are often chatting outside of my door. Not sure of what I heard, I sat up in bed, removed my earplugs and listened intently. Suddenly, I heard a subtle high-pitched tone. Still not sure of what I was hearing, I quietly made my way to my bedroom door and opened it slowly. The hall was pitch black and my eyes had begun to adjust to the light when I saw movement on the floor. Someone was in the bathroom. Then the sound began again, a soft whining, followed by a series of loud thuds, Bang! Bang! Bang! My heart was jolted into another dimension. Something was wrong, very wrong!

I rushed to the bathroom door, afraid of what I would find, but even more afraid of not knowing. Unaware of what is happening, I avoided turning on the light. As I reached the bathroom, Rita came into view. Her body was drenched with sweat; her hair was pressed against her face. Screaming and banging her head against the wall with an intensity that it hurt me to witness, I rushed to her. When she saw me she screamed out, "WHY?!!!! Why did my mother leave me? Those men hurt me! She let those men hurt me! I don't want to sleep! They're here again! I fucking hate myself!" Bang! Bang! Bang! She slammed her head against the wall over and over again. *All of a sudden I am twelve again. I am in the bathroom; my dad is at the door. "I fucking hate you! I hate you God!" I throw myself against the wall and scream, "I fucking hate you! I hate you, God!" My head hits the wall over and over and over again…. Bang! Bang! Bang!*

I am shaking. Having processed no thought of what to do next, I am catapulted back into the bathroom with Rita. *Do not turn on the light, scary…no light…Talk quietly…No noises…No big noises…quiet voices… Do not touch…Touch is scary…*

On the floor with her now. I quietly whisper into the darkness. "I am here with you sweetie…it is okay now…the bad man is gone…The bad man is gone…we protect children here…we don't hurt children… We are on the other side now…no more hurt honey…no more bad people here…Please don't hurt Rita anymore…" *The creaking of a door behind me interrupted the intensity of the moment. My eyes now adjusted, I turned my head. I see Mary quietly tiptoeing from her room. Her large eyes tell me she is scared.*

I put my finger over my lips as if to say, *shhhh*. Now Yvette is coming. Quietly they collapse to the floor, falling into the darkness by Rita. The only sound is Rita's heavy rhythmic, breathing. She is rocking back and forth slowly with her arms wrapped tightly around her legs and her head tucked between her knees. The girls gently put their hands on Rita and they too begin to cry. They are hugging each other. Rita lets out a soft cry and hugs them in return. Although the small room still remained dark, the light in the room that night was undeniably brilliant as we walked together out of the darkness. Wiping the tears from Rita's face, we all stood up together and walked downstairs. Although I don't normally encourage smoking, this is one night I would let the mountains be mountains and the little things lie. As they sat in the garage, passing the cigarette around with their wet faces, I closed my eyes and thanked God. *Thank you God for letting me be twelve again, thank you God for my father. Thank you for my little bathroom so long ago, for it is in the pain of my childhood that I have been blessed with the power to take the hand of a child who is in the darkness; and lead them out. Thank you for having me go before them and showing me the way out…*

Rita was one of my harder cases, but also one of my favorites. I learned a long time ago with Jodi that in order to help the children, I had to set clear boundaries and stick to them, or I wasn't helping anyone. I had to learn tough love. Struggling with drugs, alcohol and stealing,

I kicked her out and accepted her back several times. Tormented by the memories, she used drugs to escape. Today she is twenty-one, sober and lives in transitional housing. When she was with me, her sister returned to her life. We went on vacations together and spent holidays together as much as we could. Today she is one of the cutest, bubbly, happy kids you could ever meet.

Mary came to live with me when she was sixteen. She had been previously placed with her aunt and it didn't work out. Unable to get her to follow the rules, her aunt was done. Mary had been molested by her father since she was five and continued to allow him to molest her in the hope that it would keep him from getting to her little sister. While Mary was with me she worked with Sandy, my therapist, to heal from the abuse she endured as a child. Mary left shortly after her 18th birthday. They had changed her father's trial date so many times, she was becoming mentally handicapped by the anxiety of what was coming. Frozen in fear, she had graduated high school, but would not move forward. Weekly visits from a team of workers to plead with her to get into action had no effect. Six months after graduation, refusing to leave the house for school or work, I knew I had to do something. Unable to get her to budge, I suggested she move in with her best friend. Then she would have to get a job. Against her own will, after about four months of living with her friend, she was forced to rejoin the living due to lack of funds.

Within six months, Mary's day finally came. Terrified, but firm in her commitment to protect the lives of the other children he could hurt, and with courage that I couldn't even begin to imagine, she spoke out in "truth" to a room of strangers in the presence of the man who had terrorized her. Her father was sentenced to life in prison. If you ask Mary today if she loves her dad, she would most likely say, "Yes, he is my dad. But loving someone and speaking in truth can exist simultaneously in a healthy world." Mary's heroic words healed not only her wounds, but also that of her siblings. She was the eldest of five. With the absence of a healthy parent, she bore the load and protected them; she broke the chain. Although her sister was profoundly aware of what she had done that day, her brothers were still too small. Adopted out to another family, they would spend their young lives unaware of what had happened. But someday, when they get older, they will search out their family and discover that they had a big sister who loved them so much, that she stood up with courage against the monster who beat them to ensure he never hurt them or any other child again. As for her father, hearing the truth that day in court, he would be forced to look inward and begin to deal with the person he had become. The chain would finally be broken. Because of one brave girl, many future generations within that family will be forever free.

"Other" people say to me all the time, "You take in troubled teens? What, are you crazy?" And all I can think is: *You don't? Are you crazy?* I will never be able to transmit the magnitude of gifts I receive from each child who enters my home. The gift of seeing the eyes of a child transition from a hopeless, lifeless state to being excited about the brilliance of everything life has to offer. The moment they realize the cap is off! The moment they realize they are free! It is the most magnificent experience in the world. If I had a dollar for every time my entire body, every cell, has lit up with chills, I would be the richest woman alive. Now when they say, "Are you crazy?" I simply reply, "No I am blessed." I have met some of the bravest children in the world and I am deeply honored that they have let me be part of their lives.

About four years ago I was sitting in a recovery group meeting with friends and chatting. Excited to see each other after a few weeks of working and kid stuff, we failed to focus on anything other than each other. Whispering back and forth, we were more of a disruption than anything else. Realizing that people were looking at us, I decided to be a part of the group and break out of my little crew. I raised my hand to speak. The leader picked on me. I don't know what I said that day, but I remember it was something for the new people in the group. Something about how your life can change if you stop doing drugs. Feeling like I had put my two cents in, I continued to chat with my friends. After the meeting ended, we bolted out of the door to chat some more in the parking lot. I was outside just seconds when she appeared.

Walking up to me with teary eyes and nervous as can be, this young girl about thirty five stood in front of me. Distracted by her apparent need to say something, I turned from my friends and looked at her. "Is your name Lauri?" She said. "Yes" I responded. "Is it Lauri Burns?" She said. "Yes," I responded. It was at that moment that she lunged on me, wrapping her arms around me shaking and weeping. In a muffled voice with her head buried in my hair, she said, "I can't believe I found you!" When she pulled away, she looked at me and barely able to speak, she said, "You used to sit with me when I was a little girl. My name is Lauren. You used to sit with me when my mom did drugs. My mom committed suicide and my father died of a drug overdose. You were all I had. I thought I would never see you again."

I couldn't believe it. How she recognized me, I would never know. I was sixteen when she knew me. I was forty now. She told me, "It is your voice. I never forgot your voice." Lauren was delivered to me by God in a town remote from where I knew her, under circumstances that seem almost impossible.

Now I knew for sure, much like the experience with Bob, the broken man who saved my life, it was clear. At a time when I was more broken than ever, I delivered love and hope to a child at a level that would leave her forever changed. At that moment, I realized, I was her angel. I will never again question my ability to be "the person" for someone else. Today I realize that all it takes to save a life is love. Lauren and her children remain an integral part of our family today.

Over the next few years, I met the remainder of the thirteen people who would prepare me for my life's purpose. One was my friend and coworker, Nate. I met Nate while my team and I were working on a computer network at a hospital. Nate and I had a good deal of commonality right off the bat. He was Jewish, had been a foster parent in the past and was a single parent. It was immediately apparent to me that not only was Nate a great engineer, but even more than that, he was a great visionary. He had always had some kind of great invention or idea. About the time I met him he had an idea for a computer site where disabled and out of work engineers could work from home and provide computer support online.

He talked about it all of the time. Much like Nathaniel had described, he talked about it so vividly that even though I never actually saw it, I knew what it looked like. All along, I figured someday he would stop talking about it, and build it. I was dumbfounded when I learned that he never had to build it. He was so clear in his description that one day he walked into a room with a group of prominent business men and brought it to life so well that a week later he sold the idea to them in exchange for a check for $300,000 and an agreement to help them design it. Nate was my fourth teacher. Nate taught me that circumstances are not limiting unless you perceive them to be. People will invest in you simply because they believe in you. If you're trustworthy and reliable and people know it, they will want to help you. Lacking a product or goods, if they believe in you, they will invest in *you*.

My "aha" moment came about six years ago. I remember the very moment it hit me. I was attending a seminar. The man running the event told the audience to seek out areas of their life where we had failed to make amends to someone. He went on to explain that any unhealed relationships, no matter how small, would limit us. If you are carrying resentments towards others, you need to clear that to be successful. You don't have to allow them to be part of your life, but you need to let it go. Anger will kill you. Like wishing someone else would die and drinking the poison yourself, you are the only person the negative energy is affecting. Searching my head, with all of the work I had done, I came up dry. A few minutes later, it hit me so hard, it nearly broke me.

Standing up at a microphone in front of more than two hundred people, I made my formal amends directly to God. I cried and told him I was sorry. Sorry for not understanding why he put me with my father, sorry for abusing the beautiful body he blessed me with through drugs, suicide attempts and disgusting acts of sex. I was crying so hard I could barely breathe. He had given me so much and I had cursed him for the first twenty three years of my life. I apologized for hating him.

Sitting down in my chair, completely humiliated about what I had just shared and my outburst of emotion, he spoke to me through my thoughts. *Lauri, I was with you…I was always with you…It was a path* *that only few could endure, but I needed you to go there…I needed you to understand the depths of hating yourself…the lonely desperation of selling your body and feeling worthless…the loss of your child…I needed to prepare you…*And lastly he said something that I had yet to understand on that day, but today is clear. *Your task is much bigger than you could possibly understand now. But someday you will know that the depths you fell are equally powerful to the heights I need you to reach. You were chosen before you started. You have always been mine.*

It was at that moment that the "aha" hit. Convinced I had been a witch in a past life that was being punished by God as a child, I realized that day that my purpose was hidden in the punishment itself. When I looked back it was clear. I needed to draw from my experience as a child to heal the girls. Without my childhood, I would've never arrived here. It was so obvious, I don't know how I missed it. As I took in the miracle of everything that had transpired, I thought back to that verse I read in the bible so many years ago. "God can turn all bad to good." And now I knew.

God brought Jodi to me because he knew her mom was dying. The day she didn't return, he already knew she would leave. The day she died, he had me accept the call. How a stranger from the streets would know to call me, we would never know. But God knew. He always knew.

My whole perception shifted. Where I used to think I was being punished for being a witch in a past life, I saw that my whole life up until this point was preparing for what I would be in *this* life. I was not cursed, I was blessed. My whole life was *the study of the path out.*

If I used it to bring others out, my childhood would be the most powerful tool I had ever been given. When my mindset shifted, I became grateful for every single moment of my life…my dad, the institution, the streets… Only a person who has tapped into their own pain to heal others would ever understand. In the deepest, darkest valleys existed the greatest treasures of Heaven.

52

EVEN THOUGH I WAS ON TOP OF THE WORLD, I STILL HAD A FEW more people to meet before I would be ready to fulfill my purpose. I was at my mom's office one day when she referred me to a man a few doors down with a broken computer. Knowing that I was in the habit of fixing them, she always had a friend or a coworker in need. The man was a hypnotherapist of some sort. Luckily he didn't try to work his magic on me, but while I attempted to make his computer mouse work, he chatted excitedly. Even though I never learned his name, something he shared with me that day dramatically altered the rest of my life. I will never understand how a stranger's simple words took on such priority that they permeated my entire life, but for reasons I can't explain they did.

He told me that if you put fleas in a small jar and close the cover, they will jump so high that they will hit their heads on the cover. After a few hits they will learn to adjust their jump to avoid hitting their heads. When you release them, they will continue to jump "short." No matter how long they're out of the jar, they will never return to their full capacity for fear of hitting their heads again.

He explained to me that most people tend to live their lives this way. They limit their future based on what happened in the past. If they had been hurt in a relationship, they might say "I will never get that close again." If someone stole from them, they might say, "I will never trust anyone again." If a marriage ended badly, they may swear off marriage forever. He explained that when you limit your future based on what happened in your past, your future starts to look a lot like the very thing you are trying to avoid: Your past.

He solidified this statement by saying "If the fleas are going to continue to jump short, they might as well stay in the jar." Like the fleas, in order to live your life to the fullest, you must take note and realize the cap is off! Everything is available to you.

Now that I started thinking about it, I could see where my past still affected me. Even though my business and home life were great, there were other blind spots. First of all, I had limits on how close I would let a boyfriend get; and I certainly didn't need to get married. After all I was successful, and completely happy. I called it being "independent." In reality it was fear. Also, I had pets that I loved immensely, but none that I was really attached to since Pepper. I realized it was for fear of something happening to them. I didn't think I could handle the loss, so I avoided the attachment. Lastly, I was known for trying to fix everything myself, rather than reaching out to ask for help. Again, it looked like independence, but it was really not feeling worthy.

Because of these limits, I would never get to experience a close relationship, I would completely miss the joy of bonding with my animals, and I would never know what it is like to be nurtured by another human being, because I couldn't allow it. The bottom line is that a large portion of my life had been on "shutdown" for over twenty years. When I really starting processing what that man said, I realized I was missing out on parts of life that could bring me the greatest joy, for fear of things that had long since passed.

This man was my fifth teacher. Without this information, I would have allowed fear from the past to continue to define me. The end result would have been a limited life. I decided I wanted to have access to everything in life; I had to play "full out." It was after his talk that day that every time I heard my inner voice making a 'no' decision based on fears from the past, I did just the opposite. I decided I would risk it all. I lifted the lid off of my life. Over the next few years, one risk after another, I experienced a freedom of self expression I never knew possible.

My next teacher was Scotty. Scotty was one of the most energetic, happy people I knew. He was so happy and energetic that Madie nicknamed him "popcorn." Excited about life, he was literally unable to sit still for long. Scotty spent years studying models of success and common philosophies used by heroes. Scotty taught me about the three most powerful heroes that ever lived. Martin Luther King, Jr., Gandhi and Mother Theresa. Citing the life of Gandhi, he spoke of a short man who stopped a war by simply refusing to eat and speaking a "vision of peace." Then he went on to teach me about a black man who would change the history of the world by sharing his dream of freedom. And lastly he spoke of Mother Teresa, a poor nun with no money who would someday be known as "the most powerful woman alive" for the millions of suffering people she helped. After teaching me all of this, he said "Do you know the only difference between them and you? There is no difference. They, like you and I, were just people. Some people sit around thinking about how bad things are, and others get up and change them. It is you who will decide which kind of person you are." I really got what Scotty said, and I believed it. I knew if I had a mission, I could use this information boldly.

My next teaching came from a seventy year old Indian woman. She was a psychic whom my mom had taken me to for my birthday. Although her psychic capabilities were powerful, they had nothing to do with what she taught me. When she completed my reading, I reached into my purse to get the money and when I set it on the table, she looked at me with seriousness in her eyes and said, "One moment you will be a child swinging on a swing set, and the next moment you will be an old woman. Make sure to complete the important things before it is over." The message could not have been any clearer. The day God revealed my mission. I would act with an urgency I would not have had otherwise.

It was about five years ago when I began telling my story of transformation and the techniques that landed me where I am today. From the first time I recounted the details to a small group of women, I was aware there was something in the telling that people needed to hear. Over the past five years, I have been requested to speak at over two hundred venues. I show up wherever they request my presence in the hopes that God will transmit his healing powers through me and touch the hearts of those who so desperately need it. It has become customary after I speak for people to thank me. They often say, "It's so great everything you do. You are an angel." Clearly I never felt like an angel. The bottom line is I found my first family at the age of thirteen in a small group home in Stony Brook New York. Unable to bond with my birth family, those kids were the first family I ever knew. So, just like other people go home to their family, I go home to mine. I never felt like I was doing anything "great," I was only doing what was natural for me. Like breathing and eating, I longed to be with my family.

The more people praised me, the more aware I became that there was something else, something I had to do, something bigger. If this had been "the thing" I was supposed to do, I would feel it. I would know. But I didn't. I had an ongoing feeling that something was missing. When I told others, they thought I was crazy. Some even suggested that it was due to a lack of self-esteem, that I never felt good enough. I knew that wasn't it. They didn't get it. Like wind at my back, I could feel it. It was real.

It was about six months later that I began waking up at three a.m., one night after another. Confused by the fact that it was the same time every night, I was sure I was being woken by the sprinklers in the backyard. When I finally checked the system, it was set for six a.m. A few weeks later, very tired and frustrated, I was acutely aware that it was "time." My purpose was called and I needed to begin. The frustrating part was that I still had no idea what the heck I was supposed to do. I was only clear on the fact that it had something to do with system kids. A month later, extremely tired, I became angry with God. My prayer that night went something like this; "*OK, I understand you need me, but this waking me up in the middle of the night thing is killing me...I can't focus at work...I am an emotional wreck...I am completely frustrated and angry...And why wake me up if you're not going to tell me what to do? I need a freaking sign!!! Any sign! Or just let me sleep!*"

Before I knew it, the signs started rolling in. I would like to tell you that I figured it out immediately, but the sad truth is, that still having no idea, I showed up everywhere and anywhere I was invited to "investigate." The first sign was a voice mail on my phone machine: A woman from the county supervisor's office. She said I was recommended to serve on the Foster Care Advisory Board at social services. When I called her back and asked her who recommended me, she said she never got that information. Then next call I received was from another foster mom inviting me to a class on how to build a facility similar to Boys Town. The funny thing was that I had dreamt of building a place like Boys Town, but I never told anyone. Why did she call my phone? I would never know. I continued to be invited to numerous events. Not understanding why, but in search of the answer, I attended everything.

It was shortly after that time that I was attending a board meeting at social services and I overheard two men talking. They had been following three children who had aged out of the foster care system. Saddened by the outcome they announced, "We have lost them all." Deeply affected and not fully understanding what they were saying, I rushed home, turned on my computer and was devastated to learn that foster children all over the nation were being released to the streets on their eighteenth birthday with nothing. I was aware that when they turned eighteen their funding ran out, but I hated courts, so I never actually went to the final court date. For that matter, neither did my kids. Like a regular family, we just went with the flow. Other foster kids had independent living classes to teach them how to be adults, handle check books, balance a bank account; things of that nature. But my kids never went; they learned that kind of stuff at home. Like regular kids, they had their own accounts. I could never understand the ludicrous thought that going to a class could teach you how to do life. I assumed that was the job of the parent. Now I would know what really happens at those court dates. It turns out the classes are meant to prepare them for the day when they are sent out on their way. No money, no parents, no job, at eighteen years old, they just walk out! Sixty-five percent of foster children leave the only home they know with nothing. One in five goes straight to a homeless shelter. Over twenty thousand abused children exit the system every year in America. Nationally, 27% of our homeless population has spent time in foster care. How did I miss this?! How did everyone miss this?! I phoned my best friend Linda crying, "I can't read anymore, you need to see this! It is f***ing criminal!" Our poor babies, we took them from their parents, and said we would protect them, and at the most important time of their life, we are dumping them!

Over the next few months, overwhelmed by the fact that nothing was being done, Linda and I got into action. Using all of the tools I had been given by my teachers, we walked out big-time into the world, on a mission from God. We met with transitional housing agencies and the kids. We found out there was enough housing for one out of eight kids being released. The majority of transitional housing programs, with the exception of a few up north, had no curriculum for sober living. Kids were failing everywhere. One very successful provider that I really thought was making a difference went as far as to say, "Sure we have residents that use drugs, but it is none of our business. They are not kids anymore, they are adults." I was horrified. What kind of parent would let their kids use drugs no matter what their age?

We also realized that the primary focus of the home was on getting a job, not education. They would subsidize the kid's rent while they worked. What happened when the subsidy ran out and they were working for eight dollars an hour? Believing that they were just delaying the homelessness, we knew we had to do better. In order to really prepare them, the focus should be on education so they can obtain a life-sustaining career. I wanted to give them everything I had. Without my grant for school and my sobriety, I never would have made it. The statistics we found showed that most foster kids suffer from Post Traumatic Stress Disorder at five times the rate of Vietnam Vets and are predisposed to substance abuse. If we were going to help them, we had to do it right. Give them everything they needed! Wasting no time, I now used all of the tools I had been given. For the first time in my life I would MASTER something completely. I would step up like Cindy, be the change I wanted to see to in the world and model the examples set by the biggest world heroes!

When we weren't at work during the day, we were talking about it constantly! Within a few months, over twenty dedicated volunteers joined us! Our first meeting was amazing. Since we all had day jobs, we met at night. One girl said, "I am an artist; I can create your brochures!" A man who worked for a TV station said, "I will make a short promotional DVD for you!" A young businessman whose mother was a heroin addict and left him homeless as a child, gave us our first donation of $100 and said, "I will create your website!" People from all walks of life were inspired by our mission and stepped up to help us!

Unable to come up with a name, every time I talked about it, I would say, "You know *the teen project thing* we've been working on." Finally, a man on our team, said, "Oh, you have a name alright, you just don't know it. It is called 'The Teen Project.' Heck, you say it every time you talk about it!"

Within a month, we had a small stack of donations from over twenty people, amounting to $400. We had submitted the paperwork for our corporation and then a nonprofit. Three months later, we got our approvals. We walked into the bank with a handful of small checks. Linda and I were so excited that people cared! But we never could have imagined how much they cared…

One year later, we had a group of community members and concerned parents who had joined us. We have raised over $180,000 in donations. We knew we wanted to buy a home, but who would lend money to an organization that had no employees, no income and no history? I picked up the phone and started telling our story to the mortgage companies. The first day I found a woman who was so inspired; she said she would present it to the board at her firm. Two weeks later they called to say they would fund us! The next thing we knew, an organization that helps the homeless called and said, "We want to help!" We started looking for the first Teen Project Home. We put in one offer after another, but with all the crazy short sales and bank owned properties, they just kept falling through. The entire team was utterly confused. Not able to figure out why we couldn't get a house to save our lives when everything else went so smoothly, we talked daily to keep our sanity and faith alive. Late one Sunday, I was sitting in a support group. I couldn't even hear the man talking because I was so stressed that we couldn't find a home. Struggling to come up with an answer, it hit me. I remembered my God Box from years ago.

Seconds after it hit my mind, the man who was speaking, literally said, "And sometimes when I am confused, I drop things into my God Box." I was in complete shock! I ran out and called Gary, one of our team members, and told him what happened. I rushed home to find a suitable box. As I entered my room, I saw it was right there in front of me. My daughter Chantel had made me a plain wood box in wood shop. It was sitting right on my counter. I was so touched she had made it for me, but for the life of me, I couldn't figure out what to do with it! Now I knew. I grabbed a piece of paper out of my drawer, scribbled the words TEEN PROJECT HOUSE on it and dropped it in.

Two weeks later, we were out viewing homes with our realtor. This was the third home of the day. The majority of the homes we saw were in bad shape. When the realtor walked outside to answer her phone, I started to poke around. The first thing I noticed was that there was a very different feeling about this place. It felt safe. When I entered the bathroom, I saw the towels. They had little angels on them and they were neatly folded with care. I ended my tour in the kitchen. On the front of the refrigerator was a printed list of phone numbers. Above the numbers there was a note: *John, we are sorry to hear about your father's passing. Please keep the meeting list so that you can call another sober person.*

We put in an offer and it was accepted immediately. Committed to the fact that none of us should ever benefit monetarily from the foundation; we put the home in the name of the project.

Excited about the home, we still needed to figure out what to do with the other 20,000 children walking the streets! We were all aware that the real mission was much larger. In an effort to come up with an answer, over the next few months, I used my God Box extensively and our team hit the streets to find out more. What we found out was this: There were two drop-in centers in our county. Each center was visited by kids who lived within the general vicinity of the center. Lacking transportation, the more remote children weren't able to make it there. So we went out on the streets and found the kids. Kids in shelters, transitional housing, parks, living on the streets—anywhere we could find them, we talked to them, and all of the kids had one thing in common. Even though they had no food, no cell phone and no shelter, they still communicated with their friends through computers. Even the teens living on the street visit the local libraries to access the internet. With twenty years of experience in computer networks, and childhood abuse, I knew we had been chosen to take them home. By the time this book is finished, we will have the power and knowledge to create one of the most dramatic social changes for emancipated youth in America. "Be the change you want to see in the world."

Just a few more small miracles to tell you about and then I will leave you to take the lid off your own life….

It was just few months later that I was promoted to Senior Management at the Fortune 100 company where I had been consulting for the past ten years. With over 180,000 employees, I was a nervous wreck. Shortly after my promotion, they decided that the building we had been in for several years was too expensive. With the economy failing, "the powers that be" decided to move the facility to a less expensive area and made a deal for a ten-year lease in a nearby city for 120 million dollars. My job was to move the computer equipment that would support the personnel moving in. Working with my team to ensure we had all of the electrical and networking equipment ordered and onsite, we were set to move in just four days. That was when I ran into a hiccup. When I dropped the last of the equipment at the facility we were moving to, the engineer receiving it said, "Where is the L20/21?" Just like you're probably saying, I thought, *Huh?* Not very familiar with electrical terms, I said, "Oh, I am sure you have it." He assured me that it was over four feet in length and definitely had not come in. When I asked how critical it was, he told me that without it, no electricity and no move. Completely panicked, I rushed back to the office to order it online. One vendor after another, I got the same response. L20/21s are special ordered and right now it's backordered three weeks. There was no way! Just imagining that this strange electrical part could be the downfall of my entire career was more than

I could bear. Facing the failure of what could be hundreds of thousands of dollars in penalties, I called one of my friends from my still ongoing Pussy on the Porch meeting. I quickly brought her up to speed on this very critical situation, and then I laid the mother lode on her. "Colleen, what do you think about putting an electrical cord in the God Box? Do you think I am using it like a 'magic' box? I mean like not respecting it?" I was surprised when she responded, "Anything that keeps you up at night is a viable candidate for the box." Delighted with her answer, but still skeptical, I slammed down the phone, ran over to the drawer and with a broken pencil scratched the words L20/21 POWER CORD and dropped it in the box.

The next morning I arrived to work with only three days until the move, and resumed my online search for the power cord. As I booted up my computer, an engineer who sat in the cube next to me said, "Hey, I heard you talking about an L20/21 power cord yesterday. I know a guy up north that makes custom cords. I emailed you his number. He will have it for you by tomorrow." I couldn't believe it! The God Box worked again!

In awe of everything that was happening in my life, a few nights later, as was customary for me to do every night since New Life, I knelt down beside my bed to thank God for my day, but on this night I wanted to tell him just how happy I was. When I talk to God, it's not a lot of thou's and fancy stuff. Much like I began with George, it is just plain down and dirty like talking to a friend. My prayer went something like this: God I just want to thank you for everything; my home, my wonderful kids, my animals, my wonderful job and you know what God? If I *never* meet a man or get married, I don't care. I am the happiest woman alive! Then he spoke to me. Like I always say, when he speaks to me, I know it is Him, because it surely isn't something I would come up with. He said, "Drop HUSBAND in the box."

I thought, *WHAT*?! Are you freaking kidding? Husband? I would consider boyfriend, but HUSBAND? Are you kidding?! Then he said, "If I deliver the man who was made for you, you will not be afraid anymore Lauri. You will know the minute you see him, he is the one.

As much as I trusted God, I thought this was ludicrous. I never wanted to get married; but if he was perfect? I am not sure…crap…married?! Going back and forth with the idea, I finally said OK! OK! Already!!!! If he is "perfect" for me… Scared to death of the result, I tentatively grabbed a marker, wrote the word "husband" on it and dropped it in the box. As I walked away, I thought, *what have you done?!*

It was six months prior that I had returned to Sandy's office and said, "I am frustrated with the dating thing!" After a long chat about having dated some very nice men, but not "the" man, we updated my original list with my new specs: *Must like children!* And for once in my life, I made a commitment that I wouldn't take a date unless on the surface he looked like a match for the "list." In an effort to keep my commitment fresh in my mind, I typed the updated list into my Blackberry before I left the session that day.

The reality is, I always knew men I dated weren't "the list" at the outset. I saw the red flags before we even started. Wanting nothing more than to make him "the right guy" I unconsciously painted the red flags green in my mind each and every time. I'd minimize his liabilities and emphasize his assets. Months later, the flags I painted green would start to look a bit orange and before I knew it, the original red flags were staring me in the face, and I knew it wouldn't work. I did this over and over again. That day I left Sandy's office with a commitment to stop wasting my time dating the wrong men and to wait for the right guy or to live happy ever after with my kids. By the time I had knelt down on the floor to pray that night, it had been six months without so much as a coffee date and as stated, I was perfectly content with my life.

Three weeks later the local newspaper printed an article about me and The Teen Project. My picture was on the front page. That weekend a man I had admired from afar approached me. From the initial looks of it, he had all of the specs on the "list." On our first date he told me that he had been sober for twenty two years. He had gotten sober two months before I did in 1987. He also told me his daughter was a social worker who worked with teens in the foster care system. One week into knowing him we were on the phone chatting, when he mentioned

God. I knew I had to tell him that my God was different than most. I told him about my breakdown with God before I got sober and my lack of trust. Then I told him about the assignment at New Life and how I searched for something I could trust. When I finally ended with the fact that I initially used George Burns, he began to laugh.

Hurt by his lack of understanding, I said, "Hey, hey, cool it, you have no idea!" He then cleared his voice and said, "Oh no, *you* have no idea. I used George too." A week later, I sent him a text with a picture of my God box. Within minutes, he responded with a picture of his God box. They could have been carved from the same tree. Three weeks later he proposed to me. Six months later we were married.

As the result of my story, God boxes have sprouted up everywhere. Sarah, who is on our board for The Teen Project, dropped "proposal" in her box and weeks later her boyfriend, who would never drop the question, proposed. Linda dropped "job" in her box, and two days later she had two offers. One after another I kept hearing people I know say, "Then I dropped it in my God Box!" I don't know how all these boxes sprouted up over night. All I can think is that after seeing the most independent woman they know get married overnight, they ran out to get boxes!

⁓

Standing in line aboard the Royal Caribbean cruise ship, I answered the phone call I had been dreading.

"Lauri Burns? This Michael Gold. There was an incident involving your father and he's been here with us for a few days. Up until yesterday he told us he had no family, but now he's saying he has one daughter. Now he's saying he did some bad things and he's going to be put away. Do you know what he's talking about?"

When the man pressured me for information, I gave him a very high level view of what you already know. Then he said, "But that was thirty years ago. Surely, he can't think he would be in trouble now? He has been in an irrational, almost non communicative state for the past few days, but he is better today. Not good, but better. Would you like to talk to him?"

The broken man who got on the phone was foreign to me. His uncontrollable sobbing made it difficult to comprehend his words. "What have I done? They are going to lock me up and throw away the key! Oh God, what have I done to you? I am so sorry! I don't deserve you!" He was weeping so loudly it was heart-wrenching to hear.

"It's okay Dad. I love you Dad. That was thirty years ago. Dad please, I forgive you. It is okay. I love you Dad." Like a small child he wept and said, "Thank you honey…thank you…I don't deserve you…I never deserved you…Oh God, I am a mess.

"You should see this place they have me in. There are crazy people in here. They have me drugged up. I could barely walk until today." Then he began sobbing heavily again. "Oh God…I am a mess…I didn't mean to hurt anyone…Really, I just…I didn't mean to hurt anyone…"

The social worker retrieved the phone again. "It looks like we are going to have to keep him here." In the background I heard my father yelling, "Keep me! In this fucking place?!"

The man said, "Hold on while I go to my office." From there he told me, "I am not comfortable with his state of mind. I am afraid he may hurt himself or someone else. I am going to keep him here for a psychological evaluation for a few days."

Two days later he called again. "Your father is demanding to be let out. I am not feeling good about his condition." He ended by saying, "The only way I will release your father is if you agree to take custody and get him into therapy."

So here we were. The man who locked me up and put me in the Looney bin was now in one himself, and his only rescue—me. Life is funny sometimes isn't it? You already know what I did.

I said, "Yes, no problem, you can release my father to my custody. I will take full responsibility."

Today I know that if I had not been "the change" for my dad, this never would have occurred. On this day, the whole world shifted. Who would have thought the cowering child hiding in the closet would someday be the strong woman who would save the man who brutalized her? My father was released to my custody and put on a plane.

Over the next few weeks, I parented my father and discovered who he really was. My father's mother was a single woman who was dating a married man. Ashamed of having a child, she hid him for as long as she could. When he was three she walked him to a large building with a bunch of children. She said, "Charlie, I will be back to get you soon. You be good until I return." She had no intention of ever returning. Little Charlie sat at the big window in the orphanage every day for weeks waiting for his mother to return. The more time passed, the more terrified he became. The staff made several attempts to get him to leave the window, but it was fruitless.

A year or so later, my father was adopted by what would be the only grandparents I ever knew. Living in a tiny apartment with three daughters, they could barely afford another child, but they wanted a boy. My father never had a bedroom. He slept on a foldout cot in a tiny kitchen. My father insists that his foster mom was the most loving woman in the world, but hesitates to speak about his foster father. The only thing he ever mentioned was the frequent trips to the dentist to get drilled without Novocain. Knowing my father as a child affected me on many levels. The most important thing I learned was that until someone is "the change" in your family, the patterns will continue for generations to come. At the age of seventy three, my father made his first appointment with a therapist. He is still in therapy today and working hard.

Today my Grandma Ana's picture sits proudly on my living room shelf, right next to my award for Foster Parenting. Some foster kids take longer than others to heal, but now having been loved by two foster moms, my dad was finally going to make it to the other side of his childhood abuse.

53

IT WAS ABOUT A YEAR AGO THAT I MET MY LAST TEACHER. IT WAS Sunday night about 3:00 pm and I was due to arrive at a center to meet friends in about fifteen minutes and I was twenty minutes away. Basically, I was running late. For reasons I cannot explain none of that mattered a few minutes later.

I was driving down a street by my home that I had driven down hundreds of times before, but this was the first time I saw it. As I pulled up to the stop light, I looked to my right and I saw the words "Chabad" on a big sign outside of a brick building. Looking more intently now, I noticed people going in and out of the glass doors carrying things. It looked as though they were preparing for a party. For the life of me, I couldn't figure out what Jewish people would be doing in temple on a Sunday.

Even though I didn't remember much from my childhood, I knew the important days were Friday and Saturday. What happened next was best described as the type of "listening" Ron Johnston had taught me so long ago. Something in my mind said, *go in there.* Rationally it didn't make any sense. I was already late to meet my friends and I had no reason whatsoever to go in there.

Fighting the powers that guide me for a logical explanation, *I thought then what? I go in there and say what?* The answer came quicker than I could have imagined. *Just ask for a brochure.* Fine.

With no insight into why I would go in there, or what I was looking for. I pulled into the parking lot, parked the car and walked in looking for a "brochure."

People were rushing around setting up tables. The first person who noticed me was a lady in her early fifties. She said "Can I help you?" "Oh, I responded, I am looking for a brochure." She said, "I don't think we have brochures, but let me ask the Rabbi. Sorry about the craziness, but the Rabbi's son Yaakov is getting his first haircut today."

They were celebrating a haircut? As confused as I was, I just said "Oh, ok." She then darted off to locate the Rabbi. She returned with a man in a dark suit with long tassels hanging down the sides, a big black hat, and a long beard. He appeared to be in his early thirties. He looked at me and said "I hear you are looking for brochures. We really don't have any, but I would love to have someone call you to tell you about our temple. Can you leave me your number? They will phone you tomorrow when things calm down." I pulled my newly created Teen Project card with my cell number on it and handed it to Rabbi Marcus.

The next day, he called me directly. I couldn't believe it. He called me himself? I was as nervous as can be. I knew nothing about the Jewish religion despite the fact I was a Jew. Afraid of what he was going to ask me, I just listened. He said, "Hey, Lauri, I looked at your website about The Teen Project and all I can say is "Mazel Tov!" You are doing great work!" He said one of the few words I remembered from Hebrew School. Mazel Tov means something like congratulations, great job.

"I would love for you to come for a class at our temple," he said. As he rattled off the names of the classes, he told me the one called "Introduction to the Tanya" was a beginner's class. The next weekend, I attended temple for the first time in over thirty years. When I got to class, I noticed they were on Volume Four. At the end of the class I approached the Rabbi and said, "When are you starting over at Volume One again?" A man nearby chuckled and said "We started three years ago and there are twelve volumes, so we might start over again in fifteen years." That was when I realized how serious this was.

Although I can't fully explain it, the moment the class ended and I heard the congregation singing the Hebrew songs, something inside of me came alive. Like ET when his fellow aliens came to get him. As the spaceship closed in and his chest lit up with a red glow, something inside of me ignited that day.

For the next several months, I showed up each weekend. I was hungry for the Rabbi's teachings. I hung onto his every word. His teachings were around being "the chosen few." I always knew the Jews were chosen, but in my juvenile mind, I thought most Jews were chosen to go straight to Heaven. Where other people had to qualify, I figured good Jews were an "auto-in." Thinking about it now, I realized how silly that was.

Through the Rabbi's teachings I would learn that the Jews were chosen to bring God's light to the darkest places on the earth. And that the "chosenness" refers to our responsibility. God was counting on us. Through our connection with God, we would deliver his love to the wounded people and restore life. Now I knew. It made everything clear. God brought me here so that I could absorb all that he had for me to do through a man that spent his whole life in knowing him, my Rabbi.

He told me that Teshuvah means to return, to return to God. Each one of us needs to return. No one is perfect. Who is greater he asked? The sinner who returns and mends his ways or the very righteous who never sins? In Jewish tradition the returnee is greater. The power of Teshuvah can turn our mistakes into the greatest acts of goodness. Teshuvah is a generous gift from God, which allows us to erase our improper actions. The Torah tells us that no matter how far we stray or how many times we sin, God will wait for us to return to him. Teshuvah means we return to the path God set for us when we were born, the path that our souls know. Even though I didn't remember in my mind, when my something in me ignited that day, I knew I was home. My soul remembered.

Over the past twenty three years, our family has experienced true healing. My mother and I talk almost every day and are closer than ever. My little sister Alyssa finally caught on to the sobriety thing and has over 12 years sober today. She is a well-known fashion designer in Los Angeles and lives with her two puppies. Nadine is married and has four children and lives in the Midwest. She has over 19 years of sobriety.

54

I WANTED TO END WITH THE BEST PART OF MY LIFE: MY DAUGHTER Madie. Thanks to the people who have taught me how to love myself and others and how to speak out in truth, Madie was healed from the trauma of her first few years of life. It was during the meetings at our home for mothers and children that I first noticed Madie's gift. Children were drawn to her. Preparing games and snacks prior to their arrival, she was a natural. When the moms came to pick up their children, they never wanted to leave. Dorothy had always told Madie that this was her "gift."

At the age of nineteen she was attending a local college in pursuit of her AA degree, while still deciding on the "big" picture. On this particular day she was studying in the local coffee shop rather than returning home in between classes. Madie was sitting at a small round table with her books piled atop, waiting for her coffee order to be called. A four-year-old boy stood at the pastry counter with his caretaker. In a world of his own, he had no reaction to the noises or people around him. Turning away from the counter and without any eye contact, he quickly moved across the floor, closing in on Madie's table. Without notice, he grabbed hold of her hand and began to pull. Not understanding what was happening; she stood up and followed his lead. He led her across the room to a large shelf. When he stopped at the shelf, he just stared at the floor. Gazing up at the shelf filled with different knick knacks and coffee items, she immediately spotted the target, a colorful pack of stickers. Retrieving the stickers, she handed them to the child.

When she turned she noticed the child's parent watching. Dumbfounded, she looked at Madie and said, "How did you know?" She went on to say that with his limited communication, people rarely responded to him. Madie simply replied, "I could feel his pull." From that day forward, Madie knew she would dedicate her life to children with autism. Over the next few years she studied sign language and within two years she was assisting the Child Abuse Services Team with non-verbal and deaf children to communicate information about their perpetrator to the police.

Madie applied to seven schools for her Master's Degree. For her application, she wrote the story of her life. Her mom, her sixteen sisters and her gift in teaching non-verbal children to communicate. She was accepted by all of the schools she applied to, but because of her love for New York, she chose the only Ivy League school, Columbia University. Determined to make a difference in the field of autism, she enrolled in a Dual Masters Program. One Masters in Social Work and the other in Special Education. I could barely imagine having her three thousand miles away. It scared me to death. I just kept on thinking what if something happened to her...how would I get there? Knowing I had to let her grow up and chase her dreams, I dropped "protect my baby" into my God Box.

Last year she graduated from Columbia School of Social Work. During the time she was in New York, she interned at a school for children with learning disabilities. Whenever she called me to check in, she had a story about "her kids." Traumatized by the fact that she would be leaving them soon and having insight into their inability to process, she created a storybook with pictures of her family in California.

One month before she was due to leave, they called her into the office at the school. It was a Friday when she phoned me. "Mom, I know you will be mad. They offered me a job here and even though I want to come home...it's the kids....I can't leave them. I am going to stay in New York."

Although I miss her terribly, I understand only too well.

Central Islip Psychiatric Center, Islip, New York
Photos by Jason Krieger, www.hoursofdarkness.com

Lauri Burns
Photo by Leonard Ortiz, The Orange County Register

To order your own personal god box
visit www.theteenproject.com

LaVergne, TN USA
08 June 2010
185301LV00003B/2/P

9 781595 943460